Conquerors, Brides, and Concubines

THE MIDDLE AGES SERIES

Conquerors, Brides, and Concubines

Interfaith Relations and Social Power in Medieval Iberia

Simon Barton

PENN

UNIVERSITY OF PENNSYLVANIA PRESS

PHILADELPHIA

Published by
University of Pennsylvania Press
Philadelphia, Pennsylvania 19104-4112
www.upenn.edu/pennpress

Printed in the United States of America on acid-free paper
1 3 5 7 9 10 8 6 4 2

Library of Congress Cataloging-in-Publication Data
Barton, Simon, 1962–
Conquerors, brides, and concubines : interfaith relations and social power in medieval Iberia / Simon Barton. — 1st ed.
p. cm. — (Middle Ages series)
Includes bibliographical references and index.
ISBN 978-0-8122-4675-9
1. Interfaith marriage—Iberian Peninsula—History—To 1500. 2. Sexual ethics—Iberian Peninsula—History—To 1500. 3. Women—Iberian Peninsula—Social conditions—History—To 1500. 4. Iberian Peninsula—Politics and government—History. 5. Iberian Peninsula—Social conditions—History. 6. Iberian Peninsula—Religion—History. 7. Christianity and other religions—Iberian Peninsula. 8. Islam—Relations—Christianity—History—To 1500. I. Title. II. Series: Middle Ages series.
HQ1031.B345 2015
306.84'3—dc23 2014026614

In memory of my parents,
John and Muriel Barton

Contents

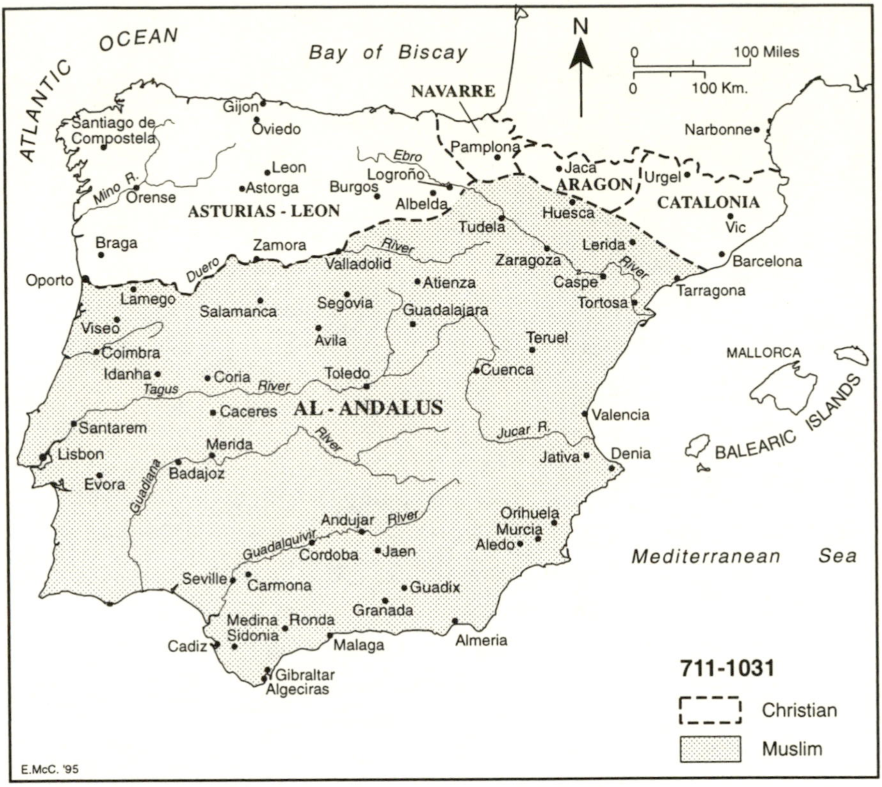

Map 1. The Iberian peninsula, 711–1031.

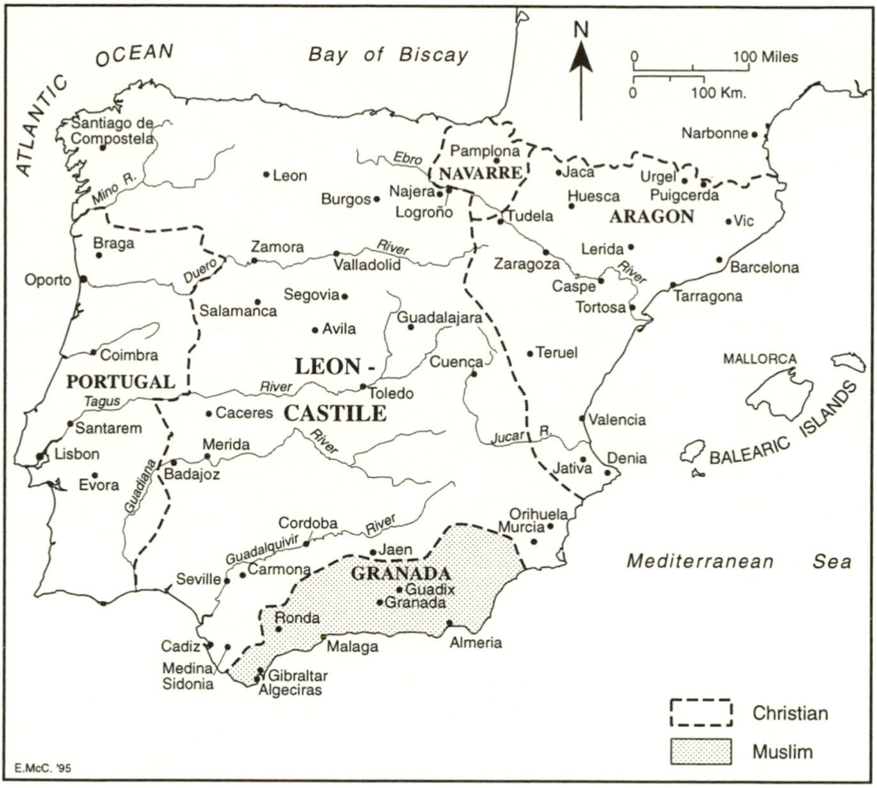

Map 2. The Iberian Peninsula, c.1350. Adapted from *Medieval Iberia: Readings from Christian, Muslim and Jewish Sources*, ed. Olivia R. Constable. 2nd ed. Philadelphia: University of Pennsylvania Press, 2011, 310.

Introduction

Every year, on the Sunday before 5 October, the feast day of St. Froilán, the inhabitants of the northern Spanish city of León celebrate a curious and eye-catching popular festival known simply as Las Cantaderas.[1] The purpose of the *fiesta* is to commemorate the agreement supposedly reached by the Christian kings of Asturias in the late eighth century, by which they undertook to deliver one hundred maidens (*cien doncellas*) to the emir of Muslim-ruled Iberia, ʿAbd al-Raḥmān I (756–88), in annual payment of tribute. Tradition records that this humiliating obligation was later expunged by King Ramiro I (842–50), who, with the miraculous assistance of St. James, defeated a large Muslim army at Clavijo in the Rioja in 844.[2] During the Leonese festivities, a theatrical ceremony takes place, as a group of young women (the *cantaderas* themselves), demurely dressed in medieval costume, are instructed to dance by a woman known as the *sotadera*, usually veiled, whose task it supposedly is to lead them on the long journey southward to join the emir's harem in Córdoba. However, the *sotadera* takes the group on an alternative route, from the square in front of the old town hall, accompanied by local dignitaries and mace bearers, as far as the cathedral. There, further singing and dancing take place, speeches are delivered by the great and the good, Mass is held, and offerings are made to the Virgin Mary to give thanks for the safe delivery of the women from the clutches of the infidel.

The origins of the festival of Las Cantaderas, which until relatively recently was held on Assumption Day (15 August), can be traced back to at least the sixteenth century. By 1596, when Atanasio de Lobera published his history of the city and church of León, the festival was already well established and the celebrations stretched over three days, combining both popular and religious elements.[3] Lobera's description of Las Cantaderas records that the four principal parishes of León—San Marcelo, Santa Ana, San Martín, and Nuestra Señora del Mercado—each sent twelve girls to the procession every year, all of them dressed to the nines in brocades and silks, and adorned with gold and silver jewelry, pearls, and other precious stones. The girls who took part in the ceremony were reportedly between ten and twelve years old, although if we are to believe Francisco López de Úbeda's picaresque novel *La pícara Justina*, published in 1605, many may have been of marriageable age, as old as eighteen or twenty.[4] As to whether they were all virgins, as was widely claimed, López de Úbeda, through his lead character Justina, expressed jocular skepticism, declaring that it would be *medio milagro* (a near miracle) if it were true.[5] López de Úbeda also paints a graphic description of the *sotadera*, whom he describes in stark terms as "the oldest and most evil thing that I ever saw in my whole life," a remark that may have been designed to underline her "otherness" to the beautiful, supposedly virginal Christian *cantaderas*.[6] This contrast may have been further reinforced if, as has been suggested, the role of the *sotadera* was typically played by a "marginalized" woman, perhaps of Morisco or gypsy stock, or even a former prostitute.[7] The *sotadera* was meant to play the key role of intermediary between Muslims and Christians, but by joining the procession to exalt the Virgin Mary she in fact became instrumental in helping to restore lost honor.[8]

On 14 August, according to Lobera's account, the girls proceeded through the city carrying large processional candlesticks to the sound of war drums, which had supposedly been captured on the battlefield of Clavijo, and then entered the cathedral. Lobera provides this earnest description:

> And although it is true that their arrival, with so much noise and din, interrupts the music and solemnity of the divine offices, the pious, Christian heart is so moved and touched, bearing in mind what it signifies and the meaning that the happy memory of the freedom of the sad maidens enshrines, represented by these joyful girls, that there is no one so hard-hearted [literally "dry-headed"] who does not shed tears to celebrate the memory of the triumph over that ancient evil. . . . Everyone present gives thanks to the Almighty for the favor He granted to Spain when He delivered it from such an ignominious tribute.[9]

The girls then sang and danced in the cathedral to the sound of a psaltery and were blessed by the bishop, before venturing outside once more to continue the celebrations. At nightfall, fireworks were set off, bonfires were lit, and musicians played trumpets. The next morning, which was Assumption Day, there were further processions and more dancing by the *cantaderas*, a solemn Mass was held, and baskets of pears and plums were offered to the bishop. This was followed by the performance of the first of two plays, which according to Lobera were written by "the best author in Spain."[10] The third and final day of the festival saw the performance of the second play, and another solemn procession took place, during the course of which a dead bull was dragged in a cart by two oxen to the cathedral and offered to an image of the Virgin.[11] This was followed by a running of the bulls—presumably "Pamplona-style"—and demonstrations of horsemanship.

The festivities in León today are less extensive and elaborate than they evidently were in the late sixteenth century, but they are no less enthusiastic and heartfelt for all that. Moreover, in their current form they are far from unique. Similar commemorative events take place in other towns and villages across northern Spain, including Betanzos in Galicia, Astorga (just down the road from León), Carrión de los Condes and Simancas in the Castilian Tierra de Campos, Santo Domingo de la Calzada and Sorzano in the Rioja, and as far to the east as Vilaseca and Bagà in Catalonia. Unlike the Leonese festival, however, many of these seem to be of relatively recent invention.[12]

As it is, the ceremony of Las Cantaderas and others like it take us to the very heart of one of Spain's most cherished national myths. The victory on the battlefield of Clavijo has traditionally been enveloped in a patriotic mystique and portrayed as a key moment in the progress of the divinely sanctioned Christian *Reconquista* (Reconquest) of Muslim Iberia. Accordingly, it has been viewed by many as an important step toward the reforging of the Spanish nation, which had supposedly been broken asunder by the Islamic conquest of the Visigothic kingdom in 711. The legend of the tribute of the hundred maidens has held the imagination of Spaniards for the best part of 900 years and has inspired an extraordinarily prolific and diverse outpouring of artistic creativity, including works of narrative history, poetry, drama (including three plays by Lope de Vega), various modern novels, painting, and even a *zarzuela* (the Spanish opera form) by Francisco Barbieri.[13] As we shall see, the legend was also the inspiration for one of the most ambitious and effective forgeries to have been carried out anywhere in the Latin West during the Middle Ages. Yet although the legend remains deeply engrained in Spanish cultural and popular tradition, and the Battle of Clavijo is widely commemorated in the names of streets and schools right across Spain, the origins, propagation, and ideological purpose of this national myth have yet to receive the sustained attention that they undoubtedly deserve.

It is partly in an attempt to explain the historical and cultural importance of the legend of the tribute of the hundred maidens, and others like it, that this book has been written. Yet its aim is even more ambitious than that. The work investigates the diverse political, social, and cultural functions that interfaith marriage alliances and other sexual encounters fulfilled within the overall dynamic of Christian-Muslim relations in the Iberian Peninsula during the medieval period, both within al-Andalus—the term by which the territory under Islamic rule was designated—and the expansionist Christian-dominated polities of the North. This study seeks to elucidate why interfaith sex mattered to such a considerable degree to secular and religious lawgivers in the Peninsula and why it impinged so significantly on the political and cultural discourse of the age. In doing so, the book also explores why the "cultural memory" of such sexual liaisons carried such a powerful resonance within Christian society during the Later Middle Ages and beyond, and considers the part that memory played in reinforcing community identity and defining social and cultural boundaries between the faiths. In pursuing this inquiry, a number of other pressing questions will be addressed. Why, for example, were anxieties about interfaith sexual mixing articulated so extensively by Christians—in law and literature—from the twelfth century on, but seldom before that date? To what extent did such fears feed on traditional Western hostility toward Islam, or conversely were a response to local attitudes and conditions? Were such attitudes the direct product of specific secular processes, such as the progress of the Christian conquest of Muslim territory, or rather did they stem from intellectual impulses emanating from beyond the Pyrenees? In short, through a close examination of the ways in which interfaith sexual relations were conducted, perceived, manipulated, and, above all, controlled, this book seeks to highlight the extent to which sex, power, and identity were closely bound up with one another in the medieval Peninsula.

In undertaking this study, I am conscious that this is not entirely uncharted territory. The extent to which restrictions were placed on interfaith sexual mixing in the medieval Peninsula, and the ways those highly charged boundaries between the faiths were patrolled or transgressed, have been the focus of some significant scholarly scrutiny in recent years. Strongly led by David Nirenberg, some of the most important research has analyzed the extent to which Christian prostitutes in the late medieval Crown of Aragon became the focal point for collective anxiety about sexual mixing with Muslim and Jewish men.[14] Other studies have examined the eroticized literary representations of Muslim women, as well as of those thirteenth-century

Christian female court entertainers called *soldadeiras*, whose licentious lifestyle and supposed cross-border sexual encounters with Muslim men made them the target of numerous scurrilous songs.[15] The process by which sexual boundaries between the faiths were erected and guarded in al-Andalus has also been subjected to revealing analysis.[16] Moreover, when this book was nearing completion, I learned of the publication of *Pluralism in the Middle Ages: Hybrid Identities, Conversion, and Mixed Marriages in Medieval Iberia* by Norwegian scholar Ragnhild Johnsrud Zorgati.[17] However, my initial fears that I had been pipped at the post and was destined to play the role of Captain Scott to Dr. Zorgati's Amundsen, so to speak, were swiftly allayed when it became clear that the scope of our respective works, as well as our methodologies, were strikingly different. Zorgati has conducted a useful comparative legal study, focusing principally on issues of conversion and mixed marriages, in which a selection of texts, ranging from Muslim *fatwās* on the one hand to the thirteenth-century Christian *Siete Partidas* on the other, are subjected to scrutiny. By exploring, through the framework of postcolonial theory, the various legal discourses that constructed or broke down boundaries between religious groups in medieval Iberia, Zorgati concludes that such boundaries were by no means static and that interfaith relationships—expressions of cultural contact and hybridity, as she puts it—might take place across them.[18]

My own investigation of interfaith sexual mixing is situated on a broader canvas, in that it explores the social, political, and cultural significance of the phenomenon from the Islamic conquest of the Iberian Peninsula in the early eighth century down to the eve of the fall of the last redoubt of independent Muslim rule, Nasrid Granada, in 1492. This study is concerned with interfaith sexuality in medieval Iberia both as a social reality and as it was imagined and manipulated in the political and cultural discourse of the time. My primary concern is less to portray interfaith sex as an expression of hybridity and cultural contact—although I do not deny that it could sometimes be such—than to highlight the numerous ways in which sexuality and politics intertwined in the medieval Peninsula. Above all, I will investigate the extent to which sexual relationships between Muslims and Christians impinged on interfaith power relations and how they might be perceived, tolerated, or feared, depending on the precise political and social contexts in which they occurred. Just as the social anthropologist Fredrik Barth has highlighted the importance of "the social processes of exclusion and incorporation" in multiethnic societies in maintaining group identity, so this work will argue that in medieval Iberia the sexual boundaries that were raised between the faiths came to perform a similar vital function.[19]

Chapter 1 examines the practice of sexual mixing between Muslim lords and Christian women in early medieval Iberia. It first considers the diverse political, social, and economic functions that marriage alliances with Visigothic heiresses or widows were designed to fulfill in the immediate aftermath of the Muslim conquest of the Peninsula. Attention is also paid to the various cross-border interfaith sexual liaisons that helped to shape Andalusi diplomatic relations with the nascent Christian realms of the North thereafter. It will be argued that, for the ruling Umayyad dynasty and for the chief ministers of the Caliphate who seized the reins of power at the end of the tenth century, as well for other élite groups, sexual relations with Christian women—be they freeborn wives or slave concubines—might serve not merely as a tool of diplomacy, but as a potent propaganda weapon and even as an instrument of psychological warfare.

Chapter 2 examines the political, religious, and cultural reasons for the decline of interfaith marriage after c.1050 and considers the wider significance of the various policies that were enacted by the Christian authorities in order to prevent interfaith sexual mixing thereafter. It questions why the matter of interfaith sex came to assume such significance for the secular and ecclesiastical lawgivers of the states of Christian Iberia from the twelfth century on, and why intercourse between Christian women and Muslim or Jewish men generated by far the greatest anxiety. Finally, it discusses whether the hardening attitudes toward social assimilation—and above all sexual interaction between Christian women and Muslim and Jewish men—can be related to the wider hostility being articulated across the Latin West at this time toward others considered to be "outsiders" at the margins of society, such as heretics, homosexuals, prostitutes, and lepers.

Chapter 3 highlights the extent to which the thorny subject of interfaith sex impinged on Christian political and cultural discourse from the twelfth century on. Christians feared for the well-being of their women who were carried off into captivity in al-Andalus or even to North Africa and voiced concern that sexual contact with Muslims would both damage their honor and pave the way to apostasy. The image of the Christian damsel in distress was repeatedly deployed by chroniclers, hagiographers, and other literary exponents in order to foster solidarity among their intended audiences. To a society that attached such importance to personal honor, literary narratives in which Christian identity and power were intimately linked to the sexual purity and honor of its women were to prove spectacularly effective and remarkably long-lasting.

Chapter 4 approaches Christian attitudes toward interfaith sex from a very different angle. In some of the texts analyzed, Christian women are portrayed not as passive victims of Muslim lasciviousness, but as wanton instigators themselves, who seek out Muslim sexual partners, with often perilous consequences. In other texts, by contrast, an alternative narrative is presented, as Muslim women surrender their bodies to Christian men and renounce Islam. At a symbolic level, this act of submission is presented as analogous to that of military surrender. Even if most of these accounts are pure fiction, their purpose was to remind their audiences that sex, power, and cultural identity were at all times closely interrelated.

This book adopts an interdisciplinary methodology that is grounded on the close reading of a wide range of source materials, including not only laws, but also charters and letters, historical narratives of various kinds, works of polemic, and hagiography, as well as literary texts in a variety of other genres. By engaging with such a broad source-base, it is possible to track Muslim and Christian attitudes toward interfaith sex across time and provide a more nuanced reading of the phenomenon, which helps to complement what could be seen as the more aspirational and normative perspectives provided by legal texts alone.[20] Among the most notable absentees from the dramatis personae of the book are the Iberian Jews, whose relationship with their Muslim and Christian neighbors has already been the object of significant scholarly study.[21] Be that is it may, this work is designed to connect with some of the most recent and lively debates in medieval Iberian studies—for example, about Christian-Muslim interaction (in peace as well as in war); and about identity formation and the reinvention of the past—and to offer some novel perspectives on the Peninsula's rich and distinctive medieval history. Furthermore, it is my hope that this study of the encounter between Islamic and Christian cultures, which continues to impinge forcefully on the consciousness of contemporary commentators and politicians both in the Muslim world and in the West, will in some way contribute to our understanding of the issues that have shaped the rich, complex, yet sometimes volatile relationship between the two.

Christianity and Islam in Iberia: From *Reconquista* to *Convivencia* and Beyond

During the course of the past century, scholarly approaches to the relationship between Christian and Islamic societies in the medieval Peninsula have undergone a number of marked shifts of emphasis.[22] Until only a few decades ago, the study of Spain and Portugal's development during this period was dominated by the concept of *Reconquista.* First coined in a Peninsular context in the nineteenth century, the term was used to denote the gradual process of territorial expansion by which, between c.720 and 1492, the Christian-dominated territories of the Peninsula—Portugal, Asturias-León, Castile, Navarre, Aragon, and the Catalan counties—wrested control of the region from Islamic authority.[23] However, it was a concept that was politically and ideologically highly charged. For many Spaniards, particularly those who espoused the idea of the "historical unity" of *la España eterna* (Eternal Spain), the *Reconquista* represented nothing less than a divinely guided patriotic and religious movement, through which Christian Spain had defended not just the Peninsula, but Christian civilization as a whole, against a rising tide of Islamic expansionism, and whose ultimate outcome was to be the creation of the modern Spanish state. It was a narrative of fall and redemption, which shaped Spanish culture, institutions, and social attitudes and helped to fulfil Spain's very own "Manifest Destiny."[24] Such ideas were articulated most forcefully and influentially by Marcelino Menéndez y Pelayo, whose bestselling *Historia de los heterodoxos españoles* (1880–82) trumpeted the view that it had been the *unidad de creencia* (unity of belief) that had sustained Spain during the dark years of Islamic occupation, and that it was thanks to the Catholic faith that "we became a nation, a great nation, rather than a crowd of assorted peoples."[25] This triumphalist, patriotic interpretation was later to be amplified by Menéndez y Pelayo's pupil, Ramón Menéndez Pidal, the doyen of twentieth-century Hispanic letters. In his essay *Los españoles en la historia* (published in 1947), a discursive meditation on the historical development of Spain and the characteristics of the Spaniards themselves, Menéndez Pidal portrayed the *Reconquista* in these exalted tones:

> The pure unfettered religious spirit which had been preserved in the north gave impetus and national aims to the Reconquest. Without its strength of purpose Spain would have given up in despair all

> resistance and would have been denationalized. In the end it would have become Islamized as did all the other provinces of the Roman Empire in the east and south of the Mediterranean. . . . What gave Spain her exceptional strength of collective resistance and enabled her to last through three long centuries of great peril was her policy of fusing into one ideal the recovery of the Gothic states for the fatherland and the redemption of the enslaved churches for the glory of Christianity.[26]

Such ideas were to prove particularly attractive to the propagandists of the authoritarian regime of General Francisco Franco, which ruled Spain with an iron grip from the end of the Spanish Civil War (1936–39) to the dictator's death in 1975.[27] The reality that Hispania—as the Peninsula as a whole had been known to the Romans—and modern Spain were not an exact fit, given the existence of an independent realm of Portugal since the twelfth century, was an uncomfortable fact that was largely overlooked.

However, the primacy of this patriotic interpretation of the Spanish past, which viewed the relationship between Christianity and Islam exclusively in terms of military, ideological, and sociocultural conflict, was soon to be challenged. Indeed, only a year after Menéndez Pidal's meditation on Spain and the Spaniards was published to great acclaim, one of his former disciples, Américo Castro, set a cat among the pigeons with his own startlingly original take on the Peninsula's medieval past. Jettisoning the intellectual baggage of National-Catholic *Reconquista* and the "eternal Spain" altogether, Castro argued that, far from being the product of intercredal conflict, Spain and the Spanish psyche were born of eight long centuries of *convivencia*, or "living together," between Christians, Muslims, and Jews. According to this analysis, rather than being uncontaminated by the Islamic conquest, Christian society was profoundly affected in culture and outlook.[28] This vision of a hybrid Spain born of coexistence and cultural symbiosis was rejected in many quarters and triggered a particularly furious riposte from another of Menéndez Pidal's pupils, Claudio Sánchez-Albornoz, who clove to the view that the essential nature of Hispania and the *homo hispanus*, the ur-Spaniard, was essentially unaffected by the Islamic "occupation."[29] Instead, he averred, the *Reconquista* was the forge in which the modern Spanish nation had been wrought.[30] In 1969, Ignacio Olagüe created a stir when he went so far as to deny that the Arabs had ever invaded Spain at all.[31]

During the course of the past four decades, however, as modern Spain has made the journey from military dictatorship to full-fledged democracy, academic perspectives on the Peninsula's medieval past have changed beyond all recognition. For one thing, the rhetoric of *Reconquista* has fallen decidedly out of fashion. Instead, influenced in particular by the approaches of the French *Annales* School and by the decentralization of political power in Spain, academic emphasis has been on the importance of socioeconomic forces rather than the power of ideology, on diversity rather than unity.[32] At the same time, Castro's vision of peaceful interfaith coexistence has been embraced anew in some quarters, albeit with some modification. [33] Some scholars have gone so far as to argue that the dynamic cultural hybridity that was supposedly the norm in the Peninsula until at least the advent of the Berber Almoravids in the late eleventh century or the pogroms of the late fourteenth century in some way prefigures modern aspirations toward multicultural dialogue and provides the present with some lessons from the past.[34]

Yet the idealizing aspects of *convivencia*, and the tendency among at least some of its proponents toward romanticized broad-brush generalization, have made the concept increasingly unsatisfactory to a number of scholars, not least because it is frustratingly elastic. Maya Soifer, in a recent bracing critique of the term, has put her finger on the nub of the problem:

> Having appeared under the guises of "peaceful coexistence," "acculturation," and "daily interaction," *convivencia* has become a byword that one can employ in any number of ways. *Convivencia* can be anything and everything: a rhetorical flourish, a nostalgic nod to a rich historiographical tradition, as well as an ambitiously construed notion that aspires to summarize the entire range of religious minorities' experiences in medieval Spain. [35]

As Soifer has observed, *convivencia* survives, but "it remains on life support."[36] The problem is not so much that interfaith social and cultural hybridity was a chimera in a medieval Iberian context—the valuable work of art historians and literary critics, in particular, provides ample evidence that such cross-fertilization could and did take place across religious frontiers[37]—but rather that the permissive use of the catch-all label *convivencia* runs the risk of oversimplifying the sheer complexity of interfaith relations in this period, and, what is worse, if it is framed according to modern multicultural sensibilities, of indulging in anachronism.[38]

It is for this very reason that a number of scholars have largely eschewed terms like *convivencia*, just as they have also given the cold shoulder to the National-Catholic rhetoric of *Reconquista*, preferring to establish new analytical categories in their stead. Brian Catlos, for example, has argued that interfaith relations in the Peninsula were above all marked by what he has dubbed *conveniencia*, an overwhelmingly utilitarian dynamic which was sustained by a complex system of reciprocal interests.[39] Some scholars have embraced socio-anthropological techniques in order to better understand the realities of interfaith interaction in medieval Iberia.[40] Yet others have promoted postcolonial theory as an important methodological tool with which to rethink such cultural contact.[41] The latter approach seeks to give voice to those marginalized peoples, the "subaltern," who have been overlooked by previous dominating ideologies, and focuses on the cultural contacts, collaborations, and resistance that arose as a result of the colonial encounter, as well as the legacies that it bequeathed. The proponents of postcolonial analysis view it as an antidote to dyed-in-the-wool historicism, by emphasizing the connectivity of the past with the present. According to Nadia R. Altschul, for example, such approaches "foster nuanced recognition of the live connection that our scholarship and medieval Iberia have with the world at large, and prepare us to better understand and challenge the inequalities of our postcolonial present."[42]

Another conceptual tool that has been much at the forefront of recent historiography on Christian-Muslim interaction in the Peninsula is that of the frontier. Numerous studies have emphasized the key role played by the militarized Christian frontier with Islam in shaping the society, economy, and culture of Central and Southern Iberia from the late eleventh century on.[43] Yet the very word "frontier" defies easy definition and is replete with ambiguity.[44] At one level, we should be aware that what passed for a frontier in the medieval world had little in common with modern concepts of hard and fast linear state borders, but is better characterized as a permeable zone of contact and typically "a complex abode of mixed loyalties," as Eduardo Manzano Moreno has put it.[45] In medieval Iberia, for example, the borderlands that separated Islamic and Christian areas of authority were regularly criss-crossed by merchants, diplomats, transhumant shepherds, political exiles, and mercenaries, to name only a few of those who made the journey.[46] Besides, it would be a mistake to conceive of the frontier purely in geopolitical terms. There were other frontiers in existence—linguistic, artistic, economic, and cultural—all highly permeable. As Benita Sampedro and Simon Doubleday have put it, "frontiers are . . . fluid, porous, and multifaceted spaces of transition. Needless to say, frontier and fluidity are not contradictory and opposed, but complementary concepts."[47] At the same time, if we over-privilege the "frontier phenomenon" as the primary form of political-military interaction in medieval Iberia, we also run the risk of oversimplifying the political dynamic of the region to a straightforward struggle between Christendom and Islam. The reality was that there were always multiple political players in the Peninsula, whose geopolitical agendas shifted over time and who did not hesitate to forge bonds of amity across the religious frontier if circumstances warranted it. A notable case in point was Alfonso IX of León (1188–1230), who allied himself with the Berber Almohads in 1196 against Christian Castile as a means to further his own territorial ambitions in the contested Tierra de Campos region, and was excommunicated by Pope Celestine III as a consequence. Medieval Iberia was always a region of multiple frontiers, never of one.

Of all the frontiers—physical or psychological—that existed in the Peninsula, religious boundaries were without a doubt among the most actively policed and, as a consequence, were probably the most difficult to cross. These religious boundaries were manifold and complex, but in general they were shaped by an overriding fear of excessive social interaction or assimilation among the three faiths that coexisted within the region. Very broadly, it is fair to say that two chief anxieties weighed heavily on the minds of the religious and secular authorities of the Christian, Jewish, and Muslim communities that dwelled on either side of the frontier between al-Andalus and the Christian-ruled realms of the North. One was their steely determination to prevent their coreligionists from renouncing their faith and embracing another; the second was their concern to prevent—or in some cases regulate—sexual relations between members of different religious faiths. This book might therefore be said to be concerned with the frontier phenomenon in at least two distinct ways. In a literal sense, it is interested in the processes by which women—either legitimate wives or slave concubines—*physically* moved from Christian- to Muslim-dominated areas of control, or vice versa, crossing the political frontier, such as it was. Equally, however, this work is concerned with those cultural, legal, or mental boundaries that the Abrahamic faiths of Iberia sought to erect in order to protect themselves from excessive social interaction or assimilation with the others and which were to loom large in the political and cultural discourse of both the Muslim- and Christian-dominated regions of the Peninsula. It is to those boundaries and to their wider function that we will now turn.

Chapter 1

Sex as Power

The circumstances surrounding the Islamic conquest of the Visigothic kingdom of Iberia between 711 and c.720 remain deeply obscure, for Muslim and Christian accounts of the invasion differ greatly in terms of chronology, detail, and emphasis. The two earliest Muslim accounts of the invasion—composed by the Maliki religious and legal scholars (*'ulamā*) Ibn Ḥabīb (d. 853) and Ibn 'Abd al-Ḥakam (d. 871) fully 150 years after the events took place—are a notable case in point. In those texts, it has been argued, the authors' primary concern appears to have been to demonstrate that the lands of the Peninsula had been conquered by force rather than by submission and, as a result, were to be regarded as the absolute property of the Muslim invaders.[1] In marked contrast, the chronicler Ibn al-Qūṭīya (d. 977), who claimed to be of Visigothic royal descent, was equally insistent that the Islamic takeover of the Peninsula had been more the fruit of a series of pacts with the Hispano-Gothic population than the consequence of a full-blown military conquest.[2] Be that as it may, there is broad consensus between the various accounts, Muslim and Christian alike, that the collapse of the Visigothic state owed as much to the invaders' skill in exploiting existing political divisions within the Peninsula as to the speed and ruthlessness with which they were able to press home their military advantage. The death of King Roderic (710–11/12) in battle and that of much of his aristocratic entourage, together with the fall of the capital Toledo soon afterward, appears to have left what remained of the Visigothic ruling élite in a state of collective paralysis, unable to coordinate further resistance.[3] In the ensuing power vacuum, some notables are said to have fled to the remote mountainous regions of the North;[4] others abandoned the Peninsula altogether and sought refuge across the Pyrenees;[5] yet others were carried off into captivity, or were even executed outright.[6]

Other Visigothic notables sought to preserve their wealth, status, and power by coming to terms with the invaders. One such was Theodemir (d. 744), lord of Orihuela, Alicante, and five other towns in the southeast of the Peninsula, who on 5 April 713 agreed on a treaty with the military commander 'Abd al-Azīz b. Mūsā, the text of which has thankfully survived.[7] Theodemir and his supporters pledged loyalty to the Muslim authorities and undertook not to succor any fugitives or enemies of the Muslim state. Furthermore, they agreed that they and the towns under Theodemir's authority would pay an annual poll tax, in return for which they were guaranteed their safety and freedom of worship. In doing so, they and the other Christian and Jewish communities who made similar undertakings acquired the status of *dhimmī* (protected peoples) under Muslim rule. The treaty may be a chance survival, but it serves to reinforce the impression given by other sources that the Islamic conquest of the Peninsula was in part a gradual and negotiated takeover, involving the active collaboration of significant elements of the Hispano-Gothic aristocracy, rather than the smash-and-grab raid presented by some of the Arabic narrative accounts.[8]

Intermarriage with the indigenous Christian population of Iberia constituted another important mechanism by which the Muslim invaders consolidated their authority over the Peninsula. Indeed, "sexual mixing" between Muslim men and Christian women—be it through marriage or the taking of slave concubines—may be said to have represented a vital element in driving the process of social and cultural change in postconquest Iberia. The purpose of this chapter is to investigate the social, cultural, and political significance of such interfaith sexual liaisons—be they consensual or forced—and the part they played within the construction of Islamic authority prior to the millennium.

Interfaith Marriage: Purposes and Consequences

According to the tenets of classical Islamic law, intermarriage between a Muslim man and a Christian or Jewish woman was entirely permissible, as long as any children born to the couple were also brought up as Muslims: "Lawful to you are the believing women and the free women from among those who were given the Scriptures before you, provided that you give them their dowries and live in honor with them, neither committing fornication nor taking them as mistresses."[9] As Jessica Coope has noted, "underlying this rule is the assumption that the husband, as head of the family, would be likely to convert his wife, whereas the wife, as the subordinate partner, would be unable to convert her husband to her religion."[10] By stark contrast, marriage or indeed any sexual relations between a Muslim woman and a Christian or Jewish man were strictly outlawed.[11] Thus, a ninth-century legal pronouncement from Córdoba ordered that any Christian found guilty of having sexual intercourse with a Muslim woman should receive corporal punishment and imprisonment; other legal authorities prescribed the death penalty for such transgressors.[12]

For its part, the Christian Church, like Judaism before it, had traditionally expressed hostility to those who engaged in sexual intercourse with people of other faiths. St. Paul had been forthright on the matter: "Do not unite yourselves with unbelievers; they are no fit mates for you. What has righteousness to do with wickedness? Can light consort with darkness?" (2 Corinthians 6:14). These prohibitions had been amplified in numerous pieces of conciliar and secular legislation promulgated during the period of the Later Roman Empire and beyond.[13] In Iberia, for example, the synod of Elvira, held c. 300–309, along with a series of church councils celebrated in Toledo under the authority of the Visigothic monarchy during the sixth and seventh centuries, had outlawed intermarriage between Jewish men and Christian women.[14] In the aftermath of the Muslim invasion and conquest of the Peninsula, however, such concerns in some quarters on the Christian side appear to have been temporarily laid to one side.

Our sources, Christian and Muslim alike, give the impression that the lead in this matter was taken by 'Abd al-Azīz b. Mūsā, who succeeded to the governorship of al-Andalus in 714 once his father Mūsā b. Nuṣayr—the Arab governor of Ifrīqīya (North Africa) and architect of the invasion of the Peninsula—had been recalled to Damascus.[15] It is widely reported that some time after taking up the reins of power 'Abd al-Azīz married King Roderic's widow (or his daughter according to some accounts), who is referred to in the *Chronicle of 754* as Egilona and by Muslim writers as Aylū or Umm 'Āṣim. The *Chronicle of 754* gives this brief account:

> After he ['Abd al-Azīz] had taken all the riches and positions of honour in Seville, as well as the queen of Spain, whom he joined in marriage, and the daughters of kings and princes, whom he treated as concubines and then rashly repudiated, he was eventually killed on the advice of Ayyūb by a revolt of his own men while he was in prayer. After Ayyūb had held Spain for a full month, al-Ḥurr

> succeeded to the throne of Hesperia by order of the prince, who was informed about the death of 'Abd al-Azīz in this way: that on the advice of Queen Egilona, wife of the late king Roderic, whom he had joined to himself, he tried to throw off the Arab yoke from his neck and retain the conquered kingdom of Iberia for himself.[16]

On the Muslim side, writing a century later, Ibn 'Abd al-Ḥakam describes these events in a far more dramatic fashion:

> After his father departed, 'Abd al-Azīz married a Christian princess, daughter of a king of al-Andalus. It is said she was the daughter of Roderic, king of al-Andalus, whom Ṭāriq killed. She brought him a great fortune in worldly things, such as cannot be described. When she came to him, she said, "Why do I not see the people of your kingdom glorifying you? They do not prostrate themselves before you as the people of my father's kingdom glorified him and prostrated themselves before him." He did not know what to say to her, so he commanded that the side of his palace be pierced with a small door. He used to give audience to the people, and for this purpose he would come to the inside of the door, so that someone entering to see him would have to lower his head on account of the smallness of the door. She was in a [hidden] spot watching the people, and when she saw this, she said to 'Abd al-Azīz, "Now you are a great king!" The people heard, however, that he had constructed the door for this purpose, and some believed that she had made him a Christian.[17]

Alarmed by this behavior, a group of prominent Arab conspirators led by Ḥabīb b. Abī 'Ubayda al-Fihrī, who was 'Abd al-Azīz's right-hand man, and Ziyād b. al-Nābigha al-Tamīmī, assassinated the governor while he was at prayer, perhaps with the connivance of the caliph Sulaymān (715–17).[18] Later authors, including the Andalusi chronicler Aḥmad al-Rāzī (d. 955), embellished this episode even farther, claiming that Roderic's widow had encouraged 'Abd al-Azīz to wear a crown studded with precious stones in order to further project his authority. It is also reported by some that the "royal couple" lived together in the church of Santa Rufina in Seville.[19]

Interfaith marriage brought with it two clear advantages for the Muslim élite that sought to consolidate its power in Iberia in the immediate aftermath of the conquest. First, it provided a means to legitimize the imposition of new lords over the Hispano-Gothic population, at a time when the pacification of the Peninsula was still precarious in the extreme and the number of Muslim settlers was relatively small. In this way, the Christian women of al-Andalus could be regarded as potential "peace-weavers" in the consolidation of Islamic rule, in the same way that intermarriage between Norman lords and local heiresses was later to provide a means to bind conquerors and conquered more closely together in the wake of the Norman conquest of England, Southern Italy, and Ireland.[20] In the case of 'Abd al-Azīz, however, the Arab governor is reported to have gone even farther, using his marriage to a member of the Visigothic ruling class as a means to associate himself with indigenous traditions of government, including perhaps crown-wearing, as part of an ambitious if ultimately doomed attempt to create a personal monarchy for himself in Iberia that might command support from the local population.[21] In short, 'Abd al-Azīz's downfall was brought about by his political ambitions, which sought to deny the caliph's authority over al-Andalus, and not by his decision to take for himself a Christian bride, as some authors would later imply. After all, Ziyād ibn al-Nābigha al-Tamīmī, one of the chief conspirators against the governor, is also said to have married a Christian noblewoman.[22]

The second advantage offered by marriage alliances between Muslim lords and Christian noblewomen was that they represented a means through which much of the landed wealth of the Visigothic magnate class could legitimately be channeled into Muslim ownership. Whereas property conquered by force of arms (*'anwatan*) would have passed automatically into the hands of the invaders, there were large swathes of the country—like Theodemir's power base in the southeast, for example—where Islamic authority had been recognized through a pact, and where the invaders had no such rights of ownership over these lands (called *ṣulḥan*).[23] Interfaith marriage offered a solution to that problem, in that the children born to such mixed faith alliances, who were to be raised as Muslims, stood to inherit the property of their Visigothic grandfathers, through their mothers, as well as the lands that their Muslim fathers might have won as the fruits of conquest.

An account of how such arrangements might have worked out in practice is provided by Ibn al-Qūṭīya. Ibn al-Qūṭīya's proud boast was that he was descended from Sara, grand-daughter of King Wittiza (694–710), whose sons had reportedly conspired against King Roderic at the time of the invasion and offered their allegiance to the Muslims. In return for this support, they had been confirmed in possession of their father's estates, totaling some 3,000 properties spread across the Peninsula, or so it was claimed.[24] Ibn al-Qūṭīya goes on to recount that when the eldest of Wittiza's sons, Almund, later died, his lands in and around Seville were seized by his brother Artabas, prompting Almund's daughter, Sara, and her younger brothers to travel to the court of the caliph Hishām I (724–43) in Damascus in search of restitution. The caliph ruled that Artabas's usurpation of Almund's legacy had been unlawful, and he also arranged for Sara to marry one of his clients, ʿĪsā b. Muzāḥim, who accompanied her back to the Peninsula and helped to recover her properties. It was from this marriage that Ibn al-Qūṭīya claimed to be descended. When later widowed in 755, Sara married again, this time to ʿUmayr ibn Saʿīd al-Lakhmī, a member of one of the Syrian *junds* (military regiments) that had arrived in the Peninsula in 742 to help prop up Umayyad authority in the wake of a major Berber revolt. It was through this second marriage, which was said to have been arranged by the first independent emir of al-Andalus, ʿAbd al-Raḥmān I, that the family of the Banū Ḥajjāj later came to enjoy extensive wealth and power in the region of Seville.[25]

How trustworthy is Ibn al-Qūṭīya's account? Given that his *History* comprises more a colorful collection of exemplary and fabulous anecdotes than a detailed account of his times, and that even his pupil Ibn al-Faraḍī is said to have disparaged him as a spinner of tales (*akhbār*) rather than as a purveyor of serious history (*taʾrīkh*), his reliability as a historian has frequently been called into question. His account of how Sara traveled to Damascus to raise her case with the caliph certainly raises all manner of doubts.[26] It has been pointed out, for example, that Wittiza's sons could only have been young boys at the time of the conquest and that it is difficult to believe that they took the lead in offering to give support to the Muslims, as Ibn al-Qūṭīya alleges.[27] On the other hand, the Christian *Chronicle of 754* does make mention of the support lent to the Muslims by Wittiza's brother, Oppa, so the idea that some of Wittiza's kin—including perhaps his widow, who had briefly held the regency before Roderic seized the throne—were instrumental in negotiating with the Muslims, and that his sons were later beneficiaries of the deal, should not be dismissed out of hand. Whether "Sara the Goth" and her brothers really did journey to the caliphal court in Damascus, as is claimed, is highly doubtful. Such stories served above all to explain to posterity the process of accommodation between conquerors and some of the vanquished that had taken place at the time of the eighth-century Islamic conquest. Yet even if embroidered, the general thrust of Ibn al-Qūṭīya's story, which illustrates how an interfaith marriage alliance provided the means by which the property of King Wittiza passed into Muslim control, is eminently plausible. As it is, a similar process of property transmission can be glimpsed in the case of a daughter of Theodemir of Murcia, who is reported to have married 'Abd al-Jabbār b. Khaṭṭāb b. Marwān b. Naḍīr, another member of the Syrian army that arrived in the Peninsula in 742. According to the chronicler al-'Udhrī, Khaṭṭāb received two villages from his bride by way of dowry, at Tarsa near Elche and at Tall al-Khaṭṭāb near Orihuela.[28] It was thanks to this alliance that the family of 'Abd al-Jabbār was able to establish itself as one of the wealthiest and most influential kin groups in the region, whose power was to endure for centuries.[29]

Interfaith marriage alliances offered the Visigothic landed aristocracy a number of advantages. Most obviously, for those like the families of Wittiza and Theodemir, who sought and found an accommodation with the Islamic invaders, marriage pacts represented a means for certain kin groups to defend their interests in the localities where they had traditionally held sway and to keep their landed wealth intact. Thus, if we are to believe Ibn al-Qūṭīya, Wittiza's son Artabas continued to be an influential power broker in the region of Córdoba even after the conquest.[30] Likewise, Theodemir's presumed son Athanagild remained a prominent figure in the southeast of the Peninsula, at any rate until the arrival of the Syrian *junds* and the appointment of the governor Abū'l-Khaṭṭār during the 740s.[31] The price to be paid for that security of tenure was to be the raising of future generations of the family as Muslims, although in the early days of the conquest, barely eighty years after the death of the Prophet Muḥammad, when the doctrines and customs of Islam were still somewhat hazily defined, the differences between the three monotheistic religions were by no means as clear to contemporaries as they would later become.[32] In short, for the members of the old Visigothic élite who were willing to collaborate with the invaders, interfaith marriage represented an attractive means to guarantee security of tenure and avoid the traumatic upheaval and loss of wealth, status, and power that had undoubtedly affected their peers in many other parts of the Peninsula.

Yet, while interfaith marriage was an important mechanism with which to encourage assimilation between Muslims and Christians in the years immediately following the conquest, it also had the potential to cause friction between the two. That, at least, is what a later account of the rebellion against Muslim authority that was hatched in the northernmost region of Asturias by the Christian warlord Pelayo (Pelagius) would have us believe. As so often, the sources for these events are both sparse and problematic in equal measure.[33] According to the *A Sebastianum* version of the late ninth-century Christian text known to historians as the *Chronicle of Alfonso III*, Pelayo was a Visigothic notable of royal descent; the Roda version of the same text, which differs in emphasis and a number of details, has him as the swordbearer of kings Wittiza and Roderic.[34] The latter version relates that in the early stages of the Muslim conquest Islamic authority over Asturias was wielded by one of Ṭāriq b. Ziyād's supporters, a Berber called Munnuza, whose center of power was the coastal settlement of Gijón.[35] During his governorship of the region:

> A certain Pelayo, who was the swordbearer of kings Wittiza and Roderic, oppressed by the authority of the Ishmaelites, had come to Asturias with his sister. On account of his sister, the aforementioned Munnuza despatched Pelayo to Córdoba as his envoy; but before he returned, Munnuza married his sister through some ruse. When Pelayo returned he by no means approved of it and since he had already been thinking about the salvation of the Church, he hastened to bring this about with all of his courage. Then the evil Ṭāriq sent soldiers to Munnuza, who were to arrest Pelayo and lead him back to Córdoba, bound in chains.[36]

This was supposedly the spark that detonated a Christian revolt in Asturias. The chronicle goes on to narrate Pelayo's flight from the Muslims, his election as *dux* (lord) of the region, and his subsequent victory at Covadonga at the foot of the Picos de Europa Mountains in 718, or possibly 722, depending on which version of events we follow. "From then on," the late ninth-century *Chronicle of Albelda* declared, "freedom was restored to the Christian people . . . and by divine providence the kingdom of Asturias was born."[37] How much of this we can take at face value is a moot point. It may be the case that claims that Pelayo enjoyed connections to the Visigothic royal house, either by blood or by service, were so much wishful thinking by later chroniclers keen to portray the Asturian realm as the legitimate successor to the Visigothic kingdom. Alternatively, it is plausible that Pelayo—like Theodemir before him—was a local noble, who had decided to come to terms with the invaders in the wake of the collapse of the Visigothic monarchy, only to repudiate those terms at a later date.[38] The motivation ascribed to Pelayo's revolt, namely his desire to avenge the dishonor brought about by his sister's marriage to Munnuza, might be construed simply as an easily understandable justification for his revolt after the event, in an age when the defense of family honor was considered essential. That said, it is by no means impossible that Pelayo's inital pact of surrender with the Muslims had been sealed by a marriage alliance between his sister and Munnuza, just as Theodemir's presumed son, Athanagild, may have engineered the marriage of his sister to Khaṭṭāb at the time of his agreement with the Syrians, when they settled in the southeast of the Peninsula.

To sum up thus far, the various strands of evidence that have survived—scattered, exiguous, and problematic though they may be—all seem to point in the same direction. They suggest that interfaith marriage between Muslim men and Christian women became a significant tool in the process of pacification and colonization that took place in the period immediately following the Islamic conquest and in the aftermath of the arrival of the Syrian *junds* in 742. Furthermore, even though only a handful of examples have come down to us, recorded by later historians because the élite protagonists were deemed particularly "newsworthy," it is safe to assume that marriage alliances of this sort occurred with frequency at other levels of society too. So commonplace indeed had the practice evidently become by the end of the eighth century, that in a letter he composed sometime between 781 and 785 Pope Hadrian I expressed dismay that so many daughters of Catholic parents in the Peninsula had been given in marriage to Muslims or Jews.[39] Hadrian's letter was a response to missives dispatched to him by the Frankish clergyman Egila, who had been consecrated bishop by Archbishop Wilcharius of Sens c.780 and sent to the Peninsula to preach.[40] Such anxieties were voiced anew at an ecclesiastical council held in Córdoba in 839, when the assembled Christian clerics denounced "the impious marriage of various faithful with the infidel, sowing crimes among our morals."[41] It is worth noting in passing that mixed marriages between Muslims and Jews are far less well documented.[42]

Other sources reinforce the impression that interfaith marriage between Muslims and Christians had become relatively frequent at lower levels of society by the middle of the ninth century. The evidence in question is provided by a clutch of Latin texts that were produced in response to the Christian "martyrdom movement" that briefly convulsed Córdoba during the 850s. The movement, which erupted in 851, appears to have been a response to the quickening pace of conversion of Andalusi Christians to Islam by the middle of the ninth century and the ongoing Arabicization of society that threatened to obliterate the traditional Latin literary heritage of the Christian Church in the Peninsula, or so some thought.[43] According to the accounts of the movement penned by the priest Eulogius of Córdoba and his disciple Paul Albar, at least forty-eight Christians deliberately courted "martyrdom" at the hands of the Islamic authorities by publicly denouncing Islam or by encouraging *muwallads* (converts to Islam) to apostatize, both of which actions carried the capital penalty under Islamic law.[44]

How much credence should be attached to these accounts is difficult to assess. The texts present—yet again!—numerous methodological problems for the historian, not least because several of the cases reported by the movement's leading light, Eulogius, appear to have been literary inventions "lifted" from various non-Hispanic martyrologies.[45] Be that as it may, it is striking that at least twelve of those Christians who were executed by command of the Umayyad authorities during this period were said to have come from religiously mixed families.[46] Not only that, the accounts also suggest that in some cases—in clear contravention of Islamic law—the children born to those couples had not been raised as Muslims. It was for this reason that the Islamic authorities regarded such voluntary martyrs as apostates.[47] Jessica Coope has gone so far as to declare that "hatred between relatives in mixed families was one of the engines that powered the martyrs' movement."[48] It is apparent that Eulogius viewed such sexual mixing as a root cause of the troubles then assailing the embattled Christian community in al-Andalus. He condemned one such mixed marriage as a "wolfish union"; elsewhere he continued the vulpine motif when he compared another interfaith marriage alliance to a wolf invading his flock.[49] In a similar vein, Paul Albar, referring to the martyr Leocritia's mixed background, declared vituperatively that she was "begotten of Gentile dregs and born from wolf's flesh."[50] Be that as it may, Eulogius and Paul Albar did not subject the women who had married Muslims to direct criticism, doubtless conscious that it was thanks to their influence that their children had embraced Christianity and later become martyrs.[51]

It seems unlikely that these mixed marriages were mere literary devices conjured up by Eulogius or Paul Albar. This impression is confirmed by the *fatwā*, or legal ruling, attributed to the jurisprudent Abū Ibrāhīm Isḥāq ibn Ibrāhīm of Córdoba (d. 965), which refers to another such marriage alliance that came to the attention of the authorities. In this case, a woman had been born to a Muslim father and a Christian mother, who had brought her up as Christian after his death. The woman had subsequently married a Christian with whom she had a child. Questioned by the judge, she claimed that her father had converted to Islam while serving elsewhere in the mercenary guard. The judge pronounced that in order that she should not be punished as an apostate, she would need to provide reliable testimony that her father's conversion had indeed occurred away from the family home.[52]

In short, the evidence outlined thus far suggests that intermarriage between Muslim men and Christian women had become relatively commonplace at lower levels of society by the mid-ninth century, that in some cases—in clear contravention of Islamic law—the children born to those couples were not raised as Muslims, and that the conversion of some but not all family members to Islam could cause considerable tensions within kin groups.[53] This might explain why the assembled clerics at the Council of Córdoba in 839, echoing Pope Hadrian's disquiet a few decades previously, considered sexual mixing of this sort sufficiently widespread to warrant explicit condemnation. In modern times the Spanish Arabist Julián Ribera went so far as to claim that the degree of interfaith sexual mixing was so extensive in Iberia during the early medieval period that the proportion of Arab blood running through the veins of the tenth-century Umayyad caliphs of al-Andalus was in fact infinitesimal.[54] According to this analysis, Andalusi society was ethnically and culturally hybrid to its very core.

There remains the possibility, however, that among the Muslim élite, at least, inter-faith marriage pacts of the kind outlined above might have been simply a short-term phenomenon born of political and economic expediency: once the Muslim conquest of the Peninsula had been consolidated the practice may have passed into desuetude. Indeed, in his pioneering work on Islamic society in the Peninsula, published in 1976, Pierre Guichard argued forcefully that, far from mixing extensively with the Hispano-Gothic population, the majority of the Arab and Berber families who had undertaken the conquest were so anxious to preserve their "pure" breeding and lineage that they went out of their way to avoid intermarriage with the local population, be they Christians, Jews, or even *muwallads*.[55] They did this, Guichard posited, by maintaining "Eastern" patterns of kinship, according to which patrilineal descent and endogamous marriage, that is, within the kin group, remained the norm. His theory seemed to be corroborated, as far as the Arabs were concerned, at least, by writers such as the Andalusi polymath Ibn Ḥazm (d. 1064), whose *Kitāb Jamharat ansāb al-ʿArab*, a genealogical account of the Arab tribes who had settled in al-Andalus after the Islamic conquest, consistently privileged the agnatic, that is to say, the male lineages of these families over the female ones.[56] It is worth noting in passing that Ibn Ḥazm also provided a number of examples of what he considered "unequal marriages" between Arab men and women of lesser social rank in his *Naqṭ al-ʿarūs*. The names of those who "married down" in this way included the vizier to the emir Muḥammad I (852–86), Tammām b. ʿĀmir al-Thaqafī, who reportedly married a daughter of the Christian Khalaf b. Rūmān.[57]

The alleged reluctance of some Muslims to intermarry with other faiths may have been reinforced by fears—articulated most powerfully by followers of the Maliki school of religious jurisprudence—of "corruption" by Christians or Jews, because it was believed that by her customs and morals the wife and mother might ultimately undermine the faith of her offspring, particularly if she lived within what was termed the *dār al-ḥarb* (the "Abode of War"), that is, the territories not under Islamic rule.[58] In his *Kitāb al-bida'*, or "The Treatise Against Innovations," Muḥammad ibn Waḍḍaḥ (d. 900) had sternly warned his coreligionists: "It is said that temptations will come with the companions of the Book, and they will be because of them."[59] Meanwhile, the religious authorities zealously patrolled the boundaries between the faiths with regard to such matters as ritual purity, food taboos, festival celebrations, or burials, in order to define and strengthen the legal and social limits between Muslims and *dhimmīs*.[60] This climate of opinion helps to explain why in their accounts of the Muslim conquest Maliki scholars such as Ibn 'Abd al-Ḥakam chose to give such prominent coverage to the doomed marriage of 'Abd al-Azīz b. Mūsā and his Christian wife, and even to echo the claim that 'Abd al-Azīz b. Mūsā had converted to Christianity. Such accounts stood not merely as a stark warning of the danger that such overmighty subjects posed to the constituted authority in the Islamic world, but also as a reminder to fellow Muslims of the serious consequences that marriage outside the Islamic *umma*, or community, might bring in its wake.[61]

However, a warning note should be sounded. In recent years several elements of the Guichard thesis have been called into question. It has been pointed out, for example, that the French scholar's research was based upon an extremely small sample of texts, drawn from only a handful of Andalusi writers active during the tenth and eleventh centuries, and that he did not take into account the ideological concerns that underpinned those writings.[62] The endogamous "Eastern" tribal structures that Guichard claimed to see across the ages may have been no more than a reflection of the political discourse of the age, which sought to emphasize the "Arabness" of the leading Peninsular families, not least that of the Umayyad caliphs of al-Andalus. The reality was that not only were many leading families ethnically hybrid, but also that most of the genealogies that were compiled during the tenth and eleventh centuries were replete with errors and imaginative inventions. As Ann Christys has observed, "many of the genealogies were more illustrious in their reconstructions than in actuality and the subject of ethnicity in al-Andalus became hopelessly confused."[63] A case in point was the Banū Khaṭṭāb family of Murcia mentioned earlier, which while proudly trumpeting its Arab ancestry did not preserve any genealogical memory of its maternal Visigothic forebears.[64] In short, the ethnic "purity" that Guichard claimed to detect among the leading Muslim kin groups of al-Andalus may be no more than a mirage.[65]

Marriage Across Frontiers

However, even if it were true that many Muslims at the level of the political and social élite later chose to eschew marriage with *dhimmī*, it is striking that a number of influential families went out of their way to seek brides who were not Muslims, and that in some cases they did so by arranging marriage alliances with the emerging Christian-ruled realms that lay to the north of the Peninsula, or even further afield.[66] The earliest recorded example of an interfaith marriage pact of this sort was that arranged by the Berber warlord known as Munnuza, the leading military figure in the northeast of the Peninsula, who rebelled against the Umayyad governor 'Abd al-Raḥmān al-Ghāfiqī in around 731, reportedly in protest at the treatment of his countrymen by Islamic administrators in Libya.[67] The *Chronicle of 754* reports that after Munnuza had raised the flag of rebellion, he sought to bolster his position in the northeast by marrying the daughter of the Frankish Duke Eudo of Aquitaine. The latter, having already suffered several attacks by Muslim forces, presumably saw the marriage as a means to forestall further aggression. Yet little good did the alliance do either of them. Munnuza was shortly tracked down by the emir's forces to Cerdanya in the eastern Pyrenees, where he was besieged and then forced to flee to the mountains, finally throwing himself to his death from a high crag. His unfortunate bride—who is referred to in later sources by the name of Lampégie—was subsequently sent to the caliph's court in Damascus. The Christian chronicler expressed unbridled satisfaction at Munnuza's demise, which he saw as retribution for having "made himself drunk on the blood of Christians," and in particular for his complicity in the murder of the local bishop of Urgel. However, he passed no judgment on Munnuza's decision to take for himself a Christian bride.[68]

Even more striking was the case of the Banū Qasī family, which dominated the area of the Upper Ebro valley from at least the late eighth century to the early tenth.[69] The Banū Qasī were *muwallads*, supposedly descended from a Visigothic count named Casius, who is said to have reached an accommodation with the Muslim authorities at the time of the eighth-century conquest, made his way to Damascus to pledge allegiance to the Umayyad caliph, al-Walīd I, and subsequently converted to Islam.[70] How much credence should be accorded to this account of the family's origins is debatable. Roger Collins has speculated that it may belong to "the spurious antiquarianism that became fashionable in the later Umayyad period," and these doubts have been echoed more recently by Jesús Lorenzo Jiménez and Maribel Fierro.[71] Even so, it is far from inconceivable that a Visigothic lord in the Upper Ebro might have brokered a pact with the Muslim invaders—just as Theodemir of Murcia is known to have done in 713—and that he or his successors later converted to Islam. The fact that some members of the Banū Qasī are later said to have renounced Islam and embraced Christianity serves to reinforce the impression that this was a *muwallad* family whose Islamic ties remained in some cases fragile.[72]

Whether or not the power of the Banū Qasī in the Ebro region predated the Muslim conquest, the family only comes sharply into focus in 788, when one member of the clan, Mūsā b. Fortun, briefly seized Zaragoza. From their power base at Tudela, the family came to enjoy a substantial degree of autonomy over the neighboring districts of Zaragoza and Huesca, and even—toward the end of the ninth century—as far west as Toledo. The power of one of the most prominent members of the dynasty, Mūsā b. Mūsā (d. 862), was such that he reputedly styled himself "the third king of Spain."[73] In the pursuit of greater autonomy, members of the Banū Qasī wove a complex web of diplomatic contacts with neighboring states, most notably with the Basque Arista family of the embryonic Christian kingdom of Pamplona-Navarre, with whom they forged numerous marriage alliances.[74] For example, we are told by the late tenth-century Christian *Roda Codex* that in 872 Mūsā b. Mūsā married Assona, daughter of Íñigo Arista, founder of the Pamplonan royal dynasty[75]; meanwhile, the chronicler al-ʿUdhrī records that Mūsā b. Mūsā's son, Muṭarrif b. Mūsā, married Velazquita, a daughter of one Sancho, "lord of Pamplona" (d. 873).[76] A few years later, in 918, another such marriage pact prompted Furtūn b. Muḥammad to ally himself with King Sancho Garcés I of Pamplona (905–25) against the then Umayyad emir ʿAbd al-Raḥmān III (912–61).[77]

A similar matrimonial strategy was pursued by another *muwallad* kin group, the Banū Shabrīṭ and its close relatives the Banū Amrūs, whose center of power lay in the Central Pyrenees around Huesca.[78] Thus, it is recorded that one of the family members, Muḥammad al-Ṭawīl, married Sancha, daughter of Count Aznar Galíndez II of Aragon.[79] The porosity of the frontier between Christian and Muslim zones of influence at this time is further demonstrated by the fact that after the death of Muḥammad al-Ṭawīl in 913, his widow Sancha left Huesca and returned to Pamplona, where she married King García Sánchez I (931–70).[80]

For their part, the Umayyad rulers of al-Andalus may have been keen to emphasize their pure Arab descent along the male line from the family of the Prophet Muḥammad, but they too are known to have sought Christian brides of high rank from across the frontier.[81] Thus, the *Roda Codex* records that the Umayyad emir ʿAbd Allāh (888–912) married Onneca (Íñiga)—known to Muslim writers as Durr—who was the widow of Aznar Sánchez of the Arista family[82]; their son Muḥammad, who also later took a Christian slave as his concubine—called Muznah in the Arabic sources—was the father of ʿAbd al-Raḥmān III, the self-styled caliph of al-Andalus.[83] The example of the Umayyads was later followed by the all-powerful *ḥājib* (chief minister) Muḥammad b. Abī ʿĀmir (d. 1002), better known by his honorific al-Manṣūr, who demanded the hand in marriage of a daughter of Sancho Garcés II of Navarre (970–94) as part of a peace deal brokered with the king, probably in 983.[84]

Unfortunately, however, our sources have practically nothing to tell us about the circumstances that gave rise to such cross-border marriage alliances. It is probably safe to assume that for the most part freeborn Christian brides were not party to the negotiations that preceded such matrimonial pacts and that their consent was rarely sought, although that did not necessarily mean that all female members of the family were completely excluded from such deliberations.[85] No marriage contracts survive, more is the pity, nor are we left with even a description of how, in the case of freeborn Christian women, the undoubtedly delicate negotiations that preceded the marriage might have been conducted between the two parties. However, a glimpse of such matters is provided by the brief and idiosyncratic *Chronicle of the Kings of León*, which was composed by Bishop Pelayo of Oviedo sometime between 1121 and 1132.[86] In his unremittingly hostile account of the reign of Vermudo II of León (982–99), the bishop makes fleeting reference to the marriage alliance that was subsequently arranged "for the sake of peace" between the king's daughter, Teresa Vermúdez, and a certain pagan (i.e., Muslim) king of Toledo by her brother Alfonso V (999–1032). According to Pelayo, the princess proved an unwilling participant in the marriage, and when the king mocked her protests and subsequently raped her, he was struck down by a vengeful angel. On his deathbed, the king ordered that Teresa be allowed to return to her Leonese homeland. It was there that she took a nun's habit and later died in Oviedo, where she was buried in the monastery of San Pelayo.[87]

We shall return to the ideological significance of this episode in a later chapter. For now, it is the historicity of Pelayo's account that concerns us.[88] Documentary sources confirm that there was indeed a Princess Teresa born to Vermudo II and his second wife Elvira García of Castile. She can first be traced in the records on 18 August 1017, when she confirmed a grant made by her mother, Queen Elvira, to the bishop and chapter of Santiago de Compostela; on 17 December of that same year, with her sister Sancha Vermúdez, she engaged in a lawsuit with one Osorio Froilaz over the monastery of Santa Eulalia de Fingoy.[89] On 1 March 1028, Teresa granted some property of her own in the city of León to the church of Santiago; and on 27 January 1030, again with her sister Sancha, she gave an estate at Serantes to the same see.[90] These Compostelan documents were later copied into the twelfth-century cartulary known today as *Tumbo A*, and a painting of the two sisters was added.[91] In both donations Teresa was styled *Christi ancilla*, which demonstrates that by 1028 she had joined a religious community, in all probability that of San Pelayo de Oviedo, as Bishop Pelayo tells us, which is where she died on Wednesday 25 April 1039, according to her epitaph.[92] However, no documentary record of Teresa's supposed marriage to a Muslim king has survived.

The identity of the "pagan king" to whom Teresa was reportedly betrothed has provoked lively but inconclusive debate among historians. The nineteenth-century Dutch Arabist Reinhardt Dozy ventured that the ruler in question was none other than the redoubtable al-Manṣūr, who was reported by the North African historian Ibn Khaldūn (d. 1406) to have married a daughter of Vermudo II in 993.[93] Dozy further speculated that it must have been in 1003—the year after the death of al-Manṣūr, when his son and successor as *ḥājib*, ʿAbd al-Malik al-Muẓaffar, made peace with Alfonso V—that Teresa must have returned to León.[94] Not all scholars have been convinced, however. Given that Vermudo II had only married his second wife Elvira of Castile in 992, their daughter Teresa could have been only a babe in arms at the time of her supposed betrothal, if indeed she had been born at all.[95] Emilio Cotarelo and Hilda Grassotti have both argued, rather, that the princess who married al-Manṣūr was the daughter of Sancho Garcés II of Navarre mentioned earlier, whose betrothal to the *ḥājib* c. 983 was recorded by other sources, and that it was the memory of that marriage agreement that reached Bishop Pelayo at the beginning of the twelfth century and was transformed into legend.[96]

However, other scenarios suggest themselves. Teresa's brother, Alfonso V, was but five years old when he succeeded to the throne of León in 999; as a result, power was initially entrusted to a regency council. During this period, the young king faced a number of challenges to his authority, including a series of aristocratic revolts, a wave of attacks on the Galician coastline by Viking marauders, and two major offensives by the forces of ʿAbd al-Malik al-Muẓaffar, in 1002 and 1005 respectively, as a result of which the Christians were forced to seek peace.[97] Is it not conceivable that it was after the second of these campaigns, by which time Princess Teresa could still have been no more than thirteen years old, that she was betrothed to al-Muẓaffar, only returning to León after his untimely death late in 1008?

An alternative—and equally intriguing—possibility is that the bridegroom in question was al-Muẓaffar's brother and successor as *ḥājib*, ʿAbd al-Raḥmān, nicknamed Shanjūl (Sanchuelo). Ibn Idhārī al-Marrākushī relates that shortly after assuming power on his brother's death on 20 October 1008 ʿAbd al-Raḥmān dispatched a letter to an unnamed "infidel king"'—in all likelihood Alfonso V of León, in the light of subsequent events—"in the same way that his brother had written to him previously."[98] This letter is likely to have sought to renew the "pact of submission" with the Leonese that had been agreed at the start of al-Muẓaffar's term in office as *ḥājib* six years earlier, and it was probably accompanied by a demand for contingents of Christian troops to supplement the caliphal army, in the same way as Leonese and Castilian forces had been required to assist al-Muẓaffar on his raiding expedition to Catalonia in 1003.[99] In January 1009, despite rumblings of discontent among some of the Umayyad aristocracy, who were affronted by both his recent nomination as successor to the caliphate and his increasing reliance on the Berber military, ʿAbd al-Raḥmān proclaimed a *jihād* and led an army of Berber mercenaries and a few volunteers from Córdoba to Toledo, from where he planned to invade the Leonese kingdom. Accompanying the expeditionary force was a group of Christians led by the Leonese Count Sancho Gómez, as well as a reported 70 members of ʿAbd al-Raḥmān's extensive harem.[100]

However, ʿAbd al-Raḥmān's plans soon unraveled. Shortly after he reached Toledo he was forced to abort the expedition when bad news reached him from Córdoba: the city had been taken over by a group of Umayyad conspirators on 15 February 1009; the caliph Hishām II (976–1013) had been deposed and replaced by the leader of the rebels, Muḥammad b. ʿAbd al-Jabbār al-Mahdī; and the palace at Madinat al-Zāhira, which had been built by al-Manṣūr, had been sacked. Given these multiple setbacks, ʿAbd al-Raḥmān opted to return south, but support for his cause soon began to crumble, and he was deserted by his Berber mercenaries. Leaving the women of his harem at his palace at Armilāṭ (Guadalmellato), to the north of Córdoba, ʿAbd al-Raḥmān fled with

Count Sancho and a force of only 50 horsemen, with the intention of escaping north. However, he was tracked down by supporters of the new caliph Muḥammad and killed, along with the count, at a nearby Christian monastery on 5 March 1009. The women of his harem were sent back to Córdoba.[101]

It seems clear enough that, like his father and brother before him, ʿAbd al-Raḥmān had sought an early military success against the Christians as a means to win personal prestige and thereby shore up his political authority at home. Whether he further attempted to emphasize his dominance over the Christians by engineering a marriage alliance with a Leonese princess, in this case Teresa Vermúdez, in the same way his father al-Manṣūr had done when he had sought the hand in marriage of Sancho Garcés II's daughter—ʿAbd al-Raḥmān's mother—is unknown but by no means implausible. ʿAbd al-Raḥmān's own status as heir to the caliphate and his Christian background on his mother's side might also have helped to seal a peace deal. According to Ibn ʿIdhārī al-Marrākushī, one of the arguments that had been employed by ʿAbd al-Raḥmān when he persuaded Hishām II to appoint him his heir was to remind him that they were both born to Navarrese mothers.[102] This might explain why it was later claimed by Christian writers, such as Lucas of Tuy (d. 1249), that the Muslim king had "pretended to be a Christian" and had sworn to provide military support to Alfonso V.[103] Conversely, one of the accusations flung at ʿAbd al-Raḥmān by his enemies within al-Andalus was that he was not a proper Muslim at all.[104] It is also noteworthy that Toledo was ʿAbd al-Raḥmān's main base of operations during the campaign against the Christians in 1009 and that after the Umayyad palace coup, faced by large-scale opposition to his authority, he apparently intended to make the city his power base from which to launch a counterattack against the rebels in Córdoba. The importance that he attached to the city can be seen from the fact that, once he had been forced to suspend the campaign and return south toward Córdoba, he sent a letter to the citizens of Toledo urging them to show loyalty to the caliph Hishām II. Subsequently, Count Sancho is said to have advised ʿAbd al-Raḥmān to escape north and ally himself with Wāḍiḥ, the governor of the Middle March, whose chief city was Toledo.[105] All this might explain the otherwise opaque comment by Archbishop Rodrigo Jiménez (d. 1247) in his *De rebus Hispanie* that the "king of Toledo" sought a political alliance with León *against* Córdoba.[106]

We cannot prove categorically that ʿAbd al-Raḥmān "Sanchuelo" was indeed the "pagan king" to whom Teresa Vermúdez was betrothed. Other plausible candidates present themselves, such as the Umayyad pretender Muḥammad b. ʿAbd al-Jabbār al-Mahdī, who, when ousted from Córdoba by

Sulaymān b. al-Ḥakam b. Sulaymān in 1010, briefly took refuge in Toledo, or even one of the various notables who sought to establish themselves as independent dynasts in Toledo in the years immediately after the fall of the caliphate.[107] What is entirely conceivable, however, is that at some point during the first decade of the eleventh century—at a time when the entire edifice of the Umayyad state was beginning to totter and when the Leonese monarchy's own grip on power was uncertain—Alfonso V, or the nobles who wielded power on his behalf, might have sought to broker a marriage alliance with a Muslim potentate, just as other hard-pressed Christian kings had done in the past. Equally, one can quite imagine why a leading Muslim with designs on the caliphal throne, like ʿAbd al-Raḥmān "Sanchuelo," keen to reinforce his own power and prestige, might have embraced such an alliance. Even if Bishop Pelayo's account clearly contains some fantastical elements, it is unlikely to be a complete fiction.

Be that as it may, one is bound to question why the Christian royal dynasties chose to enter into such interfaith marriage alliances, when the Church had traditionally preached against sexual mixing of this kind. We have seen that at the ecclesiastical council of Córdoba in 839 the assembled clerics had been at pains to denounce interfaith marriage, but if similar edicts were issued at church councils held in the Christian-dominated territories to the north of the Peninsula no record of them has survived.[108] It is entirely possible that the Muslim conquest had so utterly disrupted the apparatus of church government in the North that pastoral guidance for the laity, of the kind that had earlier been provided at regular church councils under the Visigoths, was in notably short supply. It was equally the case that prior to the eleventh century papal contacts with the bishops and churches of the Peninsula, as in most of the Latin West at this time, remained limited in the extreme. There is little evidence that any of the popes took an interest in the spiritual welfare of their Iberian flock, let alone that they voiced any concerns about the practice of interfaith marriage.[109] As Bishop Arnulf of Orléans pithily declared at the synod of Rheims in 991, "Spain knows nothing of papal decisions."[110]

Probably even more important than this, the decidedly weak political and military position in which the Christian monarchs found themselves for much of the tenth century, during which time the North was subjected to a series of devastating raids by Umayyad armies, probably meant that at times they had little room for maneuver when Muslim rulers demanded Christian brides as the price of peace.[111] In the circumstances, interfaith marriage alliances may have represented an indispensable means to achieve both peace and dynastic survival. Besides, Christian monarchs were not slow to recognize that kinship ties with the Umayyad dynasty could bring their own advantages. Thus, when Sancho I of León (956–66) was deposed from the throne in or around 958, reputedly because he was too obese to mount a horse and lead his nobles to war, he sought assistance from his grandmother Queen Toda Aznárez of Navarre. The queen promptly led a delegation to Córdoba to the court of ʿAbd al-Raḥmān III, to whom she was related through her mother Onneca's second marriage to the Umayyad emir ʿAbd Allāh. As a result of her intervention, the caliph undertook to provide Sancho with the military reinforcements he desperately needed in order to regain his throne, as well as the services of the caliph's Jewish physician Ḥasdāi b. Shaprūṭ to help him shed his excess weight.[112]

By marked contrast, it is notable that very few Muslim women are known to have crossed the frontier in the opposite direction and taken Christian husbands. True, a number of the female members of the Banū Qasī are recorded to have married prominent Christians, such as Urraca, daughter of ʿAbd Allāh b. Muḥammad (d. 915–16), who was married off to King Fruela II of León (924–25).[113] But in this the family may have constituted something of a special case, in that it was only relatively recently Islamized—which may have prompted the clan to play fast and loose with the strictures of Islamic law regarding mixed marriages. Moreover, the family's peculiar geopolitical position, sandwiched between several competing powers, apparently led it to be far more pragmatic in its marriage policy than was the case in other regions of al-Andalus. For the most part, however, it appears that cross-border marriages between Muslim women and Christian men occurred only in exceptional circumstances. Thus, when Maḥmūd b. ʿAbd al-Jabbār of Mérida (d. c.845), a longstanding rebel against Umayyad authority, who had found political asylum in the kingdom of Alfonso II of Asturias (791–842), was killed in the course of a skirmish with the king's forces, the Christian nobles of the region competed to marry his surviving sister Jamīla "on account of her ancestry, beauty and valor," according to Ibn Ḥayyān. In the end, the nobles reportedly drew lots to win her hand, whereupon she converted to Christianity and married.[114] Another Muslim woman who crossed the frontier in this manner was the princess known in Christian sources as "Zaida," who after the death of her husband al-Fatḥ al-Maʾmūn during the Almoravid attack on Córdoba on 26 March 1091, and the subsequent deposition of her father-in-law, al-Muʿtamid b. Abbād, ruler of the kingdom of Seville, fled to the Christian North and became the concubine of Alfonso VI of León-Castile (1065–1109), whom she may later have married.[115] We shall have much more to say about this interfaith liaison in Chapter 4.

Women Enslaved

Our focus thus far has been on intermarriage between Muslims and Christians. None the less, it is important to recognize that the vast majority of the Christian women who were taken as sexual partners by the Umayyad rulers and other Islamic potentates in al-Andalus were not legitimate wives at all. They were, rather, *jawārī* (singular *jāriya*), slaves of Iberian or other origin, who had been taken as concubines (*sarārī*; singular *surrīya*) on account of their beauty, or their abilities as singers, dancers, or reciters of poetry. The institution of concubinage was recognized by the Qur'ān and came to enjoy popularity in all parts of the Islamic world, with the acquisition of *jawārī* widely regarded as an important status symbol.[116] Islamic legal schools regulated the relationship between a man and his concubine and defined her rights closely. A concubine who bore a child to her Muslim master assumed the status of *umm walad* (mother of a child), which meant that she could not be sold, would enjoy permanent residence in her master's household, and would be manumitted on his death, if not sooner; their child would be regarded as a free, legitimate heir, whose legal and social status was equal to that of any siblings born to their father's free wives.

We know the names of a few of those Christian women who were taken as slave concubines in this way.[117] One was Qalam, a woman of Navarrese origin, who had been enslaved at a relatively young age and joined the harem of the emir 'Abd al-Raḥmān II (822–52), where she won renown as a skilled singer and dancer, as well as an outstanding calligrapher and storyteller.[118] Another was Ailo, who bore Muḥammad I his son and succcessor al-Mundhir (886–88).[119] By far the best known of the *jawārī*, however, was the Christian Navarrese woman known as Ṣubḥ (d. 998).[120] We have no idea of the precise circumstances that led to Ṣubḥ's enslavement, but given her reputed expertise as a singer and poetess in Arabic the likelihood is that she had been taken to al-Andalus at a relatively young age and received her education there.[121] This impression is reinforced by the fact that her brother, known as Fā'iq or Rā'iq in the sources, came to hold a series of influential posts in the caliphal administration between at least 972 and 974/5.[122] Recruited to the harem of al-Ḥakam II (961–76), Ṣubḥ bore the caliph two sons, and it was reputedly through her influence that one of them later succeeded his father to the throne as Hishām II. Such was her sway over the caliph, one source claimed, that he never opposed her will.[123] After Hishām II's accession to the throne, Ṣubḥ retained an influential role within the machinery of royal government in Córdoba, effectively acting as regent on account of her son's young age, with control over the state bureaucracy and treasury. In 996, however, she was sidelined from power by the caliph's *ḥājib*, al-Manṣūr, whose own career Ṣubḥ had earlier helped to further and with whom she was reported to have had a passionate love affair.[124]

The capture and onward sale of Christian women in the slave markets of al-Andalus is well enough documented to suggest that there was a considerable demand for such human merchandise.[125] Attractive slave girls could command high prices at market, particularly those who were accomplished singers.[126] In the vast majority of cases, such women had been taken into captivity in the aftermath of one of the many military expeditions that were launched from al-Andalus against the Christian states of the North. Whether the Christian rulers ever surrendered women to the Umayyads in payment of tribute, in accordance with the terms of a peace treaty, as Christian tradition would later claim, is unknown, but it is not entirely inconceivable. After all, the payment of tribute in the form of slaves is recorded from other regions bordering the Islamic world.[127] In other cases, the slave traffickers might have been Jews or even Christians. Thus, one source refers to the sale of a number of Christian women by Jewish merchants in ninth-century Mérida.[128] Meanwhile, a charter preserved in the cartulary of the Portuguese monastery of São Mamede de Lorvão relates how, at the time of the capture of Coimbra by al-Manṣūr in 987, a local Christian, one Ezerag de Condeixa "went to Farfon iben Abdella and became a Moor," which could either mean that he converted to Islam, or that he pledged support to the Muslim authorities.[129] Having been granted command over thirty Muslim horsemen, Ezerag is reported to have captured the Christian inhabitants of the villages in the vicinity by trickery and sold them into slavery at Santarém for six pieces of silver, in exchange for which he was later granted some property near Coimbra by al-Manṣūr.

In many cases, prisoners would have been taken in relatively small numbers, as Muslim raiding parties rampaged far and wide across Christian lands in search of easy pickings. In others, the numbers involved were clearly more substantial: when Barcelona was sacked by al-Manṣūr in 985, it was reported that all of those Christians who had taken refuge in the city at the command of Count Borrell II "for the purpose of guarding it and defending it" were either killed or taken prisoner.[130] We can get a clearer idea of how the division of such human plunder was carried out from Ibn Idhārī al-Marrākushī's relatively detailed account of the winter campaign waged by 'Abd al-Malik al-Muẓaffar in late 1007, when he besieged the castle of San Martín.[131] We are told that when, after several days of fierce fighting, the exhausted Christian defenders finally surrendered, they filed out of the castle, placing themselves and their property under the *ḥājib*'s authority. Once all had done so, al-Muẓaffar commanded that the Christians be separated into two groups: on one side the warriors and other men; on the other the women and children. The *ḥājib* then approached the prisoners on horseback, accompanied by his retinue, and was greeted by great cheers and shouts of praise from his troops. On al-Muẓaffar's command, the Christian men were then put to the sword; the women and children were shared out among the various volunteers and other troops who had taken part in the campaign, "as was the custom."[132] Doubtless some prisoners were also carried back to Córdoba with the army. A charter of Vermudo II of León reports that after the Muslim attack on Simancas in 983 those Christians who had not been executed outright were led off to Córdoba in chains.[133] For those of high social status there was always the hope that they might be ransomed.[134] But for the majority of Christian captives there was the prospect of a lifetime of servitude, either in al-Andalus or in other regions of the Islamic world. Ibn Ḥawqal, writing in the 970s, listed male and female slaves among the most important exports of al-Andalus.[135] Of course, this was not a one-way street: Muslims too were regularly enslaved in the course of Christian cross-border raids.[136]

The tenth century marked the apogee of the cross-border slave trade, as the Umayyad caliphate and the *ḥājib*s who wielded power on its behalf exerted ever greater military pressure on the Christian states of the North. According to the North African historian 'Abd al-Wāḥid al-Marrākushī (b. 1185), the fifty or so campaigns waged by al-Manṣūr from the 980s down to his death in 1002 produced such a glut of Christian slave women in the markets of Córdoba that prices collapsed, and the number of men deciding to take a free Muslim wife, as opposed to a slave concubine, slumped dramatically. The beautiful daughter of one Christian notable was said to have fetched only 20 dinars.[137] For its part, the anonymous fourteenth-century *Dhikr Bilād al-Andalus*, which preserves a catalogue of al-Manṣūr's numerous military campaigns, places particular emphasis on the large numbers of women and children captured by the *ḥājib*.[138] He claims, for example, that when Barcelona was sacked in 985 some 70,000 women and children were taken into captivity; at Zamora (981) the figure given is 40,000 women; at Pamplona (999) 18,000. These figures are doubtless so much hyperbole, but the chronicler's repeated emphasis on the numbers of prisoners taken demonstrates that the capture of Christian slaves, and in particular females and their offspring, was regarded as a specially significant and praiseworthy act. This impression is reinforced by the fact that when 'Abd al-Malik al-Muẓaffar returned from a largely fruitless campaign to Sobrarbe and Ribagorza in 1006 he was widely criticized in Córdoba for not having brought back young captives as his father had regularly done, supposedly prompting the sardonic comment from one slave trader that "the slave importer is dead."[139]

Two precious eleventh-century documents enable us to put names to a handful of those Christian women who were captured in such Muslim military operations. The first charter, probably drawn up on 4 May 1005, records the grant that was made by the layman Iaquinti and his wife Tornaánimas to the monastery of Saints Justo and Pastor in León of half of their property in Campo de Villavidel, including "in that estate the shares of our daughters named Gaudiosa and Speciosa who are captive."[140] The document says nothing about the circumstances that had led to their captivity, but one is drawn to speculate that the daughters had been carried off to al-Andalus during the course of an earlier Muslim raid into the region. This impression is reinforced by another Leonese charter, drawn up on 28 December 1023.[141] The document is remarkable for the extensive historical *narratio* inserted at the beginning, in which the nun Flora explained the background to her decision to grant all her property to the monastery of Santiago de León. She related that her grandfather Arias and her father Baldredo had earlier built the monastery of Santa Cristina within the city of León and placed the house under the control of her aunts, Justa, María, Domna Infante, and Granda, as well as her sister Honorífica and Flora herself. There then follows a vivid portrait of the devastating campaign that al-Manṣūr launched against León in 988:

> On account of the sins of the Christians, the Saracen people, the seed of the Ishmaelites, invaded all the province of the West in order to devour the earth, and to strike all with the sword, to carry off captives; thus our ambusher the most ancient serpent gave them victory. And they cast down the cities, destroyed walls and trampled us underfoot; they razed cities to the ground, they beheaded men and there was not a town, a village or castle that survived that devastation.

In the course of the raid, the nuns of Santa Cristina were carried off captive by the Muslims, with the exception of Flora's mother, the wife of Baldredo, and their son Arias. Then, Flora relates, after a long time, God took mercy on them and they left that "evil captivity," with the exception of two of them who remained in chains. Finding their monastery in León in ruins, the women chose to set up a new religious house at nearby Villar de Mazarife. In later life, after the death of her other family members, Flora recovered the remains of Arias, Baldredo, and Justa, who had been buried in the ruined monastery of Santa Cristina, and reinterred them in that of Santiago de León, whose community Flora herself joined and generously endowed. Flora's account does not tell us what became of those who were carried off to al-Andalus. Some might have been made to work in agriculture or domestic service, but it is equally possible that one or more of them had ended up in the personal harem of al-Manṣūr or in that of another Andalusi notable.

The Leonese charter of 1023 is important to us not only because it sheds some light on the precise circumstances that led to the enslavement of Christian women, but also because it demonstrates the traumatic psychological effects that the campaigns launched by al-Manṣūr had upon the Christian communities of the North. And what happened in León was replicated in Santiago de Compostela, Astorga, Zamora, Pamplona, Barcelona, and all the other major population centers that were overrun by al-Manṣūr's forces during the final two decades of the tenth century.[142]

Our sources tell us precious little about the lives of those Christian women who were taken as wives or concubines by Muslim lords. This is hardly surprising, given that, by and large, women registered but rarely on the consciousness of Andalusi writers, and those who did tended to belong to the upper classes, in particular the mothers, wives, and daughters of sovereigns. Members of the harem were not expected to meddle in political activity, and those who did—like Queen Egilona in the eighth century or Ṣubḥ in the tenth—were invariably portrayed as ambitious schemers, who used their feminine wiles to feather their own nests or those of their kin.[143] Although none of these women would have been obliged to renounce their faith, they would have been required to abide by Islamic social practices such as those concerning ritual purity and dietary laws, and their children would have been brought up as Muslims. The social pressures to convert to Islam may have been considerable, and it is likely that many women—legitimate wives and concubines alike—did so, particularly those who had borne children to their masters.[144] One woman who is known to have converted in this way was al-Manṣūr's Navarrese royal bride, known as 'Abda, of whom it was later said by the historian Ibn al-Khaṭīb that "she became a good Muslim; she was of all al-Manṣūr's wives the staunchest in faith and of most gentle birth."[145] She bore the *ḥājib* a son, ʿAbd al-Raḥmān—nicknamed Shanjūl/Sanchuelo after his paternal grandfather—who, as we have seen, came to play a key role in the events that led to the fall of the Umayyad caliphate in the early eleventh century.

Although severe restrictions were imposed on their mobility and social interaction, the brides and *jawārī* who entered the harem of the caliph or some other Muslim lord might live in some comfort. Ibn Ḥayyān, for one, mentions the fine clothes, jewels, and perfumes enjoyed by one of ʿAbd al-Raḥmān III's slave concubines, Marjān.[146] Moreover, some concubines might enjoy special status, particularly those who held the status of *umm walad*; Marjān, who bore the caliph five children, including his son and heir al-Ḥakam II, was even awarded the title of "great lady" (*al-sayyida al-kubrā*).[147] Al-Ḥakam II esteemed his own concubine Ṣubḥ so highly that in 964 he granted her an exquisite ivory container, which may now be viewed in the National Archaeological Museum in Madrid.[148] Other concubines were not so fortunate, however, and suffered victimization or even violence at the hands of their masters. According to Ibn Ḥayyān, ʿAbd al-Raḥmān III had a particularly violent streak toward the women of his harem, subjecting one unfortunate concubine who rejected his advances at his palace at Madīnat al-Zahrā' to cruel abuse, by having his eunuchs hold her while he burned her face with a candle.[149] Al-Manṣūr is reported to have had two of his slave girls executed for having recited some verses that he deemed inappropriate; while such was the ill treatment suffered by the slave concubines of Abū Marwān al-Tubnī (d. 1065) that they conspired to murder him.[150] The vulnerability of *jawārī* was magnified at times of political turmoil. For example, when Córdoba descended into the *fitna* (civil war) on the death of ʿAbd al-Raḥmān "Sanchuelo" in 1009, the members of the harems of several leading Muslims were violated.[151] Concubines might sometimes live in the lap of luxury, but for many, clearly, the experience must have been a deeply traumatic one.

The Rationale for Sexual Mixing

How are we to explain the readiness of the Umayyad rulers and other élite Muslim families of al-Andalus to enter into cross-border interfaith marriage alliances or to take Christian slave concubines? In the case of powerful kin groups such as the Banū Qasī and the Banū Shabrīṭ, marriage ties with Christian lords were clearly designed to bolster their autonomy and security vis-à-vis other regional powers, be they the Umayyad emirs to the south or the Christian Franks and Asturians to the east and west respectively, all of whom, at one time or another, had sought to impose their authority over the region of the Upper Ebro. For the Umayyads, meanwhile, as well as for the *ḥājib* al-Manṣūr, exogamous marriages acted partly as a tool of diplomacy, which could help stabilize relations with the sometimes fractious Christian states to the north. This is very much what the anthropologist Claude Lévi-Strauss had in mind when he declared that "a continuous transition exists from war to exchange, and from exchange to intermarriage, and the exchange of brides is merely the conclusion to an uninterrupted process of reciprocal gifts, which effects the transition from hostility to alliance, from anxiety to confidence, and from fear to friendship."[152]

Yet peacemaking was only part of the equation. From another perspective, Umayyad policy in this regard provides a classic example of an "aggressive" marriage strategy that seems to have been a characteristic feature of many premodern Mediterranean societies.[153] In the words of Julian Pitt-Rivers,

> Marriage strategy can be either conciliatory, defensive or aggressive. To give women in exchange for political protection and/or economic advantage involves accepting domination and profiting from its counterpart. . . . A more defensive strategy attempts to reserve its women within the group and avoid outside involvement. But the aggressive strategy aims both to deny its women to outsiders and take in their women. . . . Competition for women, however it may be conceptualised by the people themselves, is competition for power.[154]

Ruth Mazo Karras puts it more baldly: "Penetration symbolizes power. For men of one group to have sex with women of another is an assertion of power over the entire group."[155] Muslim societies were by no means unique in this respect, but it was undoubtedly the case that in early Islamic and even pre-Islamic culture it had been considered honorable for a man to acquire a wife from another kin group through force or persuasion, by conquest or alliance, and women were regarded as particularly valuable prizes of conquest.[156] Echoes of such attitudes could be found in al-Andalus too. The sexual dominance of a Muslim ruler over a Christian woman—be it a freeborn princess or a slave concubine—was portrayed by some as symbolic of Islamic political and military hegemony, as well as a humiliating reminder to the Christians themselves of their subordinate status.[157]

The prolific poetic output of the panegyrist and man of letters Ibn Darrāj al-Qasṭallī (d. 1030) provides a useful perspective on these matters.[158] Hailing from the Algarve in southern Portugal, Ibn Darrāj rose to prominence at the court of al-Manṣūr in 992, and it was in honor of the latter and of his son, 'Abd al-Malik al-Muẓaffar, that he composed a large number of panegyrics. Especially revealing for our purposes are the poems he composed for al-Manṣūr to celebrate the *ḥājib*'s military successes over the Christian armies during the final decade of the tenth century. In these works Ibn Darrāj is quick to praise the nobility, valor, piety, and generosity of his patron, but equally eye-catching is the emphasis that he places upon the capture of Christian women by Muslim armies. One such poem, which is dedicated to al-Muẓaffar, and which refers to a campaign led by al-Manṣūr against Navarre and against the territory of Miró count of Pallars, perhaps in 999, claims that the *ḥājib* had stolen the Christians' lives, "possessing the slavery of their women and dominating their souls"; he further adds that their marriage contracts had been "written with spears," a clear indication that their forcible recruitment to Muslim harems was anticipated.[159] Equally explicit is the poem written to extol al-Manṣūr's campaign to Navarre and the Rioja in 1000, which had culminated in a victory over a coalition of Christian forces. Here again Ibn Darrāj mentions the capture of Christian women, who are described as "herds of fat gazelles." Although they are chaste, the poet declares, "they would accept your offer if you wanted to marry them."[160] In another poem he wrote to celebrate the winter campaign waged against León in 995, Ibn Darrāj makes extravagant play of the vulnerability of those Christian women whose husbands had been put to the sword.[161] Furthermore, when King Sancho Garcés II of Navarre came to Córdoba at the head of a diplomatic mission in September 992, and had the opportunity to meet his grandson 'Abd al-Raḥmān "Sanchuelo," Ibn Darrāj praised the nobility of the Christian king, but left his audience in no doubt that his visit and pledge of obedience to his son-in-law, al-Manṣūr, marked a considerable humiliation for him.[162]

Since a woman's very reputation and status rested upon her honor and chastity, the sexual use of Christian female captives or even freeborn wives was designed in part to destroy solidarity among Christian families and communities, inflicting shame not only on the women themselves, but also on their male coreligionists—like King Sancho Garcés of Navarre—who had failed to protect them.[163] Simultaneously, the forcible deracination of Christian women and children to al-Andalus, and their conversion to Islam in many cases, was seemingly designed to encourage a process of assimilation which would hinder procreation among the Christians of the North and ensure a shift in cultural and ethnic loyalties in the future.[164] Sex was, perhaps, the ultimate colonizing gesture. Of course, this was by no means an exclusively medieval Iberian phenomenon. Organized sexual violence against women, with the intention of reinforcing a sense of failure and humiliation among the vanquished, has been an integral aspect of military conduct throughout the ages.[165] In a modern context, one need only recall the forcible recruitment of many thousands of "comfort women" to Japanese-run brothels during the Second World War, or the mass rapes carried out by Soviet forces in Germany in 1945 and by the participants of the Balkan and Rwandan conflicts of the 1990s, to list only some of the most shocking examples.[166] In all such cases, sexual violence acts as a political metaphor, an emblem of military hegemony, with women's bodies being used to stage the conflict.[167] "In war zones," Ruth Seifert has observed, "women apparently always find themselves on the front line."[168]

The taking of Christian prisoners—male and female alike—was regarded as a significant propaganda opportunity for the Umayyad caliphs and for the *ḥājib*s who later supplanted them. By the time of the reigns of ʿAbd al-Raḥmān III and al-Ḥakam II, the military expeditions that were regularly dispatched from Córdoba against the Christians and other enemies of the caliphate had developed into complex ceremonial occasions designed to project the caliph's power and legitimacy, as well as his commitment to the defense of the faith. Thus, we know from the detailed descriptions provided by al-Rāzī that before an army departed on *jihād* during the reign of al-Ḥakam II, its banners were customarily blessed and fixed on lances; muezzins recited verses from the Qu'rān and blessed those who would wage war on God's behalf; and the general and his army paraded through the streets of Córdoba, stopping off at the Bāb al-Sudda, one of the ceremonial gates to the royal palace, where the caliph would appear to impart his own blessing on the departing troops.[169] And the return of the army some months later was equally carefully choreographed. A report on the campaign and its achievements would be read out before the faithful in the great mosque of Córdoba; there were further parades, and the heads of some of the enemy dead, as well as prisoners of war, were conveyed in solemn procession back to the Bāb al-Sudda, along with other battle trophies such as banners, crosses, and bells.[170] The poems of Ibn Darrāj demonstrate that the many campaigns led against the Christian realms by al-Manṣūr, the victories that he won, and the plunder and captives he brought back to Córdoba were likewise regarded as opportunities for the *ḥājib* to project his own power among the populace. Significantly, the Bāb al-Sudda was the location chosen by al-Manṣūr for the mass execution of some fifty Navarrese notables by way of retaliation for an earlier Christian attack on Calatayud; indeed, we are told that the *ḥājib*'s son, 'Abd al-Raḥmān, by then no more than fourteen, personally killed one of the nobles to whom he was related through his mother.[171] By the end of the tenth century, it is apparent that *jihād* against the infidel and the large-scale enslavement of Christians that accompanied it had become significant instruments of political authority, a means to achieve social cohesion, and doubtless a significant stimulus to the local economy.[172] At the same time, the expectation was that Muslim leaders would offer protection to the women of their own community: those who failed to do so were heavily criticized. When the Muslim general Wāḍiḥ refused to rescue a Muslim girl who had been taken by a Christian soldier who had entered Córdoba in support of the would-be caliph al-Mahdi in 1010, and the girl's father was subsequently killed by the Christian despite paying a ransom, it was regarded as a particularly shameful act.[173]

We should also be aware that there were other political imperatives at play here. For the Umayyads, the taking of slave concubines or intermarriage with Christian princesses appears to have served as an important dynastic defense mechanism. Marrying a freeborn Muslim woman necessitated the paying of a dowry and even the providing of favors to her family, while divorce might lead to a costly property settlement.[174] More dangerous yet, marriage ran the risk that a Muslim wife's own kin group might at some time in the future entertain its own competing dynastic claims. Marrying a Christian princess or, even more preferable, procreating with *jawārī*, forestalled that danger. In the case of the Umayyads, D. Fairchild Ruggles has argued that "a deliberative procreative program was in effect whereby wives were denied the sexual services of their royal husbands at least until a successor (or two) had been born to a slave concubine."[175] This impression is strongly reinforced by the fact that all of the Umayyad males who came to assume the rank of emir or caliph in al-Andalus between the eighth and the tenth centuries were born to slave consorts, many of them Christian, rather than to married mothers. In his celebrated love treatise *The Dove's Neckring* Ibn Ḥazm went so far as to assert that with only one exception the Umayyad caliphs were

> disposed by nature to prefer blondes. . . . Every one of them has been fair haired, taking after their mothers, so that this has become a hereditary trait with them. . . . I know not whether this was due to a predilection innate in them all, or whether it was in consequence

of a family tradition handed down from their ancestors, and which they followed in their turn.[176]

It is striking, for example, that even though 'Abd al-Raḥmān III fathered a son from his marriage to a woman of the prestigious Quraysh tribe, the caliph chose his son born of the concubine Marjān—that is, the future al-Ḥ akam II—as heir to the caliphal throne.[177] A similar pattern of reproductive politics can be glimpsed in other regions of the Islamic world, where royal dynasties—such as the 'Abbasid caliphs or later the Ottoman sultans—went out of their way to choose slave concubines to bear their children.[178] The matrimonial policy that was adopted by the *ḥājib* al-Manṣūr is also instructive in this regard. Early in his career, as he sought to consolidate and further his political influence, he entered into advantageous marriage alliances with other powerful Muslim aristocratic families. Once he held the reins of power in al-Andalus, however, it is striking that he preferred to distance himself from the local Muslim aristocracy and underline his peninsular hegemony, in his case by marrying the daughter of Sancho Garcés II of Navarre.[179] Some writers were also of the opinion that marriage to "foreign women" (*banāt al-'ajam*) could bring benefits in terms of the physical and mental attributes of any offspring. Besides, most clove to the view that whether or not men married wives of pure Arab blood, the latter were mere "recipients" of their husband's seed: the lineage of their children was purely determined by their male ancestry.[180] As Coope has observed, "their mothers' background . . . in no way compromised their identity as Umayyads and as Arabs."[181] Even so, during the civil wars of the ninth century, there would be some who would seek to undermine the Umayyads' claim to sovereignty by asserting that their descent from non-Arab women meant that they could no longer be considered Arabs in their own right.[182]

It is time to draw the diverse threads of this chapter together. From the surviving evidence, it is clear enough that sexual mixing between Muslim lords and Christian women—be they freeborn brides or slave concubines—was commonplace in Early Medieval Iberia. In many cases, such unions were manifestly "instruments of domination," to borrow Pierre Bourdieu's phrase.[183] Thus, in the immediate aftermath of the Muslim invasion in the eighth century, marriage alliances with Christian heiresses or widows served as a means to pacify the Peninsula, legitimize the conquest, and channel the landed wealth of the Visigothic aristocracy into Muslim ownership. As far as Andalusi relations with the nascent Christian realms of the North were concerned, meanwhile, cross-border interfaith sexual liaisons served other functions. For influential *muwallad* kin groups like the Banū Qasī and the Banū Shabrīṭ, marriage pacts with their Christian neighbors were designed to bolster their local autonomy against other competing regional powers, Muslim and Christian alike. For the ruling Umayyad dynasty and for the *ḥājib*s who seized the reins of power at the end of the tenth century, meanwhile, sexual liaisons outside the *umma* served a variety of functions: as a mechanism to keep potential rivals for power within al-Andalus at arm's length; as a tool of diplomacy, with which to maintain relations with the Christian states on an even keel; as a means to reward followers who had distinguished themselves in war; and as a potent propaganda weapon—for internal and external purposes—designed to underline the dominance of the Islamic state in its dealings with the infidels of the North. Last but not least, the systematic enslavement en masse of Christian women and the recruitment of some of them as concubines to the harems of the caliphs, emirs, and other notables of al-Andalus constituted a major tool of psychological warfare, designed to sow terror among the population and sap its will to resist. As we shall see, the trauma inflicted by this policy was to endure in the Christian consciousness for generations to come.

Chapter 2

Marking Boundaries

Between c.1050 and 1300 the Iberian Peninsula was subjected to a series of powerful political and cultural impulses. There was a dramatic shift in the military balance of power after the demise of the Umayyad Caliphate in 1031, which allowed the Christian realms of the North to undertake a spectacular—if spasmodic and largely uncoordinated—movement of territorial expansion into the southern half of the Peninsula at the expense of al-Andalus, as major cities such as Toledo (1085), Zaragoza (1118), Lisbon (1147), Córdoba (1236), Valencia (1238), and Seville (1248) fell in turn. The result was to be that, with the notable exception of the Nasrid emirate of Granada (founded in 1238), Muslim authority in Iberia was almost extinguished.[1] This expansionary process was accompanied by a significant ideological transformation that saw the Christians begin to reconfigure certain aspects of their relationship with the Islamic world, a process that was accelerated and sharpened by the preaching of the Crusade. Simultaneously, a profound cultural shift occurred that prompted the religious and secular authorities of the Latin West to attempt to erect barriers to prevent social assimilation and, above all, sexual mixing between Christians, Muslims, and Jews.

As a consequence of this convergence of political, religious, and cultural trends, the practice of interfaith marriage in the Peninsula was condemned to a swift decline. Muslim rulers in al-Andalus simply no longer enjoyed the same level of political and military dominance over the northern kings as had once enabled them to demand the hands of Christian princesses in marriage as the price of peace, although the recruitment of Christian slave women to the harems of Islamic potentates was to continue for centuries to come. For their Christian counterparts, meanwhile, having so often been in the position of supplicants to the Umayyad superpower to the south, interfaith marriage was to become politically unnecessary, as well as culturally and ideologically beyond the pale. At the same time, partly as a response to the incorporation of sizeable communities of Muslims and Jews under Christian rule in the wake of the territorial conquests carried out both in the Peninsula and in the Holy Land, canon lawyers began drawing up strict injunctions against those Christians who engaged in sexual contact with infidels, pronouncements that were soon to be amplified in numerous Iberian secular law codes. The purpose of this chapter is to examine the various policies that were enacted by the Christian secular and religious authorities from the twelfth century onward with a view to restricting interfaith sex, and the wider social and ideological significance that such measures entailed.

Regulating Intimacy

As we saw in the previous chapter, the religious authorities in the Christian Latin West—in common with their Jewish and Muslim counterparts—had traditionally expressed hostility toward the practice of interfaith sex, particularly when a woman of their own faith was involved. In an Iberian context, intermarriage between Muslim men and Christian women apparently became so widespread in the decades following the eighth-century Islamic conquest that Pope Hadrian I wrote to denounce the practice, while similar concerns were voiced by the assembled Christian clerics at the council of Córdoba in 839.[2] However, there is precious little evidence to suggest that such anxieties were widely shared in the nascent Christian states of the north of the Peninsula during the Early Middle Ages. For one thing, the readiness of various Christian rulers to sanction cross-border interfaith marriage alliances with Islamic potentates—be they Umayyad dynasts or regional powerbrokers like the lords of the Banū Qasī—seems to demonstrate the primacy of pragmatism over cultural scruples at a time when Muslim al-Andalus was by far the dominant political and military player in the region. For another, it is striking that none of the handful of lawcodes issued by the Christian authorities prior to the twelfth century in any of the northern realms went out of their way to outlaw sexual mixing. Thus, among the 48 precepts that made up the extensive *fuero*, or charter of obligations and exemptions, that was granted to the city of León by Alfonso V in 1017, there was no prohibition on interfaith sex or indeed any other edict regarding the rights and obligations of religious minorities, other than a ruling on the role to be played by Jews in establishing the value of property.[3] It is similarly noteworthy that the secular and ecclesiastical magnates who attended the councils held at Coyanza near León in 1055, Santiago de Compostela in 1056, Jaca in Aragon c.1063, or Girona in Catalonia c.1068 did not consider it necessary to address the thorny subject of sexual mixing in their pronouncements; their priorities lay elsewhere.[4] The same could be said of Alfonso VI of León, who in March 1091 issued detailed instructions on the judicial procedure to be followed in legal disputes between Christians and Jews in the territory of León, but again did not consider it essential to address the matter of transgressive sexuality.[5]

The silence of the sources in this regard can be explained in various ways. At a most basic level, one might conjecture that the population of Jews and Muslims living in proximity to Christian communities in the northern realms prior to the late eleventh century was so insignificant that interfaith sex was simply not deemed a sufficiently serious risk to warrant legislation. For example, Jewish enclaves are recorded in the environs of the city of León prior to the twelfth century, but not within the urban space itself, while the Muslim population, drawn largely from slaves, was probably very small indeed.[6] We should also bear in mind that since religious minorities living under Christian rule were customarily allowed a good deal of judicial autonomy, there may have been no apparent need to incorporate these communities within Christian law, even in areas where substantial enclaves of non-Christians are known to have existed.[7] Yet we should also take account of other realities. For one thing, it might simply have been the case that a heightened sense of ethnic and religious difference, which was shortly to become a striking feature of political and cultural discourse in most parts of the Latin West, had yet to make itself felt among the Christians of the Northern Iberian realms. For another, the drive toward cultural unity and orthodoxy, which was to be a central feature of papal policy from the mid-eleventh century, and which was to see Rome ready to ride roughshod over local traditions and practices if necessary, had not yet had an impact on the north of the Peninsula. We shall return to explore these realities later in this chapter.

The dramatic military expansion of the Christian states at the expense of al-Andalus from the second half of the eleventh century onward marked a watershed moment insofar as interfaith relations were concerned. As Christian armies began to push southward, into the valleys of the Tagus and the Ebro between the 1080s and the 1140s, and then much further south toward the Guadiana, the Guadalquivir, and the Júcar a century and more later, they paved the way for an extensive program of resettlement that was designed to reinforce their control over the newly conquered territories and peoples. Kings and other lords took steps to establish the legal framework by which these Christian-ruled settlements would be governed and, with manpower at a premium, offered a variety of eye-catching inducements—including grants of property, tax breaks, and immunity from prosecution for criminals on the run—in order to attract colonists to the exposed lands that lay along the southern frontier. A case in point was the charter that Alfonso VII of León-Castile (1126–57) granted to the settlers of Oreja near Toledo in 1139 "in order to prevent the Moors from retaking it."[8] Some of the documents—known in Castilian as *fueros* (Catalan *furs*) or *cartas pueblas*—that were issued as part of this program of colonization were relatively brief statements of the obligations and privileges that would apply to settlers in the town or village in question; others were substantial compilations of municipal law and custom.[9]

Among the most striking features of this large body of customary law that was set down in writing between c.1050 and 1300 was the fact that numerous charters deemed it prudent and necessary to set out in detail the legal rights and obligations of the Jewish and Muslim communities who lived in the vicinity. On one level, this legislative initiative may be interpreted as an entirely pragmatic response to the fact that significant enclaves of religious minorities had been allowed to remain in situ in the aftermath of the Christian conquest, with a particularly high density of population in parts of Navarre, Aragon, and Valencia. With manpower scarce, there was an evident desire on the part of many Christian lords to avoid an exodus of Muslim and Jewish workers by guaranteeing their rights. In many cases *fueros* stipulated the religious, legal, and economic privileges Muslims and Jews would enjoy in a particular municipality or region, any additional taxes they might be liable to, their right in some cases to elect their own officials, or the prohibition on their holding certain posts in the local administration. A good example was the *fuero* Alfonso I of Aragon (1104–34) granted to Calatayud, south of the Ebro, in 1131, some eleven years after its conquest, in which he catalogued the various economic freedoms and legal protections that Muslims and Jews in the town would henceforth enjoy.[10]

By the late twelfth century, as economic and social interaction between the Christian, Jewish, and Muslim communities increased, laws designed to regulate intercommunal relations grew ever more detailed. Among this plethora of legislation, the monumental collections of municipal law promulgated in the towns of Teruel and Cuenca particularly stand out. Teruel, located in the Eastern Iberian Cordillera, was conquered by Alfonso II of Aragon

(1164–96) in 1171, and its substantial Latin *fuero* (the *Forum Turoli*) was promulgated five years later.[11] Cuenca, about 150 kilometers to the west, was captured by Alfonso VIII of Castile (1158–1214)—with the assistance of the Aragonese king—in 1177 and probably received its code (the *Forum Conche*) around 1190.[12] Scholars have debated at length the exact relationship between the Teruel and Cuenca codes, since there are numerous areas of convergence and similarity between the two. However, it is now considered improbable that the authorities in Cuenca directly modeled their code on the Teruel text; the likelihood, rather, is that both *fueros* drew on a common body of customary law—oral and written—then already in existence in the frontier lands under Castilian and Aragonese rule by the second half of the twelfth century.[13] Unlike the relatively limited statements of rights and responsibilities that had characterized many charters of settlement hitherto, however, the Cuenca and Teruel *fueros* set out in exhaustive detail the legal procedure that was to be followed in these towns and the system of municipal government that was to operate. Furthermore, they addressed numerous other aspects of urban life, such as the organization of the local militias whose responsibility it was to defend these communities against attack or to undertake offensive operations, regulations regarding economic activity, labor rights, the role and status of women, and so on.[14]

In common with numerous other charters of settlement of this period, the Teruel and Cuenca codes also addressed the question of interfaith relations. Muslims and Jews were welcome to settle in both towns—indeed a significant number probably remained in residence after the Christian conquest—and they shared many of the same rights and legal protections as their Christian counterparts. Yet this was no interfaith utopia. The municipal authorities in both towns were careful to draw clear lines of demarcation between the faiths in order to prevent excessive social interaction. The unvoiced fear was that social and cultural assimilation might prove a stepping-stone toward apostasy. With this in mind, Muslims and Jews at Teruel were warned not to frequent local bathhouses at the same times as Christians, with those who infringed the law facing a fine.[15] At Cuenca, the same prohibition was laid on Jews, but there is no mention of Muslims, which might suggest that apart from slaves they no longer resided in large numbers in the town.[16] Similar regulations regarding access to bathhouses were laid down in numerous other collections of frontier municipal law at this time, while the Church also added its voice to such injunctions: in 1280, at a synod in Lleida, the local bishop declared that any Christians who bathed with Muslims were to suffer excommunication.[17]

Perhaps more striking still, however, both the Teruel and the Cuenca codes contained a draconian prohibition on interfaith sex, at any rate as far as Christian women were concerned. The Teruel *fuero* has a section titled "Of the woman who sleeps with a Moor," which baldly states: "If a Christian woman is discovered with a Moor or a Jew and they can be captured, they are to be burned together."[18] The Cuenca code was equally brief and to the point: "If a woman is surprised with a Moor or a Jew, both should be burned alive."[19] These are the earliest known legal enactments from any of the northern Christian realms to regulate interfaith intimacy in this way. Their prohibition on sexual mixing was to be echoed elsewhere in the succeeding decades, as the Cuenca legal corpus came to be adopted, either partially or wholly, by dozens of other municipalities across the center of the Peninsula, from Cáceres in the west, to Soria on the Duero in the north and Baeza and Iznatoraf near the Guadalquivir in the south.[20] A good example of the legal-cultural transformation that took place in the Castilian heartlands is provided by the town of Sepúlveda, situated just south of the Duero. It is striking that when Alfonso VI granted a short *fuero* to the settlers of Sepúlveda in 1076 he made no attempt to regulate interfaith relations, let alone to target sexual mixing.[21] Yet two centuries later, when the civic authorities compiled an extensive *fuero*, which was also modeled to a large degree on the Cuenca archetype, the code included the stipulation that a Christian woman caught *in flagrante delicto* with a Muslim or Jewish man was to be burned at the stake, while her lover was to be hurled from the town's cliffs.[22] It further ruled that a Christian woman who lived among Jews and Muslims and bore a child by one of them, but was not caught in the act, was to be considered shameless, publicly flogged, and expelled from the town.[23]

Various other collections of customary law, while not drawing directly on the Cuenca corpus, also subscribed to the view that sexual liaisons between Christian women and Muslim or Jewish men were dangerous acts that deserved to be punished with the utmost rigor.[24] According to the *Costums* that were granted to the community of Tortosa on the Ebro in the 1270s, for example, if a Jewish or Muslim man were to sleep with a Christian woman, the male was to be drawn and quartered and the woman burned at the stake.[25] The thirteenth-century *Furs* of Valencia pronounced that "if a Jew or a Saracen is found to lie with a Christian woman, let both him and her be burned."[26] For its part, the *Siete Partidas*, the voluminous compendium of Roman, canon, and customary law that was compiled during the 1250s and 1260s at the behest of Alfonso X of Castile (1252–84), also promised that Jews found guilty of having intercourse with Christian women should suffer the capital penalty.[27] The penalties for Muslim male transgressors were similarly harsh and echo the punishments laid down in the various municipal *fueros*:

> If a Moor has sexual intercourse with a Christian virgin, we order that he shall be stoned, and that she, for the first offence, shall lose half of her property, and that her father, mother, or grandfather, shall have it, and if she has no such relatives, that it shall belong to the king. For the second offence, she shall lose all her property, and the heirs aforesaid, if she has any, shall obtain it, and if she has none, the king shall be entitled to it, and she shall be put to death. We decree and order that the same rule shall apply to a widow who commits this crime. If a Moor has sexual intercourse with a Christian married woman, he shall be stoned to death, and she shall be placed in the power of her husband who may burn her to death, or release her, or do what he pleases with her. If a Moor has intercourse with a common woman who abandons herself to everyone, for the first offence, they shall be scourged together through the town, and for the second, they shall be put to death.[28]

It is striking that none of these codes went out of their way to prohibit sexual relations between Christian men and Muslim or Jewish women; we will consider the significance of that omission shortly. Even so, it should be emphasized that clauses of this sort were by no means universal, since legal cultures across the Peninsula were far from uniform, and legal approaches toward religious minorities tended to reflect local conditions and priorities. A prohibition on interfaith sex was absent, for example, from major law codes such as the *Fuero General* of Navarre (1237) or the *Fori aragonum* (1247). And while numerous collections of municipal law thought it necessary to address the rights, obligations, and protections of Muslims and Jews in the economic sphere, by no means all addressed the issue of intercommunal sexuality.

Since sexual relations between Christian women and minority men were widely considered to be among the most heinous crimes that could be committed in the frontier towns under Christian control, and because of the potential gravity of the consequences for those accused and convicted on such charges, some law codes emphasized that due legal process had to be scrupulously followed. At Castelo Bom and Castelo Melhor in Portugal, as at Coria, Cáceres, and Usagre across the border in León, the local *fueros* stated that magistrates who apprehended a Jew with a Christian woman were to settle the case with two Christians and one Jew as witnesses, or two Jews and one Christian.[29] An identical procedure was followed at Sepúlveda, while in cases where a Muslim man was accused of sleeping with a Christian woman the case could be proved with two Christians and one Muslim as witnesses.[30] At Tortosa, a woman charged with conducting sexual relations with a Muslim or Jew would be pardoned if it could be established that she had been forced, or tricked because the man in question had been dressed as a Christian.[31] As we shall see, this was a defense that more than one Christian woman would have recourse to when arrested on charges of engaging in interfaith sex.

The importance that was attached to correct judicial procedure was also emphasized in the song *Quen na Virgen santa muito fiará*, one of the large collection of over 400 hymns composed in praise of the Virgin, known collectively as the *Cantigas de Santa María*, which was compiled under the patronage of Alfonso X of Castile. The song in question tells of a Christian woman whose hatred of her daughter-in-law is such that she orders one of her Muslim servants to get into bed with the woman as she sleeps, in order to make it appear that they had engaged in illicit sex. The calculating mother-in-law prevents the traumatized husband, her son, from killing the couple on the spot and instead encourages him to summon the local magistrate and others, knowing that eyewitness testimony of the crime would seal the supposed lovers' fate. The couple are duly sentenced to be burned at the stake, only for the young woman to be miraculously saved from the flames by the intervention of the Virgin; for the blameless Muslim there was to be no such deliverance, however.[32] We will return to consider the ideological significance of this episode in Chapter 4.

Although it is undoubtedly true that medieval legal enactments all too often reflected the aspirations of lawmakers as much as the social reality "on the ground," the prohibitions on interfaith sex which were inserted into the various Iberian collections of customary law that were drafted from the late twelfth century onward were by no means mere theoretical statements of ideal conduct. The rich documentary evidence from the realm of the Crown of Aragon, which has been interrogated skilfully by John Boswell, María Teresa Ferrer i Mallol, David Nirenberg, and Brian Catlos, among others, has demonstrated the zeal with which the sexual boundaries between the faiths were sometimes policed and the thoroughness with which suspected crimes might be investigated.[33] To give but one example, in January 1389 the Infante Martin of Aragon instructed the justice of the town of Arándiga, near

Calatayud, to investigate whether it was true that the previous month, on Christmas Eve, a Muslim man, Lop "el fustero" (or carpenter), had had sex with a Christian prostitute at a local inn.[34] The Infante urged the justice to undertake a thorough investigation of the case, since "we do not wish that such things should pass without due punishment," and laid out the step-by-step procedure that was to be followed. First, the justice was to interrogate the prostitute in order to establish what day and time the Muslim had come to see her; what words had been exchanged between the couple; whether he had slept with her; whether any money had changed hands; or whether the Muslim had left the woman something as security. Then the Muslim was to be questioned in the same manner, before witness statements were taken from the innkeeper and others. If the judge proved satisfied of the Muslim's guilt, he was "to do justice to him as should be done." What that meant in practice is not stipulated. Although the majority of urban *fueros* specified the capital penalty for such cases, this was by no means consistently enforced, even when guilt was firmly established, and in the majority of cases transgressors escaped by paying a fine.[35] The Aragonese Crown may have claimed jurisdiction over its subject Muslims, describing them as "Our Royal Treasure," but its kings proved notably reluctant to execute such lawbreakers. In 1322, no fewer than eighteen Muslims from the Vall d'Uxó were convicted of having had sex with a Christian prostitute, but the death penalty initially laid down was later commuted for a hefty fine.[36] When James I of Aragon issued a charter setting out his policy on interfaith relations in 1242, he allowed any Christian women then living with minority men up to two months to extricate themselves from their illegal relationships.[37] Be that as it may, on some occasions the authorities did not flinch from imposing the capital penalty. Thus, in 1311 James II of Aragon (1291–1327) confirmed that a Muslim, Muḥammad, who had been accused of trying to have sex with a Christian prostitute, was to be burned at the stake, in order that it might serve as a warning to others of his faith.[38] A similar fate befell the Navarrese Muslim Bursón, who in 1343 was found guilty of maintaining sexual relations with a Christian woman.[39]

In some cases local officials were painfully aware that they lacked the necessary legal apparatus to guide them in their investigation and sought guidance from the Crown. When, in 1300, the municipal council of Niebla near Huelva realized that their local *fuero* lacked a clause outlawing interfaith sex, they wrote to Ferdinand IV of Castile (1295–1312), who allowed them to borrow sections from the *fuero* of nearby Jerez de la Frontera for the purpose.[40] The authorities of Murcia came up against a similar problem. That much is clear from the letter that the Infante Peter, son of Sancho IV of Castile (1284–95), dispatched to the *alcaldes* of that city from Burgos on 5 August 1315.[41] The letter records that a local Muslim, Mahomat Abollexa, had been accused of having sex with a Christian woman called María Fernández, and that his Christian companion Juan de Dios (perhaps, given his name, a convert) had supposedly tricked the woman by telling her that Mahomat was a Christian. Whether María was a prostitute is not made clear, but the circumstances of her case, in particular the role of a Christian go-between who arranged the encounter with the Muslim, suggest that she may well have been. The officials duly launched an investigation into the matter and, once they had satisfied themselves of the two men's guilt, contacted the Infante to request guidance on how to proceed, since the local *fuero* did not include provision for such cases. Having considered their report and discussed it with various learned officials of the king, the Infante ruled that both men should be burned at the stake, in the case of Juan de Dios because he had played a key role in arranging the interfaith liaison and was condemned as a "besmircher of our law" (*ensuziador de nuestra ley*). The Infante further commanded that, since it appeared that María Fernández had been ensnared by Juan de Dios and was unaware that Mahomat was not a Christian, she should be released from prison. Finally, he noted that in any similar cases in the future the local authorities should proceed in the same manner.

The majority of the Christian women who were cited in the cases of sexual mixing that came before the courts appear to have been prostitutes, as in the cases from Arándiga and Vall d'Uxó mentioned above. This is not in itself terribly surprising given the nature of their profession and the fact that such women, whether they worked independently or in licensed brothels, tended to frequent areas where the faiths intermingled. The Christian authorities were well aware that prostitutes ran a particular risk of engaging in sexual relations with men of other faiths, while Muslim community leaders also protested at their presence in their midst for fear that excessive contact between the faiths might in turn lead their coreligionists to apostatize.[42] In 1304 James II of Aragon instructed his legal officials in Valencia to command the Christian prostitutes and their pimps who resided in the Muslim quarter of the city to leave, for fear they would incur "horrible sins."[43] In 1346 Peter IV of Aragon (1336–87) declared that it had come to his attention that Christian prostitutes and others had purchased houses in the Muslim quarter of the same city and warned of the danger this posed to Christians and Muslims alike; those who did so would be liable to a fine of 100 gold pieces.[44] Yet the proclamation does not appear to have had the desired effect: in 1351 the king reiterated his command that Christians were not to buy or rent houses in the Muslim quarter; yet fully 33 years later he found it necessary to return to the same theme.[45] It is striking, nonetheless, that during the final third of the fourteenth century only three cases of interfaith sex involving minority men and Christian prostitutes from licensed brothels are known to have come before the courts of Valencia. That suggests either that the harsh penalties prescribed by the law had the desired effect of dissuading Christians and Muslims from engaging in sexual mixing, or else that the authorities did not pursue malefactors with any particular sense of urgency. However, it is worthy of note that the *converso* Gil García was burned at the stake for having facilitated and covered up sexual encounters between Christian prostitutes and Muslim men, "out of great scorn for the Christian faith," as the judicial sentence put it.[46]

The readiness of the authorities to punish interfaith sex between Christian prostitutes and minority men is writ large in the legal registers of the period. If a prostitute were arrested on charges of engaging in interfaith sex, her life might depend on her being able to convince the judges that she had been unaware that her client was not a Christian. The experience of the prostitute Alicsén de Tolba, which is recorded in a detailed judicial summary drawn up on 27 November 1304, is a notable case in point.[47] Alicsén declared before the judge that when she and one of her companions had visited a shepherds' camp near Xivert (Valencia) a Muslim called Aytola was persuaded by one of his fellow shepherds, Lorenç, to sleep with her, but was told to pretend that he was a Christian named John, to speak in the accent of the mountains, and to say that he came from the port. However, when the couple slept together and Alicsén saw that Aytola had been circumcised, she realised that he was not a Christian and promptly raised the alarm, denouncing both Aytola and Lorenç to the lieutenant of the Commander of the Temple in Xivert for deceiving her to "the dishonour of God and of the Catholic faith and of Christianity." Fearing the consequences if he were brought to book, Aytola promptly skipped town; the Christian Lorenç, who had introduced his Muslim companion to Alicsén in the first place, was arrested, but later acquitted of the charge of abetting illegal interfaith sex.

To sum up thus far, the fact that Christian prostitutes were far more likely to come into sexual contact with men of another faith meant that they became a locus for collective anxiety about interfaith sex from the thirteenth century onward; they have even been portrayed as the sentinels who policed the boundaries between the faiths.[48] It was not that contemporaries were unconcerned about the sexual honor of other women, but the fact of the matter was that relationships between Christian women who were of good standing in the community and a minority male appear to have reached the courts only rarely.[49] The social space such women inhabited was far more closely controlled, with the result that the danger that interfaith sexual liaisons might occur was correspondingly diminished. In 1366, King Peter I of Portugal (1357–67) declared that since he had heard that some Christian women, deceived by the Devil, had maintained sexual relations with "men of another law," he commanded that henceforth, on pain of death, a Christian woman should only enter the Muslim and Jewish quarters of Lisbon if accompanied by a Christian man if she were a spinster or widow, or two if she were married. What is more, the king prescribed two itineraries such women were to follow.[50]

Moreover, when such cases did come before authorities, a cuckolded husband may sometimes have preferred not to press charges, for fear he would be dishonored if he did so. In 1344, a Muslim blacksmith from Lleida in Catalonia, Çalema Abinhumen, who had been accused of conducting an affair with the Christian woman, Arnaldona, was acquitted when her husband Ramon d'Aguilar flatly denied that any such relationship had taken place.[51] It is conceivable that Ramon did so to avoid public shame, although it is equally possible that in this, as in numerous other cases, the accusation of illegal sexual mixing had been brandished against a minority male not because such a relationship had actually occurred, but because it was viewed as an effective mechanism for ensuring that the accused would feel the full weight of the law.[52] Such false accusations could have devastating consequences for those implicated. In 1304, the same year as Alicsén de Tolba brought her case against the Muslim Aytola, a young Christian woman of the Aragonese town of Daroca, Prima Garsón, was accused of having pursued an affair with a local Muslim, Ali de Matero, and given birth to a child. Prima fled the town before her accusers could have her arrested, but the hapless Ali was seized and burned at the stake in her absence. When Prima was later captured and delivered into the hands of the authorities, a medical examination demonstrated that she was still a virgin and therefore innocent of the charges that had been laid against her.[53] The case demonstrates most powerfully that a determination to prevent interfaith sex was by no means the abstract preoccupation of lawgivers; it could give rise to fierce passions at the grass-roots level too.

Double Standards

If we turn our attention back to the legal prohibitions placed on sexual mixing, it is apparent that it was the conduct of Christian women and minority men that was consistently targeted. Did the same rules apply to Christian men who had sexual relations with Muslim or Jewish women? In the crusading kingdoms of the Near East, where similar multicultural realities prevailed, royal and ecclesiastical authorities took a firm line against such liaisons. The Council of Nablus of 1120, apparently inspired by Byzantine legal precedent, ruled that a Latin or Muslim man found guilty of having sex with a female of the other religion—be it voluntary or forced—should be castrated, while the woman's nose was to be cut off; Latin women who had relations with Muslim men were condemned as adulteresses.[54] Furthermore, the mid-thirteenth-century laws of the Latin Kingdom of Jerusalem warned all colonists not to marry "heretics," by which they meant non-Christians.[55] Be that as it may, numerous chroniclers of the Crusades lamented the sexual licentiousness of the participants and the frequency with which they had recourse to prostitutes or engaged in extramarital affairs with local women. The likelihood is that sexual encounters between Christian men and Muslim prostitutes or slaves occurred with some frequency, whatever the jurists of the kingdom had to say on the matter.[56]

In the Christian-dominated regions of the Iberian Peninsula the legal position regarding such sexual liaisons was notably less clear-cut. While there is ample evidence from legal and other sources to demonstrate that the authorities deplored interfaith sex where Christian women were involved, intercourse between Christian men and Muslim or Jewish women was only rarely singled out in the secular legislation of the age. According to the laws of Valencia, if a Christian man was caught sleeping with a Jewess both parties were to be burned at the stake, but in the case of a Christian man who slept with a Muslim woman, the couple would be compelled to run naked through the streets. However, whether this law was consistently implemented is doubtful, and John Boswell has observed that it "was clearly a dead letter by the mid-fourteenth century."[57] In 1276, the Infante Peter of Aragon commanded the justices of the Kingdom of Valencia that they should not allow Muslims and Christians to cohabit, on the grounds that it was "neither honest nor just."[58] The following year, Peter, now King Peter III of Aragon (1276–85), undertook before the Jews of Calatayud that any Christian man caught *in flagrante delicto* with a Jewish woman would be fined to the tune of 300 *maravedís*.[59] For his part, Sancho IV of Castile warned the Christian men of his kingdom not to commit sin with Jewish or Muslim women, "for they are women of another law and another faith."[60] He was particularly critical of his ancestor, Alfonso VIII, whose sinful seven-year relationship with a Jewess of Toledo supposedly led to his defeat at Almohad hands at Alarcos in 1195.[61] Aragonese records demonstrate that it was not unknown for prosecutions against men to be brought on such charges, and that the women in question were liable to confiscation of property and enslavement.[62] Those who denounced a Muslim woman who had engaged in interfaith sex stood to earn half her value if she were subsequently enslaved and sold. In one notorious case, in 1356, Peter IV of Aragon granted to the monks of the abbey of Rueda the right to profit from the sale of any Muslim women within its domains who had been enslaved for sleeping with Christian men, only to revoke it in September of the following year when it became known to him that it had been the monks themselves who had been engaging in sexual relations with the women in question.[63] What is abundantly clear is that legal opinion on such matters was far from consistent. In 1294, a Muslim woman of Ablitas in Navarre who was found guilty of having slept with a Christian man was merely fined the sum of thirty *solidi*.[64]

It is also worth emphasizing that the Muslim and Jewish communities of the Peninsula were equally horrified by the phantom of sexual mixing, and patrolled the social boundaries between the faiths zealously in order to protect their own women from pollution by men of another religion. The perennial fear was that if such interfaith sexual intimacy went unchecked, it would not only bring shame upon the women's families, but would also be a prelude to apostasy among their coreligionists. The late thirteenth-century Toledan rabbi Asher b. Yeḥiel decried Jewish men who carried out "harlotry with the daughter of a foreign God," and declared that those who did so were to be denounced before Jewish courts.[65] In the popular song of the beautiful Jewess Marisaltos, which is preserved among the *Cantigas de Santa María*, the young woman is thrown from a cliff by her own coreligionists, probably because she had conducted extramarital relations with a Christian man, only to be saved by the miraculous intervention of the Virgin.[66] For their part, Islamic judges regularly sentenced women found guilty of having interfaith sex or engaging in other sexual misdemeanors, such as fornication or adultery, to flogging or stoning to death, but they were not permitted to do so without the permission of the king, and such penalties were normally commuted to slavery to the Crown. Take the case of the Muslim woman Axia, who had been condemned to be stoned to death for adultery with Christians and Muslims by the *qadi* of Valencia, only to be enslaved instead by command of James II of Aragon and granted to one of his nobles.[67] Even so, in 1347, in response to lobbying by the Muslim officials in Valencia, King Peter IV of Aragon ruled that any Muslim woman convicted of pursuing an adulterous relationship with a Christian or Jew was to suffer the death penalty rather than pay a fine.[68] But such pronouncements were rare. For the most part, the execution of Muslim adulteresses remained the exception rather than the rule.

By the same token, it is apparent that on the Christian side social attitudes and legal procedures on such matters could vary substantially from region to region. Canon lawyers might have denounced the practice, but the reality was that the taking of minority women—the majority of them slaves—as concubines (*barraganas*) was widespread.[69] The *Siete Partidas* allowed a man to take a free woman or a slave as a concubine, with the proviso that he was not already married and she was not a virgin, or under twelve years of age, "or a widow who lives honourably and has a good reputation."[70] There is no indication in the code that the taking of a Jewish or Muslim woman as a *barragana* was outlawed. Similarly, no objection was raised by the lawgivers of Sepúlveda if a Christian man had a child by a minority woman; however, we have seen that a Christian woman who bore a child to a minority man was to be considered a woman of ill repute, whipped, and driven out of town.[71] The *Costums* of Tortosa contain numerous sections on the rights of minority concubines and their offspring, ruling that if the father were the owner of a slave concubine any child born to them would be considered free; if he were not the owner, the child would also become a slave, but could not subsequently be sold to a Muslim or Jew.[72] For its part, the *fuero* of Cuenca also gives the impression that such interfaith liaisons were commonplace:

> If someone has a child with another's Moorish woman, this child should be the servant of the *señor* of the Moorish woman, until his father redeems him. Also, we say that such a child should not divide with his siblings that which corresponds to the patrimony of their father, while he remains in servitude. Later should he become free, he should take a share of the goods of his father.[73]

What especially concerned some lawgivers was that any child born to a minority *barragana* should be brought up as a Christian: the laws of Soria were a case in point.[74] Similarly, the *Fuero Real* issued by Alfonso X of Castile in 1256 required a Christian man who fathered a child by a Muslim or Jewish woman to take responsibility for its upbringing and maintenance.[75] However, such children did not enjoy the same protection under the law as those of Christian *barraganas*, and if a mixed couple separated the woman might lose custody of her offspring.[76] From the fourteenth century, moreover, there is evidence to suggest that that the legal rights of such concubines and their offspring were gradually eroded.[77]

Christian men also frequented Muslim prostitutes. In Aragon the sex industry was subject to strict regulation by the Crown, which issued licenses and gleaned substantial tax revenues as a result.[78] Religious institutions, such as the Military Orders, also had a significant economic interest in Muslim prostitution, such as the Templars of Tortosa, who levied taxes on local Muslim prostitutes.[79] Municipal authorities subjected brothels to careful supervision, with premises often being walled in to prevent women from plying their trade in the public highway and to protect them from being kidnapped.[80] According to Mark Meyerson,

> Prostitution . . . was more than tolerated; it was encouraged. For why should a Christian king concern himself with the morality of Muslim women, who were, in any event, irredeemable on account of their profession of Islam? Since, according to the contemporary Catholic theological position, all Muslims were damned, the Christian authorities had no qualms about treating Muslim women as essentially soulless and exploitable objects.[81]

Many of these Muslim prostitutes were slaves, some of whom had fallen into servitude after having been condemned by local Islamic courts for sexual impropriety, or by royal or seigneurial officials for exercising prostitution without a license.[82] Others had gravitated toward prostitution after having separated from unhappy marriages or abusive husbands.[83] Social outcasts, disowned by their families and communities, vulnerable to sexual violence, for such women prostitution was one of the few economic avenues open to them if they were to survive. The experience of the Muslim woman Mariem, who left her husband in the village of Alasquer and moved to the city of Valencia in the company of another Muslim man, Cutaydal, some time prior to 1491, and was later tricked into working in the brothel of the *morería* (Muslim quarter) of Valencia, was probably not untypical.[84]

In reality, however, the boundaries between prostitution and concubinage were by no means clear-cut, and in the later medieval period there is evidence of former prostitutes entering into what have euphemistically been described as "domestic service contracts" with Christian men. The Christian Sancha Bolea, a resident of Daroca, who in her own words "became by chance a wayward woman, because a man there, in Zaragoza, took my maidenhood and dishonoured me, and I was on the verge of going to the brothels," entered into such a contract with another Christian, Juan de Madrid, in 1460. Sancha's predicament and motivation were clearly laid bare as she declared:

> In order to have some goods and not end up in the brothels, I have decided to come and live with you and serve you of my own free will. And [thus] I begged and asked you to take me into your house as housekeeper or servant, to stay with you and sleep with you, and to do with my body as you wish.[85]

In return for this undertaking, Juan de Madrid agreed to pay Sancha the sum of 200 *sueldos*. It is likely that for numerous marginalized, impoverished Muslim women similar arrangements such as these offered them a welcome, if often temporary, sense of security.[86]

The overriding impression conveyed by the Iberian *fueros* and other legal sources, therefore, was that a double standard of sexual conduct operated in the territories that lay under Christian authority.[87] The reality was that in a patriarchal, Christian society sexual relations between Christian men and minority women simply did not elicit the same level of anxiety as did those mixed faith liaisons involving Christian women. Thus, one profane song attributed to Alfonso X of Castile could say of the Dean of Cadiz, reportedly an avid collector of erotic literature, that "he fucks Moorish women whenever he feels like it" (*fod'el as mouras cada que lhi praz*); but the tone of the song is more one of jocularity than reproach.[88] The markedly asymmetrical nature of interfaith sexual relations is laid even more starkly bare by the *fuero* of Cuenca, which ruled that a Christian man found guilty of raping a Muslim woman would pay her "dower" (*arras*) amounting to 20 gold coins (*aurei*), "as if she were a married woman of the city"; if he assaulted an unmarried Christian woman, however, he faced a fine of 300 silver *sueldos* (in relative terms, a substantially higher amount) and would be outlawed, while if the woman were married her assailant would be burned at the stake.[89] The vulnerability of Muslim women to sexual assault was exemplified by the case of Fatima Curruta, which came to the attention of Peter IV of Aragon and his advisers in 1340. It was reported that Fatima had been raped by a Christian man when she was only nine years old and at a later date bore him a child. Later still, the Christian arranged for Fatima to marry a Muslim man, perhaps even providing her with a dowry, but she subsequently left that husband on account of the fact that he was squandering her property, and she finally sought and found the protection of the Aragonese Crown.[90]

At a symbolic level, David Nirenberg has observed, sex between a Christian man and Muslim woman

> Expressed and reproduced relations of domination and dependence within the household. Further, when a Christian penetrated a Muslim/woman slave he reiterated those very acts of conquest and degradation that formed much of the basis for Iberian Christian ideas of masculinity and honor. From the point of view of Christian males, then, sex with Muslim women reaffirmed religious, gendered, and economic hierarchies and created no problematic kinship ties.[91]

Whether all the Christian men who frequented Muslim prostitutes or slave concubines consciously viewed their liaisons in this way may be open to doubt, but the readiness with which they were able to engage in sexual relationships, however short-term, with minority women, set against the harsh penalties that were visited on minority males who were found guilty of illicit sexual mixing, served to underline the fact that subject Muslims and Jews did not enjoy complete equality with Christians in the eyes of the law. In this respect, sex was as much as an instrument of power over subject peoples as the forcible recruitment of Christian slave women into the harems of the Muslim caliphs and other élite males of al-Andalus had been in earlier centuries.

Sexual Mixing and the Church

The proliferation of laws prohibiting sexual intercourse between Christian women and Muslim or Jewish men was but one manifestation of the wider anxiety about sexual relations across religious lines that gripped the Christian realms of Iberia from the twelfth century onward. The contrast with the documentary silence of earlier centuries could not be greater. But secular lords were not the only ones to seek to place legal barriers in the way of interfaith sex. Equally significant was the readiness of the ecclesiastical authorities in the Latin West to denounce interfaith marriage, something that was not explicitly singled out for condemnation in most of the secular *fueros*, presumably because such matters were properly seen as falling under the authority of the Church. A notable exception was the Alfonsine *Fuero Real*, which prescribed the death penalty for a Christian woman who married a Muslim or Jew.[92] For the most part, however, clerics were at the forefront of the legislative drive to regulate marriage. From the eleventh century on, successive canon lawyers—the most prominent of whom were Burchard of Wörms, Ivo of Chartres, and Gratian—echoed the earlier prohibitions of Roman law, most notably the fifth-century Theodosian Code, by pronouncing that intermarriage between Christians and non-Christians was to be avoided at all costs, unless the Muslim or Jew in question converted to Christianity.[93] Thomas Aquinas, weighing up the pros and cons of interfaith marriage in his *Summa Theologica* (composed 1265–74), summed up the prevailing mood:

> The chief good of marriage is the offspring to be brought up to the worship of God. Now since education is the work of father and mother in common, each of them intends to bring up the child to the worship of God according to their own faith. Consequently if they be of different faith, the intention of the one will be contrary to the intention of the other, and therefore there cannot be a fitting marriage between them. For this reason disparity of faith previous to marriage is an impediment to the marriage contract.[94]

Such views were widely shared in the Peninsula. The fourth of Alfonso X's *Siete Partidas*, which likewise drew inspiration from the rulings of canon law, declared:

> A difference of religion is the sixth thing which operates as an impediment to marriage. For no Christian should marry a Jewess, Moorish woman, a heretic, or any other woman who does not profess the Christian religion, and if he does so the marriage will not be valid. A Christian can, however, be betrothed to a woman who does not profess his religion with the understanding that she will become a Christian before the marriage is consummated, and if she does not become a Christian the betrothal will be void.[95]

Tellingly, the code does not grant the same permission to Christian women.[96] However, extramarital sexual mixing was not addressed by western canonists, a fact that has led Brundage to suggest that "presumably it was not a pressing issue."[97] More to the point, it suggests that such lawyers were far less attuned to the social realities then prevailing in multicultural societies such as in the Peninsula. The secular lawgivers of Christian Iberia would in part make good that omission.

After a long silence on the matter, the papacy also began to weigh in on the argument. Pope Innocent III felt it necessary to issue two decretals dealing with the matter of interfaith marriages.[98] Even more significant, at the Fourth Lateran Council he summoned in 1215 it was agreed that henceforth, in order to avoid the risk of interfaith sexual relations, Jews and Muslims would be required to wear distinctive dress:

> In some provinces a difference in dress distinguishes the Jews or Saracens from the Christians, but in others there is such confusion that they cannot be distinguished by any difference. Thus it happens at times that through error Christians have relations with the women of Jews or Saracens, and Jews and Saracens with Christian women. Therefore, that they may not, under pretext of error of this sort, excuse themselves in the future for the excesses of such prohibited intercourse, we decree that such Jews and Saracens of both sexes in every Christian province and at all times shall be marked off in the eyes of the public from other peoples through the character of their dress. Particularly, since it may be read in the writings of Moses that this very law has been enjoined upon them.[99]

The *Siete Partidas* would later echo the papal injunction that the imposition of a dress code for minorities was necessary in order to draw visible boundaries between the faiths, thereby circumventing the danger of interfaith sex.[100] The law code's famous dictate about the perils of excessive social assimilation between Christians and Jews could equally have been applied to Muslims:

> Many crimes and offensive acts occur between Christian men and Jewish women and between Christian women and Jewish men as a consequence of their living together in towns and dressing alike. In order to avoid the errors and evils which might come about for this reason, we consider it proper and decree that all Jewish men and

> women living in our kingdom shall bear some distinguishing mark upon their heads so that all may clearly discern who is a Jew or a Jewess.[101]

By "errors and evils" it is clear enough that the law code had interfaith sex in mind.

It may be noted in passing that the corresponding section of the *Partidas* dealing with Muslims does not trouble to explain the prohibition on interfaith relationships, although this may reflect the fact that the legists who drafted the text were unable to draw on such an extensive body of theological sources, rather than any actual difference of policy.[102] Other Iberian monarchs paid lip service to such papal pronouncements by issuing vestimentary ordinances of their own, while in 1293 James II of Aragon instructed the bailiff (*baiulus*) who held jurisdiction over Lleida to enforce a special haircut for Muslims, on the grounds that it "might serve to avoid excesses and shameful conduct."[103] Yet there is little evidence that such discriminatory laws were rigorously enforced until the late fourteenth century, and in any case complete social segregation was never a serious prospect.[104] On a daily basis Christians, Muslims, and Jews might come into contact with one another in the street, in local markets, or at public utilities such as ovens or mills. They might also socialize together, in some cases gambling, drinking in taverns, and even frequenting prostitutes together.[105] The raft of legislation and other pronouncements issued by Christian, Jewish, and Muslim authorities designed to curb such social and sexual interaction across communal lines are best interpreted as an acknowledgment of that reality.

The papacy also directed its gaze toward Iberia. On 8 April 1223 Pope Honorius III dispatched a letter to the archbishop of Tarragona and his suffragans, in which he denounced the custom of those Christian kings and nobles, who—so the bishop of Zaragoza had informed him—were in the custom of handing over their noblewomen to the Muslims as a guarantee for monetary loans.[106] To make matters worse, the pope continued, "they are held excessively shamefully by those infidels, not without insult to the Christian name, [but] they do not wish to be freed from such detention." He then went on to threaten with excommunication those kings and nobles of Iberia who continued to commit such crimes. It is a startling claim. Are we to take this papal admonition at its face value? Or was the pope's letter merely a response to the widespread anxiety then abroad that had prompted the plethora of legislation against interfaith sexual mixing? The timing of the missive, which was dispatched at the very time when—as we shall see in subsequent chapters—the theme of interfaith sex was enjoying a particular literary vogue in the Peninsula, strongly suggests the latter. In reality, cross-border interfaith marriage already appears to have passed into desuetude with the collapse of the Umayyad caliphate in the early eleventh century. As the balance of power shifted decisively in favor of the Christian states of the North, the political and military leverage which had once allowed Muslim rulers to demand Christian brides as the price of peace disappeared altogether. After the reported betrothal of Vermudo II of León's daughter Teresa to an unnamed Muslim "king of Toledo"—perhaps 'Abd al-Raḥmān Sanchuelo, c.1009—which we examined in the previous chapter, no Christian monarch is known for sure to have negotiated such an alliance. The case of Sancho VII of Navarre (1194–1234), who, according to the English chronicler Roger of Howden, wished to wed the daughter of the Almohad caliph, is almost certainly a fiction.[107] Besides, the barrage of pronouncements by canon lawyers from the eleventh century onward denouncing the practice of interfaith marriage made such an alliance unthinkable in the eyes of the Church. If Christian brides of élite families were still being trafficked across the frontier into al-Andalus in the 1220s, as Pope Honorius believed, we do not hear of it from any other sources.

What we do encounter, albeit in very small numbers, are cases of Christian men marrying minority women, who were then expected to convert. The most high-profile case, as we have seen, was that of the Muslim noblewoman known to the Christians as Zaida, who after the death of her husband, al-Fatḥ al-Ma'mūn, in 1091, fled to the Christian North and became the concubine of Alfonso VI of León-Castile, whom she may later have married. A handful of cases can also be found lower down the social ladder. Thus, a document drawn up on 18 October 1270, which recorded the sale of an orchard in Oviedo by a blacksmith called Domingo Pérez and his four children for the sum of 30 *maravedís* to a minstrel (*iuglar*) called Pedro and his wife Marina "the Moor," may refer to such a marriage across religious boundaries.[108] However, conversion was not always immediately forthcoming in such cases. In 1332, a carpenter of Teruel, Gonzalo García, who had renounced his Islamic faith and converted to Christianity, was accused of having lived with his wife for over a decade while he attempted to convince her to convert, and even after the matter came before the legal authorities the king granted the woman another year's grace before she had to do so.[109] In a similar case, in 1334, Alfonso IV of Aragon allowed the Muslim woman Zobran, whose husband had earlier converted to Christianity, to continue living with him in Daroca because it was hoped he would bring about her conversion too.[110] For all that the ecclesiastical authorities might fulminate against mixed marriages, secular rulers were evidently willing to exercise a certain degree of pragmatism in their pronouncements on the question.

Faith, Power, and Sexual Control

As we contemplate the evident zeal with which Christian lawmakers in the Peninsula sought to tackle the perceived threat posed by sexual mixing, we are confronted with all manner of nagging questions. Why did the matter of interfaith sex loom quite so large in the consciousness of the secular and ecclesiastical authorities from the twelfth century onward, when lawgivers in the Northern Christian realms had been—to judge from the surviving evidence—entirely mute on the matter hitherto? Why did sexual mixing between Christian women and minority men generate by far the greatest anxiety? Was this concern to legislate against sexual mixing imposed by the ecclesiastical and secular élites "top-down," or was it, rather, a process driven by popular sectarian agitation? And to what extent was this concern to regulate intimacy born of circumstances peculiar to the Peninsula or, conversely, a response to cultural impulses generated far beyond the Pyrenees? These are complex questions which will require us to peel back the various layers of evidence with care.

First of all, let us consider the question of rationale. Perhaps unsurprisingly, given the context, the secular legal pronouncements that were issued against interfaith sex—dry and to the point—rarely sought to explain the motivation that underpinned them. However, the *Siete Partidas* were more forthcoming than most. While the Alfonsine code enshrined the right of Muslims and Jews to practice their own religions free from persecution, something that the collections of customary law never bothered to spell out, it was anxious to avoid excessive interaction between the faiths and drew the line at sexual mixing:

> Jews who lie with Christian women are guilty of great insolence and boldness, for which reason we decree that all Jews who, hereafter, may be convicted of having done such a thing shall be put to death. For if Christians who commit adultery with married women deserve death on that account, how much more so do Jews who have sexual

> intercourse with Christian women, who are spiritually the wives of Our Lord Jesus Christ because of the faith and the baptism which they receive in His name.[111]

Just as *Ecclesia*, the Church personified as a woman, was traditionally portrayed as the bride or daughter of Christ, so too through baptism were Christian women of any age or status.[112] By that definition, David Nirenberg has aptly observed, "miscegenation becomes the cuckolding of Christ."[113] From the point of view of the lawyers who framed such legislation, then, interfaith sex was nothing less than an affront, both to the natural order of Christian society and to God Himself.

Yet the policy of exclusion was not driven entirely by theological considerations of this sort. It also reflected a pragmatic anxiety that sexual relations between a Christian woman and a minority male might lead to her conversion to Islam or Judaism and that of any children subsequently born to the couple. Such fears of apostasy had deep theological roots, but they were given added potency by social realities closer to home.[114] In 1282, a Christian woman, Ona, daughter of one López Dorias, was reportedly abducted by the Muslims of Calatarao, converted to Islam, and married a Muslim.[115] The claim that Ona had been carried off against her will might have been an attempt to save face, rather than admit that she had voluntarily engaged in sexual relations with a Muslim man, which would have brought dishonor on her family. In 1311, the Christian widow Elvira of Oriola reputedly had an affair with a local Muslim of Crevillent and bore him two children, before subsequently fleeing to Granada and converting to Islam.[116] The determination of Christian lawgivers to prevent a recurrence of such cases by establishing clear legal barriers between the faiths reflected a wider concern to uphold patriarchal authority and the established social order.

Yet if we adopt a much wider perspective, we should recognize that there was nothing peculiarly Iberian, nothing especially Christian indeed, about such anxieties. The concern of certain communities to prevent sexual mixing with other groups, ethnicities, or religions is as old as history itself. As the anthropologist Mary Douglas argued in her classic work *Purity and Danger*, one of the key functions of this deep-seated fear of the defilement of a group's women by male outsiders is to reinforce the integrity of the social structure and foster group solidarity.[117] This is particularly true of patriarchal societies, in which the failure to protect the sexual honor of its women is often viewed as a direct threat to the power and prestige of the dominant males. Accordingly, when a group seeks to establish clear social boundaries vis-à-vis another group, a concern to police sexual relations is frequently one way to reinforce and secure them. And since the female body is frequently taken to represent a group's own sense of identity, a symbol of the body politic itself, one might say, the sexual behavior of its women tends to be policed with particular rigor, and misconduct severely punished.[118] By contrast, sexual relations between group males and female outsiders tend to evince notably less concern. Thus, according to Douglas:

> Both male and female physiology lend themselves to the analogy with the vessel which must not pour away or dilute its vital fluids. Females are correctly seen as, literally, the entry by which the pure content may be adulterated. Males are treated as pores through which the precious stuff may ooze out and be lost, the whole system being thereby enfeebled. A double moral standard is often applied to sexual offences. In a patrilineal system of descent wives are the door of entry to the group. . . . Through the adultery of a wife impure blood is introduced to the lineage.[119]

We have already seen that very same "double moral standard" in the pronouncements of the Iberian municipal *fueros*.

At the very root of anxiety over "social pollution," therefore, lies a sense—sometimes conscious, sometimes not—that sex, identity, and power are often all closely bound up together.[120] Allowing outsiders to engage in sexual relations with a group's own women could be construed as an act of submission, as a metaphor for external domination. We saw in the previous chapter that the enthusiasm with which the élites of al-Andalus frequently sought Christian brides or slave concubines for their harems stemmed in part from a desire to demonstrate their power and prestige, both to their own subjects and to the infidels of the North. Equally, it could be argued that the determination on the part of the Christian authorities to uphold the purity of their own women, by outlawing sexual mixing, not only sought to establish an explicit link between female sexuality and familial and communal honor, but was also a means by which the identity of the Christian community as a whole could be defined and its cohesion reinforced.[121] This chimes with the views of the sociologist Emile Durkheim, who argued that the zeal to define specific groups as deviant, that is, whose conduct is viewed as either illegal or contrary to the values of the rest of society, serves to strengthen the ties that bind that society together.[122] A similar line was taken by Georg Simmel, who was of the opinion that conflict with external enemies had historically served the key function of maintaining the unity of the Church.[123]

Such anthropological and sociological insights help to give deeper meaning to the policy of sexual control that was pursued by the Christian authorities in Iberia. However, we are bound to ask why these anxieties should have bubbled up to the surface in the twelfth and thirteenth centuries and not, say, the tenth or the eleventh. Various explanations suggest themselves. For one thing, there was the question of a rapidly changing political and demographic landscape. We might reasonably conjecture that the sudden concern by secular lawgivers to prohibit interfaith sex was in part a consequence of the dramatic shift in the Peninsular balance of power that occurred in the two centuries following the collapse of the Umayyad caliphate. The determination to prevent excessive interfaith contact that we see reflected in law codes and other texts of the period could be construed as an instinctive response to the incorporation of sizeable communities of Muslims and Jews under Christian authority, in the wake of the major territorial conquests carried out by the Christians from the late eleventh century onward. The desire to uphold and strengthen the boundaries between the faiths, be it through the regulation of clothing, social and spatial segregation, or the management of sexual relations, was to become a key component of the apparatus of colonial domination that was imposed by the Christians over their newly conquered subject peoples. It was surely no coincidence that the very same concerns to delineate clear social boundaries between the faiths and thereby avoid sexual mixing, particularly where Christian women were concerned, were being articulated in the crusading realms at the other end of the Mediterranean, where a similar colonial dynamic operated at that time.[124] Interfaith sex became the target of legislation in both regions not because it was necessarily rife, although it did undoubtedly occur, but because sexual control was viewed as an appropriate mechanism by which relative positions of power might be demarcated and Christian superiority upheld. Just as Muslim and Jewish men were thought to be challenging Christian sovereignty with "great insolence and boldness," in the words of the *Siete Partidas*, by transgressing those social boundaries, so Christian women who willingly engaged in sexual relations with minority men were considered to be not merely dishonoring their families and undermining the established patriarchal authority, but also subverting the power and prestige of Christian rule.[125] Conversely, attitudes toward sex between Christian males and minority females, in the context of concubinage and prostitution, were rather more permissive, precisely because such relationships were not seen to destabilize the hierarchies of power upon which Christian authority was based. If anything they reinforced them, by "demasculinizing" the minority men who had proved unable to prevent their own women from engaging in such sexual relations. Viewed in this light, the anxiety engendered by interfaith sexual relations could be characterized as a "political discourse" in its own right, a product of the colonial encounter between victors and vanquished.[126] Michel Foucault's famous dictum that "power is essentially what dictates its law to sex" finds ample corroboration here.[127]

Yet we should not discount the influence of external cultural forces in shaping such attitudes. For one thing, Christian expansionism in Iberia between c.1050 and 1250 was accompanied by an increased readiness on the part of its rulers and clergy to invoke sectarian rhetoric in their official documents, incendiary language that had largely been conspicuous by its absence during the preceding decades, when tribute-taking and close cross-border dealings had been the order of the day.[128] The military intervention in the Peninsula by the Berber Almoravids from 1086 appears to have acted as an important trigger in this regard.[129] In one charter, issued in 1092, King Sancho Ramírez I of Aragon (1063–94) recorded his determination to strive "for the recovery and expansion of the Church of Christ, for the destruction of the pagans, the enemies of Christ"[130]; in another, issued six years later, the Castilian nobleman Rodrigo Díaz, El Cid, the self-styled *princeps* of Valencia, was portrayed by his propagandists as a divinely appointed deliverer of the Christian people, "the avenger of the shame of His servants and the enlarger of the Christian faith."[131] Such anti-Muslim sentiments appear to have been in part a response to prompting by the papacy and other servants of Rome—the legates who became regular visitors to the Peninsula after c.1060 and the French Cluniacs and others who began to be appointed to key positions in the Iberian ecclesiastical hierarchy from the 1080s.[132] Furthermore, such attitudes soon became closely bound up with the preaching of the Crusade. After 1095, as Iberia gradually came to be regarded—both in Rome and elsewhere in Western Christendom—as a crusading theater on a par with the Holy Land, the tone of the anti-Islamic rhetoric that had begun to be trumpeted in official documents and literary texts became increasingly strident.[133] Is it not possible, then, that the desire to harden the lines of social demarcation between the faiths that is apparent in the Christian *fueros* was a direct consequence of the inflamed sectarian attitudes that had come to dominate the religious and political discourse of Western Christendom as a whole?

At the same time, we would do well to recognize that such sectarianism was merely one symptom—albeit a strikingly potent one—of a wider, much more complex "discourse of exclusion" that began to be articulated in the Latin West from the twelfth century. In his *Contra Petrobrusianos hereticos*, a tract issued against the heretical sect led by Peter of Bruis, Abbot Peter the Venerable of Cluny (d. 1156) claimed that since the time of its foundation the Christian Church had been engaged in a two-fold struggle of purgation (*purgatio*) and expansion (*dilatatio*), in the course of which internal dissidents and external enemies, be they heretics or infidels, had had to be confronted and subdued.[134] Since Christendom, which Peter conceived of in spatial as well as social terms, was destined to expand until it embraced all mankind, those who lay outside the spiritual family of the Church—in particular, heretics, Muslims, and Jews—were effectively cast to the outer margins of humanity.[135]

This exclusionary logic was fully in tune with the universalizing doctrine of ecclesiastical sovereignty that had been promoted by the reformist papacy and its supporters—many of them Cluniacs themselves—from the second half of the eleventh century.[136] The direct result of this radical shift in the world view of the clergy, what Dominique Iogna-Prat has called a "dual moment of integration and exclusion," was to be an increased tendency to identify, marginalize, and, if necessary, punish those groups who did not belong within the community of faith.[137] Those targeted were to include not only non-Christians and heretics, but also other marginalized groups, such as homosexuals, prostitutes, and lepers.[138] Thus, in the seventh of the *Siete Partidas*, Muslims and Jews were lumped together with other groups regarded as "undesirables," including traitors, slanderers and fraudsters; murderers and robbers; adulterers and homosexuals; necromancers and heretics; blasphemers and prisoners. Through the influence of the ecclesiastical hierarchy, secular rulers joined in on the act and began to legislate for difference in strikingly diverse ways. Targeting minorities through the assertion of religious authority in this way soon became a means for secular governments to display their power. It is also notable that at the very time that Christian lords in the Peninsula were taking decisive steps to delineate the rights and obligations of the Jews and Muslims in their midst, their counterparts in other regions of Europe—such as the English in Ireland and Wales, the Germans in the Baltic, or the Hungarians north of the Danube—were also engaged in an not unrelated process of legal and ethnic differentiation.[139]

For R. I. Moore, this process of social reclassification marked an important step toward the creation of what he has dubbed a "Persecuting Society" in

Europe. This development owed much to the burgeoning influence of an expanding group of clerical *literati* into whose hands new institutions of secular government were entrusted during the course of the twelfth century, at a time of rapid social and economic change.[140] It was that same educated élite, Moore argues, which "moulded the mentalities and devised the procedures which ensured that these patterns of persecution would endure in European society not just for the remainder of the middle ages, but until our own times."[141] Moore's thesis has by no means won universal scholarly support, and much more research is necessary before its broad lines can be confirmed.[142] For example, his contention that, once created, a "persecuting mentality" endured in the collective consciousness of the Latin West has been called into question.[143] Be that as it may, few would quarrel with Moore's general proposition that the drive to marginalize such a diverse range of "deviant" groups across Western Europe from the twelfth century onward cannot be interpreted as simply a "series of independent responses to real or imagined dangers," or that it was unrelated to complex changes in Christian society and government at that time, not least the papally sponsored drive to centralize ecclesiastical authority.[144] John Boswell has associated the growing intolerance toward "outsiders" with "a sedulous quest for intellectual and institutional uniformity and corporatism throughout Europe," which was exemplified by a spectacular increase in legislative production, secular and ecclesiastical alike.[145]

The implication of all this as far as this inquiry is concerned is that we should be aware that the voices that began to be raised in Christian Iberia against interfaith sex with Muslims or Jews, far from erupting ex nihilo, were themselves in part a response to heightened anxieties toward difference that emanated from beyond the Pyrenees. Key agents for the transmission of such attitudes are likely to have been the same papal legates and incoming French clerics who were helping to inculcate more sectarian attitudes toward Islam in the Peninsula. Reformers almost to a man, these foreigners sought to establish uniformity of worship and practice in the Iberian Church in order to bring it into line with the wishes of Rome and, in collaboration with the secular authorities, did much to sweep away what they regarded as outmoded rituals, customs, and attitudes, not least the "Mozarabic" or Visigothic liturgy, which was abolished in the west of the Peninsula in 1080.[146] But this was not a "cultural revolution" imposed exclusively from outside. From the twelfth century onward Iberian masters and students began to gravitate in large numbers to the law schools of Bologna and, to a much lesser degree, Paris. Such men became instrumental in ensuring that books of canon law circulated extensively in the Peninsula.[147] Moreover, as the Iberian Church began to reorient itself toward Rome from the late eleventh century, Peninsular bishops began to attend papal councils, and local clergy sought papal advice about various matters, not least regarding the laws of marriage.[148] Thus, sometime between 1187 and 1191 Pope Clement III answered a letter from the bishop of Segovia (or possibly the chapter of Ciudad Rodrigo) that questioned whether a baptized Jew or Muslim could legitimately remain married to a spouse to whom he was too closely related according to canon law.[149]

Ecclesiastical polemicists had long since used rhetoric as a means to confront and, so they hoped, confound the enemies of the Church. What was so distinctive about the exclusionary process that was enacted from the twelfth century on was the receptiveness of the secular élite to such ideas and its readiness to put them into action.[150] Even if the Christian authorities in Iberia sometimes proved lax in imposing certain segregationalist policies promoted by the papacy, such as vestimentary ordinances, their readiness to legislate against interfaith sex and the apparent thoroughness with which their legal officials investigated and prosecuted such cases speak volumes for the importance that was attached to these matters. Whether these concerns were widely shared further down the social hierarchy is more difficult to gauge. There is certainly little evidence to suggest that the drive to outlaw sexual relations between the faiths was in response to popular pressure, although the lynching of Ali de Matero at Daroca suggests that it was an issue that could cause intercommunal hostility to flare up into violence. The incendiary sermons of St. Vincent Ferrer, who warned an audience in Zaragoza in 1415 that "many Christian men believe their wife's children to be their own, when they are actually by Muslim and Jewish [fathers]," sparked panic among the local Christian community, which organized street patrols to apprehend any Muslims or Jews who were thought to be seeking to prey on Christian women.[151] Joanna Bourke's comments on the use of fear as a means to foster solidarity among communities are apt here:

> Crucially, emotions such as fear do not only belong to individuals or social groups: they mediate between the individual and the social. They are about power relations. Emotions lead to a negotiation of the boundaries between self and other or one community and another. They align individuals with communities.[152]

Yet to characterize such efforts to curb interfaith sex as constituting part of a systematic policy of persecution would be wide of the mark, not least because the regulation of intimacy was afforded equal importance by Muslim and Jewish community leaders, who similarly feared the consequences that excessive social (and sexual) contact between the faiths would bring. In this respect, it could be argued that by sponsoring the drive to proscribe sexual mixing the Christian authorities were merely bringing their own laws into line with those of the other faiths. Viewed in this light, one might even venture that the management of sexual relations by all communities and the maintenance of the boundaries between them constituted a vital mechanism by which the very stability of the multicultural societies of Iberia was preserved.[153]

Chapter 3

Damsels in Distress

During the course of the twelfth century the specter of interfaith sex came to haunt the Christian societies of the Iberian Peninsula. True, as we saw in the previous chapter, the convergence of a range of political, religious, and cultural factors after c.1050 meant that the practice of cross-border interfaith marriage among the Peninsular élites was condemned to a swift decline. Partly as a consequence of this shift in attitudes, the Christian authorities came down hard on Christian women who engaged in sexual relationships with Muslim or Jewish men, or who even prostituted themselves to non-Christians; by the same token, Christian men who had sexual liaisons with women of another faith usually did so with impunity. But the anxiety surrounding interfaith sexual mixing that appears to have gripped Christian society in the Peninsula in the Later Middle Ages was by no means articulated exclusively through the pronouncements of lawyers. Rather, it is striking that from the twelfth century onward the thorny subject was to be highlighted and explored repeatedly within an extraordinarily diverse range of texts, including works of narrative history, poetry, and hagiography, among others. The theme also provided the inspiration for one of the most ambitious and effective forgeries to have been carried out anywhere in Western Christendom during the Middle Ages. In this chapter we will subject those texts, and their ideological significance, to closer scrutiny.

The Reluctant Bride

The brief *Chronicon Regum Legionensium* (Chronicle of the Kings of León), composed by Bishop Pelayo of Oviedo, is hardly the most distinguished piece of Hispano-Latin historical literature to have come down to us.[1] The chronicle covers the history of the Leonese kingdom from the accession of Vermudo II in 982 to the death of Alfonso VI in 1109, but is a work of painfully limited scope and ambition. Not only is Pelayo's prose style laconic and unpolished, but his narrative is also both uneven and superficial in equal measure. The overwhelming impression we get is that it was flung together with some haste.[2] Yet for all its shortcomings, Pelayo's work is by no means lacking in interest for the historian, not least for the series of colorful vignettes that the bishop included, which have much to tell us about his ideological standpoint and that of the society for which he was writing. One such vignette occurs in the course of Pelayo's hostile account of the reign of Vermudo II, where he makes reference to the marriage alliance that was subsequently arranged between the king's daughter, Teresa, and an unnamed "pagan king of Toledo" by her brother Alfonso V:

> After the death of her father, Teresa was given away in marriage by her brother Alfonso to a certain pagan king of Toledo for the sake of peace, although she herself was unwilling. But as she was a Christian, she said to the pagan king: "Do not touch me, for you are a pagan. If you do touch me the Angel of the Lord will slay you." Then the king laughed at her and slept with her once and just as she had predicted he was immediately struck down by the Angel of the Lord. As he felt death approaching, he summoned his chamberlains and his councillors and ordered them to load up camels with gold, silver, gems and precious garments, and to take her back to León with all these gifts. She stayed in that place in a nun's habit for a long time, and afterward she died in Oviedo and was buried in the monastery of San Pelayo.[3]

The story of the plucky Princess Teresa and the pagan (presumably Muslim) king is shrouded by a fog of uncertainty and raises a number of intriguing questions. How much trust can we possibly place in the testimony of Pelayo, a man who is best known for having indulged in a large-scale program of forgery in defense of the rights and privileges of his episcopal see?[4] Are we really to believe that this dramatic tale was based on historical events, and if so, why did the bishop consider it worthy of inclusion in his chronicle? More broadly, what can the account tell us about twelfth-century Christian attitudes toward interfaith sexual mixing?

In Chapter 1 we saw that, for all Pelayo's reputation as a spinner of tall tales, it is by no means inconceivable that at some point during the first two decades of the eleventh century, at a time when the Leonese monarchy's grip on power was uncertain, Alfonso V—or rather the nobles who wielded power on his behalf during his minority—might have sought to broker a marriage alliance with a Muslim potentate, just as other hard-pressed Christian kings had done in the past. There is even some circumstantial evidence to suggest that the "pagan king of Toledo" referred to by Pelayo might have been the *ḥājib* 'Abd al-Malik al-Muẓaffar or his brother 'Abd al-Raḥmān "Sanchuelo," heir to the caliphal throne. There is no need to revisit that debate here. Whatever the historicity of the narrative of the marriage, the ideological *purpose* of the story within Pelayo's chronicle is of equal importance to us.

Various aspects of Pelayo's account of the betrothal of Teresa to the Muslim king immediately catch the eye. First, there is his observation that the marriage alliance was a pragmatic mechanism by which the Leonese sought to secure a peace deal. Then, there is his insistence not only that Teresa was reluctant to enter into the marriage, but also that she resolutely rejected the sexual advances of the king on the grounds that he was not a Christian. After that, there is the assurance that the king paid a heavy price for having raped the princess, being struck down by divine vengeance shortly afterward. Finally, the bishop relates that after the king's untimely death Teresa returned to her homeland bearing numerous gifts and became a nun, ending her days in the abbey of San Pelayo in Oviedo. It was conceivably from the nuns of San Pelayo that Bishop Pelayo first heard of the story. Running throughout the entire narrative we can identify a burning preoccupation with feminine sexual honor. As a broad concept, "honor" defies easy definition or categorization. In the context of twelfth-century Europe, it may suffice to say that a woman's honor—and by extension that of her family—was closely bound up with her reputation, dignity, self-esteem, modesty, and, if she was unmarried, her chastity.[5] To judge from the evidence of the Castilian municipal *fueros* of the twelfth and thirteenth centuries, for example, a woman's honor might be variously impugned by insulting her, molesting her, casting her to the ground, removing her coif, uncovering her hair, or exposing her body. Far worse, a woman might be abducted or even forced to undergo the traumatic experience of rape.[6] But there was also a widespread sense that a woman's honor was inextricably linked to that of God. In the previous chapter we saw that the Alfonsine *Siete Partidas* were notably forthright on the matter, ruling that just as Christians who committed adultery with married women deserved death, so did Jews who slept with Christian women, since the latter were seen to be "spiritually espoused to Our Lord Jesus Christ by virtue of the faith and baptism they received in His name."[7] In this way, a Christian woman's body was regarded as symbolic of God's honor and authority. It followed that a nonbeliever who violated her besmirched not merely her honor, but God's also, and that of the Christian community as a whole. As David Nirenberg has commented: "As His wives, their bodies represented the extension of His authority and community, the point at which His honor as father and husband was at risk. Because of this, women's bodies could become the site of fears concerning God's honor and that of His Church."[8] And what was true of Jews was assuredly true of Muslims too.

We should also recognize that Pelayo's denunciation of the rape of Teresa Vermúdez by the Muslim king belonged within a polemical tradition which had long sought to denigrate the Muslim faith by criticizing the depravity and violent sexuality of its followers.[9] Eulogius of Córdoba went so far as to claim that the Prophet Muḥammad had attempted to deflower the Virgin Mary.[10] Pelayo's contemporary Guibert of Nogent fulminated that the Islamic faith was nothing less than a "new license for random copulation" and denounced the numerous acts of sexual violence that the Muslims had visited on the Christians of the Near East.[11] In short, by his brutal sexual assault on the Christian princess Teresa, the Muslim king of Toledo would have been judged by many to be merely conforming to type.

One can easily see, therefore, why Pelayo's account of the forced marriage and rape of Teresa Vermúdez would have had a strong impact on his audience. Above all, the narrative was designed to highlight the dangers posed by interfaith sexual mixing. The bishop does not develop the point to any degree, but implicit in his report is that he considered the purchase of peace through the sacrifice of the chastity and honor of a high-born Christian woman to be a shameful transaction. The Muslim king, by sleeping with the Christian princess, had transgressed the social, cultural, and confessional boundaries that separated the faiths and paid the ultimate price for it. For her part, the valiant Teresa would have won admiration for the resolute manner in which she stood up to the king, but contemporaries would also have perceived that she had incurred grave dishonor by suffering rape at the hands of a Muslim, something many of her coreligionists doubtless regarded as a fate worse than death.[12] After her ordeal in al-Andalus was at an end and she had returned to her native León, the princess Teresa would have had little option but to confine herself to the cloister of San Pelayo in Oviedo.[13] For all her royal pedigree, no other man would have wished to take her as his bride. A similar attitude prevailed in the crusading kingdoms of the Latin East, where women who had had sexual relations with Muslim men found their reassimilation into Christian society difficult in the extreme.[14] Thus, when the Armenian wife of Baldwin I of Jerusalem returned from captivity in 1108, the king compelled her to enter the convent of St. Anne, suspecting—"not unreasonably," Guibert of Nogent observed—that she had been violated by her captors.[15] A similar experience befell the wife of Renier Brus, who was captured in 1132 and cast off by her husband after two years in captivity because, as William of Tyre put it, "she had not satisfactorily preserved the sanctity of the marriage couch as a noble matron should."[16]

Embroidered though it may have been, therefore, Pelayo's tale of the betrothal of Princess Teresa to the Muslim king was suffused with immense symbolic significance. It may be noted in passing that it contains certain echoes of the hagiographical accounts of the martyrdom of the Christian child-saint Pelayo, who was reportedly executed in 925 or 926, after rejecting the sexual advances of the caliph ʿAbd al-Raḥmān III, and whose remains were later translated to the nunnery of San Pelayo de Oviedo, or so it was claimed.[17] Although, unlike Pelayo, Teresa did not suffer martyrdom, audiences who heard of her story were doubtless meant to admire the fortitude with which she bore her ordeal at the hands of the Muslim king. The story of Teresa is highly significant to us, therefore, not simply because it sheds some light on the practice of interfaith marriage in Iberia shortly after the millennium, and leads us to ponder the particular circumstances under which such matrimonial pacts might have taken place, but also because it mirrors the same anxieties about interfaith sex that were beginning to be articulated by ecclesiastics and secular lawgivers in Iberia and farther afield.

What is more, the resonance and appeal of Pelayo's account were to prove notably long-lasting. The tale passed mostly word for word into the anonymous *Chronica Naierensis*, composed at the Cluniac abbey of Nájera c.1190;[18] a few decades after that it was incorporated into Lucas of Tuy's *Chronicon Mundi* (1236)[19]; and from there into Archbishop Rodrigo Jiménez's *De rebus Hispanie* (completed 1243).[20] It is worth noting that Lucas of Tuy's version of events, written a full century after Pelayo's and two centuries after the episode it purports to describe, differs in a few significant details. First, it records that the Muslim king's name was Abdella, that is ʿAbd Allāh, and that he had been attacking the Leonese kingdom at the time the marriage alliance was brokered. Second, it shifts the blame for the decision to marry off Teresa from the king to his advisors, emphasizing that Alfonso V was but a boy at the time the marriage was agreed and that he was acting on the advice of his nobles. Third, Lucas justifies the decision to betroth Teresa by alleging that the Muslim ruler in question had hoodwinked the Leonese monarch by pretending to be a Christian, and had even sworn to provide military support to Alfonso V against other Muslims. Archbishop Rodrigo Jiménez does not add a great deal of further detail to this account, although he attributes the decision to allow Teresa to be married to the Muslim ruler to be part of "a treaty that had been agreed against the king of Córdoba." Rodrigo also has Teresa declare, "I am a Christian woman and I abhor foreign marriages," a statement which neatly summed up the prevailing mood.[21] Drawing on these accounts, the story was further finessed by the compilers of the vernacular *Estoria de Espanna*, commissioned by Alfonso X of Castile, which erroneously placed the events in the year 984.[22] The Alfonsine account follows those of Lucas and Rodrigo fairly closely, but with a few differences of emphasis. In particular, the narrative accentuates the violence of the king's sexual assault, in marked contrast to Pelayo's somewhat tepid original account: "The Moorish king took no notice of what she said, and mocked her, and grabbed her, and had his way with her by force." The chronicler is keen to emphasize that no honorable Christian woman would willingly engage in sexual relations with a Muslim man: sexual mixing is portrayed as nothing less than a brutal act of rape.

The appeal of the story of the Muslim king and his reluctant Christian bride was to endure.[23] The playwright Lope de Vega addressed the episode in no fewer than three of his works—*El primer rey de Castilla* (1598–1603), *Los Tellos de Meneses* (1628), and *El labrador venturoso* (1629)—and the tale was also revisited in a number of early modern ballads. One such was the ballad which begins *Casamiento se hacía que a Dios ha desagradado* (A marriage took place which displeased God).[24] The essential elements of the story as first told by Pelayo remain the same, but the dramatic effect is heightened considerably. In the first section, the ballad tells of King Alfonso's decision, with the consent of his advisors, to marry Teresa off to a "renegade Moor" called "Audalla." Hearing of her fate, the hapless princess falls into despair, rends her clothes, tears at her face and hair, and finally faints, only reviving when her ladies in waiting splash her face with water. Later, once she has come to, the princess, while still on her knees, addresses a desperate appeal to God himself, in which she denounces her brother, who had forced her into the marriage against her will, and the prelates and nobles who advised him. She laments her fate and beseeches God to protect her and deliver her from such great peril. And there the ballad ends, with Teresa, the victim of injustice, ruing her fate, railing against her brother, and invoking divine assistance. Somewhat surprisingly, the subsequent demise of the Muslim king at the hands of a vengeful archangel, as reported by Bishop Pelayo and others, does not make an appearance.

The Tribute of the Hundred Maidens

Shortly after Bishop Pelayo laid down his pen, another account of interfaith sexual mixing was to achieve prominence, whose social and cultural resonance was to prove immeasurably greater. The origins of this account lie in the holy city of Santiago de Compostela, where sometime between 1158 and 1174 a canon of the local cathedral chapter, Cardinal Pedro Marcio, copied out what he claimed was an original charter of King Ramiro I of Asturias that had been issued on 25 May 834 at Calahorra in the Rioja.[25] It is a remarkable document indeed, quite unlike anything else of that period. After the standard preliminaries—divine invocation, intitulation, and *arenga*—there follows an extensive and dramatic *narratio*, in which the king is made to declare the following:

> In ancient times, not long after the destruction of Spain by the Saracens in the time of King Roderic, (there were) certain of our predecessors, leading men of the Christians, who were lazy, neglectful, idle, and incompetent, whose lives are certainly not worthy of being imitated by any believer. These men, it is unworthy to relate, agreed to pay the Saracens an abominable tribute, in order to avoid being disturbed by the attacks of the Saracens, namely: to give them every year one hundred maidens of extraordinary beauty, fifty from the Spanish nobility, fifty from the common people. Oh, the suffering! What a shameful example for posterity! In exchange for a temporary and short-lived peace agreement, Christianity was handed over captive in order to satisfy the lust of the Saracens.

The document goes on to relate that after King Ramiro had succeeded to the throne, he resolved to release his people from this shame. Having taken counsel with the clergy and nobles of his kingdom and having granted new laws to his subjects, he gathered a large army, which he led toward Nájera in the Rioja and camped at nearby Albelda. However, this force was soon confronted by a vast Muslim expeditionary army, made up of soldiers from both the Peninsula and North Africa. Put to flight in the face of overwhelming military power, the Christians suffered many losses and were obliged to take refuge on a nearby hilltop called Clavijo. Huddled together on that hillside, the king relates, the fearful remnants of that Christian army spent the night sobbing and praying, uncertain what to do next. However, when finally he slept, Ramiro was visited in his dreams by St. James, who is described in the charter as "protector of the Spaniards" (*Hispanorum protector*). Stretching out his hand to the king, the saint declared:

> Be of good cheer and have courage, for I will come to help you, and tomorrow, through God's power, you will vanquish that countless multitude of Saracens by whom you are besieged. However, many of your men for whom eternal rest is prepared and stand ready for battle in the name of Christ will receive the crown of martyrdom. And lest there is any room for doubt, both you and the Saracens will see me constantly dressed in white, on a great white horse, carrying in my hand a great white banner.

Sure enough, just as the Apostle had predicted, when the two armies clashed on the battlefield the next day St. James appeared, mounted on his white horse, urging on the Christian ranks and disrupting the enemy. Inspired by the sight and with shouts of "May God and St. James help us!" the Christians fell upon the enemy and won a crushing victory, killing some 70,000 Muslims in the process, or so we are told, and followed this up by capturing the nearby town of Calahorra.

After this lengthy and stirring preamble, we then reach the nub of the document. In thanks for this heaven-sent victory, and in particular recognition of the part played by his patron and protector St. James in delivering him from his enemies, the king granted to the canons of the church of Santiago de Compostela the perpetual right to receive annually quantities of wheat and wine from parishes across Christian Iberia, as well as a share of any plunder taken in future campaigns against the Muslims. This is the extraordinary tax that came to be known as the *Voto de Santiago*.

The charter known to Spanish historians as *el Privilegio del Voto* has been the subject of extensive and passionate debate.[26] The authenticity of the document and the historicity of the events it narrates have found numerous doughty defenders in the past, not least the former canon archivist of the

Figure 1. Forged charter attributed to Ramiro I of Asturias granting an annual tax (*Voto*) to the cathedral of Santiago de Compostela.

Santiago de Compostela, Archivo de la Catedral, carpeta 7, no. 1.

cathedral of Santiago de Compostela, Antonio López Ferreiro, for whom the charter was one of the key foundation texts of Spanish *Reconquista* ideology.[27] For such men, to question the events of Clavijo was akin to challenging the very essence of the Spanish nation.[28] Be that as it may, scholarly consensus today is that the charter purportedly issued by Ramiro I is a blatant forgery, in all likelihood the twelfth-century handiwork of its putative copyist, the canon, notary, and cardinal Pedro Marcio.[29] This is not the place to engage in a forensic, line-by-line analysis of the charter, but it is worth briefly enumerating a few of its most suspicious features. First, the date of the charter, 834, is impossible, in that Ramiro I had yet to come to the throne at that time; and while it appears that Christian and Muslim armies did indeed clash in battle at Clavijo, that engagement did not take place until 859, by which time King Ramiro was long since dead.[30] Second, the diplomatic—that is to say the formal style, structure, and format—of the document is utterly at odds with that of other, apparently genuine, royal diplomas of the ninth and tenth centuries.[31] Third, the list of notables who witnessed the document does not accord with the date when it was supposedly issued. Fourth, it is suspicious that the diploma was not copied into the first part of the cathedral cartulary now known as *Tumbo* A, compiled in 1129–31 under the supervision of the treasurer Bernardo, as were almost all the authentic royal charters then housed in the Compostelan archive.[32] Fifth, the protagonism attributed to the apostle James on the battlefield, along with reference to the martyrdom of Christian knights, were notable features of a number of literary texts of the twelfth century, but not of the ninth. This was a process that was closely related to the spread of crusading ideology to the Peninsula after c.1100 and to the promotion of the apostle James as Santiago Matamoros (St. James "the Moorslayer"), the "patron saint" of the military struggle against Islam.[33] Last but not least, although the legend is based around events that supposedly occurred in the late eighth and early ninth centuries, it is surely telling that none of the Asturian court chronicles composed at the end of the ninth century, all of them so keen to trumpet the achievements of the Christian kings, made any mention whatsoever of the tribute of the hundred maidens, the battle of Clavijo, or the miraculous intervention of St. James. The list could go on.

To muddy the waters even further, it is worth noting in passing that another Compostelan text, the *Chronicon Iriense*, which was perhaps completed shortly after 1120—that is, several decades before the forger of the charter of Ramiro I probably put pen to parchment—places the genesis of the *Voto de Santiago* a century later.[34] According to this source, it was King Ramiro II of León (931–51) who, after visiting the tomb of the apostle James "for the purpose of prayer" (*causa orationis*), granted an annual render to the church of Santiago de Compostela from all his territories as far east as the River Pisuerga.[35] Moreover, the chronicler establishes a clear causal link between the king's munificence to the Compostelan church and his later victory in battle over the all-powerful Umayyad caliph 'Abd al-Rahman III, presumably a reference to the battle of Simancas of 939.[36] In this version of events, however, the tribute of the hundred maidens and the military intervention of the apostle James are conspicuous by their absence.

So far, so confusing, you might say. Yet if the charter of Ramiro I is a fabrication, as is now almost universally accepted, we are bound to ask why it was forged in the first place. The answer to that question almost certainly lies in the dogged efforts that were being made by the Compostelan clergy throughout the twelfth century to promote the cult of the apostle St. James the Great, whose supposed tomb had been discovered sometime between 818 and 842 and a church built on the site. The charter of Ramiro I was in fact but one in a series of texts produced for the church of Santiago de Compostela during that period—including works of history, collections of miracle stories and hymns, and even a celebrated guide book for pilgrims—which were all designed to consolidate Santiago's status as one of Christendom's holiest cities, alongside Jerusalem and Rome.[37] But pious devotion to the Apostle alone cannot itself explain the decision to forge the charter of Ramiro I. Financial expediency might also have been a significant motivating factor. The forgery was concocted at a time when, despite the popularity of the pilgrimage to the city, the church of Santiago had been suffering a serious financial squeeze, so much so that building works on the vast Romanesque cathedral, which had been in train since the final quarter of the eleventh century, had been abruptly suspended in 1140. Is it possible that the "invention" of the *Voto* was essentially the clever ruse of a resourceful Compostelan canon anxious to make good the shortfall in funding and allow the program of construction to begin anew?[38] It is worth noting, however, that there is documentary evidence to suggest that a tax akin to the *Voto* was being levied by the Compostelan clergy in the parishes under its control many generations before the charter of Ramiro I was forged.[39] The likelihood is that Pedro Marcio sought not to conjure up an entirely new tax by fabricating the royal diploma, but rather to provide documentary justification for a fiscal imposition whose roots lay in the distant past and, even more ambitiously, to extend its reach right across the Peninsula.[40]

At the same time, the forgery should be viewed in the broader context of twelfth-century ecclesiastical power politics. This, after all, was the period when the archbishopric of Santiago de Compostela, which had only been raised to metropolitan status in 1120 thanks to the efforts of its indefatigable first archbishop, Diego Gelmírez, was locked in a bitter power struggle with its rivals, the archbishops of Braga and Toledo, over their respective rights and zones of influence.[41] Yet the decades after the death of Diego in 1140 were ones of great instability, as a series of short-lived archbishops left the Church bereft of the sustained leadership it needed, the cathedral chapter suffered divisions, the Crown and the local nobility appropriated lands and rights belonging to the see, and Compostela's relations with the archbishoprics of Braga and Toledo became bedevilled by disputes, over their suffragans in the case of the former and the primacy in that of the latter.[42] It is conceivable, then, that the forged charter of Ramiro I was designed in part to reinforce Compostela's authority, its luster even, within the Peninsular Church at a time when, holy city or not, the cathedral chapter might have feared that in some respects the see ran the risk of becoming marginalized by its rivals for power and influence, Braga and Toledo.[43] In this context, it might make sense to view the forged charter of Ramiro I as merely one element within an ambitious program of initiatives that was put in train during the second half of the twelfth century, all of them designed to burnish the reputation of both the Apostle James and the church of Santiago de Compostela itself. Of these initiatives, by far the most eye-catching was the construction of the Pórtico de la Gloria, the spectacular triple portal set within the western façade of the cathedral, which was erected between 1168 and 1188; more prosaic—but significant none the less—was the decision to expand the cathedral cartulary into a more comprehensive collection of royal privileges.[44] And the Compostelan authorities were by no means the only ones promoting such a program. King Ferdinand II of León (1157–88), who had succeeded to the throne on the death of his father Alfonso VII and the dismemberment of his Leonese-Castilian "empire," was equally determined to demonstrate his devotion to the Apostle and to promote Santiago de Compostela as the *caput* of his kingdom. In doing so, Ferdinand appears to have sought to create a counterweight to Toledo, the ancient capital of the Visigothic kingdom and seat of the Iberian Church, then under Castilian authority, in order to underpin his own pretensions—expressed in the products of his chancery—to rule in the Peninsula as *Hispanorum Rex*.[45] The later foundation of the Military Order of Santiago c.1170 was connected to this same drive to further exalt the status of St. James both in the Peninsula and further afield.

Of course, in seeking to falsify the historical record to the benefit of his see, Pedro Marcio—if indeed the forged charter was his handiwork—was acting very much in the spirit of the times. This was a period when, with ever greater weight being afforded to the written record, ecclesiastics in many parts of the Latin West were resorting to the forgery of texts in an attempt to buttress and augment the rights and privileges—real or imagined—of their institutions.[46] And in this respect, Pedro Marcio's charter might be said to have provided a veritable master class in the art of the forger, in that the Compostelan diploma, the events that it narrated, and, not least, the annual tax that it enshrined later came to be accepted as "evident truths" and incorporated into the shared cultural memory of Christian León and Castile. Not only did payment of the Compostelan tax gradually become institutionalized in parishes across Castile, León, and northern Portugal, at a time when the popularity of the pilgrimage to Compostela was in marked decline, but the church of Santiago's right to collect the *Voto* was to be confirmed at regular intervals by later Castilian and Spanish monarchs. True, payment of the tax was to provoke extensive controversy during the early modern period, but it was not until 1834 that the tax was definitively abolished, as part of a package of anticlerical measures introduced by the Liberal government of the day.[47]

Turning to the *ideological* purpose of the legend that lies at the heart of the Compostelan privilege, it is apparent that the cultural, the religious, and the political are closely intertwined. By juxtaposing, on the one hand, Christian attempts to buy peace by sacrificing the honor of its women to the Muslims, and, on the other, the abolition of that tribute through force of arms, Christian identity and power are intimately linked to the sexual purity and honor of its women. The narrative of the Compostelan charter manipulates the ideology of gender in order to warn and inspire in equal measure. The message is clear: the bodies of the Christian maidens might have been objects of exchange to begin with, the currency with which peace was bought, so to speak, but it was those same bodies which brought the Christian men to their senses and emboldened them to fight for their honor and that of the Christian community as a whole. The victory at Clavijo and the definitive suppression of the tribute of the hundred maidens thereafter are presented in the charter as a turning point in the *Reconquista*, a moment of redemption for the Christian people of the Peninsula, whose world had been turned upside down by the Islamic invasion of the eighth century. Through the influence of the maidens and the supernatural intervention of St. James, Christian men no longer had to buy peace by dishonoring their women and themselves. For their part, Christian women, those "*symbolic* instruments of male politics," to echo Bourdieu,[48] had been transformed from "peace-weavers," who bore the children of Muslim men, to "war-weavers" whose offspring would themselves take up arms in the service of Christendom in the future.[49] In short, by keeping what the Compostelan forger called the "lust of the Saracens" at bay, the boundaries—military, social, and cultural—that existed between the faiths had been strengthened anew.

From its murky beginnings in the cathedral scriptorium of Santiago de Compostela, the legend of the tribute of the hundred maidens was to be appropriated and elaborated by numerous literary exponents.[50] One of the first to do so was Lucas of Tuy. In the fourth and final part of his *Chronicon Mundi*, a history of the world down to 1236, Lucas devoted a single chapter to the story of the tribute of the hundred maidens.[51] His version of events follows that set out in the Compostelan charter fairly closely, but elaborates on some of the details. Where, for example, the charter had referred in the vaguest of terms to the "lazy, neglectful, idle and incompetent" Christian kings who had instituted the tribute, Lucas was ready to name names. He wrote of King Aurelio of Asturias (768–74), for example, that he never made war on the Muslims, but "signed a peace with them and allowed certain Christian noblewomen to join in marriage with the Saracens."[52] Later, he went on to say of King Mauregato (783–89) that "he gave many noble girls and also those of common birth in marriage due to an agreement with the Saracens so that he might have peace with them."[53] The rest of his narrative closely mirrors that of the Compostelan diploma: the demand for the delivery of the hundred maidens at the beginning of the reign of Ramiro I, with the observation that the fifty noble maidens were to be married to the Saracens, while the fifty lowborn women were to be "a source of comfort to them," that is, to be taken as concubines; the king's angry rejection of that demand and the gathering of an expeditionary force; the defeat by the Muslims near Nájera; the appearance of the Apostle James on the battlefield of Clavijo and the ultimate Christian victory; and the grant by the king of the *Voto*.[54]

In Archbishop Rodrigo Jiménez's *De rebus Hispanie*, an account in nine books of the history of the Iberian Peninsula from its origins to 1243, which drew in part on Lucas's chronicle, Mauregato is again portrayed as the villain of the piece. According to Rodrigo, it was Mauregato—reputedly the illegitimate son of Alfonso I and a Muslim slave girl—who seized the throne of Asturias from Alfonso II through the assistance of the Muslims and who agreed to deliver an unspecified number of Christian maidens "to the lechery of the Arabs" in order to retain their goodwill.[55] No mention is made here of any marriage between Muslim men and Christian brides. For Rodrigo, as for Lucas, the entire episode was one of *stupris*, which may be variously translated as "defilement," "dishonour," "disgrace," or even "outrage." By delivering the innocent maidens into Muslim hands, the "depraved" Mauregato had infringed God's law. It is striking, nonetheless, that in place of the royal grant of the *Voto* Rodrigo refers only to the various gifts that were made to St. James at the time of the battle, and he mentions opaquely that "in some places they still offer them, not out of sorrow or compulsion, but by spontaneous devotion."[56] Tellingly, that is some way short of the Peninsula-wide institutionalized tax that the Compostelan authorities claimed as their due. The archbishop of Toledo was perfectly willing to concede the part played by the Apostle in the victory for the greater Christian good at Clavijo, but he was clearly in no hurry to further the power and authority of his rival see of Santiago de Compostela.

The Compostelan account of the legend of the tribute of the hundred maidens, with its compelling narrative of defeat, humiliation, and miraculous redemption on the battlefield of Clavijo, was to become deeply engrained in later Spanish cultural and popular tradition. It was to crop up again, for example, in the late thirteenth-century *Estoria de Espanna*, which drew principally on the account of Lucas of Tuy, but with some changes of detail and emphasis.[57] Perhaps most striking of all the *Estoria*'s assertions was that the Order of Santiago had been founded at the time of the battle of Clavijo.[58] And chroniclers were not the only ones to be beguiled by the legend of the hundred maidens: there is a passing reference to them in the anonymous *Poema de Fernán González*, which was probably composed by a member of the Castilian abbey of San Pedro de Arlanza near Burgos sometime between 1250 and 1280.[59] In the early modern period, the legend also reemerged in a number of ballads and provided the inspiration for no fewer than three plays by Lope de Vega—*Las doncellas de Simancas*, *Los Prados de León*, *Las famosas asturianas*—and works by other literary exponents, including Tirso de Molina, Rodrigo de Herrera, and Luis de Guzmán.[60] The celebration of the ceremony of Las Cantaderas in the city of León, which had become well established by the end of the sixteenth century, likewise demonstrates the enduring popular appeal that the legend held during the early modern period.

We might well ask what it was that inspired our Compostelan forger to concoct a legend in which the payment in tribute of one hundred Christian maidens to a Muslim potentate lay at its heart. In the opinion of the Portuguese polymath Teófilo Braga, the legend was a conscious echo of the tribute supposedly paid by the Byzantine emperor Heraclius, who is said to have persuaded the Sassanid emperor Chosroes II to lift the siege of Constantinople in 615 by promising to pay an annual tribute of 1000 talents of gold and silver, 1000 silk robes, 1000 horses, and 1000 virgins.[61] Yet the levying of human tribute was a far older custom than that. An inscription preserved on the Kurkh Monolith, now preserved in the British Museum in London, records that when Shalmaneser III of the Assyrians captured the city of Sazabe in 858 B.C. a number of defeated kings agreed to pay him tribute, including from Sangara of Carchemish quantities of precious metals, together with livestock, dyestuffs, and "his daughter with a dowry, and 100 daughters of his nobles."[62] The same theme of human tribute crops up in Ancient Greek mythology—notably in the legend of Theseus and the Minotaur—as well as in a number of medieval popular tales.[63] Is it possible, for example, that our forger was inspired by one of the multiple versions of the tale of the tragic love affair between Tristan and Iseult much in vogue after c.1150, according to which the knight Tristan slew the Irish warrior Morholt, Iseult's uncle, who had levied an annual tribute on the kingdom of Cornwall of three hundred young men and three hundred maidens?[64]

Alternatively—and rather more plausibly, one might venture—it is possible that our forger had been inspired by more recent events. In 1135, at the ecclesiastical council of Narbonne, the bishop of Elne (in Languedoc-Roussillon), Udalgar de Castellnou (1130–47), made an impassioned speech before the other prelates, in which he reportedly bemoaned the many calamities that had befallen his diocese at that time.[65] In particular, he spoke movingly of the various attacks that had been carried out by Muslim pirates, who had killed or taken prisoner many Christians. Even worse, the bishop declared, they had demanded by way of ransom one hundred young virgins "so that they might have them and hold them and deflower them and please themselves with them in abominable concubinage." The bishop further claimed that, in order to meet these terms, Christian nobles had forcibly taken many young women from villages and towns in the vicinity in order to convey them by ship to Muslim lands, "in order that they might offer them in sacrifice to their demons, and that they might be joined sexually with perfidious peoples, and acquire knowledge of their wicked deeds, and serve them." The mothers of these young women had followed not far behind, weeping and wailing. Finally, with dramatic sighs and moans, the bishop informed the gathering that he would neither allow the Church to become contaminated nor the children of his church to perish, and voiced his hope that the faithful would rally round and help raise funds to release the hostages from captivity.

With its graphic portrayal of demon-worshipping, lascivious Muslims preying upon innocent, vulnerable Christian maidens, Udalgar's incendiary sermon was drawing on long-established polemical tropes, and it proved a veritable tour de force. Responding to the bishop's pleas, on 19 January 1135 the assembled members of the council decreed that indulgences for the remission of sins would be granted to anyone who contributed alms for the redemption of the captives. How much of this we can take at face value is uncertain. What we do know is that the redemption of Christian captives was a pressing concern for many frontier communities at this time, and that several bishops became engaged in fundraising campaigns.[66] In the case of the bishop of Elne, it is evident that he deployed the dramatic image of the hundred maidens as a skillful propagandistic tool with which to move his audience and raise the profile of his own campaign. There were lessons here from which other embattled churchmen—including perhaps Pedro Marcio of the Compostelan cathedral chapter—might profitably learn.

Variations on a Theme

Of course, we cannot know for sure that a report of Bishop Udalgar's sermon at Narbonne was indeed the direct inspiration for the forger of the charter of Ramiro I to fashion the legend of the tribute of the hundred maidens. Both "narratives," if we may characterize them as such, were manifestations of the wider preoccupation with interfaith sexual mixing that gripped Christian Iberia from the early twelfth century onward. But whatever the inspiration for the Compostelan forgery, the sheer potency of the legend that it gave birth to was such that in future it was to be eagerly appropriated and transformed by literary exponents working in other parts of the Peninsula. A notable case in point was the monk Gonzalo de Berceo of the abbey of San Millán de la Cogolla in the Rioja, who is celebrated today as the author of a clutch of vernacular devotional and theological works composed in the rhyming poetic style known as *Mester de clerecía* or *cuaderna via*.[67] In his *Vida de San Millán de la Cogolla*, an account of the life and miracles of the sixth-century founding father of his monastery, St. Aemilian, composed c.1230, Gonzalo de Berceo also addressed the theme of the annual tribute of maidens that was paid to the Muslims.[68] However, he framed the episode in a radically different manner. The action switches from Clavijo in 834 to Simancas near Valladolid in 939, where the Umayyad caliph 'Abd al-Raḥmān III suffered his most humiliating defeat. The chief protagonists are now King Ramiro II of León of Asturias and Count Fernán González (d. 970) on the one hand, and St. James and St. Aemilian on the other. Moreover, in Gonzalo de Berceo's version of events the tribute comprised sixty, not one hundred, maidens, half of them "of good breeding" (*de linaje*), the other half "of more humble stock" (*chus sorrenda*). In his poetic account we can glimpse the same indignant passion that had underpinned the Compostelan charter drawn up a few decades earlier:

> King Abderraman, lord of the pagans,
> a mortal enemy of all the Christians,
> had cast fear across hills and plains,
> they could find no recourse to escape from his hands.
>
> The accursed one commanded the Christians,
> to give him every year three score ladies in tribute,
> half of them of good breeding, half of more humble stock;
> accursed be the priest who accepts such an offering!
>
> All Christian Spain lay in this servitude,
> and gave each year this tribute by custom;
> they made an offering of great filthiness year after year,
> but they did not have the will to break free of it.
>
> All these afflictions, this deadly shame,
> had to be suffered more in León and in Castile;
> but all Christendom was distraught,
> for all alike it was a terrible wound.
>
> Never was such fierce suffering found among Christians,
> for having placed their Christian women in such evil;
> it would be wonderful thing to abandon such a terrible pact,
> such an evil tribute was never before exacted.
>
> Many noble ladies of legitimate lineage,
> were dishonoured, suffering great affront,
> it was a very bad example, and worse the deed,
> for Christians to give to Moors their women in such tribute.[69]

Yet Gonzalo de Berceo goes even farther than the forger of the Compostelan charter in denouncing interfaith sexual mixing. For the poet, the tribute of the maidens was variously a source of pain, suffering, and dishonor. He deliberately juxtaposes the terms "servitude" (*servidumne*) and "filthiness" (*suciedumne*). We are firmly in Mary Douglas territory here: interfaith sex is viewed by the poet as nothing less than social pollution.[70]

Gonzalo de Berceo's reconfigured narrative was given a further tweak when he declared that in recognition of the part played by St. Aemilian in achieving that victory, Count Fernán González had granted the monks of San Millán their own *Voto*, or tribute, which enshrined their perpetual right to receive payments in cash and kind from over two hundred communities in Castile and Navarre.[71] Two charters purportedly recording the grant by the count in 934 were also fabricated in the scriptorium of San Millán in order to further buttress the monastery's claim to this income.[72] The first, in Latin, makes no mention of the legend of the maidens, and probably predates Gonzalo de Berceo's poetic account.[73] Almost certainly, it was the pragmatic response of the monks of San Millán to the pretensions of the archbishops of Santiago de Compostela to levy the *Voto* on parishes throughout the Peninsula. Furthermore, rooted in local piety and patriotism, the Latin charter and Berceo's vernacular celebration of St. Aemilian evince a burgeoning sense of Castilian identity that was to be the hallmark of a number of texts produced in monastic contexts during the period that spanned the separation of the kingdoms of León and Castile after the death of Alfonso VII and their definitive reunification in 1230, and even beyond.[74] At the same time, it has been conjectured that the charter and Gonzalo de Berceo's decision to compose his *Vida de San Millán*, in which his effusive justification of the payment of the *Voto* lay at its heart, may have been a direct response to the economic difficulties that the abbey was experiencing by the beginning of the thirteenth century, at a time when donations by the laity and income from its lands were in decline.[75] Such views need to be nuanced. Rather like the fabricated charter of the Compostelan *Voto*, part of the function of the San Millán texts was to justify the abbey's right to an existing tribute that may have come into being as early as the 1140s, but which was being increasingly challenged after 1200, and to emphasize that it was the duty of the laity to pay it. It was not mere money-grubbing that led Gonzalo de Berceo to insert the episode of the *Voto* into his celebration of the life of San Millán. For the poet, rather, the promotion of the cult of his patron San Millán and the spiritual and economic well-being of the monastery he had founded were all part of a whole.[76]

The second version of the San Millán *Voto*, composed in Castilian, was probably drafted in the late thirteenth century and is said to have been incorporated into a royal charter of Ferdinand IV of Castile.[77] Like the Latin version before it, the charter begins by describing the various dramatic portents that could be seen in the skies above Castile in the year 934. However, while the forger of the Latin text makes no attempt to interpret those portents and does not refer to the tribute of the maidens, preferring to move directly to a description of the Christian victory at the battle of Simancas, the scribe of the Castilian version declares outright that these heavenly signs symbolized nothing less than God's displeasure with kings Ramiro II of León and García Sánchez I of Navarre and Count Fernán González of Castile, each of whom had agreed to supply the Moorish king Abderraman with sixty young women by way of tribute, thirty of them high-born and thirty daughters of laborers. Abderraman is said to have granted the women to his troops by way of payment for their service, but no one on the Christian side did anything to protect them. The author of the charter gave vent to his indignation in this way:

> The kings began to realize that they were committing a great mortal sin, and it caused sorrow to God in Heaven to see His Christian women in this way in the hands of the infidel Moorish dogs, on account of the little faith and little hope and very little charity that the kings and their nobles and vassals who were with them showed, and on account of the little concern that the aforesaid kings and their armies showed about placing the souls and the blood—bought and redeemed by the glorious blood and holy Passion—of their forlorn virgin sisters, who had been dishonoured and vilified, in the hands of the wicked and vile Moorish dogs, and who continuously with bitter sighs and tearful, sorrowful eyes and very troubled hearts as faithful Christian women called to God to save them from all the anguish and evils that their bodies and souls suffered every day.

Then, we are told, Jesus Christ took pity on these "poor, sad women" (*tristes pobresillas*) and inspired King Ramiro and the nobles of his curia to take up arms, having them declare, "it is better to die well than to live a dishonorable life." When the Muslims came to collect the human tribute, they were beheaded by the Christians, prompting Abderraman to launch a punitive expedition, encouraged by the words of the supposedly infallible wise man

Alfaramí, who lived in Mecca, who interpreted the heavenly signs as portents of an imminent Muslim military victory. Alfaramí went on to declare that such was the size and power of the Muslim expeditionary force that had been mustered that the Christians would not dare to face the king on the battlefield, and recommended that a proclamation be sent out encouraging Christians to convert to Islam, with the promise that those who did so would be given weapons and horses and would receive great rewards. But the promise was accompanied by a harsh warning too: of those who would not convert to Islam, the men would be flayed alive, the women's breasts would be twisted and removed from their bodies, and they would die by being thrown from crags, and the children would be taken by their feet and their heads dashed against rocks and walls, so that there would be no more seed of the Christians. The action builds to a gradual climax. King Ramiro makes his way to Simancas and sends letters to Count Fernán González and King García of Navarre, informing them of the approach of the Muslim army. Men, women, and children gather at Simancas, fearing that they will be beheaded by the enemy. King Ramiro prays to Christ and to St. James, beseeching them to take pity on the Christians; for their part, Count García and Count Fernán González invoke their lord, "Sant Millán de la Cogulla." Their prayers are answered: an angel is sent in the night to comfort the Christian rulers and reassure them that God, through his servants St. James and St. Aemilian, would rescue them from the despair and peril in which they found themselves. When the two armies do battle the next day, the two saints, accompanied by a heavenly host, attack the Muslim battle lines and rout them. The Christians pursue the fleeing Muslims to Aza, capture Abderraman and his wise man, and behead them. "From the great fear and tribulation that there was among Christendom," the forger writes, "there was great joy and happiness. And they said: 'Let us make them aware that these two saints were our kings and our lords.'" There then follows a detailed account of the abundant plunder that was shared out and, in particular, of the *Voto* the grateful count of Castile made to St. Aemilian.

It hardly needs saying that this is another extraordinary document, redolent with rhetorical and ideological significance. Particularly striking is the fact that, whereas the payment of the tribute of the Christian maidens is merely one element within Gonzalo de Berceo's wide-ranging celebration of the miracles of the saintly patron of his monastery, in the vernacular charter the women take center stage. The levels of indignation and hostility displayed toward the Muslims who supposedly levied the tribute are ratcheted up as never before. Echoes of the Compostelan version of the legend still survive, notably the description of the divine visitation to the anxious kings in their sleep on the eve of battle and the miraculous intervention of the saints on the battlefield, but for the most part the narrative has been entirely reshaped in accordance with the needs of the monks of San Millán. What remains, above all, is the passionate belief that the plight of the Christian maidens was a source of immense shame to Christendom, providing a *casus belli* like none other; and that the Muslim attack threatened the very survival of the Christian community. Likewise, in case any were tempted to cast doubt, the miraculous intervention of St. Aemilian on the battlefield of Simancas furnished ample justification for the abbey's right to levy the *Voto.* Just as at Santiago de Compostela, a heady brew of local piety, mixed with a dash of credal hostility, was served up in order to burnish the reputation of the monastery of San Millán and enhance its wealth and authority even more.

Yet churchmen were to be by no means alone in seeking to associate themselves with the memory of the Christian damsels in distress. By the sixteenth century, towns had begun to develop their own local variations on the theme too. At Simancas, for example, a tradition came into being which claimed that seven young women from the town, who had been chosen to be handed over to the Muslims in part payment of the tribute of the hundred maidens, preferred to cut off their hair, disfigure their faces, and cut off their own hands, so that the Muslims would not wish to take them as sex slaves. This gesture of self-sacrifice so enraged the citizens that they rose up against the Muslims and freed the maidens.[78] This was supposedly the spark for the Christian revolt that was to culminate in victory on the battlefield of Clavijo. The very name Simancas, so legend erroneously has it, derives from *siete mancas*, the seven one-handed women; in fact, the toponym is of Roman origin. The legend was later enshrined by Lope de Vega in his stage play *Las doncellas de Simancas.*[79] In fact, such "sacrificial self-mutilation" as a defense against sexual assault was a popular trope of medieval hagiography.[80] Thus, the legend of Simancas bears close similarity to another sixteenth-century account, which tells of the self-sacrifice of the three hundred nuns of the convent of St. Florentine, near Écija in Andalusia, at the time of the eighth-century Muslim conquest:

> The abbess and nuns . . . realizing that the infidels wished to attack their monastery, feared the danger of being shamed and of losing the treasure of their virginity which they had preserved for so many years, so they decided to lacerate their faces in an attempt to make themselves ugly and detestable. Their strategy and extraordinary

> plan turned out very well because with it they accomplished their intention and defeated and triumphed over the Moors, their honour and purity remaining intact. For when those barbarians saw them bloodstained and ugly, they became angry because of this and killed all the nuns with the sword, and to the halo and crown of virginity was added that of martyrdom, which they all suffered.[81]

At nearby Carrión de los Condes, meanwhile, another tradition had arisen by the sixteenth century which claimed that when, some time in the past, a contingent of Muslim soldiers had arrived at the town in order to carry off a number of local maidens, a group of wild bulls had charged at them, freeing the women from the clutches of the infidel.[82] It is possible that this belief was inspired by the distinctive bulls' heads that had been carved on either side of the west door of the church of Santa María del Camino in the twelfth century, together with what might be construed as a group of women on one of the nearby capitals. The possibility that the carvings were themselves inspired by the legend of the maidens appears unlikely, however.[83]

Aristocratic families also sought to gain prestige by associating themselves with the hundred maidens in ever more imaginative ways. By the sixteenth century, the Asturian Quirós family had incorporated the heads of five maidens onto its heraldic arms, in order to commemorate the liberation of these women from the custody of the Muslim tribute collectors by their illustrious forebears.[84] For its part, the Villalobos family of Astorga claimed to possess the banner that one of their ancestors had carried onto the battlefield of Clavijo.[85] Another local legend, this time from Galicia, related how a group of nobles, hearing that thirty local maidens were being led into captivity by the Muslims, defeated their captors near A Coruña and freed the women.[86] Since the military clash supposedly occurred near a group of fig trees, the nobles were henceforth said to have adopted the family name "Figueroa"and added a group of five fig leaves on a field of gold to their coat of arms, or so the story ran. Further variations on the theme spread to a number of towns in neighboring Portugal.[87] The *Canção do Figueiral*, perhaps of fourteenth-century origin, tells of one Guesto Asur, who went to the assistance of six maidens whom he saw weeping as they were carried off into captivity as part of the annual tribute to the Muslims. Overcome with anger, Guesto seized a branch of a nearby fig tree and drove away the Muslim troops escorting the women, winning the heart of one of the maidens in the process.[88]

The tribute of the hundred maidens was also to emerge in a late medieval Catalan context, albeit in a form far removed from the twelfth-century

Compostelan version. According to a tradition first set down in writing in 1431, which apparently drew on the oral testimony of the inhabitants of the town of Bagà, the tribute had been instituted in the year 1147, when a Catalan expeditionary force, then in alliance with Leonese, Navarrese, and Genoese troops, besieged and conquered the Mediterranean port city of Almería.[89] During the course of the hostilities one of the Catalan nobles, Galceran de Pinós, is reported to have been captured by the Muslims and led into captivity, where he remained for five years. When Count Ramon Berenguer IV of Barcelona tried to secure his release, the Muslims demanded a hefty ransom of 100,000 gold coins, one hundred pieces of brocade, one hundred white horses, one hundred head of cattle, and, last but not least, one hundred maidens. We are told that Galceran's parents managed to amass most of the ransom demanded, with the exception of the maidens, whereupon his vassals nobly agreed to send their own daughters in order to secure his release. In the meantime, however, Galceran himself had managed to escape from prison, thanks to the miraculous assistance of St. Stephen, and as he made his way back toward Tarragona he met a group of nobles who were by then journeying toward Muslim territory with the maidens and the rest of the tribute. On learning of their intentions, Galceran broke down and sobbed, before leading them in honor, first to Barcelona to see the count, and then to his home town of Bagà, where the legend ends. The geographical context and the dramatis personae of the legend might be markedly different from those circulating further to the west, but the ideological intent is familiar. Once again we can see the vulnerable, pure Christian maidens as the symbolic currency with which peace, or in this case freedom, is to be bought. Thanks to the timely intervention of St. Stephen, Galceran's release from captivity saves the honor of those women and that of the Catalan nobles, and ensures that the frontier between Christian and Muslim will not be dissolved. It is worth noting, moreover, that although the earliest known written account of the legend dates from the early fifteenth century, the tale was clearly circulating well before then. Thus, among the scenes depicted on the altarpiece which was painted for the Catalan monastery of Sant Esteve de Gualter by the artist Jaume Serrer in 1385, is one of St. Stephen liberating Galceran from his chains to the approbation of the onlooking maidens, whose delivery into slavery had thereby been prevented.[90]

The story of the hundred maidens was developed yet further by the Basque chronicler Lope García de Salazar, who compiled his *Libro de las bienandanzas y fortunas*, a history of Spain incorporating numerous legends, while a prisoner between 1471 and 1476.[91] In his account of the legend, García de Salazar depicts the hundred maidens making their way sadly toward Muslim territory "with much pain and dishonour."[92] Knowing that some of them are destined to become the Muslim ruler's concubines and others to serve in the households of his chief men, the most beautiful and wisest among the noblewomen is inspired by the Holy Spirit to shame her Christian compatriots into action by taking off all her clothes. The noblewoman's attendants are scandalized at her behavior, thinking that she has lost her mind, and beg her to get dressed, warning her that she makes them feel ashamed and that she might be stoned to death by the Moors on account of her insanity, and that the other maidens will suffer on her account. When the party finally reaches Muslim territory, the maiden gets dressed again and explains to her perplexed attendants that the reason she has removed her clothes was that in Christian lands she could not feel any sense of dishonour, because there were no true men to be found. When her attendants dispute her claim, she drives home the point relentlessly:

> If there were any men in the land of the Christians they would not carry [their women] as slaves to the land of the Moors, where their virginity would be corrupted and made filthy by infidel peoples who are enemies of the true faith, which would make them apostatize and renounce their Saviour Jesus Christ and his Mother the Virgin St. Mary, and it is because the Moors were men that they took them this way.

Unlike Princess Teresa, who in Bishop Pelayo's account bravely confronts the Muslim king of Toledo, García de Salazar's heroine directs her ire at her coreligionists in an attempt to shame them into action. Her message was stark: by failing to stand up to the Muslims and by giving away their women to infidels, the warriors of the Asturian kingdom were sullying not just the individual honor of those women, but also the collective honor of Christian society as a whole. In short, Emily Francomano observes:

> God's reprimand, delivered through a seemingly defenceless, naked and beautiful female body, is a clear call to arms and a call for the restoration of gender roles: the Christian men must demonstrate that they *are* men through war-making so that their women may be women on the Christian side of the frontier.[93]

The Christians spring into action, and with divine help, despite suffering an initial defeat at Muslim hands, they ultimately prevail, thereby preventing a new destruction of Spain.

García de Salazar's account of the legend, and his history as a whole, drew considerable inspiration from various oral legends and ballads then circulating. One such may have been a version of the ballad *En consulta estaba un dia*, in which one of the unhappy maidens storms into the court of King Ramiro, berates him for agreeing to the tribute of the hundred maidens, and accuses him of being a Moor in disguise (*Debes ser moro encubierto*). Worse still, she casts doubt on the virility of the Christian men, warning the king that while the daughters of Christians given in tribute are each giving birth to five or six Muslim sons and warriors, the Christian men are merely fathering more daughters who will in turn be given in tribute.[94] What the ballad and García de Salazar's version both make abundantly clear, just as earlier versions of the legend—from the Compostelan charter to Rodrigo Jiménez de Rada—had either stated or implied, is that it was the responsibility of Christian men to defend the honor of their women and, by extension, of Christendom as a whole.

Given the proliferation of legends relating to the tribute of the maidens, it is not entirely surprising that they also began to reach the ears of foreigners from quite an early date. Thus, a group of German texts, which describe the operations conducted in 1217 by a force of crusaders to capture the southern Portuguese fortress town of Alcácer do Sal from the Muslims, make reference to the levying of human tribute. The *Chronica regia Coloniensis*, for one, claimed that prior to the conquest the Almohad caliph had required the town to surrender one hundred Christian captives every year, and this was echoed by a poetic celebration of the capture of Alcácer, the *Gosuini de expugnatione Salaciae carmen*.[95] Two other German sources inflated the number of prisoners delivered annually to one thousand.[96] However, in none of these cases were the captives specifically said to have been females.

To sum up thus far, it is apparent that by c.1500 numerous versions of the legend of the tribute of the hundred maidens had begun to circulate in the Iberian Peninsula. By far the most influential of these was the Compostelan version, in which Ramiro I of Asturias and St. James were the chief protagonists. Imaginative and embellished though they may have been, these accounts were not entirely without historical substance: they fed upon a shared awareness that in the past interfaith marriages and other sexual liaisons had indeed occupied a significant place in the overall dynamic of Christian-Muslim relations in the Peninsula. Be that as it may, fears over the dangers posed by interfaith sex were by no means focused exclusively on the distant past; they were also firmly rooted in the here and now.

Women on the Front Line

During the first half of the thirteenth century, the military balance of power between the states of the Christian North and al-Andalus shifted dramatically in favor of the former. The stunning victory by a crusading army of Castilian, Aragonese, and Navarrese troops over the Berber Almohads at the battle of Las Navas de Tolosa in the Sierra Morena on 16 July 1212 was to be the prelude to a period of rapid Christian expansionism on all fronts.[97] By c.1250 independent Muslim political power in the Peninsula was almost at an end, with the exception of the realm of Granada and a handful of minor enclaves on the Atlantic coast. One consequence of this profound shift in the geopolitical landscape was that Muslim military pressure on the Christian-dominated lands north of the Tagus valley subsided considerably thereafter. Although major operations were still periodically launched from what remained of al-Andalus—such as the various large-scale campaigns conducted by the Berber Merinids in alliance with the Nasrids of Granada in 1275 and 1340—for much of the later medieval period military activity took the form of maritime piracy and opportunistic hit-and-run raids across the borderlands that separated the Christian and Islamic zones of power. While piracy impacted particularly on the Balearics and the Kingdom of Valencia, which had been conquered by James I of Aragon between 1229 and 1245, raids across land frontiers were commonplace along the borders that separated Castile from Muslim Granada, with the district around Jaén proving a particular hotspot. In the course of this sporadic conflict thousands of individuals on either side of the religious divide had the misfortune to fall into captivity.[98] Many of those captured in the course of such raids were soldiers,[99] of course, but laborers, shepherds, merchants, fishermen, sailors, travelers, friars, or simply women or children who found themselves in the wrong place at the wrong time, were also vulnerable.[100] Some Castilian law codes also expressed the fear that Christians might sell their unwanted children or any other person into slavery and promised fierce punishment for those who did so. At Cuenca and Teruel, for example, convicted miscreants were to be burned at the stake.[101] In December 1355 Peter IV of Aragon commanded the *baiulus* of Valencia, who wielded judicial authority over the region, to prosecute and punish those Muslims who had reputedly for a long time been in the custom of capturing Christians and conveying them across the frontier to Nasrid Granada for sale, a practice that the king denounced as "horrible and worthy of the maximum punishment."[102]

For most of those who were captured a life of grinding poverty beckoned. Living conditions were often desperately harsh, with many captives being forced to wear chains, labor long hours in the fields or on public works, and sleep in damp, unsanitary underground grain silos, known as *mazmorras*. Food was often scarce, and, as a consequence, malnutrition and disease were probably rife. The luckier ones lived in the houses of their masters, such as the women who were taken as wives or concubines, or who worked as domestic servants.[103] We cannot be sure just how many Christians fell into captivity in this way, since no systematic records were kept, but the research carried out by Jarbel Rodriguez, who has explored in depth the experiences of Christian captives from the Crown of Aragon and the efforts that were made by their coreligionists to free them, suggests that as many as 2,300 Aragonese Christians might have been held in captivity in any given year in Iberia and North Africa. More sobering still, only a tiny minority—perhaps less than ten per cent—of these prisoners were ever released.[104] The plight of these captives aroused considerable concern and sympathy on the Christian side of the frontier. Families, municipal officials, merchants, royal ransomers (called *exeas* or *alfaqueques*), and Christian ransoming orders, notably the Trinitarians and Mercedarians, devoted a huge amount of time, effort, and money toward releasing their fellow Christians from captivity.[105] It was a similar story on the Muslim side, where a variety of cooperative networks engaged in ransoming those unfortunate Muslims who had themselves been captured by Christian raiding parties.[106]

The perennial anxiety on the Christian side was not simply that their coreligionists were suffering in humiliating subjugation to infidels, but that the women among them were in acute danger of losing their honor, either by being raped during their capture and transportation to Muslim-controlled territory, or by being forced into marriage or concubinage against their will. Equally dire, there was the prospect that some captives—male and female alike—might seek to improve their pitiful living conditions by renouncing their faith and converting to Islam.[107] These fears are reflected in one of the Alfonsine *Cantigas de Santa María*, which tells of the case of two Christian women who were held captive by a wealthy Muslim lady in Tangiers.[108] The latter, on her deathbed, advises the women to become Muslims and renounce Christianity, in return for which

> they would be set free, and she would grant them money and property and would marry them both to rich Moors. If they refused to do this, she would put them both in chains and submit them to

> such great tortures that not a sound bit of skin or nerves or veins would remain in their bodies, and in addition she would have them beheaded.

Out of fear, one of the Christian women is willing to accede to these demands, but the other angrily declares her devotion to the Virgin and more specifically to the church that had been dedicated to her honor at Tudia in the Sierra Morena. The song goes on to relate that as the second woman slept she was miraculously transported by St. Mary to the town of Silves in southern Portugal, then under Christian authority. When she later visited the church of Tudia, the iron collar she wore on her neck fell to the ground.

Audiences of the *cantiga* were, of course, meant to celebrate the constancy of the second captive who held firm to her faith, but they would also have been mindful that there were many—like the first woman of the song—who would have viewed conversion to Islam as a means to escape captivity, and that any children such women bore in the future would in turn become Muslims. These were by no means empty fears. At least five of the Nasrid sultans were reportedly born to Christian mothers who had been captured and recruited to the harem at the Alhambra palace in Granada.[109] A similar fate was experienced by the Valencian woman who, after being taken captive, was sold as a concubine and later gave birth to the future Ḥafsid Sultan Uthman (1435–88) in North Africa.[110] Yet another Christian woman, who had been captured by a Granadan raiding party early in the 1470s while still only a girl of around ten to twelve years old, and who came to serve as a maid in the household of a daughter of the Nasrid ruler Abū'l-Ḥasan (1464–85), is reported to have converted to Islam when the sultan took her as his consort.[111] At a less exalted social level, we also encounter the case of the woman from Huelma near Jaén, who married a Muslim after she converted and refused to return to the Christian fold even after a visit by an *alfaqueque*; what is worse, she subsequently abandoned her husband and eloped with another Muslim man.[112] Such was the concern that captive women were more likely to convert to Islam that ransoming orders, such as the Mercedarian friars, assigned particular priority to securing their release.[113]

These anxieties are also manifest in one of the *Miráculos romançados*, a collection of miracles relating the experiences of over seventy Christians, who had reportedly been delivered from captivity by the thaumaturgical powers of St. Dominic, whose cult center was situated at the monastery of Silos in eastern Castile.[114] Most of the miracles narrated in the collection cover the period between 1277 and 1287, with some forty-four being recorded from 1285 alone, apparently reflecting the heightened sense of anxiety that took hold of Castile at the time of the Merinid invasions. Although the primary concern of narratives of this type was to publicize the miraculous powers of St. Dominic, the *Miráculos* provide detailed information on the circumstances that led to the taking of such captives, the conditions under which they were held, the labor they were obliged to carry out, and, most important of all, as far as the narrator was concerned, the miraculous manner of their escape from captivity. As Anthony Lappin has observed, such accounts are not to be regarded as word for word accounts dictated by the freed captives themselves, but rather as "the end products of an interaction between shrine-recorders and former captives, the result of the precise questioning of the freed captive by the monks at the shrine, an interrogation which might best be considered a de-briefing."[115] One such story relates the experience of Caterina from Linares near Jaén, who had been captured in the local vineyards, together with four female companions, on 1 September 1280 by the forces led by one Muḥammad "Abenmencal," brother of the sultan of Granada.[116] The account records that after the women were conveyed by their captors to Granada, Caterina was taken to the king's palace, where Muḥammad slept with her. He then took her to a separate house, where he kept her as his concubine for four years, during which time she bore him two sons. The story relates that after that time had elapsed, Caterina prayed to God, the Virgin Mary, and St. Dominic, beseeching them to forgive her, take pity on her, release her from captivity, and deliver her from that state of sin in which she found herself. In return for her freedom, she promised that she would not eat meat on Wednesdays, would fast every Saturday for the rest of her life, and would journey barefoot to the shrine of St. Dominic at Silos. After she made this promise on Saturday 1 July 1285, St. Dominic is said to have appeared before Caterina in a dream and said to her: "Caterina, keep to what you have promised, for God has taken mercy on you, and take your youngest son, and go, you and these other women, to my house, and arrange it so that you make your son a Christian in my church."

The narrative relates that when Caterina woke up, she took her son and, accompanied by four other women and two men, left through the doors which were all found to be open, as well as the main gate into the city which had also been left unguarded. The group traveled six leagues through the night until they reached the castle of Cabra near Jaén. Caterina finally reached the monastery of Silos on 1 September, where her younger son was baptized. It was a deeply symbolic moment, marking as it did the final stage of Caterina's deliverance from forced concubinage and her son's renunciation of his Islamic ancestry on his father's side.[117] One can only conclude that Caterina had been forced to leave her elder son behind, perhaps because he had already joined his father's family.[118]

Since it was widely assumed that female captives would be subjected to sexual abuse by their captors, Christian women who gave up their own lives rather than lose their chastity and honor were regarded as martyrs in their own right. Thus, it was claimed that, in the course of an attack on Jaén in 1298, various nuns from the convent of Santa Clara were killed by their Muslim captors when they refused to yield their virginity to them.[119] Other nuns from that convent are said to have suffered the same fate when Jaén came under renewed attack from Nasrid forces in 1368, while yet others were carried off to Granada, where they supposedly suffered a long and arduous captivity.[120] It was further reported that in 1396 two women from Torredonjimeno near Jaén, named Juana and María, were captured by Muslim raiders as they did their washing near the village and taken to Granada.[121] According to a much later account set down in the seventeenth century by a pious historiographer of Jaén, Martín de Ximena Jurado, their captors sought to "pervert them to their sect by whatever means, be it by gifts or by threats, and to marry them." When the maidens demurred, they were taken before the local judge, who accused them of denigrating the Prophet: "Is it possible, mad women, that you value misery more than abundance? Ignominy and insults to honour and respect? These two Moors are rich and noble, you are vile and their slaves. Why don't you renounce the faith of Jesus Christ and take them for your husbands?"

When the maidens flatly refused to renounce their faith, the judge ordered that they be beheaded at the Alhambra. When the execution had been carried out, two stars are said to have appeared in the sky and shone down on the bodies of the women; much later a chapel would be founded on the site of their martyrdom. For later generations, the commemoration of the supreme sacrifice of the maidens of Torredonjimeno, like that of the nuns of Jaén before them, would serve as a warning of the perennial danger posed to the honor of their women and to the wider Christian community by the Muslims of the South.

The same theme of the maiden who lays down her life rather than see her honor besmirched was also revisited in a charter dated 13 January 1375, by which Henry II of Castile (1369–79) is recorded to have made a grant of money and other privileges to his steward (*maestresala*), Rodrigo Sánchez Cepero.[122] The charter sets out in detail the various deeds that the nobleman—and before him his father—had performed in royal service. Particular mention was made of Rodrigo's victory over the forces of one Hosmin Hali, when he had suffered various wounds. Even more eye-catching, the king made mention of the fact that when Jaén had been sacked by the forces of Muḥammad IV of Granada (1354–83) in 1368, Rodrigo's daughter had been carried off by a "Moorish dog," one Abomelique. The king goes on to declare with admiration: "And because she did not wish to carry out disservice and treason to God by losing her virginity, as Abomelique wished, he killed her with many wounds, which caused us great sadness."

According to the charter, the matter did not end there, for Rodrigo promptly sought and received the king's permission to challenge Abomelique to a duel, which is said to have taken place near Algeciras. Rodrigo duly vanquished his opponent and celebrated his victory by cutting off his head, thereby regaining his lost honor.

How much of this are we to believe? The editor of the charter has apparently accepted the events recounted at their face value, but we should do well to be wary. The content and tone of the charter, with its tales of epic duels and aristocratic derring-do, are highly reminiscent of the chivalric romance. Equally suspicious is the fact that in 1505 Rodrigo's descendent, Martín Sánchez Cepero, had submitted the document in support of his *petición de hidalguía*, that is to say, the formal process by which a man could seek to have his noble status confirmed by law.[123] The original charter supposedly granted by Henry II does not survive. It is tempting to conclude that the charter was a fabrication designed to uphold the honor and reputation of the Sánchez Cepero family. Yet forged or not, the document demonstrates that, for laymen as well as members of the clergy, the image of the vulnerable Christian maiden seeking to defend her honor remained a potent one.

Besides, the concern displayed by Henry II for the plight of captive Christian women is demonstrated by another source. In the will he had drawn up on 29 May 1379 the king bequeathed money for the liberation of one hundred female captives from Moorish lands, stipulating that all were to be below forty years of age.[124] Presumably it was deemed of particular importance to redeem those who were still sexually active and capable of bearing children. Similar fears can be detected in other royal documents. In a charter he issued on 15 December 1386 Peter IV of Aragon voiced the fear that Christian virgins who had been imprisoned would be deflowered by their Muslim captors.[125] Monarchs also used the image of Christian women in captivity as a means to galvanize diplomatic support abroad. Thus, in the letter James II of Aragon sent to Pope Clement V in 1309, in which he sought to secure support for a new crusade against Granada, the monarch warned the pontiff that the harems of the Muslims were full of captive Christian women, and that many had already converted to Islam.[126] In a similar vein, when Peter IV tried to persuade Benedict XII to grant crusading indulgences for a campaign against Morocco in 1340, he warned the pope that Christian maidens would be raped by Muslim raiders if such a campaign were not mounted.[127]

From the foregoing it will have become clear that the subject of interfaith sex loomed large in the consciousness of Christian writers in Iberia from the twelfth century onward, just as it did in that of numerous lawgivers during the same period. This anxiety manifested itself in various ways. Christians genuinely feared for the physical well-being of their women, particularly those who were being held in captivity in Islamic territory, and voiced concern that sexual contact with Muslims would not only besmirch their honor and that of their communities, but would also be the prelude to apostasy. Moreover, as Christians looked back to the distant past, to the time when interfaith marriage had been relatively commonplace and the enslavement of Christian women had apparently taken place on an altogether higher scale, they commemorated the plight of such women in numerous and inventive ways. The image of the Christian damsel in distress was deployed by chroniclers, hagiographers, and other literary exponents, including forgers, precisely because such authors felt sure that it would arouse solidarity and indignation in equal measure among their intended audiences. To a society that set such great store by personal honor, the failure of Christian men to protect their women meant that their enslavement and, worse still, their recruitment as concubines to the harems of Islamic lords—whether in reality or in the literary imagination—was a source of profound shame and humiliation. It was for this very reason that the legend of the tribute of the hundred maidens was to prove so spectacularly effective—in cultural as well as fiscal terms—and so remarkably long-lasting. In choosing a theme in which Christian identity and power were intimately linked to the sexual purity and honor of its women, the Compostelan forger artfully touched a nerve among his coreligionists. The legend and others like it not only tapped into deep-rooted contemporary anxieties about interfaith sexual mixing, but they also constituted a stark warning from the past, and even a call to arms for the present. Rather like the numerous tales that surrounded the demise of Roderic, the last king of the Visigoths, they served to remind Christians of all ranks that the consequences of military failure against the armies of Islam had been and always would be dire, and would be paid for not only in the currency of lives, lands, and castles, but also in that of feminine sexual honor, which would in turn impinge directly on the collective honor and identity of the Christian people as a whole.[128] It was up to the soldiers of the Christian realms to prove themselves as men, in order that henceforth the memory of that past shame might be avenged and the barriers that had latterly been erected between the faiths could never be breached again.

Chapter 4

Lust and Love on the Iberian Frontier

The focus in the previous chapter was on Christian women as perceived victims of interfaith sexual mixing. We have seen that by artfully deploying the potent image of the vulnerable "damsel in distress," whose personal honor had been tainted through sexual contact with a Muslim man, Christian churchmen and others sought to elicit pity and indignation in the hearts of their coreligionists in the Peninsula as a means to foster solidarity among their communities. However, not all narratives involving interfaith sexual relations were configured in this way. In some, it is the women themselves who become the protagonists, seeking out Muslim sexual partners, with unpredictable and often dangerous consequences; in others, the tables are turned, as Muslim women surrender their bodies to Christian men. In all cases, however, the relationship between interfaith sex and power remains an intimate one.

Dangerous Liaisons

The legend of *La condesa traidora*, or "The Treacherous Countess," is set in Castile at the very end of the tenth century, during the lifetimes of Count García Fernández of Castile (970–95) and his son Count Sancho García (995–1017).[1] The legend, which is first recorded in the *Chronica Naierensis*, relates that the wife of Count García was sent a letter by a "king of the Saracens," Almanzor (that is, the all-powerful *ḥājib* al-Manṣūr), asking "with deceitful words of love" whether she would like to remain a countess or would prefer to become his queen.[2] The countess is seduced by the offer and decides to do away with her husband by feeding his horse bran instead of barley every night, so that it would collapse in battle. She further persuades the count to allow his knights to go home to spend Christmas with their loved ones, in order that his forces will be weakened. Informed of these developments by the duplicitous countess, Almanzor launches a lightning attack on Castile on Christmas Day. In the ensuing battle, as anticipated, Count García's "knobbled" horse collapses, and the Castilians are overwhelmed by the Muslim army. The count is severely wounded and captured in the struggle and dies four days later; his body is taken to Córdoba, where it is buried, and the remains are later repatriated to the Castilian abbey of Cardeña. The sequel to the story comes as Almanzor, described as "the staff of the wrath of the Lord over the Christians" (*uirga furoris Domini super Christianos*) by the chronicler, launches another series of attacks against Castile, forcing Count García's son Sancho to take refuge with his family at Lantarón near Álava. Sancho tries to buy peace by betrothing one of his sisters to Almanzor, but his mother the countess, still wishing to join the Muslim potentate "in order to satisfy her desire for vainglory and to give herself over to her lust," decides to poison her son. However, the plot is thwarted through divine intervention, when a Muslim girl warns the count of his mother's evil intentions. When Sancho returns to his palace with his men-at-arms and is brought something to drink, he insists that his mother drink it first. When, finally, after much prevarication, the countess drinks the potion, she drops dead, "falling into the very trap that she had laid," the chronicler notes with grim satisfaction. Finally, Almanzor does battle with Count Sancho and is forced to flee, dying shortly afterward at Medinaceli in 1002.

The Legend of *La condesa traidora* was to reappear in a number of later chronicles. In his *De rebus Hispanie*, Archbishop Rodrigo Jiménez refers in passing to the attempted poisoning of Count Sancho by his mother, but not to her attempt to bring about the death of her husband Count García.[3] The legend is also reported in various versions of the Alfonsine *Estoria de Espanna*.[4] For example, the *Versión crítica* (compiled between 1282 and 1284) follows Archbishop Rodrigo's "slimmed down" version of the narrative fairly closely, although after its account of the failed poisoning of Sancho it adds the jocular comment that since that day on it had been the custom in Castile always to make women drink first.[5] However, a later redaction of the *Estoria*—conventionally known to scholars as the *Versión amplificada* (carried out in 1289)—goes much farther.[6] According to its version of events, Count García Fernández had two wives, both equally troublesome. The first was a beautiful French noblewoman called Argentina, whom Count García had met as she went on pilgrimage to Santiago de Compostela with her parents. However, this bride turned out to be a *mala muger*—which could be translated as either "wicked woman" or "bad wife," although given Argentina's reported conduct both could equally apply. Six years later, we are told, as Count García lay ill, the countess eloped back to her homeland with a French count she had met as he journeyed on pilgrimage to Santiago de Compostela. However, García tracked the adulterous couple down, and with the assistance of the Frenchman's daughter, Sancha, who had earlier fallen out with her father and stepmother, wrought terrible revenge by decapitating them while they slept. As the price of her assistance, Sancha immediately slept with the count and soon became his wife. However, although Sancha began her married life well, she later harbored ill will toward the count, we are told. The narrative then closely matches that of the *Chronica Naierensis*, as Sancha, "desiring to marry a king of the Moors," went on to facilitate her husband's demise on the battlefield and later unsuccessfully sought to bring about that of her son by poisoning.[7]

Despite being embedded in a variety of historiographical works, the legend of *La condesa traidora* is a piece of "pseudo-history," which is set in a broadly recognizable historical framework.[8] Scholarly discussion of the legend has tended to focus on four principal areas. Firstly, there are its origins and development. The fact that the *Chronica Naierensis* did not include the story of Count García and his adulterous wife Argentina has led some to postulate that there were originally two separate tales that were subsequently combined by the compilers of the *Estoria de Espanna*.[9] It has also been suggested that the account of the marriage of Count García and Argentina had its origins in the Castilian abbey of San Pedro de Cardeña and was later fused to the older Najeran legend.[10]

Second, questions of historicity and genre have attracted much attention. Was the legend actually a poetic reworking of a much older historical core? Does it contain echoes of a now lost epic work, or is it better regarded as simply an assemblage of novelesque elements or folk-motifs?[11] The ambitious, powerful woman, whose transgressive sexuality and thirst for power challenge the very foundations of the patriarchal society of the day, is by no means a literary topos that was unique to Iberia. It has been pointed out that the legend bears similarities with the history of Rosamunda, queen of the Lombards, or even with that of Cleopatra, queen of Syria.[12] Wicked, ambitious, adulterous queens and female poisoners also abound in Old French epic poems.[13] As it is, there are elements of the narrative that draw clear inspiration from other Hispano-Latin historiographical texts. Thus, the account of the defeat and death of Count García in the *Chronica Naierensis* reproduces almost word for word the version preserved in the set of annals known as the *Annales*

Compostellani, which were themselves produced in the Rioja[14]; meanwhile, the description of the defeat and death of al-Manṣūr appears to have been inspired in part by the accounts preserved in the *Historia Silensis* and Bishop Pelayo of Oviedo's *De Legione*.[15] The strong suspicion is that the legend of *La condesa traidora* owed its development more to the work of prose historiographers, who simply appropriated a series of folkloric elements, than to the creativity of one or more epic poets.[16]

Third, and of particular significance as far as this inquiry is concerned, the ideological underpinnings of the legend have been subjected to analysis. Parallels can be seen between the narrative of the flight and refuge of Count Sancho at Lantarón, as reported by the *Chronica Naierensis*, and that of the rebellion of the Visigothic warlord Pelayo in Asturias in the early eighth century, as narrated by the Asturian royal chronicles.[17] Just as the Muslim invasion of 711 had been blamed on the sins of the Visigoths, so the attacks of al-Manṣūr in the late tenth century were portrayed as divine punishment for the transgressions of the Christians, and those of King Vermudo II of León in particular.[18] Like Pelayo's uprising and subsequent victory at Covadonga, Sancho's deliverance from Muslim oppression through divine intervention—signaled by his victory in battle and al-Manṣūr's death shortly afterward—was regarded as a moment of redemption, which heralded the beginning of better times for the Christians of Castile. Count Sancho is said by the chronicler of Nájera—with some hyperbole—to be the figure on whom "the entire salvation of Spain" depended, just as Pelayo is said to have voiced his intention to bring about the "salvation of Spain and the restoration of the army of the Gothic people."[19] Besides, while Pelayo's victory was said to have saved Hispania and prefigured the creation of a new Gothic dynasty, so Sancho's is framed as the moment that paved the way to a period of Castilian supremacy in the Peninsula, following the accession of Ferdinand I in 1035.[20] In this respect, the eagerness of the chronicler of Nájera to move away from hitherto dominant Astur-Leonese historiographical models by privileging the importance of Castile was symptomatic of a broader political and cultural assertiveness on the part of Castilian monastic houses that can be detected during the decades that followed the separation of the realms of León and Castile after the death of Alfonso VII in 1157.[21] Viewed in this context, the legend of *La condesa traidora*, far from being simply a novelesque interlude amid the heavy-duty political narrative, appears to have fulfilled an important historiographical and ideological purpose.

The centrality of sexuality to the narrative is another aspect of the legend that has attracted comment.[22] Particular attention has been drawn to the sexual assertiveness of the female protagonists of the tale in its various forms, and it has even been speculated that it is Count García's sexual inadequacy that leads his wives to commit adultery.[23] Equally noteworthy, however, and less remarked upon, is the close association between sexual desire and political ambition. According to the chronicler of Nájera, both motivations are what prompted Count García's wife to engineer the death of her husband and then seek that of her son, Sancho. Ramón Menéndez Pidal argued that since Count García's historical wife, Aba, was from the comital dynasty of Ribagorza, the portrait of the treacherous countess in the *Chronica Naierensis* was a deliberate attempt to highlight the contrast between what he dubbed the "relaxed political ideas" (*ideas políticas relajadas*) that the count's wife wished to introduce into Castile—by which Menéndez Pidal was alluding to the readiness of certain élite families of the Pyrenean region to intermarry with Muslim kin groups across the frontier—and the "heightened nationalist feeling" (*el alto sentido nacional*) of the Castilian counts, who were implacably opposed to such a policy.[24] However, this rather overlooks the fact that in the narrative of the legend Count Sancho actually offers his sister in marriage to al-Manṣūr in an attempt to buy peace. Rather than seeking to distinguish between Castilian patriots on the one hand and Pyrenean "miscegenists" on the other, the Najeran version of the legend appears to act as a general warning of the dangers posed by interfaith sex. The countess's adulterous conduct in seeking a Muslim sexual partner is not regarded simply as morally reprehensible, in that it represented a wholesale betrayal of her husband, her son, and her faith, but also as politically dangerous. Her lust—both for sexual gratification and for power—and her readiness to breach the cultural borders between the Christian and Islamic communities in order to attain both almost destroys the comital dynasty of Castile and places the independence of the entire Castilian region in jeopardy. It is only once that mixed union is thwarted with the death of the countess and that of al-Manṣūr soon afterward that the peril to Castile subsides. What we have here, then, is a counterpoint to the legend of the tribute of the hundred maidens and variations on that theme. The sexually predatory and vainglorious countess may appear to have little in common with the defenseless, innocent Christian maidens being forced against their will to enter into sexual relations with Muslim men, but the context and consequences of both forms of sexual mixing are identical. Interfaith sex is portrayed as a symptom of military failure and a collapse of political cohesion and will on the Christian side, which if unchecked would fatally undermine its ability to resist Muslim attack. Once again, Christian identity and power are closely bound up with the sexuality of its women.

The Christian noblewoman who crosses the military frontier into al-Andalus and engages in a sexual relationship with a Muslim lord on account of sexual desire and a thirst for power reappears in a number of other texts. One such account is preserved in the short work known as the *Crónica de la población de Ávila*, an account of the deeds of the *caballeros* of the Castilian city of Ávila, which was probably composed some time during 1256.[25] The *Crónica* relates how on the feast day of St. Leonard (6 November) a Muslim raiding party from Talavera, west of Toledo, comes to Ávila and captures a number of Christians outside its walls, among them the wife of a local commander, Enalviello, that is, Nalvillos Blázquez.[26] This woman later marries the leader of the Muslims. When Enalviello learns of this, he carries out a retaliatory raid against Talavera with a force of fifty horsemen. Reaching the outskirts of the town, he instructs his companions to wait there in hiding and to come to his aid if he blows his hunting horn; he then proceeds into the town, disguised as a farmer with a load of hay on his back. When he reaches the town fortress, he spies his wife at the window and is taken to see her by a servant. When he encounters his wife once again, Enalviello professes his love for her: "So great is the love that I have for you that if I can no longer have you I would rather be dead than alive." At this point, however, the Muslim leader returns to the fortress, and Enalviello is forced to hide. The Muslim and his wife then go to bed, and in the midst of their lovemaking we are told that the woman completely forgets about Enalviello's declaration of love for her. The woman then pointedly asks the Muslim what he would give her if she were to deliver Enalviello into his hands, and he replies that he would give her half his lordship. Faced with this tempting offer, the woman promptly betrays Enalviello to the Muslim, who vows to kill him and asks how he wishes to die. Enalviello tells him that the shame he had suffered was so great that if their positions were reversed he would take the Muslim to the highest point outside the city and burn him alive in public. The Muslim declares that Enalviello will suffer that very fate. The townsfolk are summoned to witness the public execution, but before Enalviello is consigned to the flames he is allowed to blow on his hunting horn, which summons his companions to come and save him. The citizens of Talavera are massacred, the Muslim leader is burned alive, and his Christian wife meets the same fate shortly afterward.

A markedly similar dynamic of adultery and revenge can be seen in the Portuguese narrative known as the *Lenda de Gaia* (The Legend of Gaia). The legend is preserved in the works known as *Livros de Linhagens* (Books of Lineages), collections of genealogies of leading Portuguese aristocratic families, which contain within them a variety of historical or legendary elements which were designed to add luster to these noble dynasties.[27] Three such collections have survived from the medieval period: the *Livro Velho* (compiled between 1286 and 1290), the *Livro do Deão* (compiled between 1290 and 1343), and the *Livro de Linhagens do Conde D. Pedro* (compiled between 1340 and 1343, with later additions in 1360–65 and 1380–83).[28] The *Lenda de Gaia* is preserved in the first and last of these. In the version narrated in the *Livro Velho*, the action begins as the Muslim king Abencadão kidnaps the wife of King Ramiro (II) of León and carries her off to his castle at Gaia.[29] When King Ramiro hears of this affront to his honor, he mounts a naval expedition down the River Duero to rescue his queen. Reaching the castle, the king leaves his son Ordoño and his vassals outside and approaches the fortress dressed as a beggar. The next day he is discovered by one of the queen's Muslim ladies-in-waiting, Ortiga, who has come to fetch water, and the king speaks to her in Arabic. Subsequently, Ortiga takes Ramiro into the castle, only for the queen to have him locked up in a room, with the intention of handing him over to the Muslim king. When Abencadão arrives at the castle, he has dinner and then has sex with the queen. When the queen reveals the presence of her husband, Ramiro blows the hunting horn he has brought with him to summon his son and vassals. In the ensuing battle the Christians prevail, decapitate all the Muslims, and raze the castle to the ground. Taking his queen and her ladies back to their ships, King Ramiro falls asleep on his wife's lap as they make their way home. When the queen begins to sob and wakes the king, she tells him, "I weep for the good Moor that you killed."[30] The king's response is brutal: tying a millstone to his wife's neck, he pushes her into the water and drowns her. Returning to his court, King Ramiro baptizes Ortiga and marries her. A child is later born to the couple and baptized with the name Alboazar.

The version of the legend preserved in the *Livro de Linhagens do conde D. Pedro* is even more elaborate. It begins by relating that King Ramiro, hearing of the beauty and good qualities of the sister of King Alboacer Alboçadam, declares his intention to marry her and convert her to Christianity. When King Alboacer refuses, saying that she had already been betrothed to the king of Morocco, Ramiro kidnaps her with the assistance of the sorcerer Aaman and takes her back to León, where he baptizes her and she takes the name Artiga. In retaliation, Alboacer Alboçadam launches an attack of his own, kidnaps Ramiro's queen—here called Aldora—and carries her off to his castle at Gaia, together with a number of other women. The story then broadly follows that of the *Livro Velho*: Aldora imprisons her husband with the intention of handing him over to the Muslim king; Ramiro saves himself by summoning his son and other troops, who defeat the Muslims and burn down the castle; on the journey home Aldora bursts into tears on account of her Muslim lover and is thrown into the sea. Once he returns to León, Ramiro marries the sister of Alboacer Alboçadam.[31]

These colorful accounts of cross-border sexual liaisons in turn share thematic similarities with a short narrative which is preserved within a fragment of an Aragonese chronicle, which was compiled at the request of a prominent noble family from the area of Teruel, the Martínez de Marcilla, sometime during the reign of John II of Aragon (1458–79).[32] The chronicle relates how one Count Rodrigo de Alfambra clashes in battle with the Muslim king of Camañas. Before beating a hasty retreat, the king brazenly takes out his penis and asks the count: "What do you think of this spear?" ("Que te parece de esti venablo?"). When the count later relates this to his wife over dinner she resolves to become the king's lover. There then follows an extraordinary tale: the king, learning of the countess's desire for him, has her drugged so that it appears that she has died. Later she is taken to his residence at Camañas, where the lovers live together secretly for eight months. When the count later learns that his wife is in fact residing with the king, he journeys to see her dressed as a pilgrim. Not long after the countess meets him, she discovers his identity and persuades him to hide in a chest; when the Muslim king arrives they have sex on top of it. The rest of the story follows the narrative structure of the episode recorded in the *Crónica de la población de Ávila* very closely. The count is betrayed by the countess and is taken out to be burned at the stake, but he is able to blow his hunting horn, summoning his followers to come and save him. The king and the countess, who by then had converted to Islam, are seized by the Christians and consigned to the flames.

All these legends—Castilian, Portuguese, and Aragonese alike—are replete with common folk-motifs: the adulterous wife who hides her husband and meets her lover; the king or noble who travels incognito dressed as a beggar; the man who is captured through feminine wiles; the woman who appears to be dead; the woman who falls in love with a captive knight or prince; the hero who summons help with a hunting horn, to name but a few.[33] The legends have been mostly regarded as offshoots of a common tradition which drew ultimate inspiration from the biblical account of King Solomon, who is said to have incurred divine displeasure by marrying Pharaoh's daughter, vernacular versions of which were widely reproduced in France, Germany, and Iberia between the thirteenth and fifteenth centuries.[34] Although the manner in which the Avilan, Portuguese, and Aragonese accounts is framed is less overtly political than the tale of *La condesa traidora*, which we have seen played a key role within the historiographical project being pursued by the chronicler of Nájera, these narratives do share a common thematic thread involving adultery, interfaith sex, and political treachery. In each case, the adulterous wife meets a terrible end—poisoning, drowning, or burning—on account of her sexual transgression and faithlessness. It is the willingness of the Christian woman to engage in illicit sexual mixing across religious lines that is the catalyst for the unravelling of events and the ultimate recourse to violence. Furthermore, in all the narratives the death of the adulterous couple has positive political-military consequences for the Christians. In *La condesa traidora* Count Sancho survives the assassination plot that is hatched by his mother, defeats Almanzor, and goes on to capture many towns from the Muslims.[35] In the *Crónica de la población de Ávila*, the death of the Muslim governor and his Christian wife is accompanied by the massacre or capture of the citizens of Talavera, thereby neutralizing the threat that town posed to nearby Ávila. In the *Lenda de Gaia*, King Ramiro not only converts his new wife to Christianity, but she later bears the king a son—nicknamed Cide Alboazar—who in the future is said to have gone on to fight with distinction against the Muslims and to conquer many towns. In the Aragonese legend, it is the count's victory in battle and the subsequent execution of the Muslim king and the adulterous countess at Palomera that pave the way for the Christians to capture the nearby towns of Argente and Visiedo.

However, interfaith sexual liaisons were by no means portrayed in the literary record as the exclusive preserve of powerful women. The mordantly satirical, breathtakingly slanderous, and frequently downright obscene *Cantigas de escarnio e de maldezir*, composed in Galician-Portuguese by court entertainers (*trovadores*)—many of them noblemen—between the late twelfth and late thirteenth centuries, refer to a number of what are called *soldadeiras*. The latter were female performers, whose licentious lifestyle—some of them reputedly worked as prostitutes as a means to supplement their incomes—made them the target of numerous barbed attacks.[36] In a direct parody of the heroic tales (*cantares de gesta*) of the period, several of these songs depict the *soldadeiras* departing to the frontier "to make war on the Moors" (*moiros guerreiar*), but thanks to the numerous double entendres which are deployed in such songs it is made abundantly clear that it is sexual struggle, not armed conflict, that the poet has in mind.[37] A case in point is Domingas Eanes, who after a prolonged sexual "duel" with a Muslim African horseman (*genete*) "vanquishes" her foe, only for her to be infected with venereal disease:

> Domingas Eanes fought with an African horseman and was seriously wounded; but she was so ardent that she eventually won, without a doubt, and certainly she defeated a good knight; nonetheless, he is so strong that she ended up getting hit.
>
> The blow got to her through a weak spot in her coat of mail, which was untied; and it bothers me, because in this attack, since she was braver (may God aid me), she won; but the knight did it with his weapons; he was so sly that forever she will be scarred.
>
> And that Moor brought with him, like a studly man, two companions to this combat; and he is famous for never missing when giving a great blow with his lance; and he tumbled her on her back and gave her such a blow from above, that the wound will never close.
>
> And the doctors who understand such matters say that such a wound can never heal, not by warming it with all the wool in this land or with oil; the wound doesn't go straight down, but in circles, like a screw, so that it's been seriously infected for a while.[38]

"By engaging with the *genete*," Denise Filios has commented, "Eanes collaborates with the enemy, allowing him to shaft Christian Spain in an erotic-symbolic reenactment of the Muslim conquest."[39] Another *soldadeira* who is reported to have engaged in interfaith sexual relations and paid a heavy price for her transgression is Maior Garcia. In an attempt to settle her debts, she is depicted selling her body to a Christian, a Jew, and a Muslim all in the same day, with the latter leaving her pregnant as a result.[40]

Perhaps the most celebrated of all the *soldadeiras* was María Pérez, known by the nickname "la Balteira," who was the object of several such scurrilous songs.[41] In one of these, two *trovadores*, Pedr'Amigo of Seville and Vaasco Pérez Pardal, indulge in a poetic "debate" about María. It is said that she had received her famed sexual powers—which are referred to euphemistically as her ability to "excommunicate" or "absolve" men—from an elder of the Banū Ashqilūla, one of the foremost families of the Nasrid kingdom of Granada.[42] Ultimately, however, those same powers are said to have been received direct from Mecca itself, by which it is presumably meant that María had converted to Islam, and it is even claimed that she had been responsible for the subsequent uprising by the Banū Ashqilūla against Alfonso X in Jerez and Jaén in 1275. Thus, Pedr'Amigo declared to his counterpart: "Vaasco Pérez, this power truly comes from Mecca; and since the patriarch granted it to her, she brought on herself all the blame for what happened in Jaén and in Jerez, where much evil was done, so she excommunicates anyone at all, or releases anyone at all that she wishes."

When Vaasco Perez casts doubt on this assertion, Pedro'Amigo is quick to retort: "Vaasco Pérez, she did find this power in Mecca, and the power God gave in Rome Balteira says is worth nothing at all."[43]

How much basis in fact there is in this song has been much debated.[44] Antonio Ballesteros-Beretta, following Menéndez Pidal, went so far as to speculate that María Pérez had been dispatched by Alfonso X in 1264 as part of a secret diplomatic embassy to the Banū Ashqilūla, with the intention that she use her sexual "arts"—almost like a Mata Hari *avant la lettre*—to engineer an alliance with Castile.[45] Not all have been convinced. "It would be an historical document of great importance, if we were to take it seriously," Lapa has commented drily.[46] Yet even if the figure of María la Balteira is nothing but a mirage, the product of the fevered imagination of comic entertainers at the court of Alfonso X, her figure remains highly significant for what she represents: a fear of apostasy and sexual mixing with the religious enemy is coupled with a dread that those who crossed the frontier and transgressed in this way might ultimately conspire with the infidel to bring down Christian power.[47]

Viewed from one angle, the *cantigas* and the Castilian, Portuguese, and Aragonese "adventures" described above can be said to have a certain ludic quality, even if there is nothing in them to suggest that the authors in any way condoned the interfaith sexual liaisons they described.[48] There is nothing playful whatsoever, however, about another case of supposed interfaith adultery which is the subject of one of the Alfonsine *Cantigas de Santa María*. Cantiga 186 (*Quen na Virgen santa muito fiará*) tells of a happily married couple whose connubial bliss is shattered by the machinations of the man's mother, who harbors ill will toward her daughter-in-law.[49] The mother-in-law orders one of her Muslim servants to get into bed with the wife as she sleeps and then summons her son to catch the couple—supposedly in flagrante delicto—declaring: "Come here. If you saw your wife, whom you loved more than yourself, as I just did, with a Moor beside her in bed, I imagine it would grieve you greatly. . . . See what your wife is up to!" Seeing the couple in bed, the husband vows to kill his wife on the spot, but is dissuaded from doing so by his mother, who advises him to inform the local magistrate and let justice take its course. When the magistrate and other townsfolk discover the couple in bed they exclaim: "What will become of this woman who does such a vile thing, for she has forgotten God and the world and honor and committed a low and shameful deed. For this she will burn in the fire, for she deserves it."

The woman and the Muslim, who is described "as black as pitch," are seized and taken to the town square, where a fire is lit and the couple are cast into the flames. The woman, who had earlier appealed to the Virgin for deliverance from her deadly predicament, is protected from the fire through divine intervention; however, no such mercy is shown toward the "false, treacherous Moor [who] burned . . . until not a single sign of him remained." The song is accompanied by a series of six illustrations, in five of which the Muslim is depicted. Albert J. Bagby comments of the pictures: "In the third the townspeople are gathered around the bed looking on, and the Moor is still there, mouth agape, with an expression that might be considered savage but could also be regarded as that of a simpleton. His teeth look like fangs."[50]

The fact that the Muslim man was a mere pawn in the machinations of the wicked mother-in-law and was executed despite being innocent of the crime he was accused of was clearly of no concern to the poet, who was otherwise transfixed by the "beautiful miracle"(*miragre bel*) that had occurred.

In all their different ways, the narratives that we have surveyed thus far are symptomatic of the profound sense of anxiety that the very thought of Christian women engaging in sexual relations with Muslim men—besmirching their honor and that of their husbands—induced in the ranks of Christian society in the Later Middle Ages. It was bad enough for innocent unmarried females to be handed over to the Muslims or taken prisoner, as in the legend of the hundred maidens, but in some respects the adulterous woman who willingly gave herself to a Muslim man represented an even greater threat to the good order of society. Interfaith adultery undermined the patriarchal authority that men wielded over their women, as well as the politics of interfaith segregation that was enshrined in law. It was for this very reason that Christian municipal law codes prescribed such harsh punishments for those who transgressed in this way. The fact that real-life cases of interfaith adultery appear to have come to court only rarely does not diminish the ideological significance of these legends.[51] By breaking her marriage vows, by surrendering her body to a Muslim man, by embracing—in some cases—Islam, the adulterous woman of literature was portrayed as the "insider" who seeks to destroy her community by consorting with the Islamic "Other" across the frontier. She was, one might say, the liminal figure through which fears about the threat posed to Christianity by Islam more generally might be articulated. In this way, the fictionalized sexual transgressions committed by Christian women can be said to

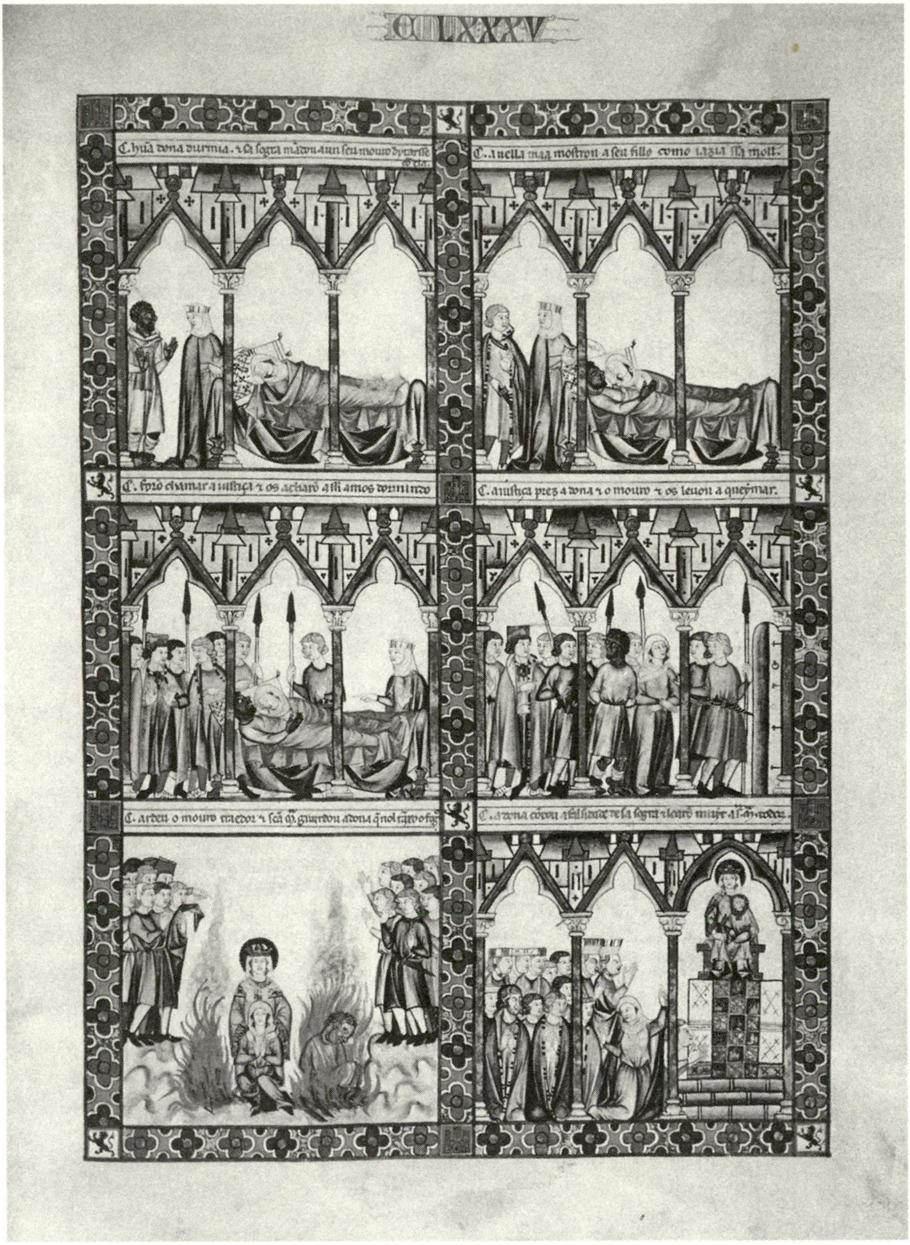

Figure 2. A Christian woman, falsely accused of adultery with a Muslim man, is saved from burning by the intervention of the Virgin Mary.

Cantigas de Santa María, no. 186: Real Biblioteca del Monasterio de Escorial, Ms T.I.j.
Reproduced with the permission of the Oronoz Picture Agency, Madrid.

have served as yet another mechanism by which the cultural lines of difference that existed between Christians and Muslims were highlighted and reinforced.

The Power of Love

In his *Chronicle of the Kings of León*, Bishop Pelayo of Oviedo provides a characteristically brief—almost telegraphic—account of the five "legitimate marriages" that were contracted by that champion of the Leonese-Castilian *Reconquista* and serial monogamist, Alfonso VI of León-Castile. The queens in question were listed as Agnes, Constance, Berta, Elizabeth, and Beatrice. The bishop then went on to add: "He also had two concubines, although they were most noble: the first was Jimena Muñoz . . .; the second was Zaida, the daughter of Abenabeth king of Seville, who was baptized and named Elizabeth, by whom he fathered Sancho, who died at the battle of Uclés."[52]

Given Pelayo's somewhat shady reputation as a spinner of tall tales and an accomplished purveyor of forged documents, it is tempting to dismiss these accounts of a Muslim noblewoman renouncing her faith and being baptized as so much wishful thinking on the bishop's part. But in the case of the woman known traditionally to Spaniards as *la mora Zaida*, Pelayo's assertion is corroborated by a number of other sources.[53] One such was the contemporary *Chronicon Floriacense*, produced at the monastery of Fleury in the Loire Valley, which in its account of the Almoravid victory over Leonese-Castilian forces at the battle of Uclés in 1108 records the death of King Alfonso's son, Sancho, "who had been born of a most noble Saracen maiden who had earlier been baptized."[54] On the Muslim side, meanwhile, Ibn Idhārī al-Marrākushī refers in his account of the Almoravid victory at Uclés to Alfonso VI's ill-fated son, Sancho, "whom he had by the wife of al-Ma'mūn ibn 'Abbad, she who had converted to Christianity."[55]

Bishop Pelayo's brief narrative of the liaison between Alfonso and Zaida passed almost word for word into the *Chronica Naierensis* and after that into Lucas of Tuy's *Chronicon Mundi*.[56] Both authors repeated Pelayo's assertion that Zaida was a concubine, Lucas stating that the king had taken her "almost as a wife" (*quasi pro uxore*). However, some thirteen years before he composed his chronicle, Lucas had already included the episode of the conversion of Zaida in his *De Miraculis Sancti Isidori*, a collection of the miracles of St. Isidore, which he compiled while he was still a canon of San Isidoro in León in 1223.[57] In this account, he not only declares that Zaida wished to be baptized, "banishing all doubt and the error of her infidelity . . . renouncing Muhammad and his falsehoods," but also that she had been moved to do so by having witnessed for herself the miracles wrought by St. Isidore. Lucas attempted to give further credence to his claim by noting that Zaida's father "Benabeth," that is, al-Muʿtamid b. Abbād, ruler of Seville,

> was somewhat inclined towards the Catholic faith, because it is said St. Isidore had manifested it to him one night, when he appeared to him in a dream, and he kept that inclination secret on account of his fear of the Hagerenes, because if they knew that he was a Christian they would have taken away the temporal kingdom that he held.[58]

According to Lucas, when "Benabeth" became aware of his daughter's love for Christ, he discreetly made contact with Alfonso VI, sending him many gifts and riches and beseeching him to send his knights to collect Zaida because she was so willing to become a Christian. Hearing the news, Alfonso VI dispatched his knights who, in accordance with the wishes of both kings, made it appear that they had carried off Zaida against her will. Once at the Leonese court, Zaida converted and took the name Elizabeth, and, "as she was very wise and beautiful," King Alfonso took her as his wife. When she died, she was buried in the abbey of San Isidoro in León. Her unfortunate father, Lucas noted, died where he was, living among the Moors, on account of his desire to rule. In short, in Lucas's account the thaumaturgical power of St. Isidore was the driving force in bringing about the conversion of Zaida and her subsequent relationship with Alfonso VI. In this case, the act of sexual mixing was viewed as entirely legitimate, since the woman concerned had converted to the Christian faith.

In his *De rebus Hispanie*, Archbishop Rodrigo Jiménez of Toledo developed the story further still. He recorded that after the death of Alfonso VI's fourth wife, Elizabeth, the king "took" (*duxit*) "Ceyda," daughter of "Abenabeth prince of Seville," who was baptized and changed her name to María. According to the archbishop:

> She [Ceyda], having heard of the great deeds of Alfonso, although she had not met him, fell deeply in love with him, to the point that she embraced the Christian faith and placed under Alfonso's authority the castles that her father had granted to her. The castles which

> she gave to her husband were these: Caracuel, Alarcos, Consuegra, Mora, Ocaña, Oreja, Uclés, Huete, Amasatrigo and Cuenca. And he had by her a son called Sancho, whom he had entrusted to Count García of Cabra so that he might raise him.[59]

Rodrigo's narrative is distinctive on a number of counts. Quite apart from the fact that he is the only chronicler to state that Zaida changed her name to María—not Elizabeth—after her baptism, he is also the first to record that a substantial "dowry"—comprising a number of key strong points in the territory south of Toledo—was delivered to Alfonso VI when Zaida entered into her relationship with the Leonese king. Even more eye-catching, perhaps, the narrative introduces an element of love interest that is utterly absent from the earlier accounts, while the thaumaturgical role ascribed to St. Isidore by Lucas disappears entirely. It is also important to note that at no point is Zaida described as Alfonso's legitimate wife.[60]

A few decades later, the archbishop's narrative was adapted and reworked by the compilers of the vernacular *Estoria de Espanna*. In the *Versión crítica* of that chronicle it is stated unambiguously that Zaida was the *amiga*, or concubine, of King Alfonso; that she was the daughter of "Hauen Hamet, king of Córdoba"; that Alfonso took her as his partner in order that Toledo might be better defended; and that he later converted her to Christianity.[61] The love affair between the couple, in which Zaida manifestly took the lead, as described by Archbishop Rodrigo, was eliminated altogether; Alfonso's decision to take Zaida as his partner was attributed to pragmatic power politics rather than to passion. The chronicle goes on to state that when Zaida converted to Christianity the king asked the clergy not to christen her Mary, because it did not seem proper for her to have the same name as the Mother of God, and she asked instead to be baptized Elizabeth. Zaida is then said to have surrendered to Alfonso the various castles that her father had placed under her authority.[62] In short, what we seem to have here is an attempt by the chronicle's compilers to reconcile the contradictory accounts of Zaida's baptism provided by Pelayo (via Lucas of Tuy) and Rodrigo Jiménez.

However, the later *Versión amplificada* of the same chronicle revises the account of the *Versión crítica* in several respects.[63] First, it corrects the earlier Alfonsine account by stating that Zaida's father was the king of Seville, not of Córdoba. Second, it is keen to emphasize that the princess in question was not the king's concubine, as all previous commentators had either baldly stated or at least implied, but his *mugier velada*, that is, his "secret wife."[64] This may have been done with a view to upholding the reputation of the king's only son, Sancho, who later died in the disaster of Uclés. It also reintroduced the love element that the previous editors of the *Estoria* had suppressed. It related that King Abenabeth of Seville had "a maiden daughter who was great and beautiful and of very good manners," whom he loved greatly and to whom he granted Cuenca and other towns and castles in order that she could marry well. For her part, Zaida

> heard so much about King Alfonso, that he was a great knight and very handsome and skilled in arms and in all his other deeds, that she fell in love with him; and without even seeing him, for she never saw him, Doña Çayda fell deeply in love with him, with his good fame and his reputation, which grew by the day and resounded ever more, so much so that she went further.

The account goes on to relate that Zaida sent some messengers to the Leonese king in order to arrange a meeting between the two, with the promise that if the king agreed to marry her she would deliver to him Cuenca and all the other castles and fortresses her father might give her in dowry. The king responded positively to these overtures, and a meeting between the two took place at Consuegra or Ocaña, south of Toledo, or even Cuenca to the east—the compilers of the *Estoria* candidly admit their uncertainty—and reportedly led to love at first sight: "And as soon as they both saw each other, she was enamoured and smitten with King Alfonso, and he was no less smitten, for he saw her as great and beautiful and cultured, and of very good bearing, just as they had spoken of her."

Alfonso is reported to have said that if the agreement were to be fulfilled, Zaida would have to convert to Christianity, to which she readily agreed and repeated her promise that she would hand over Cuenca and the other towns that her father had given her if the king would marry her. The chronicle also records that Alfonso, ever the pragmatist, seeing that the strongholds promised by Zaida would help to reinforce his control over Toledo, consulted with the counts and other magnates of the kingdom. He then had her baptized and married her, and she bore him a son. Once again, we can see the royal chroniclers attempting to combine and rationalize diverging narrative accounts. The passionate love affair between Zaida and Alfonso is restored to its rightful place, but the king's watchful concern for the well-being of his kingdom is also given its due.

Unlike the other cross-border interfaith relationships we have examined thus far, the historicity of the relationship between King Alfonso and Zaida does not appear to be in doubt, even if certain aspects of it remain obscure. However, one thing we can be sure about is that "Zaida" was almost certainly not the woman in question's real name: it derives, rather, from the Arabic *sayyida*, the title by which all Muslim ladies of noble blood were known.[65] Furthermore, while there is unanimity that the "Abenabeth" of Seville referred to in most Christian accounts was al-Muʿtamid b. Abbād, ruler of the *taifa* kingdom of Seville, who was toppled from his throne and exiled to Morocco by the Berber Almoravids in 1091, Zaida was definitely not his daughter, as Bishop Pelayo and others claimed.[66] Instead, as Lévi-Provençal, drawing on the testimony of Ibn Idhārī al-Marrākushī, pointed out long ago, Zaida was in fact the widow of al-Muʿtamid's son, al-Fath al-Maʾmūn, who was killed on 26 March 1091, in the course of the Almoravid attack on Córdoba.[67] While the siege of that city was still in progress, al-Maʾmūn reportedly sent his wife and children, as well as his treasure, to nearby Almodóvar del Río. It was after that town in turn fell to the Almoravids, on 22 April 1091, that his widow presumably sought asylum at the court of Alfonso VI, perhaps fleeing north to Toledo with the troops of Álvar Fáñez, who had earlier tried to intervene on al-Muʿtamid's behalf and had been defeated by the Almoravids near Almodóvar del Río in the late spring or early summer of that year.[68] In short, we get the impression that Zaida was a woman acting in desperation. Shortly after arriving at the Leonese court, as numerous chroniclers attest, she became King Alfonso's concubine, converted to Christianity, and at an unknown date, probably between 1093 and 1095, bore the king a son, Sancho.[69] Moreover, if the princess in question was indeed a member of the Toledan royal house, as María Jesús Rubiera Mata has suggested, then the alliance with Alfonso VI begins to sound rather less of a love-match than the chroniclers would have us to believe and more the product of hard-nosed power politics.[70] As the compilers of the *Versión amplificada* of the *Estoria de Espanna* suggested, Alfonso's relationship with a Muslim princess might well have been viewed as a means to reinforce the king's authority over the city and region of Toledo, conquered only six years before. Even so, the suggestion that al-Muʿtamid of Seville had delivered to Alfonso VI a series of castles as a means to seal the relationship between Zaida and Alfonso has been called into question. Not only did the grant of such a dowry run entirely counter to Islamic custom, but the fortresses listed by Rodrigo Jiménez and others—Caracuel, Alarcos, Consuegra, and so on—were never under the authority of al-Muʿtamid to begin with.[71]

Whether Zaida also eventually became Alfonso VI's legitimate wife has been the subject of extensive but inconclusive debate.[72] Bernard Reilly has argued that in an attempt to secure the legitimacy of his son Sancho Alfonso VI married Zaida, who took the name Elizabeth, some time between March 1106 and the second half of 1107, that is, after the death of Alfonso's French queen, also named Elizabeth.[73] For his part, Gonzalo Martínez Díez has suggested that the Queen Elizabeth mentioned by Pelayo and "Zaida" were one and the same person.[74] The fact remains, however, that Bishop Pelayo of Oviedo, himself a regular visitor to the court of Alfonso VI, was careful to distinguish between the king's legitimate wives and his concubines and their respective progeny. In any case, it appears that the unfortunate Zaida herself later died in childbirth, probably on 12 September 1107, whereupon she was buried in the monastery of Sahagún, according to a now lost funerary inscription, or in that of San Isidoro in León, as Lucas later claimed.[75]

Whatever the precise circumstances that led to the sexual liaison between Zaida and Alfonso VI, and whether or not the couple were subsequently joined in matrimony, one can easily imagine why the episode—as related and embroidered by Lucas of Tuy, Rodrigo Jiménez, and others—would have caught the imagination of later generations. The tale presented by Archbishop Rodrigo, in particular, is a beguiling one of interfaith contact across the frontier in which love and, ultimately, the Christian faith triumph, as Zaida agrees to be baptized. Menéndez Pidal believed that Archbishop Rodrigo's embellished account of the love affair must have drawn on a now lost epic poem, which he dubbed the *Cantar de Zaida*.[76] However, his theory has little hard evidence to back it up. Just as likely, the archbishop's tale might have been inspired by another popular orally transmitted tale of interfaith love, a number of which had begun to circulate in France during the twelfth century.[77]

Among the most popular of these accounts was that known in France as *Mainet* and in Castilian as *Mainete*, one of many epic tales associated with the *Enfances* of the Carolingian emperor Charlemagne, which enjoyed widespread popularity across much of Europe from the the twelfth century onward.[78] The Castilian version of story begins as the French prince Mainete, or Carlos—the future Charlemagne—goes into exile following a quarrel with his father, Pippin. Crossing the Pyrenees into the Peninsula, he takes up service with Galafre, the Muslim king or governor of Toledo. Another Muslim potentate, Bramante, then demands the right to marry the king's daughter, Galiana, but when the king refuses, a battle erupts between Bramante and his soldiers on the one hand and those loyal to Galafre and Mainete, who was himself in love with the Muslim princess. However, Mainete himself is asleep and initially oblivious to the battle raging outside; when he finally awakes Galiana accuses him of cowardice. Stung by these words, Mainete prepares for battle and demands a horse and arms. Before he plunges into the fray, however, Galiana asks him to take her back with him to France and marry her, promising that she will convert to Christianity if he does so. Mainete gladly accedes to her request. As he makes his way toward the battlefield he encounters his cousin Ainart, mortally wounded, and pledges to wreak vengeance on his behalf. Charging into the fray, Mainete kills more than a dozen of Bramante's followers and then engages in single combat with Bramante himself, finally slaying and decapitating him. He then ties Bramante's severed head to his horse's bridle and offers it to Galiana as a wedding gift. The princess later follows Mainete back to France, after a perilous and difficult journey in which she is briefly captured by Muslim troops before being saved by the French knights. Once in France, the various promises that had been made on both sides are fulfilled: Galiana converts to Christianity and marries her lover, who is shortly crowned King Charles.

The surviving Castilian versions of *Mainete*—contained in the *Versión crítica* and the *Versión amplificada* of the *Estoria de Espanna*, among others—have been subjected to revealing analysis by Francisco Bautista, who has argued convincingly that that a poetic Castilian *Cantar de Mainete*, which drew on a late twelfth-century French version of the same tale, was circulating in the Peninsula well before it was summarized in prose by the compilers of the *Estoria de Espanna.*[79] The fact that Archbishop Rodrigo Jiménez makes passing reference to the legend in Book IV of his *De rebus Hispanie* demonstrates the currency that the tale must have had in Toledo by the early thirteenth century.[80] It is perfectly possible, indeed, that *Mainete*, with its account of warfare, interfaith love, conversion, and marriage served in part to inspire the archbishop's own colorful presentation of the supposed love affair between Zaida and Alfonso VI. Of course, there are considerable differences between the two accounts. *Mainete* is a patently fictitious epic tale, whose principal purpose was doubtless to entertain and inspire; by contrast, for all the romantic embroidering by Archbishop Rodrigo and others, the account of Alfonso VI and Zaida had a strong historical underpinning. In the case of Zaida, military success—in this case the capture of Toledo—is actually the precursor to conversion and sexual conquest, bringing with it towns and castles by way of dowry: it is the power and prestige of the Leonese king that win Zaida's heart. In *Mainete*, it is the defeat of the Muslim Bramante and his followers in battle that ultimately brings wealth and honor to the French knights and facilitates Galiana's conversion and subsequent marriage.

Another king who was said to have indulged in a cross-border interfaith love affair was Sancho VII of Navarre. In 1199, Sancho found himself caught between a rock and a hard place. His disastrous political and military strategy of previous years, which had seen him ally himself in 1195–96 with Alfonso IX of León and the Almohad caliph Yaʿqūb al-Manṣūr against his neighbour Alfonso VIII of Castile, had brought precious little by way of territorial advantage. To make matters worse, on 20 May 1198, at Calatayud, Alfonso VIII and Peter II of Aragon (1196–1213) had agreed a military alliance against Navarre.[81] Later that year, Castilian and Aragonese armies invaded the kingdom, captured a number of minor strong points, and besieged the strategically important city of Vitoria. At this point, perhaps doubting that the city could hold out for long, the Navarrese king sought salvation in a renewed military alliance with the Almohads. According to Archbishop Rodrigo Jiménez, who was himself Navarrese and was doubtless well informed about these events, King Sancho resolved to take matters into his own hands:

> A man of proven valour and strength, but obstinate by nature, having left his kingdom to fate, he set off to join the Arabs, accompanied on his journey by a few nobles, and stayed there for some time waiting for the return of certain messengers whom he had sent to the Miramamolín [caliph] on the other side of the sea. Once [the messengers] had returned, weighed down with money and gifts, the king continued through those lands going from one city of the Arabs to another with the only aim of raising funds.[82]

Meanwhile, the archbishop reports, the citizens of Vitoria, ground down by continual fighting and hunger, were on the point of surrender, which led Bishop García of Pamplona to set out for al-Andalus in search of the king.[83] Once he had finally tracked him down, the bishop obtained permission from the king for the citizens of Vitoria to surrender. At the same time, Alfonso VIII of Castile brought under his authority a number of other territories, including the county of Treviño, and the Basque territories of Álava and Guipúzcoa. As for the king of Navarre, the archbishop noted acidly, "he returned furnished with gifts from the Hagarene, but deprived of all of the above and of glory." By March 1201, Sancho had returned to his kingdom, when he can be traced at Tudela.[84]

The archbishop's narrative is broadly confirmed by the work conventionally known as *The Latin Chronicle of the Kings of Castile*, probably composed by the royal chancellor of Castile, Juan, bishop of Osma and later of Burgos, and completed some time between 1236 and 1239. The chronicler recorded Sancho's decision to flee his kingdom and seek help from the "king of Morocco," by which he meant the Almohad caliph. He further claimed that the king traveled as far as the caliphal court in Marrakesh to do so and that he was rewarded with a sum of money and "certain revenues assigned to him in Valencia, where he remained for a long time."[85] For its part, the *Versión amplificada* of the *Estoria de Espanna* translated Rodrigo Jimenez's account into the vernacular almost word for word, but was much more forthright in its judgment of the king's conduct, preferring to label him a "coward" (*cobarde*), rather than "stubborn" (*obstinatus*), as the archbishop had done.[86]

However, the English chronicler Roger of Howden had a strikingly different story to tell.[87] In his *Chronica*, which he completed in 1201, he recounted the tale of a daughter of one Boyac Almiramimoli, the "Emperor of the Africans," who "having heard by popular report of the outstanding qualities of Sancho, king of Navarre, brother of Berengaria Queen of England, fell so deeply in love with him that she passionately wished to have him as her husband." She eventually told her father of her desire and vowed that she would hang herself unless Sancho took her as his wife. According to Roger, the caliph asked his daughter how such an alliance could possibly be brought about when she was a pagan and the king a Christian. Her response was direct:

> I am ready to adopt the Christian faith, and to live according to their Law, provided that I can have the king of Navarre as my husband; and that, dear father, can easily be achieved through you. Everybody goes in awe of you, everyone stretches out arms towards you; send him requests and presents, and you will secure him for me.

The caliph was beset with doubts, declaring that he would prefer the princess to marry one of his own people, but his daughter was implacable, so he dispatched messengers to King Sancho, "asking him to come and marry his daughter, promising that he would give him all the money that he wanted, and in addition all of al-Andalus." Roger then recorded that while King Sancho was still en route to the court the caliph died and was succeeded by his young son, who on account of his age was unready to take on the governance of his realm and threatened by numerous, unnamed enemies:

> Since the king of Navarre had arrived hoping to be accepted as the spouse of the princess, the young man who was to succeed to the throne told him that if he wished to help him, and serve him in the task of recovering the land, he [the caliph] would give him his sister according to the promises of his father; but if he refused to help, he would hold the king in captivity and he would never escape from it.

Faced with such a dilemma, Roger reported, Sancho pledged to aid the new caliph, who after three years was to rule in his own right. Whether Sancho and the Muslim princess were ultimately joined in matrimony we are not told, for the story breaks off, but Roger later records that Sancho returned to his kingdom and agreed a truce with his Christian neighbors.[88]

There are echoes of some of the later renditions of the story of Alfonso VI and Zaida here. Roger's account, interlaced as it is with quotations from Ovid's treatises on love, is fanciful in the extreme. The historian Munárriz y Velasco dismissed it as "an absurd story."[89] It hardly needs saying that it is highly unlikely that a Muslim princess would have taken the lead in proposing such a marriage alliance, or that the caliph would have countenanced it. Besides, the suggestion that Sancho crossed to Africa and spent three years there fighting on behalf of the caliph's son is not borne out by Muslim sources, Archbishop Rodrigo's account, or by the evidence of Sancho's own chancery. Be that it as it may, it is by no means inconceivable that Sancho crossed the frontier into Muslim territory in search of assistance, just as other monarchs—like Sancho I and Alfonso VI of León—had done in the past. Yet Roger is careful to frame the narrative in a way that would meet the expectations of his Christian audience. By presenting the Muslim princess as the ardent suitor, who out of love and admiration for the Christian king promised to convert to Christianity in order that her love might be fulfilled, and with the additional promise from the caliph of money and authority over the whole of al-Andalus, Sancho's image is utterly transformed from that of desperate asylum-seeker to powerful, charismatic king.

How the romanticized story of the love match between Sancho and the unnamed Muslim princess ultimately reached Roger of Howden is unknown. One possibility is that the story was broadcast by Bishop García of Pamplona, who traveled to England in 1201 to iron out problems concerning the dowry of the widowed Queen Berengaria, who had earlier married Richard I of England. Alternatively, the story about King Sancho's journey might have been recounted by a member of Sancho's entourage when the king met King John of

England, at Chinon, in October 1201.[90] Viewed in this context, it is tempting to conclude that the colorful account of interfaith love was part of a concerted Navarrese diplomatic effort to "spin" King Sancho's otherwise inglorious sojourn in Muslim territory in the very best possible light.

A very different dynamic operates in the celebrated French metrical romance known as *Floire et Blancheflor*, which first appeared toward the middle of the twelfth century and came to enjoy extraordinary popularity in western Europe during the Later Middle Ages.[91] The earliest Castilian rendering of the legend, known as *Flores y Blancaflor*, which drew on the earlier aristocratic, *Conte* version of the romance, probably dates from the late thirteenth century.[92] It tells of the recently widowed and pregnant countess Berta, who travels with her father on pilgrimage to Santiago de Compostela. In the course of an ambush Berta's father is killed, and she is enslaved by the Muslim king of Almería and becomes a servant to his queen, although she does not convert to Islam. It transpires that both women give birth on the same day (Easter Sunday): the queen to a boy, Flores; the countess to a girl, Blancaflor. As the children grow up together they fall in love, prompting the king to fear it would not be possible to arrange a dynastic marriage for Flores and that by the nature of her birth and status Blancaflor was "a poor creature of low station," incommensurate with the honor, rank, and religion of his son. To solve this problem, Blancaflor is arrested on trumped up charges of trying to poison the king and is sold into slavery, ending up in the harem of the emir of Babylon in Cairo. Flores is made to believe that Blancaflor has died, and his parents continue the subterfuge by erecting a sumptuous tomb in her honor. However, so great is Flores's grief at his loss that his mother eventually reveals the truth, and he sets off to search for Blancaflor. When he finally makes his way to Cairo, he is smuggled into the Tower of Maidens, where the emir keeps his harem of 140 beautiful women. When the lovers are discovered, the king is first tempted to have Flores summarily executed, but then decides to put the couple on trial. Found guilty and sentenced to death, the couple are led away to be beheaded, only for the emir to relent and allow them to go free, declaring that he will instead marry Gloris, daughter of the emperor of Germany. By the time Flores and Blancaflor return to the Peninsula, the Muslim king and his wife have died and Flores succeeds to the throne. There is a final twist in the tale, however, as before his coronation Flores converts to Christianity and insists that his people should do the same. It is an extraordinary finale. While most of the legend of Flores and Blancaflor seems to speak of intercultural assimilation, a world in which the boundaries between the faiths have become so highly porous that the daughter of the Christian countess succumbs to the charms of a Muslim prince, the ending in which Flores converts and Christianity triumphs over Islam returns us to the familiar territory we have already explored in the cases of Zaida and Galiana.[93]

What is striking about the story of the love affair between Flores and Blancaflor in an Iberian context is not merely its long and varied literary life—which was a feature shared by many of the legendary episodes that have been examined in this chapter—but its representation in visual forms too. Thus, a figurative version of the tale of the two lovers appears in the magnificently carved corbels of the chapter house of Burgos cathedral, which were probably executed some time between 1336 and 1345.[94] In one of these sculptures, on the southern wall of the chapter house, Flores and Blancaflor are depicted seated together in Cairo, reunited at last, she wearing the crown that befits her status as queen and holding a lion cub on her lap; he wearing a turban, a striking signifier of his cultural "otherness" and an indication, perhaps, that his assimilation into the Christian community is not yet complete.[95] In another of the sculptures, however, this on the northern wall, the story is brought to a close, as Flores is now crowned and dressed in Western manner, looking every inch the Christian king.[96] By depicting the love story through such a visual formulation, the artisans who created the Burgos corbels were trumpeting in spectacular fashion the triumph both of love and of the Christian faith as a whole. Equally striking, Cynthia Robinson has identified elements of the story of Flores and Blancaflor among the extravagant paintings that adorn parts of the ceiling of the Alhambra's Hall of Justice.[97] In this case, however, the tale was adapted and altered for its Nasrid audience, with particular emphasis being placed on the courtly behavior and ethics displayed by the élite protagonists.[98] The final, happy marriage of the lovers is ignored, as is, unsurprisingly, Flores's subsequent conversion to Christianity, as related in Christian versions of the tale.

All the accounts of interfaith love affairs that we have examined thus far take place within the exalted ranks of the social élite. But Muslim princesses were not the only ones to be portrayed surrendering to the power of love and that of the Christian faith too. At the end of a brief, anonymous *Vita* of Bishop—later Saint—Peter of Osma, which was probably composed by stages during the twelfth and thirteenth centuries, there follows a list of the miracles that were attributed to the saint's power.[99] Particularly noteworthy for our purposes is the story of the Christian man from Berlanga de Duero who is captured by Muslim troops in the course of a skirmish.[100] Taken into

Figure 3. Carved corbel depicting the lovers Flores and Blancaflor.
Burgos cathedral chapter house.

captivity, he is brought across the frontier into al-Andalus and made to serve a Muslim family. He makes great efforts to earn the kindness of his new masters, so much so that a Muslim girl falls in love with him and promises to free him if he would marry her. The girl carries out her side of the bargain, leaves her family home, and the couple cross the frontier back to Castile where the Muslim converts. Here, however, the man encounters determined opposition to the impending nuptials from his own family, which views a marriage to a convert to be unworthy of them. The couple then approach Bishop Peter, who gives them a dowry and wedding clothes to enable them to get married. When the woman suffers paralysis in later life and her husband threatens to abandon her if she does not get better, she finds a miraculous cure at the tomb of the saintly bishop. It is a simple story, but its ideological message has much in common with that of the more imaginative and extravagant tales we have already surveyed: it is not simply that love conquers all, but that its ultimate strength derives from the power of the Christian faith.

The incorporation of love motifs in a wide variety of medieval literary narratives was by no means a uniquely Iberian phenomenon, of course. The theme of "courtly love" in all its various manifestations enjoyed huge popularity in aristocratic circles throughout much of the Latin West from the late eleventh century onward.[101] Courtly romances typically portray a nobleman adoring and worshipping his beloved lady—who was often already married—from afar, seeking to win her favor by performing heroic deeds, sometimes incurring her public indifference or even scorn, and only rarely consummating his love for her. The lyrics of *amor de lonh* composed by the Provençal troubador Jaufré Rudel (d. c.1170), in which he declared his love for a far-away and unattainable lady, are a notable case in point.[102] In the interfaith love affairs between Christian nobles and Muslim princesses, however, the roles are frequently reversed, as it is the Muslim woman who takes the initiative in the amorous relationship. Thus, in the account of the love affair between Alfonso VI and Zaida, as retold by Archbishop Rodrigo Jiménez and the *Versión amplificada* of the *Estoria de Espanna*, it is the princess who falls in love with the Leonese king *de lonh* on account of his reputation, who sends messengers to arrange a meeting between them, and who demonstrates the power and depth of her love by converting to Christianity and by delivering to the Leonese king a string of strategically important towns and castles. Similarly, in Roger of Howden's imaginative account it is the Almohad princess who expresses her love for Sancho of Navarre, declares her intention to convert to Christianity, and effectively blackmails her father, the caliph, into allowing her to marry the Navarrese king.

The Muslim princess who falls in love with a Christian lord and subsequently converts to Christianity was a popular trope of twelfth- and thirteenth-century Western literature, particularly in the Old French *chansons de geste*.[103] In such "love narratives" conversion not only represents an acknowledgement of the superiority of a new faith on the part of the Muslim, but also a conscious change of political and cultural allegiance. The Muslim women involved are required to renounce Islam, abandon their families, and, more often than not, adopt a new name. From the point of view of their Christian paramours, meanwhile, such interfaith sexual liaisons often bring tangible rewards in their wake: wealth, territory, and power. Furthermore, the symbolic significance of the act of conversion is greater still. As Amy Remensnyder has observed:

> Implicit in the spiritual conquest enacted by conversion is the appropriation of the convert by his or her new religion—and it is one thing to appropriate the men belonging to the enemy camp and entirely another to appropriate the women. The domination, whether

> real or imagined, of the enemy's women often expresses triumph as eloquently as any victory won through the clash of arms can. As a narrative trope, it draws its power in part from the equivalence so often made between the female body and a territorial polity or a people.[104]

Far from being opposites, therefore, love and war could be presented as related parts of an overall strategy of domination and conquest.[105] When Muslim women like Ortiga, Zaida, and Galiana surrender their bodies to Christian lords and agree to convert to Christianity, their actions are both an implicit reproach to the Muslim fighting men who had failed to protect them and metaphors for the submission of the whole of Muslim al-Andalus to Christian power. The same explicit connection between military and sexual domination was also underscored by Christian poets, who portrayed Muslim cities as women ripe for conquest/seduction.[106] Conversely, when the Muslim prince Flor converts to Christianity he commands that all his Muslim subjects should follow his example on pain of death. In the literary imagination, therefore, love and conversion were envisaged as tools of domination, the means by which the Islamic "Other" could be both tamed and assimilated.

Hybridity and Revenge

The legend of the *Siete Infantes de Lara* is a stirring tale of family feud, treachery, and vengeance set in late tenth-century Castile. The story begins in Burgos, where the seven Infantes, or young noblemen, of Lara become embroiled in fighting at the wedding celebrations held in honor of their uncle, Ruy Velázquez, and his blushing bride, Doña Lambra. When Gonzalo González, the youngest of the Infantes, gets involved in an argument with Lambra's cousin, Álvar Sánchez, and ends up killing him, there follows an escalating spiral of tit-for-tat violence. A temporary truce is imposed by Count García Fernández, but ill feeling between the Infantes and Lambra does not dissipate. When Gonzalo González strips down to wash his goshawk in a garden fountain in plain view of Lambra, she is outraged at this affront to her honor and commands one of her manservants to throw a cucumber soaked in blood at Gonzalo. In retaliation, the Infantes kill the manservant, even as he clings to Lambra. Considering that that their collective honor has been gravely damaged, Ruy Velázquez plots to bring about the Infantes' downfall. Velázquez persuades the Infantes' father, Gonzalo Gustios, to go to Córdoba on his behalf, to the court of Almanzor (al-Manṣūr), ostensibly with a request for financial assistance to help defray the elevated cost of the recent wedding celebrations. In reality, the letter reveals that Velázquez plans to betray the Infantes to the Muslims when they next go on campaign to the Campo de Almenar, and asks Almanzor to behead Gustios once he has read the letter. When, shortly afterward, the Infantes set out on campaign, they are duly ambushed, captured, and beheaded in Velázquez's presence, and their heads are sent to Córdoba, together with that of their faithful guardian, Muño Salido. Almanzor delivers the grisly consignment on a white sheet to the distraught Gonzalo Gustios, now his prisoner, who, as he recognizes the eight heads, erupts with grief and talks mournfully to each in turn, recounting the great deeds that they had performed while alive. Gustios flies into a rage and slays a number of Muslims, and asks Almanzor to kill him once and for all. However, Almanzor, moved by this display of paternal grief, takes pity on Gustios, spares his life, and later sets him free. In a dramatic sequel to the tale, Velázquez and Lambra are made to pay for their perfidy. Some years later, Mudarra González "the Avenger," the illegitimate son of Gustios and a Muslim princess who had looked after him in prison, travels to Castile, slays the treacherous Velázquez, and later burns Lambra alive.

One can quite imagine the frisson of excitement, not to mention the profound sense of pity and revulsion, that medieval audiences must have felt as they listened with rapt attention to this dramatic and bloody tale. Treachery is an especially reprehensible—and therefore intrinsically fascinating—crime among humankind; but the crime must have seemed all the greater when the turncoat in question happened to be hand-in-glove with a common enemy across the religious-military frontier.

The earliest known version of the legend of the *Siete Infantes de Lara* was embedded in the *Versión crítica* of the *Estoria de Espanna*.[107] A more extensive version of the tale was subsequently included in the *Versión amplificada* of the same work and in the *Crónica Geral de Espanha de 1344*.[108] It was also incorporated into a range of other texts, including a number of late medieval and early modern ballads and dramas.[109] Among modern scholarship, Menéndez Pidal argued forcefully that the prose version of the legend that has come down to us was in fact a recasting of a much earlier epic poem—what he called a *canto noticiero*—composed orally c.1000.[110] However, not all scholars have been convinced, and more recent research has viewed the *Cantar* as very much a product of the thirteenth century.[111] Its date of composition aside, scholarly focus has been on the historicity of the *Cantar*[112]; its relationship with the medieval French epic[113]; and its perceived religious symbolism, among other things.[114] The sexual symbolism of the legend has also come in for close scrutiny. Critics have drawn attention to the sexual undercurrents that underlie the early exchanges between Lambra and her nephew Gonzalo González, as well as to the erotic symbolism of certain aspects of the narrative.[115] For example, the scene where Gonzalo González washes himself and then his goshawk in full view of Lambra has been interpreted as symbolic of an act of public masturbation, just as the bloody cucumber that was flung at him in riposte has been read as his figurative emasculation.[116]

There are, of course, important differences between this narrative of cross-border treachery and those that we examined earlier in this chapter. Lambra may be portrayed as calculating and vengeful, seemingly glad for her husband to negotiate with Castile's Muslim enemies in order to exact bloody retribution on the Infantes who had dishonored them both, but she is not an adulteress, and she does not engage in sexual relations with a Muslim man. Instead, it is a Christian male, Gonzalo Gustios, who, while still a prisoner in Córdoba, takes the initiative in an interfaith sexual encounter. The version of the legend preserved in the *Versión crítica* of the *Estoria de Espanna* relates that while Gustios is languishing in prison Almanzor sends a Muslim noblewoman (*una mora onrrada*) to serve him and comfort him. She tries to console him by saying—untruthfully—that she herself had twelve sons who had been slain in battle by the Christians. The couple fall in love and sleep together, with the result that the woman falls pregnant. Later, before he returns to Castile and to his legitimate wife, Sancha (Velázquez's sister), Gustios tells the Muslim woman that if their yet-to-be born child is a boy he should journey to Salas when he is old enough to see his father with half a gold ring to identify himself.

In the version preserved in the *Crónica geral de Espanha de 1344*, meanwhile, the Muslim woman who comforts Gustios in prison is said to be none other than Almanzor's own sister, who is described as "a very beautiful and very young woman, and a virgin maiden, who spoke very well and eloquently."[117] The woman is initially reluctant to visit Gustios, declaring that she wished that all the Christians in Spain found themselves in such a situation, but she finally accedes to her brother's imprecations after he threatens her. She takes Gustios in her arms and comforts him, telling him of her seven sons who had also supposedly died in battle. She then observes that Gustios is not too old to father more sons who might exact revenge on his behalf. Gustios's response is immediate and brutally direct: "With you I will father the son who will avenge the others." The Muslim princess demurs, but Gustios will not be denied:

> And Don Gonzalo said that he would not stop for all the Moors that there were in Spain. . . . And he grabbed her and lay with her. And God decided that from that union she should end up pregnant with a son, whom they later called Mudarra Gonçalvez, who was later a very good Christian and at God's service, and was the most honourable man that there was in Castile, apart from Count García Fernandez, who was the lord of that place.

According to this account, therefore, Mudarra was the product, not of an interfaith love affair, but of a brutal act of rape.[118] And in case any were tempted to cast aspersions, the *Crónica* is quick to emphasize that the violent sexual encounter between Gustios and the princess had God's blessing, just as it was also at pains to emphasize that Mudarra, the offspring of this relationship, became a "good Christian" in later life.[119] Either way, the Muslim noblewoman who bears the couple's illegitimate son, Mudarra González, becomes an instrument in the calculated act of vengeance that Gonzalo Gustios plans.

Consensual or not, the sexual encounter between Gonzalo Gustios and the Muslim princess is a key moment in the narrative of the legend of the *Siete Infantes de Lara*. It is not just the trigger for the process of retribution that Gustios—through his son Mudarra—will put in train in the future, but it is also a telling assertion of Christian power, even if it takes place in a squalid prison cell rather than on the battlefield. The fact that Almanzor is depicted as willingly giving the virginity and fertility of his sister to Gustios as consolation for the loss of his sons, and that he later welcomes the birth of Mudarra, is a tacit acknowledgment by the Muslim of the status and power of the Christian. The fact that the princess is not even named in any of these accounts simply goes to underline the impression that she is regarded as a particularly valuable object of exchange in a power relationship between two élite males, rather than an individual with her own motivation and agency.[120] In the same way, Gustios's decision to have sex with the Muslim woman and to father a child by her—without any recourse to Almanzor, or even seeking the woman's own consent, according to one version of the legend—can itself be interpreted as a starkly hegemonic gesture. As Louise Mirrer has observed with regard to the late medieval ballad *Pártese el moro Alicante,* which is in turn based upon the legend of the *Siete Infantes de Lara,*

> what may at first glance appear to be a gesture of cross-border sympathy—the Muslim king generously makes a present of his own

> sister as consolation to a grieving Christian—on closer inspection demonstrates Christians' desire for the total possession of Spain. . . . The *morica*, a stand-in for Muslim Spain, is to be possessed exclusively by Christians.[121]

We should not be too surprised by any of this. The Muslim princess who assists a Christian nobleman to escape from captivity was a popular topos of medieval *chansons de geste* and romances, and its literary roots may be traced back to biblical, classical, and Islamic sources.[122] Among the best known examples, the Anglo-Norman chronicler Orderic Vitalis, writing in 1135, recounted the tale of the Saracen princess Melaz, who supposedly engineered the release from captivity of Prince Bohemond of Taranto (d. 1111), lord of Antioch, and later married one of Bohemond's followers, Richard of Salerno.[123] In the late twelfth-century *chanson de geste La Prise d'Orange*, meanwhile, Orable, wife of the Muslim ruler of Orange, helps the Christian nobleman William to escape from captivity and take control of the town; she also later converts and becomes his wife.[124] In Orderic's account, Melaz is the means by which Bohemond's humiliating captivity is transformed into what Simon Yarrow has called "a triumphal story of his heroic deeds as a model of Christian manhood."[125] In *La Prise d'Orange*, Orable's marriage to William is in large part a device to help legitimize his act of conquest. Unlike Melaz and Orable, however, the Muslim princess of the legend of the *Siete Infantes de Lara* does not convert to Christianity, and her sexual liaison with Gonzalo Gustios is not the prelude to immediate Christian military victory. However, her son Mudarra will indeed convert and go on to attain wealth, status, and power in Christian society, eschewing his Islamic heritage for good. Rather like the Muslim Flores, who embraces Christianity at the end of his love affair with Blancaflor, so Mudarra, the hyper-masculine, hybrid hero, is assimilated into the Christian fold; his celebrated military prowess will henceforth be deployed in the service of the count of Castile.[126]

In the course of this chapter we have encountered interfaith sexual liaisons in many diverse literary contexts. Most of the episodes related are entirely fictional; a few are framed in a historical context that is broadly recognizable; many adapt literary tropes that enjoyed popularity in other parts of the Latin West and even further afield. The protagonists of these tales include calculating adulteresses, whose lust—for sex and power—leads them to consort with Muslims and even to convert to Islam; *soldadeiras* of dubious morals; ardent Muslim women, whose professed love for Christian men is such that they are willing to leave their families and be baptized; complicit sexual partners; and even a victim of rape. When viewed up close it is hard to see that women such as the *condesa traidora*, María la Balteira, Princess Zaida, the lover/victim of Gonzalo Gustios, or any of the other female participants in these literary liaisons have much in common, beyond the obvious fact that their sexual partners are of another faith; indeed, we might be more struck by the differences rather than the commonalities of such tales. Yet if we take a step backward, it is possible to see a common ideological thread running through all these narratives of sexual mixing. Time and again, we are reminded of the symbolic importance of the relationship between sex, power, and cultural identity. Christian women who crossed the physical and cultural boundaries that existed between the Christian and Islamic worlds to engage in sexual intercourse with Muslim men were seen to undermine the foundations of traditional patriarchal authority and to threaten the very independence of Christian rule. Conversely, Muslim women who converted to Christianity and surrendered their bodies to Christian men were not merely embracing a new faith, but also—symbolically—submitting to a new power, a process that Sharon Kinoshita has aptly dubbed one of "conquest-by-seduction."[127] By seeking to exercise sexual control over their own women, as well as those of the enemy across the frontier, Christian chroniclers and poets were staking a claim on behalf of their coreligionists to exercise political as well as cultural hegemony in the Peninsula as a whole.[128] In all of these literary accounts, sexual possession and Christian power march to the beat of the same drum.

Conclusion

The ethnoreligious communities of the medieval Iberian Peninsula—whether they dwelled in al-Andalus or in the Christian-ruled realms of the North—did not and could not exist in complete isolation from one another, whatever their religious leaders might have preferred. The fact of the matter was that in areas where the mixed faith population was relatively dense, such as the Ebro valley or the cities of Córdoba or Toledo, interfaith social interaction was frequent, extensive, and by no means necessarily antagonistic. Christians, Muslims, and Jews could be next-door neighbors, engage in commerce with one another, share public amenities such as mills or ovens, or cooperate in agriculture or irrigation; they might even socialize with one another. These, as Brian Catlos has observed, were "low complexity" activities, which had little or no ritual content and did not generally imply any sense of domination by one group over another.[1] Even so, we should not automatically assume that mundane coexistence between the faiths necessarily blurred the multifarious sociocultural boundaries which demarcated an individual's background. As Richard Fletcher has noted:

> Where you lived, how you dressed, along which streets you walked, where you shopped or bathed or disposed of domestic refuse, your language and gestures, what food you ate and how you prepared it, the pets you kept, how you brought up your children, what expletives you might use in anger. . . . All of these gave off signals indicative of cultural allegiance, indicative therefore of frontiers which might or might not be negotiable, thresholds which needed to be approached, if at all, with wariness.[2]

Yet of all the various ways the faiths met and intermingled, sexual contact was undoubtedly the one that carried the greatest ideological "charge" and stirred up the highest level of anxiety.

This book has investigated the multiple and complex ways in which interfaith sexuality, power, and group identity intersected in medieval Iberia. We have seen that in the aftermath of the eighth-century Islamic conquest exogamous marriages between Muslim élite men and Christian women served to legitimize and consolidate Islamic authority over the region; in later decades, such interfaith unions may have become relatively commonplace further down the social order, too. The cases of the family of Wittiza and Theodemir illustrate that interfaith marriage was also the mechanism by which the landed wealth of the Visigoths could be legitimately channeled into Muslim ownership. Furthermore, such marriage alliances subsequently became a tool of diplomacy for the ruling Umayyad dynasty of al-Andalus and for other élite families of the region, such as the Banū Qasī, Banū Shabrīṭ, or Banū Amrūs, in their relations with the emerging states of the Christian-dominated North. The taking of a Christian bride or even a slave concubine by a Muslim ruler might serve as a dynastic defense mechanism, designed to forestall the danger that a Muslim wife's family might at some point in the future stake its own claims to political power. It was also presented by court poets, such as Ibn Darrāj al-Qasṭallī, as a sign of Islamic political and military (as well as sexual) dominance. At the same time, the enslavement of large numbers of Christian women during the course of Muslim attacks on the states of the North, which led to some of them—like al-Ḥakam II's adored concubine Ṣubḥ—later being recruited to the harems of the Muslim male élite, constituted nothing less than a practical and symbolic weapon of warfare, designed to erode community cohesion on the Christian side and reduce its will to resist.

It is notable, by contrast, that very few Muslim women are known to have crossed the frontier in the opposite direction and taken Christian husbands, and that those who did so may have been acting in desperation. Muslim patriarchal society viewed sexual relations between its own women and men of another faith as anathema and issued stern judicial sanctions against those who transgressed in this way. The Christian bishops who gathered in council at Córdoba in al-Andalus in 839 similarly fulminated against "impious marriage" between the faiths; yet, there is no evidence that either the secular or the ecclesiastical authorities of the Christian-dominated realms of the North of the Peninsula shared such concerns at this time.

This analysis of interfaith sexual mixing in Iberia has suggested that attitudes toward such liaisons did not remain fixed throughout the medieval period. Rather, on the Christian side, there was a marked change in outlook and custom from the late eleventh century. A range of political, social, and cultural forces—a marked shift in the Peninsular balance of power in favor of the Christian states of the North; papally sponsored ecclesiastical reform; the growing influence of canon lawyers; and the dissemination of a more militant brand of anti-Islamic ideology in the Latin West—converged to condemn the practice of interfaith marriage in Christian Iberia to a swift decline. The cross-border arrangements of times past, which had seen Christian brides sent to join the harems of the emirs, caliphs, and other potentates of al-Andalus, came to be considered godless and immoral acts of surrender and pollution. Even so, Muslim rulers—in both the Peninsula and the Maghreb—would continue to acquire slave concubines through the spoils of war for generations to come.

One of the most striking manifestations of this transformation in Christian attitudes was to be the proliferation of legal enactments by the secular authorities of the Christian states, which were designed to prevent social assimilation and, above all, sexual mixing between Christian women and Muslim and Jewish men. Yet another symptom of change was the propagation of a plethora of Christian legends relating to interfaith sex, of which the story of the tribute of the hundred maidens—which was to form the basis of Compostelan claims to the exaction of the *Voto de Santiago*—was by far the most potent. Other legends which highlighted the same theme, like the dangerous liaisons pursued by the *condesa traidora*, reflected a different anxiety. Women who sought out Muslim lovers were judged guilty of treachery on two counts: by undermining the foundations of traditional patriarchal authority, they were seen to be not only besmirching their familial and communal honor, but also threatening the very ability of the Christian states to remain independent of their Muslim foes. Conversely, Muslim women who supposedly converted to Christianity and surrendered their bodies to Christian men, like the princess known to Christian authors as "Zaida," did not arouse the same misgivings, precisely because their actions were viewed as a physical and symbolic acknowledgment of Christian military, religious, and sexual potency.

The women we have encountered in this study occupied all levels of the social hierarchy. They included élite women, such as Queen Egilona of the Visigoths, the *condesa traidora*, and the Princesses Teresa and Zaida, as well as females whose social and economic horizons were decidedly more limited, like Caterina de Linares, who was captured by a Muslim raiding party as she toiled in a vineyard near Jaén, or the various marginalized Christian prostitutes whose activities brought them to the attention of local judges. Yet it is important to recognize that our perspective on these women and others is distorted to a very large degree by the nature of our sources. The diverse texts that have been examined in this book overwhelmingly reflected the views of the patriarchy. The women who emerge from the pages of secular or ecclesiastical lawbooks, or from the works of chroniclers, hagiographers, court poets, or even clerical forgers, were mostly ciphers, whose significance was above all symbolic. It is only in the case of women such as Ṣubḥ, or the nun Flora, or the prostitute Alicsén de Tolba that we are dealing with real-life characters, and even then the details of their lives have reached us through the pens of male authors.

We should also be mindful of the fact that our perception of these "processes of cultural differentiation"—as sociologists might categorize the various policies deployed by the authorities in Iberia to control interfaith sexuality—is itself obscured. While legal, religious, and artistic sources have a good deal to tell us about the collective strategies and discourses which were intermittently deployed by those in power in order to exercise control over sexual activity, or by others to create and defend collective identities, we know far less about how interfaith sexuality was regarded at the "microlevel" of individuals, families, and intimate relationships.[3] The accounts of the lives of the Cordoban martyrs hint at the family tensions that conversion and mixed marriages might engender in ninth-century Córdoba; and legal records of investigations into illicit interfaith relationships demonstrate that passion—whether momentary or more enduring—could impel men and women to transgress those lines of cultural demarcation that their coreligionists had established. Social attitudes toward sexual boundary-crossing were far from homogeneous, but it is difficult for us to trace the contours of that reality in any great detail at the level of the individual or the group. The legal records of the Crown of Aragon, which have been subjected to illuminating analysis by María Teresa Ferrer i Mallol, David Nirenberg, and others, are our best guide to understanding the attitudes and actions of individual participants "on the ground," as it were.

The determination to erect boundaries in order to prevent interfaith sexual relations was the product of a set of overlapping anxieties shared by Christians, Jews and Muslims alike. Robert I. Burns puts it neatly:

> The élites of each of the three groups obsessively feared assimilation. Each fostered its own world of symbol, praxis, and pervasive public expression, while restricting entry into or sharing in the religiously defined societies of the other two peoples. The paradox of daily mingling, economic activities, and osmotic interchanges involving all three peoples did not cancel out this more elemental orientation.[4]

While there were significant differences in the Christian, Islamic, and Jewish legal treatment of women, their respective law codes were patriarchal to their very core and were in agreement that their own women should not marry or indeed indulge in any sexual relationships with men of other faiths. The fear, at a pragmatic level, was that such liaisons would inevitably lead to apostasy on the women's part, which would in turn undermine religious and social cohesion in their own communities. Just as significant, however, such sexual encounters were construed symbolically—on all sides—as an acknowledgement of submission. They were considered acts of dishonor, humiliation, and pollution, both to the women themselves and to their menfolk who had failed to protect them. By explicitly linking the security, sexual honor, and purity of a group's women with the collective honor and identity of their community as a whole, lawgivers and others imbued such sexual unions with intense political meaning. Interfaith sex was targeted by lawgivers, therefore, not because it was rife, although it did undoubtedly occur, but because sexual control was widely regarded as an appropriate instrument by which relative positions of power might be clearly differentiated. In Muslim and Christian Iberia, as in many other religiously or ethnically plural societies, sexuality served as "a loaded metaphor for domination."[5] To consider it part of a "persecuting discourse" is probably wide of the mark. It was precisely because sex was considered such a potent marker of intercultural power relations that Maliki scholars, Christian lawyers, poets, and others felt the need to remind their coreligionists—time and again—of the potential dangers posed by such relationships. As Fredrik Barth has observed, if the social boundaries that a group erects toward other groups serve as a mechanism to maintain its identity, those boundaries will require "continual expression and validation" if they are to remain effective.[6]

For those who transgressed society's rules, like the Muslim or Jewish men who slept with Christian prostitutes, the consequences could be severe. The shepherds who propositioned Alicsén de Tolba in 1304 were acutely conscious that they were breaking the law, which is why the Christian companion of the Muslim Aytola suggested that the latter should adopt a different accent, give a false name, and lie about his background. Yet interfaith sexual politics were almost always asymmetrical. In al-Andalus, Muslim men were able to take Christian wives or concubines with the full acquiescence of Islamic law, whatever misgivings it induced among the religious authorities; in the Christian-ruled realms, the Church may have frowned upon the practice of Christian men taking Muslim or Jewish concubines or frequenting minority prostitutes, but such relationships were not considered to undermine the existing hierarchies of power—indeed, they could be said to have strengthened them—and were rarely punished in law. As Ann Laura Stoler has observed, such sexual asymmetries "convey what is 'really' going on elsewhere, at another political epicenter. They are tropes to depict other centers of power."[7] At the same time, it would be a mistake to regard the discourse of anxiety about interfaith sex as being a constant, unchanging state of mind. Attitudes toward sexual boundary-crossing might vary substantially, depending on the specific context in which they occurred, and could be amplified at times of crisis.[8]

The zeal with which the Christian authorities of the Peninsula sought to police the boundaries between the faiths through the management of sexual relations was by no means a uniquely Iberian phenomenon. The very same concerns to prevent excessive social assimilation and, above all, sexual relations between the faiths can be observed in the crusading realms of the Near East, where an analogous colonial dynamic had come into being at the beginning of the twelfth century. Indeed, one can go a step further and situate the drive to legislate against interfaith sexual mixing within a much broader "discourse of exclusion" that was being articulated in many parts of the Latin West at this time, from the shores of the Baltic to the Mediterranean, as the center began to exert pressure on the periphery. Such exclusionary attitudes were the product of complex and far-reaching changes in Christian society and government. Not least of these was the drive by the reformist papacy to consolidate ecclesiastical authority, which seems to have encouraged a tendency to identify and marginalize those "outsiders" who were not seen to belong within the community of faith. The anxiety toward difference that is plain to see in the Iberian municipal *fueros* of the twelfth and thirteenth centuries, or in the various legendary accounts of interfaith sexual mixing that circulated at the same time, was probably conveyed to Iberia by a variety of routes: by reformist papal legates and French clerics, who visited the region in significant numbers from the late eleventh century onward; by canon lawyers, whose pronouncements began to be widely disseminated south of the Pyrenees at this time; and by Iberian clerics, who had either studied abroad, or had attended papal councils, or were at least well informed about their deliberations. One consequence of the transformation that such men wrought in the structures, practices, and outlook of the Iberian Church was to be the development of markedly more sectarian attitudes toward Islam and Judaism in the Peninsula, which would soon filter down to the level of secular law and custom too.

The demise of the Islamic emirate of Granada in 1492 and the subsequent assertion of Christian religious supremacy—through a program of forced mass conversion or outright expulsion targeted at Jews and Muslims alike—was to mark the death-knell of religious heterodoxy in the Peninsula. Even so, the marked sensitivity toward cultural difference that had been such a striking feature of Christian statecraft and cultural production from the twelfth century onward did not disappear thereafter. During the early modern period, the Spanish Crown and Church, through the institution of the Inquisition, kept watchful guard over the *converso* (converted) population, seeking to root out the "infidelity, apostasy and heretical depravity" of the *conversos*, "persecuting and punishing them to the fullest extent that law and custom allow."[9] Such anxieties were shared by many official institutions (including city councils, universities, and religious orders), which adopted statutes of *limpieza de sangre* (purity of blood) in an attempt to debar anyone of Jewish or Muslim ancestry from holding public office.[10]

In the cultural sphere, meanwhile, two countervailing tendencies were at work. On the one hand, there was increasing engagement with the "Moorishness" of the Peninsula's medieval past, both in the literary imagination and in the realm of material culture.[11] On the other, the militant Christianity of the *Reconquista* was an ever-present source of artistic inspiration, spawning an abundance of works exalting the deeds of martial heroes like El Cid or commemorating such signal events as the expunging of the tribute of the hundred maidens on the battlefield of Clavijo.

Nowhere was the legacy of the medieval past more obvious than in the proliferation of local festivals of *moros y cristianos* (Moors and Christians), those highly choreographed visual spectacles, involving processions, dances, speeches, challenges, and mock battles, in which key episodes of the *Reconquista* were celebrated and reenacted.[12] Such festivities not only came to enjoy popularity in towns and villages across the Peninsula during the late medieval and early modern periods, but also crossed the Atlantic in the wake of the Spanish and Portuguese conquest of the Americas too.[13] The festival of Teotihuacán in colonial New Spain, which commemorated the Battle of Clavijo, provides a striking case in point.[14] The "narrative" of the festival began, somewhat bizarrely, with the character of Pontius Pilate, in the role of the emir of Granada, bemoaning the fact that King Ramiro had refused to honor the terms of the treaty that had been agreed with his predecessor and deliver the stipulated annual tribute of one hundred Christian maidens. Pilate later gathers a Muslim army, while on the Christian side St. James summons King Ramiro, El Cid, and his ambassador, and they resolve to fight to deliver the Christians from the Muslim yoke. First, however, a face-to-face meeting is arranged between the saint and Pilate, at which the former denounces the tribute of the maidens as being "very offensive to a Christian of Castile." St. James sets out his demands, which include the stipulation that Pilate is to convert to Christianity. When Pilate rejects these outright, the Apostle launches a furious riposte in which he denounces both Pilate and the Muslim faith and promises that the emir will suffer a crushing defeat. Sure enough, when battle is joined, the Christians prevail, and the vanquished Muslims pledge allegiance to the Cross.

Festivals like that of Teotihuacán were redolent with symbolic meaning for participants and spectators alike. Although at first sight one might be tempted to view such ceremonies as yet another manifestation of the growing cultural "maurophilia" of the early modern period, their purpose was primarily to reinforce a sense of group identity among Christian communities—on whichever side of the Atlantic they found themselves—by reasserting the ideology of tradition. By performatively deploying the imaginary of the predatory "Moor," threatening and lascivious by turns, Christians were reminded of the threat that had been posed to their communities in the past by the Islamic "Other" and might yet be posed again if the boundaries that had been erected between the faiths were not defended. Such attitudes were given added potency by the fact that from the sixteenth century Islamic military forces continued to threaten Spanish interests, this time in the shape of the Ottoman Turks and Barbary corsairs, whose raids regularly struck Spain's Mediterranean coastline, and with whom Spanish forces repeatedly crossed swords.[15] In the Americas, meanwhile, such festivals similarly served to strengthen group identity among the Spanish colonists, reminding them of their common cultural heritage. They also provided an opportunity to demonstrate to the indigenous peoples the power of the Apostle St. James and other heroes of the faith, and the strength of Christian authority as a whole.[16]

In the modern age, festivals of *moros y cristianos* continue to be celebrated, and indeed have enjoyed a surge in popularity and extravagance in recent times.[17] One factor contributing to this development has been the spectacular growth of the tourist industry since the 1960s, which has led many local communities—particularly in the southeast of the Peninsula—to see the festivals as an opportunity to put their localities "on the map." Equally important, the transition to democracy and the large-scale decentralization of political power since the death of General Franco in 1975 have also encouraged far greater pride in local traditions. Moreover, the fact that Spain's own relationship with the Islamic world has in some respects entered a difficult phase in recent years—exacerbated by Spanish military intervention in Iraq and

Afghanistan, large-scale Moroccan immigration, and the Madrid bombings by Islamist militants in 2004—has given such festivals a heightened ideological "edge."[18]

In their modern incarnation, the festivals defy easy analysis or categorization. While at one level such ceremonies reflect an enduring fascination with Spain's exotic "Moorish" past and very often display a ludic rather than a confrontational tone, at another the participants can be seen to be reaffirming the age-old connection between identity, locality, and tradition.[19] In doing so, they are maintaining—symbolically—clear boundaries between the faiths, restating Christian proprietary rights, both to the locality and, by extension, to the Peninsula as a whole.[20] In this way, maurophilia and maurophobia each continue to shape the identity and outlook of Spaniards today. The rhetoric of "otherness" which was forged by men like Pedro Marcio, over 800 years ago, continues to resonate. That is why to this day, every October, the *cantaderas* sing, dance, and process through the streets of León in honor of their patron saint Froilán. Through such regular acts of commemoration and performance, local communities are not only reminded of the strength of their common cultural roots, but are also brought closer together in the present.

Appendix

The *Privilegio del Voto*

The *Privilegio del* Voto is a forged charter attributed to Ramiro I of Asturias, purportedly issued on 25 May 834 at Calahorra, according to which the king granted an annual tax to the cathedral of Santiago de Compostela (Ms: Santiago de Compostela, Archivo-Biblioteca de la Catedral, carpeta 7, no. 1).

The text here is based on the edition of Antonio López Ferreiro, *Historia de la Santa A.M. Iglesia de Santiago de Compostela*, 5 vols. (Santiago de Compostela: Impr. y Enc. del Seminario Conciliar Central, 1898–1902), 2: 132–37, but has been corrected in places.

In nomine patris et filii et spiritus sancti amen. Antecessorum facta per que successores ad bonum poterunt erudiri, non sunt pretereunda sub silentio, uerum pocius debent comitti monumentis litterarum ut eorum recor / datione ad imitationem bone operationis inuitentur posteri. Ea propter ego rex Renemirus et a Deo michi coniuncta Urracha regina, cum filio nostro rege Ordonio, et fratre meo/mee rege Garsia, oblationem nostram / quam gloriosissimo apostolo dei Iacobo fecimus cum assensu arciepiscoporum, episcoporum abbatum, et nostrorum principum et omnium Hispanie Christianorum litterarum committimus obseruationi, ne forte successores nostri / quod a nobis factum est, per ignorantiam temptent irrumpere, et ut etiam per recordationem nostre operationis, ad similiter operandum moueantur. Causas etiam quibus ad faciendum istam oblationem conpul / si sumus, scribimus ut ad noticiam successorum reseruentur in posterum. Fuerunt igitur in antiquis temporibus, circa destructionem Hispanie a Sarracenis factam rege Ruderico dominante, quidam / nostri antecessores, pigri, negligentes, desides, et inertes Christianorum principes, quorum utique uita nulli fidelium extat imitanda. Hi, quod relatione non est dignum, ne Sarracenorum infestationibus inquietarentur, consti / tuerunt eis nefandos redditus de se annuatim persoluendos, centum uidelicet puellas excellentissime pulcritudinis. Quinquaginta de nobilibus Hispanie, quinquaginta uero de plebe, pro dolor et exemplum posteris non / obseruandum. Pro pactione pacis temporalis et transitorie tradebatur captiua Christianitas luxurie Sarracenorum explende. Ex predictorum principum semine nos perducti, ex quo per Dei misericordiam regni suscepimus guberna / culum, diuina inspirante bonitate predicta nostre gentis obprobria cogitauimus abolere. Hac de tam digna cogitatione perficienda, communicauimus consilium, primo archiepiscopis, episcopis, abbatibus et religiosis uiris, post modum / uero uniuersis nostri regni principibus. Accepto tamen sano et salubri consilio, dedimus apud Legionem legem populis, et posuimus consuetudines per uniuersas nostri regni prouincias obseruandas. Deinde uniuersis nostri / regni principibus edictum commune dedimus quatinus quosque robustos et ad preliandum fortes uiros, tam nobiles quam ignobiles, tam milites quam pedites, ab extremis nostri regni finibus euocarent, et usque ad constitutum / diem in expeditionem facerent congregari. Archiepiscopos etiam et episcopos, abbates et religiosos uiros ut interessent rogauimus quatinus eorum orationibus nostrorum per Dei misericordiam augmentaretur fortitudo. Completum est / itaque imperium nostrum, et relictis ad excolendas terras tantum mode debilibus, et ad bellandum minus idoneis, congregati sunt in expeditionem ceteri, non de nostro imperio

In the name of the Father and the Son and the Holy Spirit. Amen. The deeds of ancestors should not be consigned to silence in order that their successors may be educated in good deeds; rather, on the contrary, they should be consigned to written documents so that, with their memory, those in the future might be invited to imitate good examples. For this reason, I, King Ramiro and the wife that God gave me, Queen Urraca, with our son King Ordoño and my brother King García, submit to writing the gift that we made to the most glorious Apostle of God, James, with the agreement of the archbishops, bishops, and abbots and of our nobles and of all the Christians of Spain, so that our successors should not seek to undo what we have done through ignorance, but rather by remembering our deed they should be inspired to imitate it. We also record the reasons that moved us to make this donation, so that notice of it might reach our successors in the future.

In ancient times, not long after the destruction of Spain by the Saracens in the time of King Roderic, (there were) certain of our predecessors, leading men of the Christians, who were lazy, neglectful, idle and incompetent, whose lives are certainly not worthy of being imitated by any believer. These men, it is unworthy to relate, agreed to pay the Saracens an abominable tribute, in order to avoid being disturbed by their attacks, namely: to give them every year one hundred maidens of extraordinary beauty, fifty from the Spanish nobility, fifty from the common people. Oh, the suffering! What a shameful example for posterity! In exchange for a temporary and short-lived peace agreement, Christianity was handed over captive in order to satisfy the lust of the Saracens.

From the day in which we, descended from the aforementioned princes, took over government, by the grace of God, divine goodness inspiring us to do so, we resolved to abolish such a disgrace from our people. With the aim of carrying out such a worthy undertaking, we communicated our purpose, first to the archbishops, bishops, abbots and holy men, and then to all the nobles of our kingdom. Once such prudent and healthy counsel had been taken, we issued at León a law for the people and established customs, which were to be kept in all the provinces of our kingdom. At the same time, we issued a general decree to all the nobles of our kingdom that they might muster from all the regions of our kingdom men who were strong and ready for war, nobles and commoners alike, horsemen and footsoldiers, gathering them all together on the agreed day to go on campaign. We also asked the archbishops, bishops, abbots and holy men to be present, in order that through their prayers, the strength of our men might be increased by God's mercy.

Once our command had been carried out in this way, and having left behind

sicut solent inuiti, sed Deo ducente per Dei / amorem spontanei. Cum his ego rex Ranamirus de misericordia Dei pocius quam de gentis nostre multitudine confidens, peragiatis inter iacentibus terris, iter mei exitus direxi in Nageram. Hac inde declinaui in lo /cum qui nuncupatur Aluella. Interim autem Sarraceni nostrum aduentum fama precone cognoscentes, omnes cismarini in unum contra nos congregati sunt. Transmarinis etiam per litteras et nuncios in suum auxi /lium conuocatis, inuaserunt nos in multitudine graui et manu ualida. Quid plura? Quod sine lacrimis non recordaremur peccatis exigentibus, multis ex nostris corruentibus, percussi et uulnerati, conuersi sumus in fu- /gam, et confusi peruenimus in collem qui Clauillium nominatur. Hac ibi in una mola congregati, totam fere noctem in lacrimis et orationibus consumpsimus, ignorantes ex toto quid in die essemus postea aucturi. / Interea sompnus arripuit me regem Ranemirum cogitantem multa et anxium de periculo gentis Christiane. At michi dormienti, beatus Iacobus Hispanorum protector corporali specie est se presentare dignatus. Quem / cum interrogassem cum admiratione quisnam esset, apostolus Dei beatum Iacobum se esse confessus est. Cumque ad hoc uerbum ultra quam dici potest obstupuissem, beatus apostoli ait: Numquid ignorabas quod do / minus meus Ihesus Christus alias prouincias aliis fratribus meis apostolis distribuens totam Hispaniam mee tutele per sortem deputasset, et mee commisesset protectioni? Et manu propria manum meam astrigens: Con / fortare inquit et esto robustus. Ego enim ero tibi in auxilium et mane superabis in manu Dei Sarracenorum a quibus obsessus est innumerabilem multitudinem. Multi tamen ex tuis quibus, iam parata est eterna / requies, sunt instanti pugna pro Christi nomine martirii coronam suscepturi. Et ne super hoc detur locus dubitationi, et uos et Sarraceni uidebitis me constanter in albo equo dealbata grandi specie, maximum ue / xillum album deferentem. Summo igitur mane facta peccatorum uestrorum confessione et accepta penitentia, celebratis missis, et accepta Dominici corporis et sanguinis communione armata manu ne dubitetis inuadere / Sarracenorum acies inuocato nomine Dei et meo; pro certo enim noueritis eos in ore gladio ruituros. Et his dictis euanit a conspectu meo uisu desiderabilis Dei apostolus. Ego autem pro tanta et tali uisione uehementer / e sompno excitatus, archiepiscopis, episcopis, abbatibus et religiosis uiris seorsum uocatis, quicquid michi fuerat reuelatum, cum lacrimis et singultibus, et nimia contrictione cordis eodem ordine propalaui. Illi ergo in oratione / prius prouoluti Deo et apostolo pro tam admirabili consolatione gracias egerunt innumeras, ac deinde rem administrare prout nobis fuerat reuelatum, festinarum. Armata itaque et ordinata nostrorum acie, uenimus cum / Sarracenis in pugnam et beatus Dei

to till the fields only those who were weak and least capable of fighting, the others mustered for the departure, not by our command, but spontaneously by the love of God who guided them. Having crossed the neighbouring lands with this small number of people, relying more on God's mercy than on the multitude of my army, I, King Ramiro, set out towards Nájera, from where I came to a place called Albelda. In the meantime, hearing the news of our arrival from a scout, the Saracens gathered together all those on this side of the sea and, having also summoned by letters and messengers those who live across the sea, they attacked us in great numbers and with strong force. What else? The result—which we cannot recall without the tears demanded for our sins—was that when many of ours had fallen, we fled exhausted and wounded, and in confusion we reached the hilltop which they call Clavijo. There we spent almost the whole night crammed together on a rock ledge, sobbing and praying, completely unsure what we were going to do the next day.

Meanwhile, I, King Ramiro, was taken by sleep, as I thought anxiously about the threat to the Christians. And while I slept, there deigned to appear before me in bodily form the blessed James, protector of the Spaniards. And when I, astonished by what I could see, asked him who he was, he assured me that he was the apostle of God the Blessed James. And when I was stunned beyond expression by these words, the blessed apostle said: "Do you not know that my Lord Jesus Christ, handing out the other provinces of the world to my brothers, the other apostles, allotted to my care and placed under my protection all of Spain?" And pressing his hand on mine, he continued: "Be of good cheer and have courage, for I will come to help you, and tomorrow, through God's power, you will vanquish that countless multitude of Saracens by whom you are besieged. However, many of your men for whom eternal rest is prepared and stand ready for battle in the name of Christ will receive the crown of martyrdom. And lest there is any room for doubt, both you and the Saracens will see me constantly dressed in white, on a great white horse, carrying in my hand a great white banner. And so, just before dawn breaks, having received the sacrament of penitence by confessing your sins, Mass having been held and having received the Communion of the body and blood of the Lord, do not fear to attack the battle lines of the Saracens, invoking the name of the Lord and mine, sure of the fact that they are about to fall by the edge of your sword." Having said all of this, the welcome vision of the apostle of God disappeared from my presence.

Then I, having been woken suddenly by such an extraordinary vision, with tears and sobs and great palpitations of the heart, informed the archbishops, bishops and religious men whom I had summoned. So, having first

apostolus apparuit, sicut promiserat utrisque instigando, et in pugnam animando nostrorum aciem, Sarracenorum uero turbas impediendo et diuerberando. Quod quam cito nobis apparuit, cog / nouimus beatissimi apostoli promissionem impletam, et de tam preclara uisione exhilarati, nomen Dei et apostoli in magnis uocibus et nimio cordis affectu, inuocauimus dicentes: Adiuua nos Deus et sancte Iacobe. Que quidem inuocatio ibi tunc / prima fuit facta in Hispania, et per Dei misericordiam non in uanum; eo namque die corruerunt circiter septuaginta millia Sarracenorum. Tunc etiam euersis eorum municionibus eos insequendo ciuitatem Kalaforram cepimus et Christiane re- /ligioni subiecimus. Tantum igitur apostoli miraculum post inopinatam uictoriam considerantes, deliberauimus statuere patrono et protectori nostro beatissimo Iacobo donum aliquod in perpetuum permansurum. Statuimus ergo per totam His / paniam, ac uniuersis Hispaniarum partibus, quascumque Deus sub apostoli Iacobi nomine dignaretur a Sarracenis liberare, uouimus obseruandum, quatinus de uno quoque iugo boum, singule mensure de meliori fruge ad modum primi /ciarum et de uino similiter, ad uictum canonicorum in ecclesia beati Iacobi commorantium annuatim ministris eiusdem ecclesie in perpetuum persoluantur. Concessimus etiam et similiter in perpetuum confirmauimus quod Christiani per / totam Hispaniam in singulis expeditionibus de eo quod a Sarracenis acquisierint ad mensuram porcionis unius militis, glorioso patrono nostro et Hispaniarum protectori beato Iacobo fideliter attribuant. Hec omnia donatiua, uota et / oblationes, sicut superius diximus per iuramentum nos omnes Christiani Hispanie promissimus annuatim ecclesie beati Iacobi, et damus pro nobis et successoribus nostris canonice in perpetuum obseruanda. Petimus ergo pater omnipotens Deus eterne quati- / nus intercedentibus meritis beati Iacobi, ne memineres Domine nostrarum iniquitatum sed sola tua misericordia nobis prosit indignis, et ea que ad honorem tuum beato Iacobo apostolo tuo dedimus et offerimus, de eis que per te ipso opitulante / acquisiuimus, nobis et successoribus nostris proficiant ad remedium animarum, et per eius intercessionem recipere digneris cum electis tuis in eterna tabernacula qui in trinitate uiuis et regnas in secula seculorum amen. Uouemus etiam et in / perpetuum statuimus tenendum quatinus quicumque ex genere nostro descenderint, semper suum prestent auxilium ad pretaxata beati Iacobi donatiua. Quod si quis ex genere nostro uel aliorum ad hoc nostrum testamentum uiolandum / uenerit, uel ad implendum non adiuuerit, quisquis ille fuerit, clericus uel laicus, in inferno cum Iuda traditore et Datan et Abiron quos terra uiuos absorbuit, dampnetur in perpetuum, et filii eius fiant orfani, et uxor eius uidua, et reg / num eius temporale accipiat alter,

offered countless thanks to God in prayer and to the Apostle for such marvellous consolation, they then hurried to put into practice the order that had been given to me. So having armed and arranged our battlelines, we joined battle with the Saracens and the Blessed Apostle of God appeared just as he had promised, goading both sides on, urging on our forces in the battle, and truly hindering and striking the Saracens' hordes. As soon as we saw this, we understood that the promise of the blessed Apostle had been fulfilled and, greatly overjoyed by such a splendid vision, we began to give great shouts which emerged from the depths of our hearts, invoking the name of God and of the Apostle: May God and St. James help us! This, in that place, was the first time that such an appeal had been made in Spain; and by God's mercy not in vain, for this day around seventy thousand Saracens fell on the battlefield. Subsequently, we pursued them, having destroyed their fortifications, and conquered the town of Calahorra and subjected it to the Christian faith.

Reflecting on this unexpected victory by the Apostle's great miracle, we decided to establish for our patron and protector, the most Blessed James, some gift that would last forever. We therefore established throughout Spain, all the regions of the Spaniards, every one of which God had deemed worthy of deliverance from the Saracens in the name of the Apostle James, to pay every year in perpetuity, by way of first fruits, from each yoke of land a measure of the best crops, and the same of wine, to feed the canons who reside in the church of the Blessed James and for the ministers of the same church. We also grant and equally confirm in perpetuity, that the Christians throughout Spain, from the plunder that on each of the expeditions they seize from the Saracens, should give to our glorious patron, the protector of Spain, the Blessed James, exactly that part and portion that corresponds to a knight.

We, all the Christians of Spain, have promised on oath to give every year to the church of the Blessed James all these grants, gifts and offerings that are listed above and thus we have canonically determined that it should be observed by us and our descendants in perpetuity. Therefore, we beseech you Omnipotent Father, Eternal God, that through the merits of the Blessed James you do not remember our wickedness, Lord, but rather that only your mercy should benefit us, though we do not deserve it. And that whatever we give and offer in your honour to the Blessed Apostle James, of the things that through you and his aid we have acquired for ourselves and for our successors, may serve as the remedy of our souls, and through your intercession may you deign to admit us into the eternal dwelling-places with your chosen ones, where you live and reign in Trinity for ever and ever. Amen.

et a communione corporis et sanguinis Christi fiat alienus, eterni uero regni participatione priuetur perhenniter. Insuper regie magestati et ecclesie beati Iacobi per medium pariat sex mille libras argenti. Et hoc scriptum semper maneat in robore. Nos etiam archiepiscopi, episcopi, abbates, qui illud idem miraculum, quod Dominus noster Ihesus Christus famulo suo illustri regi nostro Ranemiro per apostolum suum Iacobum monstrare dignatus est propriis occulis Deo iuuante / uidimus, predictum ipsius regis nostri et nostrum, et totius Hispanie Christianitatis factum, in perpetuum confirmamus et canonice sanccimus observandum. Quod si quis ad hoc scriptum, et ecclesie beati Iacobi apostoli donatiuum ad inrumpendum / uenerit uel persoluere renuerit, quisquis ille fuerit, rex uel princeps, rusticus, clericus, uel laicus, eum maledecimus et excommunicamus, et cum Iuda traditore Gehennali pena dampnamus in perpetuum cruciandum. Hoc idem succes / sores nostri archiepiscopi, episcopi faciant deuote annuatim. Quod si renuerint, omnipotentis Dei patris et filii et spiritus sancti auctoritate et nostra dampnentur et excommunicatione et potestatis sibi a Deo tradite rei teneantur.

Facta scriptura con / solationis, donationis, et oblationis huius, in ciuitate Kalaforra. Noto die VIII kalendarum iunii, era DCCCLXXII. Ego rex Ranemirus cum coniuge mea regina Urracha, et filio nostro rege Ordonio et fratre meo / rege Garsia, hoc scriptum quod fecimus proprio robore confirmamus. Qui presentes fuerunt:

[Column 1]:

Ego Dulcius Cantabriensis archiepiscopus qui presens fui, confirmo.

Ego Suarius Ouetensis episcopus qui presens fui, confirmo.

Ego Oueco asturicensis episcopus qui presens fui, confirmo.

Ego Salomon astoriensis episcopus qui presens fui, confirmo.

Ego Rodericus lucensis episcopus qui presens fui, confirmo.

Ego Petrus hiriensis episcopus qui presens fui, confirmo.

[Column 2]:

Ego regina Urracha, confirmo.

Ego rex Ordonius eius filius confirmo.

Ego rex Garsia frater regis Ranemirus, confirmo.

[Column 3]:

Osorius Petrici regis maiordomus qui presens fui, confirmo.

Pelagius Guterrici regis armiger qui presens fui, confirmo.

Menendus Suarizi potestas terre qui presens fui, confirmo.

Rudericus Gunsaluiz potestas terre qui presens fui, confirmo.

Gudesteus Osorici potestas terre qui presens fui, confirmo.

We also wish and establish that it should be forever observed that whoever descends from our lineage should lend his favour and help to the aforementioned gifts of the Blessed James. And if anyone from our family or of any other should come to break this our testament or does not help to carry it out, whoever he may be, cleric or layman, may he forever be condemned to Hell with Judas the traitor and Dathan and Abiron, whom the earth swallowed whole; and may his children be orphans and his wife a widow; and may his temporal kingdom be possessed by another; and may he be deprived of the Communion of the body and blood of Christ; and may he be forever denied a share in the eternal kingdom. Besides which, let him pay half of six thousand pounds of silver to the royal majesty and the church of the Blessed James. And may this document remain in force always. Furthermore, we the archbishops, bishops and abbots, who with God's assistance saw with our own eyes that very miracle, that our Lord Jesus Christ, through the intercession of his Apostle James, deigned to show his servant, our illustrious king Ramiro, confirm in perpetuity the abovementioned act of donation and gift of the same king, of us and of all the Christians in Spain, and we canonically sanction its observance.

And if anyone should violate this document and donation of the church of the Blessed James or refuse to pay it, whoever he might be, king or nobleman, peasant, cleric or layman, we curse him and excommunicate him, and we condemn him to be tormented in Hell in perpetuity with Judas the traitor. May all our successors as archbishops or bishops do the same faithfully every year. And if they refuse, may they be condemned by our authority and that of God the Father and the Son and the Holy Spirit, and may they, criminals, be held in excommunication and handed over to God's own power.

This charter of confirmation, donation and offering was written in the city of Calahorra on the day known as the eighth of the kalends of June, Era 872 [= 25 May 834]. I, King Ramiro, together with my wife Queen Urraca and our son King Ordoño and my brother King García, confirm this document which we have made with our own sign. These men were present:

[Column 1]:

I, Archbishop Dulcius of Cantabria, who was present, confirm it.

I, Bishop Suero of Oviedo, who was present, confirm it.

I, Bishop Oveco of Astorga, who was present, confirm it.

I, Bishop Salomon of Asturias, who was present, confirm it.

I, Bishop Rodrigo of Lugo, who was present, confirm it.

I, Bishop Pedro of Iria, who was present, confirm it.

Suarius Menendiz, potestas terre qui presens fui, confirmo.
[Column 4]:
Guterre Osoriz potestas qui presens fui, confirmo.
Osorius Guterrici potestas qui presens fui, confirmo.
Ranemirus Garsia potestas qui presens fui, confirmo.
[Column 5]:
Martinus testis.
Petrus testis.
Pelagius testis.
Suarius testis.
Menendus testis.
Vincentius sagio regis testis.
Nos omnes Hispanie terrarum habitatores populi que presentes fuimus et superscriptum miraculum patroni et protectoris nostri gloriosissimi apostoli Iacobi propriis oculis uidimus, et triumphum de Sarracenis per Dei misericordia obtinuimus, quod superius / scriptum est, sanccimus, et in perpetuum confirmamus permansurum.
Ego Petrus Marcius Dei gratia ecclesie beati Iacobi cardinalis, sicut inueni in alio scripto quod in beati Iacobi thesauro et in eius titulo permanet ita scripsi, et hoc translatum feci, et proprio robore confirmaui.
Gondisaluus notuit.

[Column 2]:
I, Queen Urraca, confirm it.
I, King Ordoño his son, confirm it.
I, King García, brother of King Ramiro, confirm it.
[Column 3]:
Osorio Pérez, the king's *maiordomus*, who was present, confirm it.
Pelayo Gutiérrez, the king's *armiger*, who was present, confirm it.
Menendo Suárez, magnate, who was present, confirm it.
Rodrigo González, magnate, who was present, confirm it.
Gudesteo Osóriz, magnate, who was present, confirm it.
Suero Menéndez, magnate, who was present, confirm it.
[Column 4]:
Gutierre Osoriz, noble, who was present, confirm it.
Osorio Gutiérrez, noble, who was present, confirm it.
Ramiro Garcés, noble, who was present, confirm it.
[Column 5]:
Martin, witness.
Pedro, witness.
Pelayo, witness.
Suero, witness.
Menendo, witness.
Vicente, the king's *sayón* [judicial official], witness.
We, all the inhabitants of the lands of Spain, who were present and saw with our own eyes the aforementioned miracle of our patron and protector the most glorious Apostle James and achieved triumph over the Saracens through God's mercy, as is written above, sanction and confirm (this) so that it may remain forever.

I, Pedro Marcio, by the grace of God cardinal of the church of the Blessed James, wrote and made this copy and confirmed it with my own signature as I found it in another document in the treasury of the Blessed James and which remains in its possession.
Gonzalo wrote this.

Abbreviations

AEM	*Anuario de Estudios Medievales*
AHDE	*Anuario de Historia del Derecho Español*
CCCM	*Corpus Christianorum. Continuatio Mediaeualis*
CEISI	Centro de Estudios e Investigación San Isidoro
CEM	*Cantigas d'escarnho e de mal dizer dos cancioneiros medievais galego-portugueses*, ed. Manuel Rodrigues Lapa, 2nd ed. ([Vigo]: Editorial Galaxia, 1970).
CSIC	Consejo Superior de Investigaciones Científicas
CSM	*Corpus scriptorum Muzarabicorum*, ed. Juan Gil. 2 vols. (Madrid: CSIC, 1973)
EEMCA	*Estudios de Edad Media de la Corona de Aragón*
EI²	*Encyclopaedia of Islam*, 2nd ed., ed. P. Bearman, Th. Bianquis, C.E. Bosworth, E. van Donzel, W. P. Heinrichs, et al. 12 vols. (Leiden: Brill, 1960–2009)
JMIS	*Journal of Medieval Iberian Studies*
MGH	*Monumenta Germaniae Historica*

Notes

INTRODUCTION

1. Concepción Alarcón Román, "La antigua ceremonia de las doncellas *Cantaderas* en León," *Revista de dialectología y tradiciones populares* 50 (1995): 179–95; see further Ana Isabel Arias Fernández, "Las cantaderas o el tributo de las cien doncellas," *Argutorio* 15 (2005): 11–15; Ofelia Rey Castelao, "Historia e imaginación: la fiesta ficticia," in Manuel Núñez Rodríguez, ed., *El rostro y el discurso de la fiesta* (Santiago de Compostela: Universidad de Santiago, 1994), 185–96.

2. The legend will be explored in depth in Chapter 3.

3. Atanasio de Lobera, *Historia de las grandezas de la muy antigua e insigne ciudad y Iglesia de León y de su Obispo y Patrón sant Froylan, con las del glorioso San Atilano, obispo de Zamora* (Valladolid: Diego Fernandez de Cordoua, 1596), fols. 215r–220r. On the significance and purposes of Lobera's account, see further Rey Castelao, "Historia e imaginación," 187–92. A century later, the ceremony of Las Cantaderas was also briefly described by Francisco Cabeza de Vaca Quiñones y Guzmán, *Resumen de las políticas ceremonias con que se gobierna la noble, leal y antigua ciudad de León, cabeza de su reino* (Valladolid: Imprenta de Valdivielso, 1693), 36–37. The municipal accounts from León shed further light on the organization and nature of the festivities: see Ana Isabel Arias Fernández, "Tradiciones y celebraciones en León, 1690–1700," in María Antonia de Morán Suárez and María del Carmen Rodríguez López, eds., *La documentación para investigación: homenaje a José Antonio Martín Fuertes* (León: Universidad de León, 2002), 71–97.

4. Francisco López de Úbeda, *La pícara Justina*, ed. Bruno Mario Damiani (Madrid: José Porrúa Turanzas/Studio Humanitatis, 1982), 244.

5. Ibid., 244–45.

6. Ibid., 246.

7. Alarcón Román, "La antigua ceremonia," 186–87, 194–95.

8. Ibid., 195.

9. Lobera, *Historia*, fols. 216v–217r.

10. Ibid., fols. 218r–v. A century later, however, in 1695, the municipal accounts of León record that no fewer than fifteen *comedias* were performed in the city as part of the festivities of Las Cantaderas: Arias Fernández, "Tradiciones y celebraciones," 82 n. 26.

11. The Leonese festivities were but one manifestation of the burgeoning cult of the

Virgin Mary that enjoyed great popularity during the later medieval and early modern periods. The nature of that cult and its social and cultural implications are considered in full by Amy Remensnyder, *La Conquistadora: The Virgin Mary at War and Peace in the Old World and the New* (Oxford: Oxford University Press, 2014).

12. The festivities at Sorzano are subjected to scrutiny by Jesús Gonzalo Moreno, who sees the roots of the present festival in a local fertility ritual: "Aproximación a la procesión de las cien doncellas de Sorzano: orígenes y sentido actual," *Berceo* 122 (1992): 117–26, at 117.

13. For a useful, yet far from comprehensive, introduction, see M. Manzanares de Cirre, "Las cien doncellas: trayectoria de una leyenda," *PMLA* 81 (1966): 179–84; José María Roca Franquesa, "La leyenda 'El tributo de las cien doncellas,'" *Boletín del Instituto de Estudios Asturianos* 5 (1948): 129–63.

14. David Nirenberg, *Communities of Violence: Persecution of Minorities in the Middle Ages* (Princeton, N.J.: Princeton University Press, 1996), 127–65; idem, "Religious and Sexual Boundaries in the Medieval Crown of Aragon," in Mark D. Meyerson and Edward D. English, eds., *Christians, Muslims, and Jews in Medieval and Early Modern Spain: Interaction and Cultural Change* (Notre Dame, Ind.: University of Notre Dame Press, 2000), 141–60; idem, "Conversion, Sex, and Segregation: Jews and Christians in Medieval Spain," *American Historical Review* 107 (2002): 1065–93. See also John Boswell, *The Royal Treasure: Muslim Communities Under the Crown of Aragon in the Fourteenth Century* (New Haven, Conn.: Yale University Press, 1977), 343–53; María Teresa Ferrer i Mallol, *Els sarraïns de la corona catalano-aragonesa en el segle XIV: segregació i discriminació* (Barcelona: CSIC, 1987), 17–39; Brian A. Catlos, *The Victors and the Vanquished: Christians and Muslims of Catalonia and Aragon, 1050–1300* (Cambridge: Cambridge University Press, 2004), 305–12.

15. Louise Mirrer, *Women, Jews, and Muslims in the Texts of Reconquest Castile* (Ann Arbor: University of Michigan Press, 1996), 17–30. On the *soldadeiras*, see Benjamin Liu, "'Affined to love the Moor': Sexual Misalliance and Cultural Mixing in the *Cantigas d'escarnho e de mal dizer*," in Josiah Blackmore and Gregory S. Hutcheson, eds., *Queer Iberia: Sexualities, Cultures, and Crossings from the Middle Ages to the Renaissance* (Durham, N.C.: Duke University Press, 1999), 48–72; Denise Filios, *Performing Women: Sex, Gender, and the Medieval Iberian Lyric* (New York: Macmillan, 2005), 33–82.

16. Janina M. Safran, "Identity and Differentiation in Ninth-Century al-Andalus," *Speculum* 76 (2001): 573–98; eadem, *Defining Boundaries in al-Andalus: Muslims, Christians, and Jews in Islamic Iberia* (Ithaca, N.Y.: Cornell University Press, 2013); Ana Fernández Félix, *Cuestiones legales del islam temprano: la 'Utbiyya y el proceso de formación de la sociedad islámica andalusí* (Madrid: CSIC, 2003), 436–92.

17. Ragnhild Johnsrud Zorgati, *Pluralism in the Middle Ages: Hybrid Identities, Conversion, and Mixed Marriages in Medieval Iberia* (New York: Routledge, 2012).

18. Ibid., 171–78.

19. Fredrik Barth, "Introduction" in Fredrik Barth, ed., *Ethnic Groups and Boundaries: The Social Organization of Culture Difference* (Boston: Little, Brown, 1969), 9–37, at 10.

20. On the question whether normative texts may reflect "historical reality," see the discussion in Zorgati, *Pluralism*, 16–20.

21. Nirenberg, "Conversion, Sex, and Segregation"; idem, "Deviant Politics and

Jewish Love: Alfonso VIII and the Jewess of Toledo," *Jewish History* 21 (2007): 15–41; Jonathan Ray, *The Sephardic Frontier: The* Reconquista *and the Jewish Community in Medieval Iberia* (Ithaca, N.Y.: Cornell University Press, 2006), 165–74. On sexual mixing between Muslims and Jews, see Nirenberg, *Communities of Violence*, 182–88; idem, "Love Between Muslim and Jew in Medieval Spain: A Triangular Affair," in Harvey J. Hames, ed., *Jews, Muslims, and Christians in and Around the Crown of Aragon: Essays in Honour of Professor Elena Lourie* (Leiden: Brill, 2004), 127–55.

22. José María Jover Zamora, "Corrientes historiográficas en la España contemporánea," in idem, *Historiadores españoles de nuestro siglo* (Madrid: Real Academia de la Historia, 1999), 273–310; Ignacio Peiró Martín, "La historiografía española del siglo XX: aspectos institucionales y políticos de un proceso histórico," in Antonio Morales Moya, ed., *Las claves de la España del siglo XX*, vol. VIII. *La cultura* (Madrid: España Nuevo Milenio, 2001), 45–73; Jaume Aurell, "Le médiévisme espagnol au XXème siècle: De l'isolationnisme à la modernisation," *Cahiers de civilisation médiévale* 48 (2005): 201–18.

23. On the development of the notion of *Reconquista* in the modern age and its attendant political baggage, see Martín F. Ríos Saloma, *La Reconquista: una construcción historiográfica (siglos XVI–XIX)* (Madrid: Universidad Nacional Autónoma de Mexico/Marcial Pons, 2011). See also Adam J. Kosto, "Reconquest, Renaissance, and the Histories of Iberia, ca.1000–1200," in Thomas F. X. Noble and John Van Engen, eds., *European Transformations: The Long Twelfth Century* (Notre Dame, Ind.: University of Notre Dame Press, 2012), 93–116.

24. John Tolan, "Using the Middle Ages to Construct Spanish Identity: 19th and 20th Century Historiography of Reconquest," in Jan Piskorski, ed., *Historiographical Approaches to Medieval Colonization of East Central Europe* (Boulder, Colo.: East European Monographs, 2002), 329–47.

25. Marcelino Menéndez y Pelayo, *Historia de los heterodoxos españoles*, 2 vols. (Madrid: Biblioteca de Autores Cristianos, 1956), 2: 1193. See further Douglas W. Foard, "The Spanish Fichte: Menéndez y Pelayo," *Journal of Contemporary History* 14 (1979): 83–97; Peter Linehan, "History in a Changing World," in Linehan, *Past and Present in Medieval Spain* (Aldershot: Ashgate, 1992), Part 1, 1–22, at 11–12.

26. Ramón Menéndez Pidal, *The Spaniards in Their History*, trans. Walter Starkie (London: Hollis & Carter, 1950), 143–44.

27. On Menéndez Pidal's trajectory as a historian, see Simon Barton, "In Search of the Eternal Nation: Ramón Menéndez Pidal and the History of Spain," in Juan-Carlos Conde, ed., *Ramón Menéndez Pidal After Forty Years: A Reassessment*, Papers of the Medieval Hispanic Research Seminar 67 (London: Department of Hispanic Studies, Queen Mary, University of London, 2010), 97–112. On the impact of his work on El Cid on Francoist ideology, see Eukene Lacarra Lanz, "La utilización del Cid de Menéndez Pidal en la ideología militar y franquista," *Ideologies and Literature* 3 (1980): 95–127. However, Menéndez Pidal himself was not an apologist for the Francoist regime and suffered numerous privations at its hands: see further Joaquín Pérez Villanueva, *Ramón Menéndez Pidal: Su vida y su tiempo* (Madrid: Espasa-Calpe, 1991), 381–88; Peter Linehan, "The Court Historiographer of Francoism? *La Leyenda oscura* of Ramón Menéndez Pidal," *Bulletin of Hispanic Studies*

(Glasgow) 73 (1996): 437–50; José Ignacio Pérez Pascual, *Ramón Menéndez Pidal: Ciencia y pasión* (Valladolid: Junta de Castilla y León, 1998), 285–312; Prudencio García Isasti, *La España metafísica: Lectura crítica del pensamiento de Ramón Menéndez Pidal (1891–1936)* (Bilbao: Real Academia de la Lengua Vasca/Euskaltzaindia, 2004), 602–8.

28. Américo Castro, *España en su historia. Cristianos, moros y judíos* (Buenos Aires: Editorial Losada, 1948); trans. Edmund L. King, *The Structure of Spanish History* (Princeton, N.J.: Princeton University Press, 1954). A revised and expanded edition was published as *La realidad histórica de España* (Mexico City: Porrúa, 1954); trans. Willard F. King and Selma Margarretten, *The Spaniards: An Introduction to Their History* (Berkeley: University of California Press, 1971).

29. Claudio Sánchez-Albornoz, *España: un enigma histórico*, 5th ed. (Barcelona: Editora y Distribuidora Hispanoamericana, 1976); trans. Colette Joly Dees and David-Sven Reher, *Spain, a Historical Enigma*, 2 vols. (Madrid: Fundación Universitaria Española, 1975). The debate between Sánchez-Albornoz and Castro has been subjected to scrutiny by José Luis Gómez Martínez, *Américo Castro y el origen de los españoles: historia de una polémica* (Madrid: Gredos, 1975); J. N. Hillgarth, "Spanish Historiography and Iberian Reality," *History and Theory* 24 (1985): 23–43. Sánchez-Albornoz's standpoint has been discussed by Reyna Pastor de Togneri, "Claudio Sánchez-Albornoz y sus claves de la historia de España," *Revista de Historia Jerónimo Zurita* 73 (1998): 117–31.

30. Claudio Sánchez-Albornoz, *Mi testamento histórico-político* (Barcelona: Planeta, 1975), 91.

31. Ignacio Olagüe, *Les Arabes n'ont jamais envahi l'Espagne* (Paris: Flammarion, 1969). His thesis was thoroughly dismantled by Pierre Guichard, "Les Arabes ont bien envahi l'Espagne: les structures sociales de l'Espagne musulmane," *Annales. Economies. Sociétés. Civilisations* 29 (1974): 1483–1513.

32. Aurell, "Le médiévisme espagnol," 212–16.

33. For a defense of the continuing relevance of *convivencia* as a category of scholarly analysis, see Thomas F. Glick and Oriol Pi-Sunyer, "*Convivencia*: An Introductory Note," in Vivian B. Mann, Thomas F. Glick, and Jerrilyn D. Dodds, eds., *Convivencia: Jews, Muslims, and Christians in Medieval Spain*, (New York: George Braziller, 1992), 1–10. On the historiography of *convivencia*, see John Tolan, "Une *convivencia* bien précaire: la place des Juifs et des Musulmans dans les sociétés chrétiennes ibériques au Moyen Âge," in Guy Saupin, Rémy Fabre, and Marcel Launay, eds., *La tolérance: colloque international de Nantes, mai 1998, Quatrième centenaire de l'édit de Nantes*, Centre de Recherche sur l'Histoire du Monde Atlantique (Rennes: Presses Universitaires de Rennes, 1999), 385–94; Kenneth Baxter Wolf, "*Convivencia* in Medieval Spain: A Brief History of an Idea," *Religion Compass* 3 (2009): 72–85; and Maya Soifer, "Beyond *convivencia*: critical reflections on the historiography of interfaith relations in Christian Spain," *JMIS* 1 (2009): 19–35; Simon Doubleday, "Hacia la descolonización del concepto de *convivencia*: algunos apuntes sobre el contexto norteamericano," in Ariel Guiance, ed., *La influencia de la historiografía española en la producción histórica americana* (Madrid: Marcial Pons, 2011), 59–75.

34. See in particular, María Rosa Menocal, *The Ornament of the World: How Muslims, Jews and Christians Created a Culture of Tolerance in Medieval Spain* (Boston: Little, Brown,

2002); David Levering Lewis, *God's Crucible: Islam and the Making of Europe, 570–1215* (New York: Norton, 2005); Simon Doubleday and David Coleman, eds., *In the Light of Medieval Spain: Islam, the West, and the Relevance of the Past* (New York: Palgrave, 2008).

35. Soifer, "Beyond *convivencia*," 21–22.

36. Ibid., 21.

37. See, for example, Jerrilynn D. Dodds, María Rosa Menocal, and Abigail Krasner Balbale, *The Arts of Intimacy: Christians, Jews, and Muslims in the Making of Castilian Culture* (New Haven, Conn.: Yale University Press, 2008); David Wacks, *Framing Iberia: Maqāmāt and Frametale Narratives in Medieval Spain* (Leiden: Brill, 2007).

38. On the difficulties raised by modern interpretations of medieval tolerance, see Glenn Olson, "The Middle Ages in the History of Toleration: A Prolegomena," *Mediterranean Studies* 16 (2007): 1–20; Alex Novikoff, "Between Tolerance and Intolerance in Medieval Spain: An Historiographical Engima," *Medieval Encounters* 11 (2005): 7–36; Cary J. Nederman, "Introduction: Discourses and Contexts of Tolerance in Medieval Europe," in John Christian Laursen and Cary J. Nederman, eds., *Beyond the Persecuting Society: Religious Toleration Before the Enlightenment* (Philadelphia: University of Pennsylvania Press, 1998), 13–24; Soifer, "Beyond *convivencia*," 22–23.

39. Brian A. Catlos, "Contexto y conveniencia en la corona de Aragon: propuesta de un modelo de interacción entre grupos etno-religiosos minoritarios y mayoritarios," *Revista d'História Medieval* 12 (2001–2): 259–68; idem, *The Victors and the Vanquished*, 407. The primacy of pragmatism in shaping interfaith relations is also emphasized by Christopher Lowney, *A Vanished World: Medieval Spain's Golden Age of Enlightenment* (New York: Free Press, 2005), 189, 204.

40. Those who have embraced anthropological approaches include Pierre Guichard, *Al-Andalus: estructura antropológica de una sociedad islámica en occidente* (Barcelona: Barral Editores, 1976); Catlos, *The Victors and the Vanquished*; Thomas F. Glick and Oriol Pi-Sunyer, *Islamic and Christian Spain in the Early Middle Ages*, rev. 2nd ed. (Leiden: Brill, 2005).

41. For an overview see Nadia R. Altschul, "Postcolonialism and the Study of the Middle Ages," *History Compass* 6, 2 (2008): 588–606; eadem, "The Future of Postcolonial Approaches to Medieval Iberian studies," *JMIS* 1 (2009): 5–17.

42. Altschul, "The Future," 14.

43. The primacy of the frontier in Iberian history is writ large in Angus MacKay, *Spain in the Middle Ages: From Frontier to Empire, 1000–1500* (London: Macmillan, 1977) and Charles J. Bishko, *Studies in Medieval Spanish Frontier History* (London: Variorum, 1980). See further Elena Lourie, "A Society Organized for War: Medieval Spain," *Past and Present* 35 (1966): 54–76; Manuel González Jiménez, "Frontier and Settlement in the Kingdom of Castile (1085–1350)," in Robert Bartlett and Angus MacKay, eds., *Medieval Frontier Societies* (Oxford: Oxford University Press, 1989), 49–74; James F. Powers, *A Society Organized for War: The Iberian Municipal Militias in the Central Middle Ages, 1000–1284* (Berkeley: University of California Press, 1988); Philippe Sénac, *La frontière et les hommes (VIIIe–XIIe siècle): Le peuplement musulman au nord de L'Ebre et les débuts de la reconquête aragonaise* (Paris: Maisonneuve et Larose, 2000); Carlos de Ayala Martínez, Pascal Buresi,

and Philippe Josserand, eds., *Identidad y representación de la frontera en la España medieval (siglos XI–XIV)* (Madrid: Casa de Velázquez/Universidad Autónoma de Madrid, 2001); and Pascal Buresi, *La frontière entre chrétienté et Islam dans la péninsule Ibérique: du Tage à la Sierra Morena (fin XIe–milieu XIIIe siècle)* (Paris: Publibook, 2004), to name only a few of the most significant works. For an incisive critique of "frontier interaction" in the Peninsula, see Peter Linehan, "At the Spanish Frontier," in Peter Linehan and Janet L. Nelson, eds., *The Medieval World* (London: Routledge), 37–59.

44. David Abulafia, "Introduction: Seven Types of Ambiguity, c.1100–c.1500," in David Abulafia and Nora Berend, eds., *Medieval Frontiers: Concepts and Practices* (Aldershot: Ashgate, 2002), 1–34. For a survey of historiographical approaches to the medieval frontier, see Nora Berend, *At the Gate of Christendom: Jews, Muslims and "Pagans" in Medieval Hungary, c.1000–c.1300* (Cambridge: Cambridge University Press, 2001), 6–17.

45. Eduardo Manzano Moreno, "The creation of a medieval frontier: Islam and Christianity in the Iberian Peninsula, eighth to eleventh centuries," in Daniel Power and Naomi Standen, eds., *Frontiers in Question: Eurasian Borderlands, 700–1700* (Basingstoke: Macmillan, 1999), 32–54, at 51. Cf. Eduardo Manzano Moreno, *La frontera de al-Andalus en época de los omeyas* (Madrid: CSIC, 1991), 25–26.

46. See, for example, Ann Christys, "Christian-Muslim Frontiers in Early Medieval Spain," *Bulletin of International Medieval Research* 5 (1999): 1–19; eadem, "Crossing the Frontier of Ninth-Century Hispania," in Abulafia and Berend, eds., *Medieval Frontiers*, 35–53; Robert I. Burns, "Renegades, Adventurers and Sharp Businessmen: The Thirteenth-Century Spaniard in the Cause of Islam," *Catholic Historical Review* 58 (1972): 341–66. On the passage of mercenaries across the frontier, see Simon Barton, "Traitors to the Faith? Christian Mercenaries in al-Andalus and the Maghreb, 1100–1300," in Roger Collins and Anthony Goodman, eds., *Medieval Spain: Culture, Conflict and Coexistence: Studies in Honour of Angus MacKay* (Basingstoke: Palgrave Macmillan, 2002), 23–45; idem, "From Mercenary to Crusader: The Career of Álvar Pérez de Castro (d. 1239) reconsidered," in Julie Harris and Therese Martin, eds., *Church, State, Vellum and Stone: Essays on Medieval Spain in Honor of John Williams* (Leiden: Brill, 2005), 111–29; Brian Catlos, "Mahomet Abenadalill: A Muslim Mercenary in the Service of the Kings of Aragon (1290–1291)," in Hames, ed., *Jews, Muslims, and Christians*, 257–302.

47. Benita Sampedro Vizcaya and Simon Doubleday, "Introduction," in Benita Sampedro Vizcaya and Simon Doubleday, eds., *Border Interrogations: Questioning Spanish Frontiers* (New York: Berghahn, 2008), 1–14, at 2–3.

CHAPTER 1. SEX AS POWER

1. ʿAbd al-Malik b. Ḥabīb, *Kitāb al-Taʾrīkh (La historia)*, ed. Jorge Aguadé (Madrid: CSIC, 1991), 136–49; *The History of the Conquest of Egypt, North Africa, and Spain. Known as the Futūḥ Miṣr of Ibn ʿAbd al-Ḥakam*, ed. Charles C. Torrey (New Haven, Conn.: Yale University Press, 1922), 204–13; English translation in *Christians and Moors in Spain*, vol. 3, *Arabic Sources*, ed. and trans. Charles Melville and Ahmad Ubaydli (Warminster: Aris &

Phillips, 1992), 14–17; *Medieval Iberia: Readings from Christian, Muslim and Jewish Sources*, ed. Olivia R. Constable, 2nd ed. (Philadelphia: University of Pennsylvania Press, 2011), 36–40. On the purposes of these and other authors, see Eduardo Manzano Moreno, "Las fuentes árabes sobre la conquista de al-Andalus: una nueva interpretación," *Hispania* 202 (1999): 389–432; idem, *Conquistadores, emires y califas: los omeyas y la formación de al-Andalus* (Barcelona: Crítica, 2006), 35–39; Alejandro García Sanjuán, "Formas de sumisión del territorio y tratamiento de los vencidos en el derecho islámico clásico," in Maribel Fierro and Francisco García Fitz, eds., *El cuerpo derrotado: cómo trataban musulmanes y cristianos al enemigo vencido* (Madrid: CSIC, 2008), 61–112; Nicola Clarke, "Medieval Arabic accounts of the conquest of Córdoba: Creating a narrative for a provincial capital," *Bulletin of the School of Oriental and African Studies* 74 (2011): 41–57; eadem, *The Muslim Conquest of Iberia: Medieval Arabic Narratives* (Abingdon: Routledge, 2011).

2. Ibn al-Qūṭīya, *Taʾrīkh iftitāḥ al-Andalus*, ed. Ibrāhīm al-Abyārī (Cairo: Dār al-Kitāb al-Miṣrī; Beirut: Dār al-Kitāb al-Lubnānī, 1982); English translation by David James, *Early Islamic Spain: The* History *of Ibn al-Qūṭīya* (London: Routledge, 2009). On his purpose in writing, see María Isabel Fierro, "La obra histórica de *Ibn al-Qūṭīya*," *Al-Qanṭara* 10 (1989): 485–511; Ann Christys, *Christians in al-Andalus, 711–1000* (Richmond: Curzon, 2002), 158–83; James, *Early Islamic Spain*, 38–41.

3. On the Islamic conquest, see Roger Collins, *The Arab Conquest of Spain 710–797* (Oxford: Blackwell, 1989); Hugh Kennedy, *Muslim Spain and Portugal: A Political History of al-Andalus* (London: Longman, 1996), 3–18; Pedro Chalmeta Gendrón, *Invasión e islamización: la sumisión de Hispania y la formación de al-Andalus*, 2nd ed. (Jaén: Universidad de Jaén, 2003); Manzano Moreno, *Conquistadores*.

4. *Crónica mozárabe de 754*, ed. and trans. José Eduardo López Pereira (Zaragoza: Anubar Ediciones, 1980), 72–73. The chronicle is translated into English by Kenneth Baxter Wolf, *Conquerors and Chroniclers of Early Medieval Spain*, 2nd ed. (Liverpool: Liverpool University Press, 1999), 111–60. One such noble may have been Pelayo, on whom see further below.

5. Bishop Sindered of Toledo, who is reported to have abandoned his flock and fled to Rome, is a case in point: *Crónica mozárabe*, 70–71.

6. It is reported that Mūsā b. Nuṣayr took with him a large number of captives on his return to Syria: for example, *Crónica mozárabe*, 74–75. This is confirmed by the testimony of the English pilgrim Willibald, later bishop of the German see of Eichstätt, who reportedly met one such Spaniard when he visited Syria in 723: Huneberc of Heidenheim, *Vita Willibaldi episcope Eichstetensis*, ed. Oswald Holder-Egger, *MGH, Scriptores* 15:1 (Hanover: *Impensis Bibliopolii Hahniani*, 1887), 80–117, at 86–88; trans. C. H. Talbot, *The Anglo-Saxon Missionaries in Germany* (London: Sheed and Ward, 1954), 162–63; reprinted in Thomas Noble and Thomas Head, eds., *Soldiers of Christ: Saints' Lives from Late Antiquity and the Early Middle Ages* (University Park: Pennsylvania State University Press, 1994), 141–64. For executions, see *Crónica mozárabe*, 70–71; cf. *Ajbar Machmuâ (Colección de tradiciones)*, ed. and trans. Emilio Lafuente y Alcántara (Madrid: Rivadeneyra, 1867), 9–11, 23–27 (Spanish translation).

7. Melville and Ubaydli, eds., *Christians and Moors in Spain*, 10–13 (with English

translation); *Medieval Iberia*, ed. Constable, 45–46. The *Chronicle of 754* provides a lengthy tribute to Theodemir, whom it describes as a "warlike man" (*uir belliger*): *Crónica mozárabe*, 112–14. See further Eduardo Manzano Moreno, "Árabes, bereberes e indígenas: al-Andalus en su primer período de formación," in Miquel Barceló and Pierre Toubert, eds., *L'Incastellamento: Actas de las reuniones de Girona (26–27 November 1992) y de Roma (5–7 May 1994)* (Rome: École française de Rome; Escuela española de historia y arqueología en Roma, 1998), 157–77, at 166. On the reliability of such capitulation treaties, see Chase F. Robinson, *Empire and Elites After the Muslim Conquest: The Transformation of Northern Mesopotamia* (Cambridge: Cambridge University Press, 2000), 6–15; cf. Collins, *The Arab Conquest*, 39–40; Chalmeta Gendrón, *Invasión e islamización*, 213–20; García Sanjuán, "Formas de sumisión," 74–76.

8. Manzano Moreno, "Árabes, bereberes e indígenas," 167.

9. Qur'ān 5:5, trans. N. J. Dawood, *The Koran*, 4th ed. (Harmondsworth: Penguin, 1974). On Islamic legislation concerning mixed marriages, see Yohanan Friedmann, *Tolerance and Coercion in Islam: Interfaith Relations in the Muslim Tradition* (Cambridge: Cambridge University Press, 2003), 160–93; Zorgati, *Pluralism*, 104–13. See also Maya Shatzmiller, "Marriage, Family, and the Faith: Women's Conversion to Islam," *Journal of Family History* 21 (1996), 235–66, at 243–44; Safran, *Defining Boundaries*, 103–6.

10. Jessica A. Coope, *The Martyrs of Córdoba: Community and Family Conflict in an Age of Mass Conversion* (Lincoln: University of Nebraska Press, 1995), 12. That said, there is evidence from other parts of the Islamic world to suggest that in comparison to men Christian women were more likely to resist conversion: Shatzmiller, "Marriage, Family, and the Faith," 236–37.

11. Friedmann, *Tolerance and Coercion*; Zorgati, *Pluralism*, 109–13.

12. Vincent Lagardère, *Histoire et société en occident musulman au moyen age: analyse du* Mi'yār *d'al-Wanšarīsī* (Madrid: Casa de Velázquez; CSIC, 1995), 72; al-Qayrawānī, *Risala ou traité abrégé de Droit Malékite et Morale Musulmane*, trans. Edmond Fagnan (Paris: Geunther, 1914), 193. See further Fernández Félix, *Cuestiones legales*, 436–92; Zorgati, *Pluralism*, 142–56.

13. Usefully summarized by Nirenberg, *Communities of Violence*, 129–33. On Iberian Jewish attitudes toward sexual mixing, see Yitzhak Baer, *A History of the Jews in Spain*, 2 vols. (Philadelphia: Jewish Publication Society, 1961), 1: 322–33; Ray, *The Sephardic Frontier*, 165–75; Nirenberg, *Communities of Violence*, 134–36.

14. On the canons of the council of Elvira, see *La colección canónica hispana* 4: *Monumenta Hispaniae Sacra*, ed. Gonzalo Martínez Díez and Félix Rodríguez (Madrid: CSIC, 1984), 247, 267. For the Visigothic prohibitions, see III Toledo, canon 14; IV Toledo, canon 63; X Toledo, canon 7, in *La colección canónica hispana* 5: *Concilios hispanos: segunda parte*, ed. Gonzalo Martínez Díez and Felix Rodríguez (Madrid: CSIC, 1992), 120–21, 239–40, 551.

15. On 'Abd al-Azīz b. Mūsā, see Chalmeta Gendrón, *Invasión e islamización*, 242–54; Guichard, *Al-Ándalus*, 187–97.

16. *Crónica mozárabe*, 76–78.

17. Ibn 'Abd al-Ḥakam, *Futūḥ Miṣr*, 212; trans. in Constable, ed., *Medieval Iberia*, 39–40.

18. Ibn al-Qūṭīya claimed that the assassination was carried out on the direct orders of the caliph: *Ta'rīkh*, 36–37; trans. James, *Early Islamic Spain*, 53.

19. Al-Rāzī's *Akhbār Mulūk al-Andalus* survives in later Romance reworkings: see *Crónica del Moro Rasis: versión del ajbār mulūk al-Andalus de aḥmad ibn muḥammad ibn mūsa al-rāzī, 899–955; romanzada para el rey don Dionís de Portugal hacia 1300 por mahomad, alarife, y Gil Pérez, clérigo de don perianes porçel*, ed. Diego Catalán and María Soledad de Andrés (Madrid: Editorial Gredos-Seminario Menéndez Pidal, 1970), 363; and *Edición crítica del texto español de la Crónica de 1344 que ordenó el Conde de Barcelos don Pedro Alfonso*, ed. Diego Catalán and María Soledad de Andrés (Madrid: Gredos-Seminario Menéndez Pidal, 1970), 161. The episode of the crown-wearing by 'Abd al-Azīz is also recounted by, among others, *Ajbar Machmuâ*, 20 (Arabic), 31–32 (Spanish); *Fatḥ al-Andalus*, ed. Luis Molina (Madrid: CSIC, 1994), 42; Ibn al-Qūṭīya, *Ta'rīkh*, 36–37; trans. James, *Early Islamic Spain*, 53. For a useful analysis of the sources, see Manzano Moreno, "Las fuentes árabes," 409–12; and see further Maribel Fierro, *La heterodoxia en al-Andalus durante el periodo omeya* (Madrid: Instituto Hispano-Árabe de Cultura, 1987), 17–18; eadem, "Pompa y ceremonia en los califatos del Occidente islámico (ss. II/VIII–IX/XV)," *Cuadernos del CEMYR* 17 (2009): 125–52, at 127–28.

20. "Marriage and the control of inheritance are . . . the very heart of the solution to the conquerors' problems": Eleanor Searle, "Women and the legitimisation of succession at the Norman Conquest," in R. Allen Brown, ed., *Proceedings of the Battle Conference 1980* (Woodbridge: Boydell, 1981), 159–70, at 169. However, Elisabeth van Houts has recently emphasized that exogamous marriages appear to have been relatively rare in England: "Intermarriage in Eleventh-Century England," in David Crouch and Kathleen Thompson, eds., *Normandy and Its Neighbours 900–1250: Essays for David Bates* (Turnhout: Brepols, 2011), 237–70. On the importance of intermarriage as a strategy of conquest by the Normans in Italy, see Joanna H. Drell, "The Aristocratic Family," in Graham Loud and Alex Metcalfe, eds., *The Society of Norman Italy* (Leiden: Brill, 2002), 97–113, at 110–11. On marriage as a political tool in Norman Ireland, see Gillian Kenny, *Anglo-Irish and Gaelic Women in Ireland* (Dublin: Four Courts Press, 2007), 85–91.

21. Collins, *The Arab Conquest*, 37–38.

22. *Ajbar Machmuâ*, 20 (Arabic), 32 (Spanish); Ibn 'Idhārī al-Marrākushī, *Al-Bayān al-mughrib fi akhbār al-Andalus wa'l-Maghrib*, ed. Évariste Lévi-Provençal, Georges S. Colin, and Iḥsān 'Abbās, 4 vols. (Paris: Geuthner, 1930; Leiden: Brill, 1948–51; Beirut: Dār al-Thaqāfah, 1967), 2: 23. For other examples of interfaith marriage in al-Andalus, see Manuela Marín, *Mujeres en el-Ándalus: estudios onomástico-biográficos de al-Andalus*, 11 (Madrid: CSIC, 2000), 141–47.

23. Manzano Moreno, "Las fuentes árabes"; Chalmeta, *Invasión e islamización*, 202–13.

24. For what follows, see Ibn al-Qūṭīya, *Ta'rīkh*, 29–32; trans. James, *Early Islamic Spain*, 49–51.

25. Guichard, *Al-Ándalus*, 187–92.

26. See the discussion in Christys, *Christians in al-Andalus*, 158–83; Manzano Moreno, *Conquistadores*, 44–46.

27. Roger Collins, *Visigothic Spain, 409–711* (Oxford: Blackwell, 2004), 138.

28. Al-ʿUdhrī, *Nuṣūṣ ʿan al-Andalus min kitāb Tarṣī al-akhbār wa-tanwīʿ al-āthār wa l-bustān fī garāʾib al-buldān wa-al-masālik ilā jamīʿ al-mamālik.*, ed. ʿAbd al-ʿAzīz al-Ahwānī (Madrid: Instituto de Estudios Islámicos, 1965), 15. See further Luis Molina, "Los Banū Jaṭṭāb y los Banū Abī Ŷamra (siglos II–VIII/VIII–XIV)," in Manuela Marín and Jesús Zanón, eds., *Estudios onomástico-biográficos de al-Andalus*, vol. 5 (Madrid: CSIC, 1992), 289–307, at 289–90 and n. 6.

29. Guichard, *Al-Ándalus*, 192–96; Manzano Moreno, *Conquistadores*, 107–8.

30. Ibn al-Qūṭīya, *Taʾrīkh*, 57–60; trans. James, *Early Islamic Spain*, 75–77.

31. *Crónica mozárabe*, 114. The chronicler claimed that Abūʾl-Khaṭṭār levied a fine of 27,000 *solidi*, on prompt payment of which Athanagild was restored to the favor of the governor. However, the suspicion remains that the terms of the pact agreed by Theodemir had lapsed by that stage: Collins, *The Arab Conquest*, 191.

32. Manzano Moreno, *Conquistadores*, 115–16.

33. There has been extensive discussion of the problems raised by the early Christian sources. See, in particular, Manuel Gómez Moreno, "Las primeras crónicas de la Reconquista: el ciclo de Alfonso III," *Boletín de la Real Academia de la Historia* 100 (1932): 562–623; Jan Prelog, *Die Chronik Alfons' III: Untersuchung und kritische Edition der vier Redaktionen* (Frankfurt am Main: Peter Lang, 1980). For the texts themselves, see *Crónicas asturianas*, ed. and trans. Juan Gil Fernández, José L. Moralejo, and Juan I. Ruiz de la Peña (Oviedo: Universidad de Oviedo, 1985). For an English translation of the Roda version of the *Chronicle of Alfonso* III, see Wolf, *Conquerors and Chroniclers*, 161–77.

34. *Crónicas asturianas*, 122.

35. By the late thirteenth century it was being claimed that Munnuza was a Christian who had pledged support to the Muslims; the much earlier Asturian chronicles do not support this assertion: *Primera crónica general de España*, ed. Ramón Menéndez Pidal, 2 vols. (Madrid: Editorial Gredos, 1977), 1: 319[a].

36. *Crónicas asturianas*, 122–24.

37. Ibid., 173.

38. Collins, *The Arab Conquest*, 149.

39. *Epistolae Merowingici et Karolini Aevi*, ed. Wilhelm Gundlach, Ernst Dümmler, et al., *MGH: Epistolae* 3 (Berlin: Weidmann, 1892), 643.

40. On Egila and his activities in the Peninsula, see Collins, *Arab Conquest*, 219–21, 222; John C. Cavadini, *The Last Christology of the West: Adoptionism in Spain and Gaul, 785–820* (Philadelphia: University of Pennsylvania Press, 1993), 138 nn. 32, 37–38, 139 nn. 39, 41–42.

41. *CSM* 1: 136.

42. Marín, *Mujeres*, 141–42.

43. The martyrdom movement has generated a sizeable bibliography. Good starting points are Kenneth Baxter Wolf, *Christian Martyrs in Muslim Spain* (Cambridge: Cambridge University Press, 1988); Coope, *The Martyrs of Córdoba*; Christys, *Christians in al-Andalus*, 52–79. For an estimate of the rate of conversion to Islam in al-Andalus, see Richard Bulliet, *Conversion to Islam in the Medieval Period* (Cambridge, Mass.: Harvard University Press, 1979), 114–27. On the problems raised by Bulliet's methodology, see Alwyn Harrison,

"Behind the Curve: Bulliet and Conversion to Islam in al-Andalus Revisited," *Al-Masāq* 24 (2012): 35–51.

44. Eulogius, *Memoriale sanctorum, Documentum martyriale, and Liber apologeticus martyrum*, in *CSM* 2: 363–459, 459–75, 475–95; trans. María Jesús Aldana García, *Obras completas de San Eulogio: Introducción, traducción, y notas* (Córdoba: Universidad de Córdoba, 1998). Paul Albar, *Indiculus luminosus* and *Vita Eulogii*, in *CSM* 1: 270–315, 330–43; the latter is translated by Carleton M. Sage, *Paul Albar of Cordoba: Studies on His Life and Writings* (Washington, D.C.: Catholic University of America Press, 1943), 190–214.

45. Christys, *Christians in al-Andalus*, 52–79.

46. Wolf, *Christian Martyrs*, 23–35; Coope, *Martyrs of Córdoba*, 11–31, 70–79.

47. Fierro, *La heterodoxia*, 53–57. On the legal status of children born to such mixed marriages, see Ana Fernández Félix, "Children on the Frontiers of Islam," in Mercedes García Arenal, ed., *Conversions islamiques: identités religieuses en Islam méditerranéen* (Paris: Maisonneuve & Larose, 2002), 61–72, at 62–65.

48. Coope, *Martyrs of Córdoba*, 29.

49. *Documentum martyriale*, 20.9: *CSM* 2: 471; *Memoriale Sanctorum*, I.1.19: *CSM* 2: 370.

50. *Vita Eulogii*, 13: *CSM* 1: 337. Muslims are again compared to wolves in Albar, *Indiculus Luminosus*, prologue, 10: *CSM* 1: 271, 283; Eulogius, *Memoriale Sanctorum*, I, 1: *CSM* 2: 370. The topos of the predatory wolf as a symbol of heresy was well established in Christian tradition.

51. Coope, *The Martyrs*, 14.

52. See Lagardère, *Histoire et société*, 53–54; Safran, *Defining Boundaries*, 122–24.

53. Coope, *The Martyrs*, 30–31; Shatzmiller, "Marriage, Family, and the Faith," 257–58.

54. Julián Ribera y Tarragó, *El cancionero de Abencuzmán*, in *Disertaciones y opúsculos*, 2 vols. (Madrid: Imprenta de Estanislao Maestre, 1928), 1: 12–26. Cf. Évariste Lévi-Provençal, *Histoire de l'Espagne Musulmane*, 3 vols. (Paris and Leiden: G.-P. Maisonneuve; Brill, 1950–53), 3: 174.

55. Guichard, *Al-Ándalus*, 20–23, 55–85, 181–240.

56. Ibn Ḥazm, *Kitāb Jamharat ansāb al-ʿArab*, ed. ʿAbd al-Salām Muḥammad Hārūn (Cairo: Dār al-Maʿārif, 1962). Partial Spanish trans. by Elías Terés, "Linajes árabes en al-Andalus, según la 'Ŷamhara' de Ibn Ḥazm," *Al-Andalus* 22 (1957), 55–112; and Fernando de la Granja, "La marca superior en la obra de al-'Udrí," *EEMCA* 8 (1967): 447–545, at 532–34. On the purposes of the work, see Jessica Coope, "Marriage, Kinship, and Islamic Law in Al-Andalus: Reflections on Pierre Guichard's *Al-Ándalus*," *Al-Masāq* 20 (2008): 161–77, at 165–68.

57. Ibn Ḥazm, *Naqṭ al-ʿarūs*, ed. C. F. Seybold, trans. Luis Seco de Lucena (Valencia: Anubar Ediciones, 1974), 94–95 (Spanish), 160–61 (Arabic).

58. Safran, "Identity and Differentiation," 583–84; eadem, *Defining Boundaries*, 129.

59. Muḥammad b. Waḍḍaḥ, *Kitāb al-bidaʿ (Tratado contra las innovaciones)*, ed. María Isabel Fierro (Madrid: CSIC, 1988), 205.

60. The essential guide is Safran, *Defining Boundaries*.

61. See above, nn. 17 and 19. Manzano Moreno, "Las fuentes árabes," 411.

62. Gabriel Martinez-Gros, *Identité andalouse* (Paris: Sindbad, 1997), 115–66.

63. Christys, *Christians in al-Andalus*, 171. Jessica Coope has further challenged the Eastern kinship model defended by Guichard, arguing that bilateral kinship, which allowed women to inherit property, was established well before the late tenth century: Coope, "Marriage, Kinship, and Islamic Law," 161–77.

64. Maribel Fierro, "Genealogies of Power in al-Andalus: Politics, Religion and Ethnicity During the Second/Eighth-Fifth/Eleventh Centuries," *Annales Islamogiques* 42 (2008): 29–55, at 34.

65. A riposte to Martinez-Gros may be seen in Pierre Guichard, "A propos de l'identité andalouse: quelques éléments pour un débat," *Arabica* 46 (1999): 97–110. This in turn was followed by Gabriel Martinez-Gros, "Comment écrire l'histoire de l'Andalus? Réponse a Pierre Guichard," *Arabica* 47 (2000): 261–73. Manuela Marín has used the evidence of biographical dictionaries to argue that the *'ulamā* of al-Andalus frequently married outside their extended families: Manuela Marín, "Parentesco simbólico y matrimonio entre los ulemas Andalusies," *Al-Qantara* 16 (1995): 335–56.

66. Abdurrahman Ali El-Hajji, "Intermarriage Between Andalusia and Northern Spain in the Umayyad Period," *Islamic Quarterly* 11 (1967): 3–7; Guichard, *Al-Ándalus*, 181–86.

67. For what follows, see *Crónica mozárabe*, 96–98.

68. Collins, *The Arab Conquest*, 88–89.

69. For an overview, see Alberto Cañada Juste, "Los Banu Qasi (714–924)," *Príncipe de Viana* 48–49 (1980): 5–95; idem, "El posible solar originario de los Banū Qasī," in *Homenaje a José María Lacarra en su jubilación del profesorado: Estudios Medievales*, 2 vols. (Zaragoza: Anubar, 1977), 1: 33–38. See also Roger Collins, *The Basques*, 2nd ed. (Oxford: Blackwell, 1990), 123–24, 140–43; Manzano Moreno, *La frontera*, 110–24, 293–304.

70. Ibn Ḥazm, *Jamharat*, 502; trans. De La Granja, "La marca superior," 532.

71. Collins, *The Arab Conquest*, 204; Roger Collins, *Early Medieval Spain: Unity in Diversity, 400–1000*, 2nd ed. (Basingstoke: Macmillan, 1995), 188; Collins, *The Basques*, 141; Julia Pavón Benito, "Muladíes: Lectura política de una conversión: Los Banū Qasī (714–924)," *Anaquel de Estudios Árabes*, 17 (2006): 189–202; Jesús Lorenzo Jiménez, "Algunas consideraciones acerca del conde Casio," *Studia Histórica: Historia Medieval* 27 (2009): 173–80; idem, *La dawla de los Banū Qasī: Origen, auge y caída de un linaje muladí en la Frontera Superior de Al-Andalus* (Madrid: CSIC, 2010); Maribel Fierro, "El conde Casio, los Banu Qasi y los linajes godos en al-Andalus," *Studia Histórica: Historia Medieval* 27 (2009): 181–89.

72. Ibn Ḥazm, *Jamharat*, 502–3; trans. De La Granja, "La marca superior," 533–34. On the probable Visigothic origins of the Banū Qasī, see now Eduardo Manzano Moreno, "A vueltas con el conde Casio," *Studia Histórica: Historia Medieval* 31 (2013): 255–66.

73. *Crónicas asturianas*, 146–47.

74. Guichard, *Al-Ándalus*, 231–32. The extensive marriage ties of the Banū Qasī with their neighbors are usefully displayed in the table compiled by Lévi-Provençal, *Histoire de l'Espagne*, 1, between 388 and 389.

75. José María Lacarra, "Textos navarros del Códice de Roda," *EEMCA* 1 (1945): 194–283, at 229. On the content of the *Codex* and its depiction of Muslims, see Philippe Sénac,

"Note sur les musulmans dans les *Génealogies* de Roda," in Amaia Arizaleta, ed., *Poétique de la chronique: L'écriture des textes historiographiques au Moyen Age (Péninsule Ibérique et France)* (Toulouse: Université de Toulouse-Le Mirail, 2008), 37–46.

76. Al-'Udhrī, *Nuṣūṣ'an al-Andalus*, 62; trans. De La Granja, "La marca superior," 516.

77. Al-'Udhrī, *Nuṣūṣ'an al-Andalus*, 68; trans. De La Granja, "La marca superior," 525.

78. On the Banū Shabrīṭ and the Banū Amrūs, see María Jesús Viguera, *Aragón musulman* (Zaragoza: Mira Editores, 1988), 76–78, 96–97, 105, 112–15, 122–24, with genealogy at 114; Philippe Sénac, "Les Seigneurs de la Marche (*aṣḥābu al-ṭagri*): les Banū 'Amrūs et les Banū Šabrīṭ de Huesca," *Cuadernos de Madīnat al-Zahrā* 7 (2010): 27–42.

79. Lacarra, "Textos navarros," 243–44.

80. Ibn Ḥayyān, *Al-Muqtabas V*, ed. Pedro Chalmeta et al. (Madrid-Rabat: Instituto Hispano-Arabe de Cultura, 1979), 468; Spanish translation by María Jesús Viguera and Federico Corriente, *Crónica del califa 'Abarraḥmān III an-Nāṣir entre los años 912 y 942 (al-Muqtabis V)* (Zaragoza: Anubar Ediciones/Instituto Arabe de Cultura, 1981), 352.

81. El-Hajji, "Intermarriage"; Guichard, *Al-Ándalus*, 185–86.

82. Lacarra, "Textos navarros," 231.

83. Lévi-Provençal, *Histoire*, 2: 2.

84. *Una descripción anónima de al-Andalus*, ed. and trans. Luis Molina, 2 vols. (Madrid: CSIC, 1983), 1: 187 (Arabic), 2: 198 (Spanish); idem, "Las campañas de Almanzor a la luz de un nuevo texto," *Al-Qanṭara* 2 (1981): 209–63, at 246–47. The princess is called 'Abda in some sources: El-Hajji, "Intermarriage," 4, n. 9.

85. Marín, *Mujeres*, 564–65 and n. 597.

86. Pelayo de Oviedo, *Crónica del Obispo Don Pelayo*, ed. Benito Sánchez Alonso (Madrid: Centro de Estudios Históricos, 1924; trans. Simon Barton and Richard Fletcher, *The World of El Cid: Chronicles of the Spanish Reconquest* (Manchester: Manchester University Press, 2000), 74–89. For an introduction to the life and works of Pelayo, see Francisco Javier Fernández Conde, *Libro de los Testamentos de la catedral de Oviedo* (Rome: Iglesia Nacional Española, 1971), 35–80; Barton and Fletcher, *The World of El Cid*, 65–74.

87. Pelayo, *Crónica*, 63–65.

88. For what follows, see also Simon Barton, "Marriage across frontiers: sexual mixing, power and identity in Medieval Iberia," *JMIS* 3 (2011): 1–25, at 12–17.

89. Manuel Lucas Álvarez, ed., *La documentación del Tumbo A de la catedral de Santiago de Compostela: Estudio y edición* (León: CEISI, Caja España de Inversiones, Caja de Ahorros y Monte de Piedad, Archivo Histórico Diocesano, 1997), no. 90; José María Fernández del Pozo, "Alfonso V, rey de León," in *León y su historia: miscelánea histórica*, vol. 5 (León: CEISI, 1984), 9–262, at 243–44.

90. Lucas Álvarez, ed., *La documentación del Tumbo A*, nos. 93–94.

91. Ghislaine Fournes, "Iconologie des infantes (*Tumbo* A et *Tumbo* B de la cathédrale de Saint-Jacques de Compostelle et *Tumbo* de Touxos Outos)," *e-Spania* (6 December 2008): http://e-spania.revues.org/index12033.html (last accessed 24.7.13)

92. Hilda Grassotti, "Vindicación de doña Teresa," in Hilda Grassotti, *Estudios medievales españoles* (Madrid: Fundación universitaria española, 1981), 449–58, at 453.

93. Reinhardt Dozy, *Recherches sur l'histoire et la littérature de l'Espagne pendant le*

Moyen Age, 3rd ed., 2 vols. (Paris: Brill, 1881), 1: 184–92, at 186–87. The story was also echoed by a later writer, who put into Teresa's mouth the following stinging riposte: "A people should entrust its honour to the spears of its warriors and not to the thighs of its women": Lévi-Provençal, *Histoire*, 2: 243–44.

94. Dozy, *Recherches*, 1: 187. His view was supported by Justo Pérez de Urbel, "Los primeros siglos de la Reconquista (años 711–1038)," in Justo Pérez de Urbel and Ricardo del Arco y Garay, *España cristiana: Comienzo de la Reconquista (711–1038). Historia de España [dirigida por Ramón Menéndez Pidal]*, vol. 6 (Madrid: Espasa Calpe, 1956), 1–348, at 173.

95. Emilio Cotarelo, "El supuesto casamiento de Almanzor con una hija de Bermudo II," *La España Moderna* 169 (1903): 42–55; Claudio Sánchez-Albornoz, "El ejército y la guerra en el reino asturleonés, 718–1037," *Settimane di Studio del Centro Italiano de studi sull'alto medioevo* 15 (1968): 293–428, at 421 n. 450; Grassotti, "Vindicación"; Fernández del Pozo, "Alfonso V," 38; José María Fernández del Pozo, *Alfonso V (999–1028). Vermudo III (1028–1037)* (Burgos: La Olmeda, 1999), 29–33. Menéndez Pidal also discussed the episode, although he did not pass judgment on the reliability of Pelayo's account: Ramón Menéndez Pidal, *Historia y epopeya* (Madrid: Junta para Ampliación de Estudios e Investigaciones Científicas; Centro de Estudios Históricos, 1934), 18–21.

96. See above n. 84; Cotarelo, "El supuesto casamiento," 54–55; Grassotti, "Vindicación," 451.

97. Fernández del Pozo, "Alfonso V," 41–50, 69–78, 84–87. On al-Muẓaffar's campaigns, see Fernández del Pozo, "Alfonso V," 54–56. A charter of 5 February 1003 records that it had been drawn up "in presentia qui ibi fuit zacbascorta Eben Bacri quando uenit de Cordoba pro pace confirmare ad Romanos in Domnos Sanctos": Marta Herrero de la Fuente, ed. *Colección diplomática del monasterio de Sahagún (857–1230): II (1000–1073)* (León: CEISI, Caja de Ahorros y Monte de Piedad, Archivo Histórico Diocesano, 1988), no. 380.

98. Ibn Idhārī al-Marrākushī, *Al-Bayān*, 3: 39; trans. Felipe Maíllo Salgado, *La caída del Califato de Córdoba y los Reyes de Taifas (al-Bayān al-Mugrib)* (Salamanca: Estudios Árabes e Islámicos, Universidad de Salamanca, 1993), 44.

99. Ibn Idhārī al-Marrākushī, *Al-Bayān*, 3: 5; trans. Maíllo Salgado, *La caída del Califato*, 13–14.

100. On Count Sancho Gómez, see Margarita Torres Sevilla-Quiñones de León, "Un tradicional ejemplo de confusión genealógica: a proposito de la muerte de Abd al-Rahman 'Sanchuelo' y Sancho ibn Gómez (1009)," *Estudios humanísticos: Geografía, historia, arte* 19 (1997): 67–73; eadem, *Linajes nobiliarios de León y Castilla (siglos IX–XIII)* (Valladolid: Junta de Castilla y León, Consejería de Educación y Cultura, 1999), 255. For an alternative identification, see Peter Scales, *The Fall of the Caliphate of Córdoba: Berbers and Andalusis in Conflict* (Leiden: Brill, 1994), 53–54.

101. On the expedition and death of 'Abd al-Raḥmān, see Ibn Idhārī al-Marrākushī, *Al-Bayān*, 3: 49–50, 66–74; Maíllo Salgado, *La caída del Califato*, 53–55, 68–74. See also the account of al-Nuwayrī, in Aḥmad b. Muḥammad al-Maqqarī, *The History of the Mohammedan Dynasties in Spain*, trans. Pascual de Gayangos, 2 vols. (London: Oriental Translation Fund of Great Britain and Ireland, 1840–43), 2: 486–90.

102. Ibn Idhārī al-Marrākushī, *Al-Bayān*, 3: 42; trans. Maíllo Salgado, *La caída del Califato*, 47. See further Maribel Fierro, "On Political Legitimacy in al-Andalus: A Review Article," *Der Islam: Zeitschrift für Geschichte und Kultur des islamischen Orients* 73 (1996): 138–50, at 141.

103. Lucas of Tuy, *Chronicon Mundi*, ed. Emma Falque, *CCCM* 74 (Turnhout: Brepols, 2003), 274–75.

104. Ibn Idhārī al-Marrākushī, *Al-Bayān*, 3: 68; trans. Maíllo Salgado, *La caída del Califato*, 70.

105. Ibid., 71.

106. Rodrigo Jiménez de Rada, *De rebus Hispanie sive Historia Gothica*, ed. Juan Fernández Valverde, *CCCM* 72 (Turnhout: Brepols, 1987), 167; Spanish translation by Juan Fernández Valverde, *Historia de los hechos de España* (Madrid: Alianza Editorial, 1989), 210.

107. David Wasserstein, "The Emergence of the Taifa Kingdom of Toledo," *Al-Qanṭara* 21 (2000): 17–56.

108. See above, n. 41.

109. See, for example, Richard Fletcher, *The Episcopate in the Kingdom of León in the Twelfth Century* (Oxford: Oxford University Press, 1978), 181–82; Thomas Deswarte, *Une Chrétienté romaine sans pape: l'Espagne et Rome (586–1085)* (Paris: Garnier, 2010), 313–49. For the wider picture, see Gerd Tellenbach, *The Church in Western Europe from the Tenth to the Early Twelfth Century*, trans. Timothy Reuter (Cambridge: Cambridge University Press, 1993), 72–73.

110. Cited by Richard Fletcher, *Saint James's Catapult: The Life and Times of Diego Gelmírez* (Oxford: Oxford University Press, 1984), 192.

111. For an overview of the political situation, see Collins, *Early Medieval Spain*, 181–265.

112. On Queen Toda, see Roger Collins, "Queens-Dowager and Queens-Regnant in Tenth-Century León and Navarre," in John Carmi Parsons, ed., *Medieval Queenship* (Basingstoke: Palgrave Macmillan, 1997), 79–92, at 87–89. On the queen's embassy to Córdoba, see Lévi-Provençal, *Histoire*, 2: 70–73.

113. Ibn Ḥazm, *Jamharat*, 503; trans. De La Granja, "La marca superior," 534.

114. Ibn Ḥayyān, *Crónica de los emires Alḥakam I y ʿAbdarraḥmān II entre los años 796 y 847 [Almuqtabis II–1]*, trans. Maḥmūd ʿAlī Makkī and Federico Corriente (Zaragoza: Instituto de Estudios Islámicos y del Oriente Próximo, 2001), 304–6. On this episode, see Christys, "Crossing the Frontier"; María Jesús Viguera Molins, "Una andalusí en Galicia y sus cuatro 'transgresiones,'" in Francisco Toro Ceballos and José Rodríguez Molina, eds., *VIII Estudios de Frontera. Mujeres y fronteras. Homenaje a Cristina Segura* (Jaén: Diputación de Jaén, 2010), 497–516.

115. Évariste Lévi-Provençal, "Hispano-Arábica: la 'Mora Zaida,' femme d'Alphonse VI de Castille et leur fils l'infant D. Sancho," *Hespéris* 18 (1934): 1–8; Alberto Montaner Frutos, "La mora Zaida, entre historia y leyenda (con una reflexión sobre la técnica historiográfico alfonsí," in Barry Taylor and Geoffrey West, eds., *Historicist Essays on Hispano-Medieval Narrative in Memory of Roger M. Walker* (London: Maney Publishing; Modern Humanities Research Association, 2005), 272–52.

116. Qur'ān, 4:3; 23:6; 33:50–52; 70:30. On the institution of Islamic concubinage, see Joseph Schacht, "Umm al-Walad," *EI*², 10: 857–59; Robert Brunschvig, "'Abd," *EI*², 1: 24–40; S. E. Marmon, "Concubinage, Islamic," in *Dictionary of the Middle Ages*, ed. Joseph R. Strayer, 13 vols. (New York: Scribner for American Council of Learned Societies, 1982–89), 3: 527–29; Georges Henri Bousquet, *L'éthique sexuelle de l'Islam* (Paris: Maisonneuve et Larose, 1966), 93–100; Cristina de la Puente, "Límites legales del concubinato: normas y tabúes en la esclavitud sexual según la *Bidāya* de Ibn Rušd," *Al-Qanṭara* 28 (2007): 409–33; eadem, "Entre la esclavitud y la libertad: consecuencias legales de la manumisión según el derecho māliki," *Al-Qanṭara* 21 (2000): 339–60, at 344–48; Khalil 'Athamina, "How Did Islam Contribute to Change the Status of Women: The Case of the *jawārī*, or the Female Slaves," *Al-Qanṭara* 28 (2007): 383–408; Kecia Ali, *Marriage and Slavery in Early Islam* (Cambridge, Mass.: Harvard University Press, 2010), 164–72; Zorgati, *Pluralism*, 130–34. On literary perceptions of *jawārī*, see Fedwa Malti-Douglas, *Woman's Body, Woman's Word: Gender and Discourse in Arabo-Islamic Writing* (Princeton, N.J.: Princeton University Press, 1991), 33–38. On the position of female slaves in al-Andalus, see further Guichard, *Al-Ándalus*, 170–76; Marín, *Mujeres*, 125–40.

117. D. Fairchild Ruggles, "Mothers of a Hybrid Dynasty: Race, Genealogy, and Acculturation in al-Andalus," *Journal of Medieval and Early Modern Studies* 34 (2004): 65–94, with a useful genealogical diagram at 70.

118. Guichard, *Al-Ándalus*, 173.

119. Al-Maqqarī called her "Athl," "tamarisk": *The History of the Mohammedan Dynasties*, trans. Gayangos, 2: 131.

120. Laura Bariani, "De las relaciones entre Ṣubḥ y Muḥammad Ibn Abī 'Āmir al-Manṣūr, con especial referencia a su 'ruptura' (waḥša) en 386–388/996–998," *Qurṭuba* 1 (1996): 39–57; Manuela Marín, "Una vida de mujer: Ṣubḥ," in María Luisa Ávila and Manuela Marín, eds., *Biografías y género biográfico en el occidente islámico*, Estudios onomástico-biográficos de al-Andalus 8 (Madrid: CSIC, 1997), 425–45; Nada Mourtada-Sabbah and Adrian Gully, ""I am by God, fit for High Positions": on the Political Role of Women in al-Andalus," *British Journal of Middle Eastern Studies* 30 (2003): 183–209, at 191–95; Philippe Sénac, *Al-Mansûr: Le fléau de l'an mil* (Paris: Perrin, 2006), 18–20, 29–30, 32–33, 61, 70–74.

121. Marín, "Una vida de mujer," 436.

122. Ibid., 436–37.

123. *Una descripción anónima*, 1: 174 (Arabic), 2: 184 (Spanish).

124. Cristina de la Puente, "La caracterización de Almanzor: entre la epopeya y la historia," in Ávila and Marín, eds., *Biografías y género biográfico*: 367–402, at 377–78, 386–87.

125. Charles Verlinden, *L'esclavage dans l'Europe médiévale*, 2 vols. (Bruges: De Tempel, 1955), 1: 181–247; Ribera, *Cancionero*, 17–23; Olivia Remie Constable, *Trade and Traders in Muslim Spain: The Commercial Realignment of the Iberian Peninsula, 900–1500* (Cambridge: Cambridge University Press, 1994), 203–7; eadem, "Muslim Spain and Mediterranean slavery: the medieval slave trade as an aspect of Muslim-Christian relations," in Scott L. Waugh and Peter. D. Diehl, eds., *Christendom and Its Discontents: Exclusion, Persecution and Rebellion, 1000–1500* (Cambridge: Cambridge University Press, 1996), 264–84.

126. Constable, *Trade and Traders*, 205. On the high value attached to female singers elsewhere in the Islamic world, see ʿAthamina, "How Did Islam," 400–403.

127. ʿAthamina, "How did Islam," 392 and nn. 46–48; Bernard Lewis, *Race and Slavery in the Middle East: an historical enquiry* (New York: Oxford University Press, 1990), 9 and refs therein.

128. Ribera, *El cancionero*, 1: 24–25. On Jewish slavers, see Constable, *Trade and Traders*, 204–5; eadem, "Muslim Spain and Mediterranean Slavery," 267–68.

129. *Liber testamentorum coenobii laurbanensis*, ed. Aires A. Nascimento and José María Fernández Catón, 2 vols. (León: CEISI, 2008), doc. no. 71.

130. *Diplomatari de la Catedral de Barcelona: Documents dels anys 844–1260*, ed. Àngel Fàbrega i Grau, 1 (Barcelona: Fundació Noguera, 1995), no. 172. On those taken prisoner, see Pierre Bonnassie, *La Catalogne du milieu du Xe à la fin du XIe siècle: croissance et mutations d'une société*, 2 vols. (Toulouse: Université de Toulouse-Le Mirail), 1: 344–46.

131. For what follows, see Ibn Idhārī al-Marrākushī, *Al-Bayān*, 3: 21–23; trans. Maíllo Salgado, *La caída del Califato*, 28–30. The castle in question may have been that of San Martín de Rubiales, situated on the north bank of the River Duero between Roa and Peñafiel.

132. For a discussion of the Maliki position on the treatment of prisoners, see Safran, *Defining Boundaries*, 200–201.

133. Lucas Álvarez, ed., *La documentación del Tumbo A*, no. 52.

134. On the ransom of élite Christians after the fall of Barcelona in 985, see Bonnassie, *La Catalogne*, 1: 344.

135. Ibn Ḥawqal, *Kitāb ṣūrat al-arḍ* (Beirut: Dār Maktabat al-Ḥayāh, 1964), 105–6; trans. María José Romaní Suay, *Configuración del mundo* (Valencia: Anúbar, 1971), 62. On the functioning of slave markets in the Islamic world more broadly, see Youssef Ragib, "Les marchés aux esclaves en terre d'Islam," in *Mercati e mercanti nell'alto Medioevo: l'area euroasiastica e l'area mediterránea*, Settimane di studio del centro italiano di studi sull'alto Medioevo 40 (1993): 721–63.

136. The bibliography on Muslim slaves in Christian Iberia is extensive. For a starting point, see Jacques Heers, *Esclaves et domestiques au moyen âge dans le monde méditerranéan* (Paris: Fayard, 1981); and the collection of studies in Maria Teresa Ferrer i Mallol and Josefa Mutgé i Vives, eds., *De l'esclavitud a la llibertat: esclaus i lliberts a l'Edat Mitjana: actes del col·loqui internacional celebrat a Barcelona, del 27 al 29 de maig de 1999* (Barcelona: CSIC, 2000). See further Stephen Bensch, "From Prizes of War to Domestic Merchandise: The Changing Face of Slavery in Catalonia and Aragon, 1000–1300," *Viator* 25 (1994): 63–94; Josep Hernando, *Els esclaus islàmics a Barcelona: Blancs, negres, llors i turcs. De l'esclavitud a la llibertat (S.XIV)* (Barcelona: CSIC, 2003); Ana Echevarría Arsuaga, "Esclavos musulmanes en los hospitales de cautivos de la Orden militar de Santiago (siglos XII y XIII)," *Al-Qanṭara* 28 (2007): 465–88; François Soyer, "Muslim Slaves and Freemen in Medieval Portugal," *Al-Qanṭara* 28 (2007): 489–516.

137. ʿAbd al-Wāḥid ibn ʿAlī al-Marrākushī, *Kitāb al-Muʿjib fī talkhīṣ akhbār al-Maghrib*, ed. Reinhardt Dozy, *The History of the Almohades by Abdo-'l-Wahid al-Marrekoshî*, 2nd ed. (Amsterdam: Oriental Press, 1968), 26; Spanish translation by Ambrosio Huici Miranda, in

Colección de crónicas árabes de la Reconquista, 4 (Tetuán: Editora Marroquí, 1955), 30. In the late eleventh century a white female slave in the markets of Córdoba might fetch 28 dinars, about the same as a horse: Lévi-Provençal, *Histoire*, 3: 259.

138. *Una descripción anónima*, 1: 185–95 (Arabic), 2: 196–204 (Spanish).

139. Ibn Idhārī al-Marrākushī, *Al-Bayān*, 3: 13; trans. Maíllo Salgado, *La caída del Califato*, 20–21.

140. *Colección documental del Archivo de la catedral de León (775–1230)*, III (986–1031), ed. José Manuel Ruiz Asencio (León: CEISI; CSIC-CECEL; Caja de Ahorros y Monte de Piedad; Archivo Histórico Diocesano, 1987), no. 648. The copy of the document preserved in the *Tumbo Legionense* gives the date as the Spanish Era 1003, that is, A.D. 1065, which is probably attributable to an error on the scribe's part, who seems to have omitted the *x aspado* (denoting 40) in the date: see the discussion in ibid., 186.

141. Ibid., no. 803.

142. On the trauma suffered by the Christians after the sack of Barcelona, for example, see Bonnassie, *La Catalogne*, 1: 344–45.

143. María Jesús Viguera, "Aṣluḥu li'l-ma'ālī: On the social status of Andalusī women," in Salma Khadra Jayyusi, ed., *The Legacy of Muslim Spain*, 2 vols. (Leiden: Brill, 1992), 2: 709–24, at 717–18. For a similar perspective, in an Abbasid context, see Nadia Maria El Cheikh, "Gender and Politics in the Harem of al-Muqtadir," in Leslie Brubaker and Julia M. H. Smith, eds., *Gender in the Early Modern World: East and West, 300–900* (Cambridge: Cambridge University Press, 2004), 147–61.

144. Marín, *Mujeres*, 143–44; Jarbel Rodriguez, *Captives and Their Saviors in the Medieval Crown of Aragon* (Washington, D.C.: Catholic University of America Press, 2007), 50. On the legal status of children of captives, see Fernández Félix, "Children on the Frontiers of Islam," 66–67; and Daniel König, "Caught Between Cultures? Bicultural Personalities as Cross-Cultural Transmitters in the Late Antique and Medieval Mediterranean," in Rania Abdellatif, Yassir Benhima, Daniel König, and Elisabeth Ruchaud, eds., *Acteurs des transferts culturels en Méditerranée médiévale* (Munich: Oldenbourg, 2012), 56–72, at 62–63.

145. Dozy, *Recherches*, 1: 191–92.

146. Ibn Ḥayyān, *Al-Muqtabas V*, 11–12 (Arabic), 17–18 (Spanish).

147. Ibid., 7 (Arabic), 14 (Spanish).

148. John Beckwith, *Caskets from Cordoba* (London: HMSO, 1960), 10–13 and Plate 6. The casket may be viewed on-line at http://www.discoverislamicart.org/database_item.php?id=object;ISL;es;Mus01;14;en [last accessed 24.7.2013]

149. Ibn Ḥayyān, *Al-Muqtabas V*, 37–38 (Arabic); 40–41 (Spanish).

150. Marín, *Mujeres*, 688–89, 698–700.

151. Ibid., 682–85.

152. Claude Lévi-Strauss, *The Elementary Structures of Kinship*, ed. Rodney Needham, trans. James Harle Bell, John Richard von Sturmer, and Rodney Needham (London: Eyre & Spottiswoode, 1969), 67–68.

153. See, for example, the collected papers in Raymond Cohen and Raymond Westbrook, eds., *Amarna Diplomacy: The Beginnings of International Relations* (Baltimore: Johns Hopkins University Press, 2000), in particular 79–83, 162–64, 165–73, 180–83, 197–98.

154. Julian Pitt-Rivers, *The Fate of Shechem, or The Politics of Sex: Essays in the Anthropology of the Mediterranean* (Cambridge: Cambridge University Press, 1977), 166.

155. Ruth Mazo Karras, *Sexuality in Medieval Europe: Doing unto Others* (London/ New York: Routledge, 2005), 25.

156. Guichard, *Al-Ándalus*, 85–86.

157. See also in this context Guichard, *Al-Ándalus*, 185–86; Marín, *Mujeres*, 142, 553–54. Cf. Leslie P. Peirce, *The Imperial Harem: Women and Sovereignty in the Ottoman Empire* (Oxford: Oxford University Press, 1993), 36–37.

158. Ibn Darrāj al-Qasṭallī, *Dīwān*, ed. Maḥmūd 'Alī Makkī (Beirut: al-Maktab al-Islāmī, 1969); there is a Spanish translation of selected poems by Margarita la Chica Garrido, *Almanzor en los poemas de Ibn Darrāŷ* (Zaragoza: Anubar Ediciones, 1979). On the career of Ibn Darrāj, see Régis Blachère, "La vie et l'oeuvre du poète-épistolier andalou Ibn Darrâǧ al-Kasṭallī," *Hespéris* 36 (1933): 99–121. *Hespéris,*. On the significance of his work, see also Maḥmūd 'Alī Makkī, "La España cristiana en el diwan de Ibn Darrāŷ," *Boletín de la Real Academia de Buenas Letras de Barcelona* 30 (1963–64): 63–104.

159. Ibn Darrāj al-Qasṭallī, *Diwān*, no. 104; trans. Chica Garrido, *Almanzor*, 88–90.

160. Ibn Darrāj al-Qasṭallī, *Diwān*, no. 105; trans. Chica Garrido, *Almanzor*, 90–93.

161. Ibn Darrāj al-Qasṭallī, *Diwān*, no. 111; trans. Chica Garrido, *Almanzor*, 106–9.

162. Ibn Darrāj al-Qasṭallī, *Diwān*, no. 107; trans. Chica Garrido, *Almanzor*, 96–99. On the embassy of King Sancho to Córdoba, see further Lévi-Provençal, *Histoire*, 2: 242–43.

163. Rodríguez, *Captives and Their Saviors*, 49–50.

164. For modern parallels, see Matthias Bjørnlund, "'A Fate Worse Than Dying': Sexual Violence During the Armenian Genocide," in Dagmar Herzog, ed., *Brutality and Desire: War and Sexuality in Europe's Twentieth Century* (Basingstoke: Palgrave, 2008), 16–58, at 33–41; Claudia Card, "Rape as a Weapon of War," *Hypatia* 11 (1996): 5–18, at 5.

165. For the premodern period, see Kathy L. Gaca, "Girls, women, and the significance of sexual violence in ancient warfare," in Elizabeth D. Heineman, ed., *Sexual violence in conflict zones: From the Ancient World to the era of human rights* (Philadelphia: University of Pennsylvania Press, 2011), 73–88; Corinne Saunders, "Sexual Violence in Wars: The Middle Ages," in Hans-Henning Kortüm, ed., *Transcultural Wars from the Middle Ages to the 21st Century* (Berlin: Akademie Verlag, 2006), 151–64. In an Iberian context, see Maribel Fierro, "Violence against women in Andalusi historical sources (third/ninth-seventh/thirteenth centuries)," in Robert Gleave and István Kristó-Nagy, eds., *Violence in Islamic Thought from the Qur'an to the Mongols* (Edinburgh: University of Edinburgh Press, forthcoming). I am grateful to Professor Fierro for sending me a copy of her paper prior to publication.

166. See further Ruth Seifert, "The Second Front: The Logic of Sexual Violence in Wars," *Women's Studies International Forum* 19 (1996): 35–43, at 39; Card, "Rape as a Weapon," 11; Herzog, ed., *Brutality and Desire*, passim. For a more nuanced analysis, see James Mark, "Remembering Rape: Divided Social Memory and the Red Army in Hungary 1944–1945," *Past & Present* 188 (2005): 133–61.

167. Anna Roberts, "Introduction: Violence Against Women and the Habits of Thought," in Anna Roberts, ed., *Violence Against Women in Medieval Texts* (Gainesville: University Press of Florida, 1998), 1–21, at 6.

168. Seifert, "The Second Front," 37.

169. Janina M. Safran, *The Second Umayyad Caliphate: The Articulation of Caliphal Legitimacy in al-Andalus* (Cambridge, Mass.: Harvard University Press, 2000), 76–85, 220–21.

170. Ibn Ḥayyān, *Al-Muqtabas V*, 401–2 (Arabic); 339–40 (Spanish); Safran, *The Second Umayyad Caliphate*, 78–79.

171. Ibn Darrāj al-Qasṭallī, *Diwān*, no. 116; trans. Chica Garrido, *Almanzor*, 120–22. The executions probably took place in 997: Makkī, "La España cristiana," 77–78.

172. Sénac, *Al-Mansûr*, 114–15.

173. Ibn Idhārī al-Marrākushī, *Al-Bayān*, 3: 97; trans. Maíllo Salgado, *La caída del Califato*, 91.

174. Murray Gordon, *Slavery in the Arab World* (New York: New Amsterdam Books, 1989), 88.

175. Ruggles, "Mothers of a Hybrid Dynasty," 72.

176. Ibn Ḥazm, *Ṭawq al-Ḥamāma fi al-ulfa wa-al-ullāf*, ed. Al-Tahir Ahmad Makki, 3rd ed. (Cairo: Dār al-Ma'ārif, 1980), 48–49; English trans. A. J. Arberry, *The Ring of the Dove by Ibn Hazm: A Treatise on the Art and Practice of Arab Love* (London: Luzac Oriental, 1953), 61–62. Those same physical characteristics were noted in the Umayyad princess Wallāda, daughter of caliph Muḥammad al-Mustakfī III (1025), who is said to have refused to wear a *ḥijāb* when promenading through the streets of Córdoba, so that her beauty might be displayed to all: Wilhelm Hoenerbach, "Notas para una caracterización de Wallāda," *Al-Andalus* 36 (1971): 467–73; Teresa Garulo Muñoz, "La biografía de Wallada, toda problemas," *Anaquel de Estudios Árabes* 20 (2009): 97–116.

177. Marín, *Mujeres*, 542.

178. On the 'Abbasid harem, see Hugh Kennedy, *The Court of the Caliphs: The Rise and Fall of Islam's Greatest Dynasty* (London: Weidenfeld & Nicolson, 2004), 167–68, 172–99; 'Athamina, "How Did Islam," 395–98; on Ottomans, see Peirce, *The Imperial Harem*, 28–56.

179. Marín, *Mujeres*, 555–57.

180. Henri Pérès, *La poésie andalouse en arabe classique au XIe siècle: ses aspects géneraux, ses principaux thèmes et sa valeur documentaire*, 2nd ed. (Paris: Adrien-Maisonneuve, 1953), 284–87; 'Athamina, "How Did Islam," 397; Ruggles, "Mothers of a Hybrid Dynasty," 77.

181. Coope, "Marriage, Kinship, and Islamic Law," 166.

182. Fierro, "Genealogies of Power," 30. Similar criticisms had earlier been aimed at the Umayyad rulers in the Near East, but hostility toward sons of slave women began to recede thereafter: 'Athamina, "How Did Islam," 394–98.

183. Pierre Bourdieu, *Masculine Domination* (Stanford, Calif.: Stanford University Press, 2001), 44.

Chapter 2. Marking Boundaries

1. For an overview of this process of Christian territorial expansion, see Joseph F. O'Callaghan, *A History of Medieval Spain* (Ithaca, N.Y.: Cornell University Press, 1975), 333–57.

2. *Epistolae Merowingici*, 1: 643; *CSM*, 1:136.

3. *Los Fueros del Reino de León*, ed. Justiniano Rodríguez Fernández, 2 vols. (León: Ediciones Leonesas, 1981), 2: 14–23, § 25.

4. On the Council of Coyanza, see Alfonso García Gallo, "El Concilio de Coyanza: Contribución al estudio del Derecho canónico español en la Alta Edad Media," *AHDE* 20 (1950): 275–633. Section 6 of the decrees issued at Coyanza enjoined Christians to avoid being in the same house with Jews on the Sabbath or sharing meals with them, but did not address the matter of sexual relations. On the Council of Santiago de Compostela, see Gonzalo Martínez Díez, "El concilio compostelano del reinado de Fernando I," *AEM* 1 (1964): 121–38. For the Council of Jaca, see *La colección diplomática de Sancho Ramírez*, ed. Ángel Canellas López (Zaragoza: Real Sociedad Económica Aragonesa de Amigos del País, 1993), 18–21. For the Council of Girona, *Colección de cánones y de todos los concilios de la iglesia española y de América*, ed. Francisco Antonio González and Juan Tejada y Ramiro, 7 vols. (Madrid: José María Alonso, 1849–62), 3: 125–28.

5. Andrés Gambra, ed., *Alfonso VI: cancillería, curia e imperio*, 2 vols. (León: CEISI; Caja España de Inversiones; Archivo Histórico Diocesano, 1997–98), 2: no. 114.

6. Carlos Estepa Díez, *Estructura social de la ciudad de León (siglos XI–XIII)* (León: CEISI; Archivo Histórico Diocesano; Caja de Ahorros y Monte de Piedad de León, 1977), 163–72, 173–76.

7. While the Navarrese town of Tudela on the Ebro was granted a *fuero* by Alfonso I of Aragon (1104–34) in 1127, the local Muslim enclave had received its own set of laws from the king some twelve years earlier: *Colección de fueros municipales y cartas pueblas de los reinos de Castilla, Leon, Corona de Aragon y Navarra*, ed. Tomás Muñoz y Romero (Madrid: Imprenta de Don José María Alonso, 1847), 415–17 (1115) and 420–22 (1127).

8. José Luis Martín Rodríguez, *Orígenes de la Orden Militar de Santiago* (Barcelona: CSIC, 1974), 178–80.

9. A useful catalogue of *fueros* has been compiled by Ana María Barrero García and María Luz Alonso Martín, eds., *Textos de derecho local español en la Edad Media* (Madrid: CSIC/Instituto de Ciencias Jurídicas, 1989). For an introduction to the origins and development of the *fuero* form, see Alfonso García Gallo, "Aportación al estudio de los Fueros," *AHDE* 26 (1956): 387–446.

10. *Fuero de Calatayud*, eds. Jesús Ignacio Algora and Felicísimo Arranz Sacristán (Zaragoza: Diputación Provincial-Institución Fernando el Católico, 1982), 31–53. For an overview of the treatment of Jews, see Pilar León Tello, "Disposiciones sobre judíos en los fueros de Castilla y León," *Medievalia* 8 (1999): 223–52.

11. *El Fuero de Teruel*, ed. Max Gorosch (Stockholm: Almqvist and Wiksell, 1950); *El fuero latino de Teruel*, ed. Jaime Caruana Gómez de Barreda (Teruel: Tallares Gráficos, 1974). See further Ana María Barrero García, *El Fuero de Teruel: su historia, proceso de formación y reconstrucción crítica de sus fuentes* (Madrid: Instituto de Estudios Turolenses, 1979).

12. *Fuero de Cuenca (formas primordial y sistemática: texto latino, texto castellano y adaptación del Fuero de Iznatoraf)*, ed. Rafael de Ureña y Smenjaud (Madrid: Tipografía de Archivos, 1935), which includes both Latin and Castilian versions of the code. English

translation by James F. Powers, *The Code of Cuenca: Municipal Law on the Twelfth-Century Castilian Frontier* (Philadelphia: University of Pennsylvania Press, 2000). On the date of the code's promulgation, see 18–22.

13. The matter is explored in depth by Alberto García Ulecia, *Los factores de diferenciación entre las personas en los fueros de la Extremadura castellano-aragonesa* (Seville: Gráficas del Sur, 1975), 355–452; Barrero García, *El Fuero de Teruel*, 53–137; Powers, *A Society Organized for War*, 219–29.

14. On military organisation, see Powers, *A Society Organized for War*; on women, the essential guide is Heath Dillard, *Daughters of the Reconquest: Women in Castilian Town Society, 1000–1300* (Cambridge: Cambridge University Press, 1984).

15. *Fuero de Teruel*, ed. Gorosch, §319.

16. *Fuero de Cuenca*, 2.32.

17. James F. Powers, "Frontier Municipal Baths and Social Interaction in Thirteenth-Century Spain," *American Historical Review* 84 (1979): 649–67; Maria Filomena Lopes de Barros, "Body, Baths and Cloth: Muslim and Christian Perceptions in Medieval Portugal," *Portuguese Studies* 21 (2005): 1–12. On the synod of Lleida, see Josefina Mutgé Vives, "La aljama sarracena en la Lleida cristiana: noticias y conclusiones," in *VII Simposio Internacional de Mudejarismo* (Teruel: Centro de Estudios Mudéjares; Instituto de Estudios Turolenses, 1999), 101–11, at 106 and n. 26.

18. *Fuero de Teruel*, ed. Gorosch, §497.

19. *Fuero de Cuenca*, 11.48.

20. The municipalities which adopted the Cuenca code, together with its prohibition on interfaith sexual mixing, included: Alarcón: *Les fueros d'Alcaraz et d'Alarcon*, ed. Jean Roudil, 2 vols. (Paris: Klincksiek, 1968), §256; Alcaraz: *Les fueros d'Alcaraz et d'Alarcon*, §4.49; Baeza: *El Fuero de Baeza: Edición, estudio y vocabulario*, ed. Jean Marie Victor Roudil (The Hague: G.B. van Goor Zonen, 1962), §270; Béjar: *Fuero de Béjar*, ed. Juan Gutiérrez Cuadrado (Salamanca: Universidad de Salamanca, 1975) §350; Brihuega: *El fuero de Brihuega*, ed. Juan Catalina García (Madrid: Tipografía de Manuel G. Hernández, 1887), 149; Huete: *Los fueros de Villaescusa de Haro y Huete*, ed. María Teresa Martín Palma (Málaga: Universidad de Málaga, 1984), §227; Iznatoraf: in *Fuero de Cuenca*, §270; Plasencia: *El fuero de Plasencia: estudio histórico y edición crítica del texto*, ed. Eloísa Ramírez Vaquero (Mérida: Editora Regional de Extremadura, 1987), §107; Soria: *Fueros castellanos de Soria y Alcalá de Henares*, ed. Galo Sánchez (Madrid: Junta para Ampliación de Estudios e Investigaciones Científicas; Centro de estudios históricos, 1919), §543; Villaescusa de Haro: *Los fueros de Villaescusa*, §255; Zorita de los Canes: *El fuero de Zorita de los Canes*, ed. Rafael de Ureña y Smenjaud (Madrid: Establecimiento Tipográfico de Fortanet, 1911), §272. For a full list, see Barrero García and Alonso Martín, *Textos*, 546–48.

21. *Los fueros de Sepúlveda: edición crítica y apéndice documental*, ed. Emilo Sáez et al., (Segovia: Diputación Provincial de Segovia, 1953), 45–51.

22. *Los fueros de Sepúlveda*, §68 (Muslims), §71 (Jews).

23. Ibid., §215.

24. Other *fueros* to include clauses outlawing interfaith sex included those of the Coria-Cima-Coa family, although these referred only to Jews: Coria: *El fuero de Coria: estudio*

histórico-jurídico, ed. José Maldonado y Fernández del Torco et al. (Madrid: Instituto de Estudios de Administracion Local, 1949), §135; Cáceres: *Los fueros municipales de Cáceres: Su derecho público*, ed. Pedro Lumbreras Valiente (Cáceres: Ayuntamiento, 1974), §386; Castelo Bom: in *Monumenta Portugalia Historica, a saeculo octavo post Christum usque ad quintum decimum: Leges et Consuetudines*, eds. Alexandre Herculano and Joaquim J. da Silva Mendes Leal, 2 vols. (Lisbon: Academia Real das Ciências, 1856–68), 1: 745–90, at 760; Castelo Melhor: *Monumenta Portugalia Historica: Leges*, 1: 910; *Fuero de Usagre (siglo XIII) anotado con las variantes dél de Cáceres*, ed. Rafael de Ureña y Smenjaud and Adolfo Bonilla y San Martín (Madrid: Hijos de Reus, 1907), §395.

25. *Costums de Tortosa*, ed. Jesús Massip i Fonollosa (Barcelona: Fundació Noguera, 1996), 9.2.7. On the position of Mudejars in Tortosa, see María Teresa Ferrer i Mallol, "The Muslim "aljama" of Tortosa in the Late Middle Ages: Notes on Its Organisation," *Scripta Mediterranea* 19–20 (1998–99): 143–64.

26. *Furs de València*, ed. Germà Colòn and Arcadi Garcia, 5 vols. (Barcelona: Barcino, 1970–90), 9.2.9.

27. *Las Siete Partidas: el libro del fuero de las leyes*, ed. José Sánchez-Arcilla Bernal (Madrid: Reus, 2004), 7.24.9; trans. Samuel Parsons Scott, *Las Siete Partidas*, rev. Robert I. Burns, 5 vols. (Philadelphia: University of Pennsylvania Press, 2001), 5: 7.24.9. Whether the *Partidas* were formally promulgated during King Alfonso's lifetime is controversial; for an overview of the debate, see Sánchez-Arcilla Bernal, *Las Siete Partidas*, xiii–xxx.

28. *Las Siete Partidas*, 7.25.10.

29. See above n. 24.

30. *Fuero de Sepúlveda*, §68 (Muslims), §71 (Jews).

31. *Costums de Tortosa*, 9.2.7.

32. *Cantigas de Santa María*, 3 vols., ed. Walter Mettmann (Madrid: Castalia, 1986–89), 2: no. 186; English translation by Kathleen Kulp-Hill, *Songs of Holy Mary of Alfonso X, the Wise: A Translation of the* Cantigas de Santa María (Tempe: Arizona Center for Medieval and Renaissance Studies, 2000), no. 186. See Figure 2.

33. Boswell, *The Royal Treasure*, 343–53; Ferrer i Mallol, *Els sarraïns*, 17–39; Nirenberg, *Communities of Violence*, 127–65; Catlos, *The Victors*, 305–12.

34. For what follows, see Ferrer i Mallol, *Els sarraïns*, 329–30; José Hinojosa Montalvo, *Los mudéjares: La voz del Islam en la España cristiana*, 2 vols. (Teruel: Centro de Estudios Mudéjares; Instituto de Estudios Turolenses, 2002), 2: 536–37.

35. Ferrer i Mallol, *Els sarraïns*, 34–36; Catlos, *Victors*, 308–10, 369. A similarly pragmatic approach was taken in Portugal: Lopes de Barros, "Body, Baths and Cloth," 6–7. On the policy toward Jews, see Ray, *The Sephardic Frontier*, 166–67.

36. Ferrer i Mallol, *Els sarraïns*, 35 n. 85; Nirenberg, *Communities*, 145.

37. *Colección diplomática del concejo de Zaragoza*, ed. Ángel Canellas López, 2 vols. (Zaragoza: Ayuntamiento de Zaragoza, 1972), 1: no. 66.

38. Ferrer i Mallol, *Els sarraïns*, 232; Hinojosa Montalvo, *Los mudéjares*, 2: 521.

39. Félix Segura Urra, "Los mudéjares navarros y la justicia regia: cuestiones penales y pecularidades delictivas en el siglo XIV," *Anaquel de Estudios árabes* 14 (2003): 239–58, at 255 n. 88.

40. Antonio Benavides, *Memorias del rey D. Fernando IV de Castilla,* 2 vols. (Madrid: Imprenta de José Rodríguez, 1860), 2: 210–11.

41. For what follows, see Juan Torres Fontes and Emilio Sáez, "Privilegios a la ciudad de Murcia," *AHDE* 14 (1943): 530–45, at 532–33.

42. On Muslim protests, see Nirenberg, *Communities,* 146.

43. Ferrer i Mallol, *Els sarraïns,* 216–17.

44. Ibid., 264; Hinojosa Montalvo, *Los mudéjares,* 2: 529–30.

45. Hinojosa Montalvo, *Los mudéjares,* 2: 531; Ferrer i Mallol, *Els sarraïns,* 325–26.

46. M. Carmen Peris, "La prostitución valenciana en la segunda mitad del siglo XIV," *Revista d'Història Medieval* 1 (1990): 179–99, at 183, 185 and n. 14; see also Nirenberg, *Communities,* 145 n. 67.

47. The text is edited by Hinojosa Montalvo, *Los mudéjares,* 2: 515–20; for analysis, see Nirenberg, *Communities,* 147–48.

48. Nirenberg, *Communities,* 146; idem, "Religious and Sexual Boundaries," 141–60; idem, "Conversion, Sex, and Segregation," 1075.

49. Nirenberg, *Communities,* 144.

50. *Chancelarias Portuguesas. D. Pedro I (1357–1367)* (Lisbon: Instituto Nacional de Investigação Científica; Centro de Estudos Históricos da Universidade Nova de Lisboa, 1984), no. 1131; cited in Lopes de Barros, "Body," 8.

51. Josefina Mutgé Vives, *L'aljama sarraïna de Lleida a l'edat mitjana: aproximació a la seva historia* (Barcelona: CSIC, 1992), 298–302; Hinojosa Montalvo, *Los mudéjares,* 2: 525–29.

52. Ferrer i Mallol, *Els sarraïns,* 33–34; Nirenberg, *Communities,* 37, 145.

53. Ferrer i Mallol, *Els sarraïns,* 32–33, 223–24, 225–26.

54. Benjamin Z. Kedar, "On the Origins of the Earliest Laws of Frankish Jerusalem: The Canons of Nablus, 1120," *Speculum* 74 (1999): 310–35, with an edition of the decrees at 331–34.

55. *Assises de la cour des bourgeois,* ed. Conte de Beugnot, *Recueil des Historiens des Croisades: Lois, 2* (Paris: Belles-Lettres, 1843), §158, at 107.

56. James Brundage, "Marriage Law in the Latin Kingdom of Jerusalem," in Benjamin Z. Kedar, Hans Eberhard Mayer and R. C. Smail, eds., *Outremer—Studies in the History of the Crusading Kingdom of Jerusalem Presented to Joshua Prawer* (Jerusalem: Yad Izhak Ben Zvi Institute, 1982), 258–71; idem, "Prostitution, Miscegenation and Sexual Purity in the First Crusade," in Peter W. Edbury, ed., *Crusade and Settlement: Papers Read at the First Conference of the Society for the Study of the Crusades and the Latin East and Presented to R. C. Smail* (Cardiff: University College Cardiff Press, 1985), 57–65; both reprinted in James Brundage, *The Crusades, Holy War and Canon Law* (Aldershot: Ashgate, 1991), nos. XVII and XIX.

57. *Furs,* 9.2.10; Boswell, *The Royal Treasure,* 346 n. 70.

58. Hinojosa Montalvo, *Los mudéjares,* 2: 515.

59. Nirenberg, *Communities,* 141 n. 53.

60. *Castigos del rey don Sancho IV,* ed. Hugo Oscar Bizzarri (Frankfurt-Madrid: Vervuert; Iberoamericana, 2001), §19, at 189.

61. Ibid., § 21, at 201–6. See further Nirenberg, "Deviant Politics."

62. Boswell, *The Royal Treasure*, 344–46; Catlos, *The Victors*, 306.

63. Ferrer i Mallol, *Els sarraïns*, 280–81.

64. Segura Urra, "Los mudéjares navarros," 251 and n. 65.

65. Cited by Nirenberg, *Communities of Violence*, 135. For similar denunciations, see Ray, *The Sephardic Frontier*, 169–74.

66. *Cantigas de Santa María*, 2: no. 107; translation by Kulp-Hill, *Songs of Holy Mary*, no. 107. For discussion of the episode, see Mirrer, *Women, Jews, and Muslims*, 33–44.

67. Ferrer i Mallol, *Els sarraïns*, 235–36.

68. Ibid., 270–71. See also Nirenberg, *Communities*, 137 and nn. 38–39.

69. On canon lawyers' attitude toward concubinage, see James A. Brundage, *Law, Sex and Christian Society in Medieval Europe* (Chicago: University of Chicago Press, 1987). See further Karras, *Sexuality in Medival Europe*, 100–104; eadem, "Marriage, Concubinage, and the Law," in Ruth Mazo Karras, Joel Kaye, and E. Ann Matter, eds., *Law and the Illicit in Medieval Europe* (Philadelphia: University of Pennsylvania Press, 2008), 117–29. On *barraganas*, see Dillard, *Daughters*, 127–34; Eukene Lacarra Lanz, "Changing Boundaries of Licit and Illicit Unions: Concubinage and Prostitution," in Eukene Lacarra Lanz, ed., *Marriage and Sexuality in Medieval and Early Modern Iberia* (New York: Routledge, 2002), 158–94; Zorgati, *Pluralism*, 134–41; María Teresa Arias Bautista, *Barraganas y concubinas en la España medieval* (Seville: Arcibel, 2010).

70. *Las Siete Partidas*, 4.14.1–2. However, men of high birth were warned not to take concubines of low birth, since "it is not proper that the blood of nobles should be contaminated by, or mingled with that of such infamous women," while a child born to such a union would not be recognized by the law: *Las Siete Partidas*, 4.14.3.

71. *Fuero de Sepúlveda*, §215.

72. *Costums de Tortosa*, 6.1.12, 14, 17–18. On the fate of children born to mixed parents, see Ferrer i Mallol, *Els sarraïns*, 27–28.

73. *Fuero de Cuenca*, 11.23.

74. *Fueros castellanos*, §318.

75. Alfonso X el Sabio, *Fuero Real*, ed. Azucena Palacios Alcaine (Barcelona: Promociones y Publicaciones Universitarias, 1991), 3.7.4; cf. Zorgati, *Pluralism*, 139.

76. Zorgati, *Pluralism*, 140.

77. The matter is explored by Brian Catlos, *Muslims of Medieval Latin Christendom, c.1050–1614* (Cambridge: Cambridge University Press, 2014), chap. 9.

78. Boswell, *The Royal Treasure*, 348–51; Mark Meyerson, "Prostitution of Muslim Women in the Kingdom of Valencia: Religious and Sexual Discrimination in a Medieval Plural Society," in Marilyn J. Chiat and Kathryn L. Reyerson, eds., *The Medieval Mediterranean: Cross-Cultural Contacts*, Medieval Studies at Minnesota 3 (St. Cloud, Minn.: North Star Press of St. Cloud, 1988), 87–95; Peris, "La prostitución"; Noelia Rangel López, "Moras, jóvenes y prostitutas: acerca de la prostitución valenciana a finales de la Edad Media," *Miscelánea Medieval Murciana* 32 (2008): 119–30; Lacarra Lanz, "Changing Boundaries."

79. Catlos, *The Victors*, 311. For other examples, see Lacarra Lanz, "Changing Boundaries," 182–83.

80. Lacarra Lanz, "Changing Boundaries," 176.

81. Meyerson, "Prostitution," 88.

82. See further Ferrer i Mallol, *Els sarraïns*, 19–21, 25–27.

83. Meyerson, "Prostitution," 91; Rangel López, "Moras, jóvenes y prostitutas," 121–22.

84. See "Confessions of a Muslim Prostitute (1491)," in Constable, ed., *Medieval Iberia*, 493–95; Rangel López, "Moras, jóvenes y prostitutas," 124.

85. Lacarra Lanz, "Changing Boundaries," 158–59.

86. On the legal vulnerability of concubines, see Dillard, *Daughters*, 133; cf. Zorgati, *Pluralism*, 139–40.

87. Cf. Heath Dillard, "Women in Reconquest Castile: The *Fueros* of Sepúlveda and Cuenca," in Susan Mosher Stuard, ed., *Women in Medieval Society* (Philadelphia: University of Pennsylvania Press, 1976), 71–94, at 85–86.

88. *CEM* no. 23. See further Francisco Márquez Villanueva, "Las lecturas del deán de Cádiz en una *cantiga de mal dizer*," in Israel J. Katz and John E. Keller, eds., *Studies on the* Cantigas de Santa María*: Art, Music, and Poetry. Proceedings of the International Symposium on the* Cantigas de Santa María *of Alfonso X, el Sabio (1221–1284) in Commemoration of Its 700th Anniversary Year—1981 (New York, November 9–21)* (Madison, Wis.: Hispanic Seminary of Medieval Studies, 1987), 329–54; Ingrid Vindel Pérez, "Breves apuntes a la cantiga que Alfonso X dedicó a cierto deán de Cádiz," *Espéculo: Revista de estudios literarios* 14 (2000).

89. *Fuero de Cuenca*, 11.22, 24–25.

90. Ferrer i Mallol, *Els sarraïns*, 256–57.

91. Nirenberg, *Communities*, 141. For similar views, see Dillard, "Women in Reconquest Castile," 86.

92. Alfonso X, *Fuero Real*, 4.11.3.

93. The work of the canonists is analyzed by Brundage, *Law, Sex, and Christian Society*, 195–96, 207, 238, 267–68, 340, 361, 380, 461–62; Emilio Bussi, "La condizione giuridica dei musulmani nel diritto canonico," *Rivista di storia del diritto italiano* 8 (1935): 459–94; Peter Herde, "Christians and Saracens at the Time of the Crusades: Some Comments of Contemporary Canonists," *Studia Gratiana* 12 (1967): 359–76; Henri Gilles, "Législation et doctrine canoniques sur les sarrasins," in *Islam et Chrétiens du Midi (XII–XIVs.)*, ed. E. Privat, Cahiers de Fanjeaux 18 (Toulouse: Centre d'Études Historiques de Fanjeaux, 1983), 195–213; David M. Freidenreich, "Muslims in Western Canon Law, 1000–1500," in David Thomas et al., eds., *Christian-Muslim Relations: A Bibliographic History*, 2 vols. (Leiden: Brill, 2011), 2: 41–68. In some cases legal codes referred to minorities by the generic term of "heretics" or "pagans," but it is clear enough that Jews and Muslims are meant.

94. *The "Summa Theologica" of St. Thomas Aquinas*, trans. Fathers of the English Dominican Province, 22 vols. (London: Burns Oates & Washbourne, 1920–24), 19, third part (supplement), 59.1.

95. *Las Siete Partidas*, 4.2.15.

96. Zorgati, *Pluralism*, 121–22.

97. Brundage, *Law, Sex, and Christian Society*, 207.

98. Ibid., 380.

99. *Constitutiones concilii quarti lateranensis una cum commentariis glossatorum*, ed. Antonio García y García, *Monumenta Iuris Canonici, Corpus glossatorum*, 2 (Vatican City: Biblioteca Apostolica Vaticana, 1981), 107 (canon 68); trans. from H. J. Schroeder, *Disciplinary Decrees of the General Councils: Text, Translation and Commentary* (St. Louis: B. Herder, 1937), 290–91.

100. *Las Siete Partidas*, 7.24.11.

101. Ibid.

102. Dwayne E. Carpenter, "Minorities in Medieval Spain: the legal status of Jews and Muslims in the *Siete Partidas*," *Romance Quarterly* 33 (1986): 275–87, at 282; cf. Zorgati, *Pluralism*, 162–64.

103. On the introduction of vestimentary legislation in Aragon, see Boswell, *The Royal Treasure*, 330–32; Ferrer i Mallol, *Els sarraïns*, 41–60; Catlos, *The Victors*, 300–302. On the Portuguese legislation, see Lopes de Barros, "Body, Baths and Cloth," 9–11. For the royal ordinance on haircuts, see Ferrer i Mallol, *Els sarraïns*, 213. On the vestimentary ordinances imposed on Jews during the same period, see Ray, *The Sephardic Frontier*, 156–64.

104. Catlos, *The Victors*, 300–302.

105. Meyerson, "Prostitution," 87–88; Ferrer i Mallol, *Els sarraïns*, 12–14, 230–31. It was not until 1368 that Charles II of Navarre outlawed the presence of Muslims and Jews at the gambling house of Tudela: Segura Urra, "Los mudéjares navarros," 253–54.

106. *Los cartularios de San Salvador de Zaragoza*, ed. Ángel Canellas López, 4 vols. (Zaragoza: IberCaja, 1990), 2: no. 918.

107. On this episode, see below, Chapter 4.

108. *El monasterio de San Pelayo de Oviedo. Historia y fuentes, I: Coleccion diplomatica (996–1325)*, eds. Francisco Javier Fernández Conde, Isabel Torrente Fernández, and Guadalupe de la Noval Menéndez (Oviedo: Monasterio de San Pelayo, 1978), no. 127.

109. Nirenberg, *Communities*, 143.

110. Ferrer i Mallol, *Els sarraïns*, 243.

111. *Las Siete Partidas*, 7.24.9.

112. Nirenberg, "Conversion, Sex, and Segregation," 1067.

113. Nirenberg, "Religious and Sexual Boundaries," 145. The passage is subjected to detailed analysis by Dwayne E. Carpenter, *Alfonso X and the Jews: An Edition and Commentary on the* Siete Partidas *7.24 "De los judios"* (Berkeley: University of California Press, 1986), 91–93.

114. See, for example, Deuteronomy 13:6–11; Galatians 1:8–9; Hebrews 3:12; 2 Peter 2:20–22.

115. Catlos, *The Victors*, 311.

116. Ferrer i Mallol, *Els sarraïns*, 37–38 and n. 97.

117. Mary Douglas, *Purity and Danger: An Analysis of Concepts of Pollution and Taboo* (London: Routledge and Kegan Paul, 1978).

118. Ibid., 159.

119. Ibid., 156.

120. See in this context Michel Foucault, *The History of Sexuality*, vol. 1: *The Will to Knowledge*, trans. Robert Hurley (Harmondsworth: Penguin, 1998), 81–91.

121. Nirenberg, "Conversion, Sex, and Segregation," 1069–71.

122. Steven Lukes, *Durkheim: His Life and Work* (Harmondsworth: Penguin, 1973), 160–63. Cf. R. I. Moore, *The Formation of a Persecuting Society: Power and Deviance in Western Europe, 950–1250*, 2nd ed. (Oxford: Blackwell, 2007), 100–103.

123. Georg Simmel, *Conflict*; [and] *The Web of Group-Affiliations*, trans. Kurt Wolf (New York: Free Press, 1955), 98.

124. See above, nn. 54–56.

125. cf. Liu, "'Affined to love the Moor,'" 56.

126. The preoccupation of modern colonial systems with sexuality has been the subject of extensive research in recent years. For an overview, see Linda Bryder, "Sex, Race, and Colonialism: An Historiographical Review," *International History Review* 20 (1998): 806–54; and Malia B. Formes, "Beyond Complicity Versus Resistance: Recent Work on Gender and European Imperialism," *Journal of Social History* 28 (1995): 629–41. I have found particularly useful Ann Laura Stoler, *Carnal Knowledge and Imperial Power: Race and the Intimate in Colonial Rule* (Berkeley: University of California Press, 2002), 22–111.

127. Foucault, *The History of Sexuality*, 1: 83.

128. Richard Fletcher, "Reconquest and Crusade in Spain, c. 1050–1150," *Transactions of the Royal Historical Society* 5th ser. 37 (1987): 31–47, at 35–36. For a suggestion that the ideology of Reconquest may have not entirely disappeared prior to this, see Felipe Fernández-Armesto, "The Survival of a Notion of *Reconquista* in Late Tenth- and Eleventh-Century León," in Timothy Reuter, ed., *Warriors and Churchmen in the High Middle Ages* (London: Hambledon, 1992), 123–43.

129. Jonathan Riley-Smith, *The First Crusaders, 1095–1131* (Cambridge: Cambridge University Press, 1997), 43–44; William J. Purkis, "The Past as a Precedent: Crusade, Reconquest and Twelfth-Century Memories of Christian Iberia," in Lucie Doležalová, ed., *The Making of Memory in the Middle Ages* (Leiden: Brill 2009), 441–61, at 456–59.

130. *Documentos correspondientes al reinado de Sancio Ramirez: Documentos reales procedentes de la real casa y monasterio de San Juan de la Peña*, 2 vols. (Zaragoza: M. Escar, 1907–13), ed. José Salarrullana y de Dios and Eduardo Ibarra y Rodríguez, 1: no. 48.

131. *Documentos de los Archivos Catedralicio y Diocesano de Salamanca (siglos XII–XIII)*, ed. José Luis Martín Martín et al. (Salamanca: Universidad de Salamanca, 1977), no. 1. On the circumstances that gave rise to the drafting of the charter, see Simon Barton, "El Cid, Cluny and the Spanish *Reconquista*," *English Historical Review* 126 (2011): 517–43.

132. On relations with the papacy, see Fletcher, *The Episcopate*, passim; idem, *Saint James's Catapult*, 167–70, 192–222; Joseph F. O'Callaghan, "The Integration of Christian Spain into Europe: The Role of Alfonso VI of León-Castile," in Bernard F. Reilly, ed., *Santiago, St.-Denis, and St. Peter* (New York: Fordham University Press, 1985), 101–20; Deswarte, *Une Chrétienté romaine*, 351–517. On the Cluniac presence in the Peninsula, see H. E. J. Cowdrey, *The Cluniacs and the Gregorian Reform* (Oxford: Clarendon, 1970), 214–47; the articles by Charles J. Bishko reprinted and collected in his *Spanish and Portuguese Monastic History, 600–1300* (London: Variorum, 1984); Peter Segl, *Königtum und Klosterreform in Spanien. Untersuchungen über die Cluniacenserklöster in Kastilien-León vom Beginn des 11. bis zur Mitte der 12. Jahrhunderts* (Kallmünz: Michael Lassleben, 1974); Antonio Linage

Conde, *Los orígenes del monacato benedictino en la Península Ibérica*, 3 vols. (León: CEISI; CSIC, 1973), 2: 861–997; Carlos Manuel Reglero de la Fuente, *Cluny en España: Los prioratos de la provincia y sus redes sociales (1073–ca. 1270)* (León: CEISI, 2008), with a historiographical survey at 59–100.

133. On the introduction of crusading ideology into the Peninsula, see José Goñi Gaztambide, *Historia de la bula de la Cruzada en España* (Vitoria: Editorial del Seminario, 1958); Fletcher, "Reconquest and Crusade"; Marcus Bull, *Knightly Piety and the Lay Response to the First Crusade: the Limousin and Gascony, c.970–c.1130* (Oxford: Clarendon, 1993), 96–114; Simon Barton, "From Tyrants to Soldiers of Christ: The Nobility of Twelfth-Century León-Castile and the Struggle Against Islam," *Nottingham Medieval Studies* 44 (2000): 28–48; Joseph F. O'Callaghan, *Reconquest and Crusade in Medieval Spain* (Philadelphia: University of Pennsylvania Press, 2003); William J. Purkis, *Crusading Spirituality in the Holy Land and Iberia c.1095–c.1187* (Woodbridge: Boydell, 2008), 120–78.

134. Peter the Venerable, *Contra Petrobrusianos hereticos*, ed. James Fearns, *CCCM* 10 (Turnhout: Brepols, 1968), 212, ll. 15–21; the work is subjected to illuminating analysis by Dominique Iogna-Prat, *Order & Exclusion: Cluny and Christendom Face Heresy, Judaism, and Islam (1000–1150)* (Ithaca, N.Y.: Cornell University Press, 2002), 98–261.

135. Iogna-Prat, *Order & Exclusion*, 359–60. For a useful critique of Iogna-Prat's thesis, see the articles in *Early Medieval Europe* 13 (2005) by David Nirenberg, "Engaging *Order and Exclusion*: reflections on a recent book by Dominique Iogna-Prat," 387–94; Isabelle Cochelin, "Orders and Exclusions," 395–403; Lucy Pick, "Peter the Venerable and the New World Order," 405–11, and the reply by Dominique Iogna-Prat, "Ordering Christian Society Through Exclusion: The Strange History of Cluny," 413–18.

136. On the development of the ideology of papal power, see John A. Watt, *The Theory of Papal Monarchy in the Thirteenth Century: The Contribution of the Canonists* (New York: Fordham University Press, 1965); Colin Morris, *The Papal Monarchy: The Western Church from 1050 to 1250* (Oxford: Clarendon, 1989); Jane E. Sayers, *Innocent III: Leader of Europe, 1198–1216* (London: Longman, 1994).

137. Iogna-Prat, *Order & Exclusion*, 34.

138. For an introduction to these matters, see Moore, *The Formation*; John Boswell, *Christianity, Social Tolerance, and Homosexuality: Gay People in Western Europe from the Beginning of the Christian Era to the Fourteenth Century* (Chicago: University of Chicago Press, 1981).

139. Robert Bartlett, *The Making of Europe: Conquest, Colonization and Cultural Change, 950–1350* (London: Allen Lane, 1993), 204–42; R. R. Davies, *Domination and Conquest: The Experience of Ireland, Scotland and Wales, 1100–1300* (Cambridge: Cambridge University Press, 1990); Berend, *At the Gate of Christendom*, 42–108.

140. Moore, *The Formation.* It should be noted that Moore's thesis focused principally on heretics, Jews, and lepers, and not on Muslims.

141. Moore, *The Formation*, 145.

142. For a summary of scholarly reactions to the Moore thesis, see Moore, *The Formation*, 172–96. See further the collected papers in Scott L. Waugh and Peter. D. Diehl, eds., *Christendom and Its Discontents: Exclusion, Persecution and Rebellion, 1000–1500* (Cambridge: Cambridge University Press, 1996).

143. Nirenberg, *Communities*, 5–6, 242–45.

144. Moore, *The Formation*; cf. Boswell, *Christianity, Social Tolerance*, 272.

145. Boswell, *Christianity, Social Tolerance*, 270–71.

146. On the abolition of the liturgy, see Cowdrey, *The Cluniacs*, 214–47; O'Callaghan, "The Integration," 101–20. Thomas Deswarte has emphasized the importance of the secular authorities in implementing the program of reform: *Une Chrétienté romaine*, 403–517.

147. Kosto, "Reconquest," 103–6 and references therein.

148. Fletcher, *Episcopate*, 204–6.

149. *Regesta Pontificum Romanorum ab condita ecclesia ad annum post Christum natum MCXCVIII*, ed. Philip Jaffé, 2 vols. (Leipzig: Veit, 1885–88. Reprint Graz: Akademische Druck- u. Verlagsanstalt, 1956), 2: no. 16,595; Fletcher, *Episcopate*, 211–12.

150. A point emphasised by Cochelin, "Orders and Exclusions," 403.

151. David Nirenberg, "Enmity and Assimilation: Jews, Christians, and Converts in Medieval Spain," *Common Knowledge* 9 (2003): 137–55, at 143.

152. Joanna Bourke, "Fear and Anxiety: Writing About Emotion in Modern History," *History Workshop Journal* 55 (2003): 113–33, at 124.

153. See in this context, Barth, *Ethnic Groups and Boundaries*, 14–16; Nirenberg, *Communities*, Part 2.

CHAPTER 3. DAMSELS IN DISTRESS

1. See above, Chapter 1, n. 86.

2. Barton and Fletcher, *The World of El Cid*, 71.

3. Pelayo, *Crónica*, 63–65.

4. Pelayo has been dubbed the "prince of falsifiers" by Peter Linehan, "Religion, Nationalism and National Identity in Medieval Spain and Portugal," in Stuart Mews, ed., *Religion and National Identity*, Studies in Church History 18 (Oxford: Blackwell/Ecclesiastical History Society, 1982), 161–99, at 162. For a detailed study of the Pelagian forgeries, see *Libro de los Testamentos de la catedral de Oviedo*, ed. Francisco Javier Fernández Conde (Rome: Iglesia Nacional Española, 1971). See also Luis Vázquez de Parga, *La División de Wamba* (Madrid: CSIC, 1943); Demetrio Mansilla, "La supuesta metropolí de Oviedo," *Hispania Sacra* 8 (1955): 259–74.

5. On the importance of the concepts of honor and shame in Mediterranean modes of thought, see the collected essays in John Peristany, ed., *Honour and Shame: The Values of a Mediterranean Society* (London: Weidenfeld and Nicolson, 1965); Jane Schneider, "Of Vigilance and Virgins: Honor, Shame and Access to Resources in Mediterranean Societies," *Ethnology* 10 (1971): 1–24.

6. Dillard, *Daughters of the Reconquest*, 168–92.

7. *Siete Partidas*, 7.24.9.

8. Nirenberg, "Conversion, Sex, and Segregation," 1068; see also Nirenberg, *Communities of Violence*, 151–52.

9. For an introduction to the polemical anti-Islamic tropes deployed by Christian

authors, including criticism of the supposed sexual depravity of Muslims, see Norman Daniel, *Islam and the West: The Making of an Image* (Edinburgh: Edinburgh University Press, 1960), especially 135–52; Boswell, *Christianity, social tolerance*, 279–82; John V. Tolan, *Saracens: Islam in the Medieval European Imagination* (New York: Columbia University Press, 2002), 146, 152. The same tropes were later wielded in the fiery sermons delivered by Eudes de Châteuroux against the Muslims of Lucera in Italy: Christoph T. Maier, "Crusade and Rhetoric Against the Muslim Colony of Lucera: Eudes of Châteuroux's *Sermones de Rebellione Sarracenorum Lucherie in Apulia*," *Journal of Medieval History* 21 (1995): 343–85, at 372–73.

10. *Memoriale Sanctorum*, 1.7.31–2: *CSM* 2 : 376.

11. Guibert of Nogent, *Dei Gesta per Francos et cinq autres textes*, ed. Robert B. C. Huygens, CCCM 127a (Turnhout: Brepols, 1996), 98, 102; trans. Robert Levine, *The Deeds of God Through the Franks* (Woodbridge: Boydell, 1997), 30–31, 33. On the depiction of sexual violence in crusading narratives, see Natasha Hodgson, *Women, Crusading and the Holy Land in Historical Narrative* (Woodbridge: Boydell, 2007), 97–100.

12. Cf. Yvonne Friedman, *Encounter Between Enemies: Captivity and Ransom in the Latin Kingdom of Jerusalem* (Leiden: Brill, 2002), 169–72.

13. Grassotti, "Vindicación de doña Teresa," 453.

14. Friedman, *Encounter Between Enemies*, 181–86.

15. Guibert of Nogent, *Dei Gesta per Francos*, 349; trans. Levine, *The Deeds of God*, 164. See further Bernard Hamilton, "Women in the Crusader States: The Queens of Jerusalem (1100–1190)," in Derek Baker, ed., *Medieval Women* (Oxford: Blackwell, 1978), 143–74, at 144–45.

16. Cited by Friedman, *Encounter Between Enemies*, 181.

17. On the martyrdom of Pelayo, see Manuel C. Díaz y Díaz, "La Pasión de S. Pelayo y su difusión," *AEM* 6 (1969): 97–116; Mark D. Jordan, "Saint Pelagius, Ephebe and Martyr," in Josiah Blackmore and Gregory S. Hutcheson, eds., *Queer Iberia: Sexualities, Cultures, and Crossings from the Middle Ages to the Renaissance* (Durham, N.C.: Duke University Press, 1999), 23–47. However, Oviedo was not the only Christian center to lay claim to the relics of the saint; see Christys, *Christians in al-Andalus*, 94–101.

18. *Chronica Naierensis*, ed. Juan Antonio Estévez Sola, *CCCM* 71A (Turnhout: Brepols, 1995), 147–48; Spanish translation by Juan Antonio Estévez Sola, *Crónica Najerense* (Madrid: Ediciones Akal, 2003), 153.

19. Lucas of Tuy, *Chronicon Mundi*, 274–75.

20. Rodrigo Jiménez, *De rebus Hispanie*, 167; Spanish trans. Fernández Valverde, *Historia de los hechos*, 210.

21. Rodrigo Jiménez, *De rebus Hispanie*, 167. There are biblical resonances here: see, for example, Deuteronomy 7:3, Ezra 9–10; Nehemiah 13. Similar arguments were marshalled by the Carolingians in their attempts to prevent exogamous marriages: see Walter Pohl, "Alienigena coniuga: Bestrebungen zu einem Verbot auswärtiger Heiraten in der Karolingerzeit," in Andreas Pečar and Kai Trampedach, eds., *Die Bibel als politisches Argument*, *Historische Zeitschrift*, Beiheft 43 (Munich: R. Oldenbourg, 2007), 159–88.

22. *La* Estoria de España *de Alfonso X: Estudio y edición de la* Versión Crítica *desde*

Fruela II hasta la muerte de Fernando II, ed. Mariano de la Campa Gutiérrez, *Anejos de Analecta Malacitana* 75 (Málaga: Universidad de Málaga, 2009), 356.

23. The long literary life of the story is explored by Pilar Vega Rodríguez, "Teresa, la infanta (y el rey moro de Toledo)," in Leonardo Romero Tobar, ed., *Temas literarios hispánicos (I)* (Zaragoza: Universidad de Zaragoza, 2013), 243–70.

24. *Primavera y flor de romances o Colección de los más viejos y más populares romances castellanos*, ed. José Fernando Wolf and Conrado Hofmann, 2 vols. (Berlin: A. Asher and Company, 1856), 1: no. 27. On the ballad itself, see Frank L. Odd, "Women of the Romanceros: A Voice of Reconciliation," *Hispania* 66 (1983): 360–68, at 361; Vega Rodríguez, "Teresa, la infanta," 254–55. The same story, with slight variations on a theme, appears in a number of other ballads. See, for example, *Romancero general o colección de romances castellanos*, ed. Agustín Durán, 2 vols. (Madrid: Atlas, 1945), 1: nos. 721–22.

25. Santiago de Compostela, Archivo de la Catedral, carpeta 7, no. 1. The charter was edited by Antonio López Ferreiro, *Historia de la Santa A. M. Iglesia de Santiago de Compostela*, 5 vols. (Santiago de Compostela: Impr. y Enc. del Seminario Conciliar Central, 1898–1902), 2: 132–37; a revised edition, with English translation, can be seen in the Appendix to this book. On the career of Pedro Marcio, see Fernando López Alsina, *La ciudad de Santiago de Compostela en la Alta Edad Media* (Santiago de Compostela: Ayuntamiento de Santiago de Compostela, Centro de Estudios Jacobeos, Museo Nacional de las Peregrinaciones, 1988), 91–93. It is not known when the charter was supposedly transcribed, but given that Pedro Marcio is styled cardinal the date of composition may be narrowed down to sometime between 1158 and 1174: López Alsina, *La ciudad*, 92 n. 295. It has also been suggested that Pedro Marcio might have had a hand in the compilation of the house history of his cathedral see, the *Historia Compostellana*: López Alsina, *La ciudad*, 78–93.

26. Ofelia Rey Castelao, *La historiografía del Voto de Santiago: recopilación crítica de una polémica histórica* (Santiago de Compostela: Universidad de Santiago de Compostela, 1985). See further Thomas D. Kendrick, *St. James in Spain* (London: Methuen, 1960), 34–59, 193–200; López Alsina, *La ciudad*, 175–86.

27. López Ferreiro, *Historia*, 2: 73–146. Equally vociferous in defense of the authenticity of the charter was Julián Cantera Orive, *La batalla de Clavijo y aparición en ella de nuestro patrón Santiago* (Vitoria: Editorial Social Católica, 1944; repr. Logroño: Editorial La Rioja, 1997).

28. After Clavijo, López Ferreiro roundly declared, "la existencia de la nacionalidad española quedaba asegurada": López Ferreiro, *Historia*, 2: 78.

29. "Ningún historiador digno de tal nombre tiene hoy por auténtica la tradición de la batalla de Clavijo": Claudio Sánchez-Albornoz, "La auténtica batalla de Clavijo," *Cuadernos de Historia de España* 9 (1948): 94–139, at 94. See further Louis Barrau Dihigo, "Études sur les actes des rois asturiens (718–910)," *Revue Hispanique* 46 (1919): 1–192, at 125–26; Antonio Floriano Cumbreño, *Los documentos reales del periódo astur*, 2 vols. (Oviedo: Instituto de Estudios Asturianos, 1949–51), 1: 222–35; Manuel Lucas Álvarez, *La documentación real astur-leonesa (718–1072), El Reino de León en la Alta Edad Media*, 8 (León: CEISI; Caja España de Inversiones; Caja de Ahorros y Monte de Piedad; Archivo Histórico Diocesano, 1995), 109–11.

30. Sánchez-Albornoz, "La auténtica batalla de Clavijo."

31. On Astur-Leonese diplomatic practice, see Barrau Dihigo, "Études"; Floriano Cumbreño, *Los documentos reales*; Lucas Álvarez, *La documentación real.*

32. Lucas Álvarez, ed., *La documentación del Tumbo A.* On the compilation of the Tumbo and the role played by Bernardo, see López Alsina, *La ciudad*, 28–43.

33. On St. James and the Iberian *Reconquista*, see Klaus Herbers, "Politik und Heiligenverehrung auf der Iberischen Halbinsel: Die Entwicklung des *politischen 'Jakobus'*" in Jürgen Petersohn, ed., *Politik und Heiligenverehrung im Hochmittelalter*, Vorträge und Vorschungen 42 (Sigmaringen: Thorbecke, 1994), 177–275; Francisco Márquez Villanueva, *Santiago: Trayectoria de un mito* (Barcelona: Edicions Bellaterra, 2004), 183–222; Purkis, *Crusading Spirituality*, 139–65.

34. Manuel Ruben García Álvarez, "El *Cronicón Iriense*, estudio preliminar, edición crítica y notas históricas," *Memorial Histórico Español* 50 (1963): 1–204, at 115. On the ideological concerns and dating of the *Chronicon*, see Amancio Isla Frez, "Ensayo de historiografía medieval: El Cronicón Iriense," *En la España medieval* 4 (1984): 413–32.

35. This finds corroboration in the bull Pope Paschal II granted to the church of Santiago de Compostela on 30 December 1102, in which he stated that the River Pisuerga marked the eastern boundary of the area within which the *Voto* was to be levied: *Historia Compostellana*, ed. Emma Falque Rey, *CCCM* 70 (Turnhout: Brepols, 1988), 28–29.

36. López Alsina, *La ciudad*, 175.

37 On the origins and development of the cult of St. James at Santiago de Compostela, see Fletcher, *Saint James's Catapult*, 53–101; Jan van Herwaarden, *Between St. James and Erasmus. Studies in Late-Medieval Religious Life: Devotion and Pilgrimage in the Netherlands* (Leiden: Brill, 2003), 311–54; Márquez Villanueva, *Santiago.*

38. Fletcher, *Saint James's Catapult*, 293–94.

39. López Alsina, *La ciudad*, 176–81.

40. Sánchez-Albornoz, "La auténtica batalla," 95–96; Rey Castelao, *La historiografía*, 9–10; López Alsina, *La ciudad*, 175–86.

41. For an introduction to these matters, see Fletcher, *Saint James's Catapult*, 206–12, 282–91.

42. Fletcher, *The Episcopate*, 57–59.

43. Rey Castelao, *La historiografía*, 10.

44. Lucas Álvarez, *La documentación*, 32.

45. Henrik Karge, "'Hoc ego facio ad restaurationem portus Apostoli': der Pórtico de la Gloria und die königliche *restauratio* von Santiago de Compostela in der 2. Hälfte des 12. Jahrhunderts," in Claudia Rückert and Jochen Staebel, eds., *Mittelalterliche Bauskulptur in Frankreich und Spanien: Im Spannungsfeld des Chartreser Königsportals und des Pórticode la Gloria in Santiago de Compostela* (Frankfurt and Madrid: Vervuert-Iberoamericana, 2010), 321–40, with illustrations at 315–17. For the view that the forged diploma of Ramiro I belongs to the reign of Alfonso VII, see Kendrick, *St. James in Spain*, 193–200.

46. On medieval forgery a good starting point is *Fälschungen im Mittelalter: internationaler Kongress der Monumenta Germaniae Historica, München, 16.–19. September 1986*: *Schriften der Monumenta Germaniae Historica*, 6 vols. (Hanover: Hahnsche Buchhandlung, 1988–90).

47. Ofelia Rey Castelao, *El Voto de Santiago: Claves de un conflicto* (Santiago de Compostela: Xunta de Galicia, 1993).

48. Bourdieu, *Masculine Domination*, 43.

49. Emily C. Francomano, "The Legend of the *Tributo de las cien doncellas*: Women as Warweavers and the Coin of Salvation," *Revista Canadiense de Estudios Hispánicos* 32 (2007): 9–25, at 18.

50. Roca Franquesa, "La leyenda "; Manzanares de Cirre, "Las cien doncellas"; Francomano, "The Legend."

51. Lucas of Tuy, *Chronicon Mundi*, 237–39. On the use made by Lucas of the Compostelan charter, see Emma Falque Rey, "El llamado *Privilegio de los Votos*, fuente del *Chronicon Mundi* de Lucas de Tuy," *Habis* 33 (2002): 573–77.

52. Lucas of Tuy, *Chronicon Mundi*, 231.

53. Ibid., 232.

54. Ibid., 238–40.

55. Rodrigo Jiménez, *De rebus Hispanie*, 123–24.

56. Ibid., 133.

57. *Versión crítica de la Estoria de España: estudio y edición desde Pelayo hasta Ordoño II*, ed. Inés Fernández-Ordóñez (Madrid: Fundación Ramón Menéndez Pidal; Universidad Autónoma de Madrid, 1993), 436, 442–43, 498–501.

58. Ibid., 500.

59. *Poema de Fernán González*, ed. Alonso Zamora Vicente (Madrid: Espasa Calpe, 1946), ll. 104–7.

60. On the literary "echoes" of the Legend, see Roca Franquesa, "La leyenda," 147–63.

61. Teófilo Braga, *Epopêas da raça moçárabe* (Porto: Imprensa Portuguesa, 1871), 174–75; idem, *As lendas cristãs* (Porto: Lugan & Genelioux, 1892), 270–84. The link between the Byzantine and Compostelan legends is reaffirmed by Márquez Villanueva, *Santiago*, 190. However, contemporary Byzantine sources make no mention of the tribute, and it is almost certainly a later legend. I am grateful to Dr. Mark Whittow for clarifying this point for me.

62. *Records of the Past*, 2nd series, ed. A. H. Sayce, 6 vols. (London: Samuel Bagster, 1888–92), 4 (1890), 63; online at http://www.sacred-texts.com/ane/rp/rp204/rp20413.htm (last accessed 19.11.2013).

63. On a possible link between the legend of the tribute of the hundred maidens and that of Theseus, see further José Antonio Quijera Pérez, "El tributo de las cien doncellas. Un viejo mito mediterráneo," *Revista de Folklore* 13 (1993): 128–35.

64. On the Tristan legend and its dissemination, see Joan Tasker Grimbert, ed., *Tristan and Isolde: A Casebook* (New York: Routledge, 2002).

65. For what follows, see Joaquin Lorenzo Villanueva, *Viage literario a las iglesias de España*, 22 vols. (Madrid: Imprenta Real, 1803–52), 6: 340–41; cf. Petro de Marca, *Marca Hispanica sive Limes Hispanicus* (Paris: François Muguet, 1688), cols. 494–95.

66. Bishop Gaufred of Barbastro was a case in point: see Enrique Flórez et al., *España Sagrada: theatro geográfico-histórico de la iglesia de España*, 56 vols. (Madrid: various publishers, 1747–1957), 47: 287. On ransoming activities more broadly, see below n. 105.

67. Anthony Lappin, *Gonzalo de Berceo: The Poet and His Verses* (Woodbridge: Tamesis, 2008).

68. *La "Vida de San Millán de la Cogolla" de Gonzalo de Berceo (Estudio y edición crítica)*, ed. Brian Dutton, 2nd ed. (London: Tamesis, 1984). Berceo adapted and substantially expanded a much earlier Latin Life of St. Aemilian, composed by Braulio of Zaragoza sometime between 631 and 645: *Vita S. Emiliani: edición crítica*, ed. Luis Vázquez de Parga (Madrid: CSIC, 1943); English trans, A. T. Fear, *Lives of the Visigothic Fathers* (Liverpool: Liverpool University Press, 1997), 15–43.

69. El reï Abderraman, sennor de los paganos,
un mortal enemigo de todos los christianos,
avié pavor echado por cuestas e por planos,
non avién nul consejo por exir de sus manos.

Mandó a los christianos el qe mal sieglo prenda,
que li diessen [cadanno] [tres vent] duennas en renda,
las medias de lignaje, las medias chus sorrenda;
¡mal sieglo aya preste qe prende tal ofrenda!

Yazié toda Espanna en esta servidumne,
dava esti tributo cadanno por costumne;
fazié anniversarios de muy grant suciedumne,
mas por quitarse ende non avié firmedumne.

Todos estos qebrantos, esta mortal manciella,
era más afincada en León e ên Castiella;
mas todo Christian[ism]o sedié man a massiella,
ca pora todos era una mala postiella.

Nunqua fue en christianos tan fuert qebrantamiento,
por meter sus christianas en tal enconamiento;
una serié grant cosa dexa[r] tan grant conviento,
nunqua fue sosacado tan mal sosacamiento.

Mucha duenna d'alfaya de linaje derecho,
andavan afontadas sufriendo mu[ch] despecho,
era muy mal exiemplo, mucho peor el fecho,
dar christian[o]s a moros sues duennas por tal pecho.

—*La "Vida de San Millán de la Cogolla"*, ll. 369–74.

70. For a discussion of the literary style of Gonzalo de Berceo's account of the episode of the *Voto*, see Francisco Javier Grande Quejigo, *Hagiografía y difusión en la vida de San*

Millán de la Cogolla de Gonzalo de Berceo, Logroño: Gobierno de La Rioja; Instituto de Estudios Riojanos, 2000), 145–61.

71. *La "Vida de San Millán de la Cogolla"*, ll. 461–79.

72. The numerous charters attributed to Count Fernán González which were forged in the scriptorium of San Millán are subjected to scrutiny by Manuel Zabalza Duque, ed., *Colección diplomática de los condes de Castilla* (Valladolid: Junta de Castilla y León, 1998). Cf. Julio Escalona, Isabel Velázquez Soriano, and Paloma Juárez Benítez, "Identification of the sole extant charter issued by Fernán González, Count of Castile (932–970)," *JMIS* 4 (2012): 259–88.

73. *La "Vida de San Millán de la Cogolla"*, 1–7. On the tribute of San Millán, see Antonio Ubieto Arteta, "Los "Votos" de San Millán," in *Homenaje a Jaime Vicens Vives*, 2 vols. (Barcelona: Universidad de Barcelona, 1965), 1: 304–24; *La "Vida de San Millán de la Cogolla"*, 169.

74. Pilar Azcárate, Julio Escalona, Cristina Jular, and Miguel Larrañaga, "Volver a nacer: historia e identidad en los monasterios de Arlanza, San Millán y Silos (siglos XII–XIII)," *Cahiers de linguistique hispanique médiévale* 29 (2006): 359–94, at 15–24.

75. *La "Vida de San Millán de la Cogolla"*, 183–88 and l. 479; José Ángel García de Cortázar, *El dominio del monasterio de San Millán de la Cogolla (siglos X a XIII): introducción a la historia rural de Castilla altomedieval* (Salamanca: Universidad de Salamanca, 1969), 321–23.

76. Grande Quejigo, *Hagiografía*, 248–57, 287, 319.

77. *La "Vida de San Millán de la Cogolla,"* 9–24.

78. Florián de Ocampo, *Corónica general de España que recopilaba el Maestro Florian de Ocampo coronista del rey nuestro señor Don Felipe II*, 8 vols. (Madrid: Benito Cano, 1791), 8: 327.

79. Lope de Vega, *Las doncellas de Simancas*, in *Obras de Lope de Vega*, 16, ed. Marcelino Menéndez y Pelayo (Madrid: Atlas, 1966), 395–431. Today the maidens are commemorated as part of the annual town festivities in honor of its patron St. Saviour, and a monument has been erected in their honor.

80. Jane Tibbetts Schulenberg, *Forgetful of Their Sex: Female Sanctity and Society, ca. 500–1100* (Chicago: University of Chicago Press, 2001), especially 145–49, 168–75.

81. Fray Antonio de Yepes, *Crónica general de la Orden de San Benito*, ed. Justo Pérez de Urbel, 3 vols. (Madrid: Atlas, 1959–60), 1: 138; cf. Schulenberg, *Forgetful of Their Sex*, 147. On the significance of self-inflicted facial lacerations by victims of rape, see Dillard, *Daughters of the Reconquest*, 183–84.

82. Ocampo, *Corónica general de España*, 7: 142.

83. Cantera Orive, *La batalla de Clavijo*, 126–27; cf. María Flora Cuadrado Lorenzo, "La iglesia de Santa María de Carrión de los Condes y su programa escultórico," *Publicaciones de la Institución Tello Téllez de Meneses* 57 (1987): 203–92.

84. Ocampo, *Corónica general de España*, 7: 142. The Caraveo family, originally from Cantabria but established in Ciudad Rodrigo near Salamanca by the middle of the sixteenth century, also incorporated the heads of five *doncellas* onto its family arms: Endika, Irantzu, and Garikoitz de Mogrobejo, *Diccionario Hispanoamericano de Heráldica Onomástica y Genealogía*, 32 (17) (Bilbao: Editorial Mogrobejo-Zabala, 2009), 469–70. I am grateful to Amanda Dotseth for bringing this to my attention.

85. Margarita Torres Sevilla-Quiñones de León, *Las batallas legendarias y el oficio de la guerra* (Barcelona: Plaza & Janés, 2002), 110.

86. Gonzalo Argote de Molina, *Nobleza de Andalucía*, ed. Manuel Muñoz y Garnica (Jaén: Francisco López Vizcaíno, 1886; repr. Jaén: Instituto de Estudios Giennenses, 1957), 721–22.

87. Braga, *Epopeas*, 186–90.

88. Ibid., 189–207.

89. For what follows, see Martín de Riquer, *La leyenda de Galcerán de Pinós y el rescate de las cien doncellas* (Barcelona: Talleres Gráficos Antonio J. Rovira, 1944).

90. The altarpiece can now be seen in the Museu Nacional d'Art de Catalunya, Barcelona.

91. Lope García de Salazar, *Las bienandanzas e fortunas. Códice del siglo XV*, ed. Ángel Rodríguez Herrero, 4 vols. (Bilbao: Diputación Provincial de Vizcaya, 1967).

92. Ibid., 3:11–13. The episode is subjected to revealing analysis by Francomano, "The Legend," 13–20.

93. Francomano, "The Legend", 15. Cf. Rodriguez, *Captives and Their Saviors*, 50.

94. *Romancero general*, 1: no. 617. The original date of composition of the ballad is unknown, and it did not appear in written form until 1597: Francomano, "The Legend," 22.

95. *Chronica regia Coloniensis*, ed. Georg Waitz, *MGH: Scriptores rerum Germanicarum*, 18i (Hanover: Impensis Bibliopoli Hahniani, 1880), 1–299, at 240; *Gosuini de expugnatione Salaciae carmen. In Monumenta Portugalia Historica, a saeculo octavo post Christum usque ad quintum decimum: Scriptores*, vol. I, fascículo II. Ed. Alexandre Herculano. Lisbon: Academia Real das Ciências, 1860, 101–4, at 103, ll. 63–65.

96. *Ex historia expeditionum in Terram Sanctam a. 1217–1219*, in Waitz, ed., *MGH: Scriptores rerum Germanicarum*, 18, 339–43, at 340; *Gesta crucigerorum Rhenanorum*, ed. Reinhold Röhricht, in *Quinti belli sacri: Scriptores minores* (Geneva: J.-G. Fick, 1879), 27–56, at 30.

97. For an outline of these developments, see O'Callaghan, *Reconquest and Crusade*, 66–117.

98. The phenomenon of captivity in the Peninsula has been the subject of extensive scholarly focus. The pioneering work as far as the Crown of Aragon was concerned was José María Ramos y Loscertales, *El cautiverio en la Corona de Aragon durante los siglos XIII, XIV y XV* (Zaragoza: Publicaciones del Estudio de Filología de Aragón, 1915). This may be supplemented by Maria Teresa Ferrer i Mallol, "La redempció de captius a la Corona Catalano-Aragonesa (segle XIV)," *AEM* 15 (1985): 237–97; and Rodriguez, *Captives and Their Saviors*. On the Castilian side, see Carmen Argente del Castillo Ocaña, "Los cautivos en la frontera entre Jaén y Granada," in Cristina Segura Graíño, ed., *Relaciones Exteriores del Reino de Granada. IV Coloquio de Historia Medieval Andaluza* (Almería: Instituto de Estudios Almerienses, 1988), 211–25; Emilio Cabrera Muñoz, "Cautivos cristianos en el reino de Granada durante la segunda mitad del siglo XV," in Segura Graíño, ed., *Relaciones Exteriores*, 227–36; Abdelghaffar Ben Driss, "Los cautivos entre Granada y Castilla en el siglo XV según las fuentes árabes," in Pedro Segura Artero, ed., *Actas del Congreso "La Frontera Oriental Nazarí como Sujeto Histórico (S.XIII–XVI)": Lorca-Vera, 22 a 24 de noviembre de 1994*

(Alicante: Instituto de Estudios Almerienses, 1997), 301–10. On the ideological significance of captivity, see Anthony Lappin, *The Medieval Cult of Saint Dominic of Silos*, MHRA Texts and Dissertations 56 (Leeds: Maney; Modern Humanities Research Association, 2002); and Remensnyder, "Christian Captives," 642–77. There is much useful material of a comparative nature in Friedman, *Encounter Between Enemies.*

99. Anthony Lappin's research on captivity in Castile, drawn from the evidence of miracle stories, suggests that perhaps one-third of those taken captive were men-at-arms: *The Medieval Cult*, 342–49 (table 7).

100. On the capture of children, see Cabrera, "Cautivos cristianos", 230.

101. *Fuero de Cuenca*, 11.47; *Fuero de Teruel*, §496. For other prohibitions, see Dillard, *Women of the Reconquest*, 207–8.

102. Maria Teresa Ferrer i Mallol, *La frontera amb l'Islam en el segle XIV: Cristians i sarraïns al País Valencià* (Barcelona: CSIC, 1988), 302–3; Hinojosa Montalvo, *Los mudéjares*, 2: 532.

103. On the living conditions endured by captives, see José María de Cossío, "Cautivos de moros en el siglo XIII," *Al-Andalus* 7 (1942): 49–112, at 74–83; Rodriguez, *Captives and Their Saviors*, 42–48.

104. Rodriguez, *Captives and Their Saviors*, 32–34, 176–78. Other research indicates that on the Muslim side at least 1063 captives were redeemed between 1381 and 1480: Andrés Díaz Borrás, *El miedo al mediterráneo: la caridad popular valenciana y la redención de cautivos bajo poder musulmán, 1323–1539* (Barcelona: CSIC, 2001), 287–334.

105. On the work of the Trinitarians, a good starting point is Bonifacio Porres Alonso, *Libertad a los cautivos: Actividad redentora de la orden Trinitaria*, 2 vols. (Córdoba and Salamanca: Secretariado Trinitario, 1998). On the Mercedarians, the research of James Brodman is particularly significant, especially his *Ransoming Captives in Crusader Spain: the Order of Merced on the Christian-Islamic Frontier* (Philadelphia: University of Pennsylvania Press, 1986). See also Díaz Borrás, *El miedo*; Joaquín Millán Rubio, *La Orden de Nuestra Señora de la Merced* (Rome: Instituto Histórico de la Orden de la Merced, 1992). The efficiency of their ransoming efforts is called into question by Rodriguez, *Captives and Their Saviors*, 106–7.

106. Kathryn Miller, *Guardians of Islam: Religious Authority and Muslim Communities of Late Medieval Spain* (New York: Columbia University Press, 2008), 151–75. See also Cristina de la Puente, "Mujeres cautivas en 'la tierra del Islam,'" *Al-Andalus-Magreb* 14 (2007): 19–37.

107. Rodriguez, *Captives and Their Saviors*, 81–93; idem, "Conversion anxieties in the Crown of Aragón in the Later Middle Ages," *Al-Masāq* 22 (2010): 315–24.

108. *Cantigas de Santa María*, 3: no. 325; translation by Kulp-Hill, *Songs of Holy Mary*, no. 325. On Alfonso X's devotion to the Marian cult, see Anthony Lappin, "The Thaumaturgy of Regal Piety: Alfonso X and the *Cantigas de Santa Maria*," *Journal of Hispanic Research* 4 (1995–96): 39–59.

109. Aḥmad Mukhtār 'Abd al-Fattāḥ 'Abbādī., *El reino de Granada en la época de Muhammad V* (Madrid: Instituto de Estudios Islámicos, 1973), 161. See now Barbara Boloix, *Las sultanas de la Alhambra (siglos XIII–XV): las grandes desconocidas del reino nazarí de Granada* (Granada : Editorial Comares, 2013).

110. Robert Brunschvig, ed., *Deux récits de voyage inédits en Afrique du Nord au XVe siècle: Abdalbasit b. Halil et Adorne* (Paris: Larose, 1936; repr Paris: Maisonneuve and Larose, 2001), 125. For other examples, see Marín, *Mujeres*, 129.

111. Hernando de Baeza, "Las cosas que pasaron entre los reyes de Granada desde el tiempo de el rrey don Juan de Castilla, segundo de este nonbre, hasta que los Catholicos Reyes ganaron el rreyno de Granada." In *Relaciones de algunos sucesos de los últimos tiempos del reino de Granada* (Madrid: Sociedad de Bibliófilos Españoles, 1868), 1–44, at 7–8. For a full discussion of this liaison and the later legends surrounding it, see José Enrique López de Coca, "The Making of Isabel de Solis," in Collins and Goodman, eds., *Medieval Spain: Culture, Conflict and Coexistence*, 225–41.

112. Juan de Mata Carriazo, "Relaciones fronterizas entre Jaén y Granada en el año 1479," *Revista de archivos, bibliotecas y museos* 61 (1955): 23–51, at 31.

113. Rodriguez, *Captives and Their Saviors*, 50. Jewish law accorded priority to the release of women for precisely the same reason: Friedman, *Encounter Between Enemies*, 178–79.

114. *Los "miraculos romançados" de Pero Marín: Edición crítica*, ed. Karl-Heinz Anton (Burgos: Abadía de Silos, 1988). There is an earlier edition by Sebastián de Vergara, *Vida, y milagros de el thaumaturgo español Moyses Segundo, redemptor de cautivos, abogado de los felices partos, Sto. Domingo Manso, abad Benedictino, reparador de el Real Monasterio de Silos* (Madrid: Imprenta de los Herederos de Francisco del Hierro, 1736), 128–229. The accounts are subjected to scrutiny by José María de Cossío, "Cautivos de moros en el siglo XIII," *Al-Andalus* 7 (1942): 49–112; María de los Llanos Martínez Carrillo, "Historicidad de los 'Miraculos romançados' de Pedro Marín (1232–1293): el territorio y la esclavitud granadinos," *AEM* 21 (1991): 69–96; Lappin, *The Medieval Cult*, 275–390.

115. Lappin, *The Medieval Cult*, 276–77.

116. For what follows, see *Los "miraculos romancados,"* 163–64; Vergara, *Vida, y milagros*, 214–15. Discussion in Lappin, *The Medieval Cult*, 295–96. For other female captives, see *Los "miraculos romançados"*, 115–17, 166–67, 167–68.

117. Lappin, *The Medieval Cult*, 295–96.

118. Rodriguez, *Captives and Their Saviors*, 49.

119. Martín de Ximena Jurado, *Catálogo de los obispos de las iglesias catedrales de la diócesis de Jaén y anales eclesiásticos de este obispado*, ed. José Rodríguez Molina and María José Osorio Pérez (Granada: Universidad de Granada, 1991), 320. See in this context, Carmen Argente del Castillo Ocaña, "Cautiverio y martirio de doncellas en La Frontera," in Francisco Toro Ceballos and José Rodríguez Molina, eds., *IV estudios de Frontera: Historia, tradiciones y leyendas en La Frontera* (Jaén: Diputación Provincial de Jaén, 2002), 31–72, at 59–61.

120. Ximena Jurado, *Catálogo*, 344.

121. For what follows, see ibid., 368.

122. José Rodríguez Molina, "La frontera entre Granada y Jaén fuente de agrandecimiento para la nobleza (Siglo XIV)," in Segura Graíño, ed., *Relaciones Exteriores*, 237–50, with an edition of the royal diploma at 247–50; see also *Colección diplomática del Archivo Histórico Municipal de Jaén. Siglos XIV y XV*, ed. José Rodríguez Molina et al. (Jaén: Ayuntamiento de Jaén, 1985), no. 2.

123. On the importance attached to *hidalguía*, see James Casey, *Early Modern Spain: A Social History* (London: Routledge, 1999), 139–44.

124. *Crónicas de los Reyes de Castilla. Desde don Alfonso el Sabio, hasta los Católicos don Fernando y doña Isabel*, ed. Cayetano Rosell, 3 vols. (Madrid: Ediciones Atlas, 1953), 2: 40.

125. Ferrer i Mallol, "La redempció de captius," 241 n. 23.

126. Andrés Giménez Soler, "La Corona de Aragon y Granada," *Boletín de la Real Academia de Buenas Letras de Barcelona* 19 (1905): 101–34; 20 (1905): 186–224; 21 (1906): 295–324; 22 (1906): 333–65; 23 (1906): 450–76; 24 (1906): 485–96; 26 (1907): 49–91; 27 (1907):146–80; 28 (1907): 200–25; 29 (1908): 271–98; 30 (1908): 342–75, at 22: 352–53.

127. Ángel Canellas López, "Aragón y la empresa del Estrecho en el siglo XIV: Nuevos documentos del Archivo Municipal de Zaragoza," *EEMCA* 2 (1946): 7–73, doc. 9.

128. On the myths surrounding the demise of King Roderic, see Patricia E. Grieve, *The Eve of Spain: Myths of Origins in the History of Christian, Muslim, and Jewish Conflict* (Baltimore: Johns Hopkins University Press, 2009).

CHAPTER 4. LUST AND LOVE ON THE IBERIAN FRONTIER

1. On the historical background, see Gonzalo Martínez Diez, *El Condado de Castilla (711–1038): La historia frente a la leyenda*, 2 vols. (Madrid: Junta de Castilla y León; Marcial Pons, 2005), 2: 483–656.

2. For what follows, see *Chronica Naierensis*, 144–46; Spanish translation by Estévez Sola, *Crónica Najerense*, 150–51. For an overview of the legend and its transmission in later historiography, see David G. Pattison, *From Legend to Chronicle: The Treatment of Epic Material in Alphonsine Historiography* (Oxford: Society for the Study of Mediaeval Languages and Literature, 1983), 57–69; Mercedes Vaquero, *Tradiciones orales en la historiografía de fines de la Edad Media*, Spanish Series 55 (Madison, Wis.: Hispanic Seminary of Medieval Studies, 1990), 1–64.

3. Rodrigo Jiménez, *De rebus Hispanie*, 151; Spanish translation by Fernández Valverde, *Historia de los hechos*, 194–95. The archbishop further observes that out of contrition for his role in the death of his mother Count Sancho erected the Benedictine monastery of Oña.

4. The highly complex process of textual transmission is untangled by Fernández-Ordóñez, *Versión crítica*, 73–82, 288–90; see further, however, Francisco Bautista, "Pseudo-historia y leyenda en la historiografía medieval: la Condesa Traidora," in Francisco Bautista, ed., *El relato historiográfico: textos y tradiciones en la España medieval*, Papers of the Medieval Hispanic Research Seminar 48 (London: Department of Hispanic Studies, Queen Mary, University of London, 2006), 59–101, at 79–92.

5. "Agora sabet aqui que desde alli adelante fue tomada en vso en Castilla de dar primero beuer a las mugeres": *La* Estoria de España, 358.

6. For what follows, see *Primera Crónica General*, 2: 427–28.

7. Ibid., 2: 453–54.

8. Full discussion in Bautista, "Pseudo-historia y leyenda."

9. For example, Ruth House Webber, "The Spanish Epic in the Context of the

Medieval European Epic," *Studia Riquer* 4 (1991): 333–44, at 341–42. See, however, Pattison, *From Legend to Chronicle*, 61; Alan Deyermond, *La literatura perdida de la Edad Media castellana. Catálogo y estudio I: Épica y romances* (Salamanca: Universidad de Salamanca, 1995), 69.

10. Bautista, "Pesudo-historia y leyenda," 83–92.

11. For an introduction to these matters, see Menéndez Pidal, *Historia y epopeya*, 1–27; Louis Chalon, "La historicidad de la leyenda de la Condesa Traidora," *Journal of Hispanic Philology* 2 (1977–78): 153–63. Gonzalo Martínez Díez has cast doubt on the historicity of the legend: *El Condado de Castilla*, 2: 529. On the incorporation of folkloric motifs in this and other texts, see Alan Deyermond and Margaret Chaplin, "Folk-Motifs in the Medieval Spanish Epic," *Philological Quarterly* 51 (1972): 36–53, especially 49–52.

12. William P. Shepard, "Two Assumed Epic Legends in Spanish," *Modern Language Notes* 23 (1908): 146–47; Colin Smith, *The Making of the* Poema de mio Cid (Cambridge: Cambridge University Press, 1983), 28.

13. Peggy McCracken, *The Romance of Adultery: Queenship and Sexual Transgression in Old French Literature* (Philadelphia: University of Pennsylvania Press, 1998), especially 144–70. On poison as the weapon of choice for murderous queens, see Frank Collard, "*Venenosa mulier coronata:* variations sur la figure de la reine empoisonneuse dans l'Occident médiéval," in Marcel Faure, ed., *Reines et princesses au Moyen Âge: Actes du Cinquième Colloque International de Montpellier, Université Paul-Valéry, 24–27 novembre 1999*, 2 vols. (Montpellier: Université Paul-Valéry, 2001), 1:303–22.

14. Flórez, *España Sagrada*, 23: 320.

15. Bautista, "Pseudo-historia y leyenda," 68–69.

16. Diego Catalán, *De la silva textual al taller historiográfico alfonsí – Códices, crónicas, versiones y cuadernos de trabajo* (Madrid: Fundación Ramón Menéndez Pidal; Universidad Autónoma de Madrid, 1997), 382 n. 367.

17. Bautista, "Pseudo-historia y leyenda," 63–68.

18. *Chronica Naierensis*, 146. The belief that al-Manṣūr's attacks were divinely sanctioned had been earlier expressed by the author of the so-called *Historia Silensis*: *Historia Silense: Edición crítica e introducción*, ed. Justo Pérez de Urbel and Atilano González Ruiz-Zorrilla (Madrid: CSIC, 1959), 173; English trans. in Barton and Fletcher, *The World of El Cid*, 9–64, at 35. See also Pelayo, *Crónica*, 65.

19. *Chronica Naierensis*, 145–46; *Crónicas asturianas*, 127.

20. Bautista, "Pseudo-historia y leyenda," 73–76. The political rhetoric of the chronicler of Nájera chimes with that of the chancery products of Alfonso VIII (1158–1214), which also trumpeted Castile's role as defender of Christendom: Peter Linehan, *History and the Historians of Medieval Spain* (Oxford: Clarendon, 1993), 291–95.

21. Azcárate, Escalona, Jular and Larrañaga, "Volver a nacer."

22. The pioneering study was Alan Deyermond, "La sexualidad en a la épica medieval española," *Nueva Revista de Filología Española* 36 (1988): 767–86. See also Andrew M. Beresford, "'Cortol la cabeça e atola del petral ca la querie dar en donas a Galiana': On the Relationship Between Death and Sexuality in Four Epic Legends," in David G. Pattison, ed., *Textos épicos castellanos: problemas de edición y crítica*, in *Papers of the Medieval Hispanic*

Research Seminar 20 (London: Department of Hispanic Studies, Queen Mary and Westfield College, 2000), 41–63, at 53–58.

23. Vera Castro Lingl, "The Count's Wife in *La condesa traidora*, the *Poema de Fernan González*, and the *Romanz del infant Garçía:* How Many Sanchas?" *Bulletin of Hispanic Studies* (Glasgow) 73 (1997): 373–80; and eadem, "The Two Wives of Count Garçi Fernández: Assertive Women in *La condesa traidora*," in Andrew M. Beresford, ed., *Quien hubiese tal ventura: Medieval Hispanic Studies in Honour of Alan Deyermond* (London: Department of Hispanic Studies, Queen Mary and Westfield College, 1997), 9–21. On the supposed impotence of García Fernández, see Patricia Grieve, "Private Man, Public Woman: Trading Places in *Condesa traidora*," *Romance Quarterly* 34 (1987): 317–26, at 320; see, however, the comments of Beresford, "'Cortol la cabeça'," 54 n.18.

24. Menéndez Pidal, *Historia y epopeya*, 27.

25. "Crónica de la Población de Ávila," ed. Manuel Gómez Moreno, *Boletín de la Real Academia de la Historia* 113 (1943): 11–56, at 32–34; also *Crónica de la Población de Ávila*, ed. Amparo Hernández Segura (Valencia: Anúbar, 1966), 27–29. The episode is briefly surveyed by María Jesús Lacarra, "La historia de Enalviellos (*Crónica de la Población de Ávila*)," in *Orígenes de la prosa*, vol. 4 of *Historia de la literatura española*, ed. María Jesús Lacarra and Francisco López Estrada (Madrid: Ediciones Júcar, 1993), 77–84; Laura María Rubio Moreno, "Crónica de la población de Avila: la polifonía textual en la historia de Nalvillos," in *Beatriz Díez Calleja, ed., El primitivo romance hispanico: de nuevo sobre la época de orígenes* (Burgos: Instituto Castellano y Leonés de la Lengua, 2008), 455–63. On the chronicle more broadly, see Manuel Abeledo, "La crónica de la población de Ávila: un estado actual de la cuestión desde su primera publicación," *Estudios de Historia de España* 11 (2009): 13–47.

26. In her edition of the chronicle, Hernández Segura has argued, not altogether convincingly, that the Muslim attack on Ávila probably took place in 1111: *Crónica*, 11–12.

27. For an introduction to the *Livros* and their social and cultural significance, see Luís Krus, *A concepção nobiliárquica do espaço ibérico (1280–1380)* (Lisbon: Fundação Calouste Gulbenkian; Junta nacional de investigação científica e tecnológica, 1994); Juan Paredes, *Las narraciones de los* Livros de Linhagens (Granada: Universidad de Granada, 1995).

28. *Livros Velhos de Linhagens*, ed. Joseph Piel and José Mattoso, in *Portugaliae Monumenta Historica Nova Serie* (Lisbon: Academia das Ciências, 1980); *Livro de Linhagens do Conde D. Pedro*, ed. José Mattoso, in *Portugaliae Monumenta Historica Nova Serie*, 2 vols. (Lisbon: Academia das Ciências, 1980).

29. *Livros Velhos de Linhagens*, 47–50. On the legend and its cultural context, see Raymond Foulché-Delbosc and Alexander Krappe, "La légende du roi Ramire," *Revue Hispanique* 78 (1930): 489–543; Jose Carlos Ribeiro Miranda, "A *Lenda de Gaia* dos Livros de Linhagens: Uma questão de literatura?," *Revista da Faculdade de Letras: Línguas e Literaturas* 5 (1988): 483–516; María Ana Ramos, "*Hestorja dell Rej dom Ramjro de lleom. . . .* Nova versão de *A Lenda de Gaia*," *Critica del Testo* 7 (2004): 791–843; eadem, "A intenção de inscrever na memória colectiva. O sucesso textual do motivo *a mulher de Salomão* na narrativa histórica portuguesa," in Márcio Ricardo Coelho Muniz, Maria de Fátima Maia Ribeiro, and Solange Santos Santana, eds., *Anais do XXII Congresso Internacional da Associação Brasileira de Professores de Literatura Portuguesa (2011)*, 625–53; http://www.abraplip

.org/anais_abraplip/documentos/mesas_tematicas/maria_ana_ramos.pdf; Paredes, *Las narraciones*, 107–23.

30. *Livros Velhos de Linhagens*, 49.

31. *Livro de Linhagens do Conde D. Pedro*, 204–11.

32. The chronicle was edited by Foulché-Delbosc and Krappe, "La légende," 522–25, and Martín Riquer, "Crónica aragonesa del tiempo de Juan II," *Analecta Sacra Tarraconensia* 17 (1944): 1–29; idem, "Una versión aragonesa de la leyenda de la enterrada viva," *Revista de Bibliografía Nacional* 6 (1945): 241–48. The linguistic peculiarities of the text are scrutinized by Fernando López Rajadel, *Datación de la "Historia de los Amantes de Teruel": A través de los datos socioeconómicos del "papel escrito de letra antigua" copiado por Yagüe de Salas* (Teruel: Centro de Documentación Hartzenbusch; Fundación Amantes de Teruel, 2008), 72–79.

33. On folk-motifs, the standard work is Stith Thompson, *Motif-index of folk-literature: a classification of narrative elements in folktales, ballads, fables, mediaeval romances, exempla, fabliaux, jest-books and local legends* (Copenhagen: Rosenkilde and Bagger, 1955). In an Iberian context, see also Deyermond and Chaplin, "Folk-Motifs."

34. Foulché-Delbosc and Krappe, "La légende," 534–43; Ribeiro Miranda, "A lenda de Gaia."

35. According to the chronicler, the towns conquered by Count Sancho included San Esteban de Gormaz, Gormaz, Coruña del Conde, Osma, Castrabo, Medina, Berlanga, *et multas alias*: *Chronica Naierensis*, 149.

36. *CEM*, ed. Rodrigues Lapa. On the authors of the *cantigas*, see José António Souto Cabo, *Os cavaleiros que fizeram as cantigas: aproximação às origens socioculturais da lírica galego-portuguesa* (Niterói: Editora da UFF, 2012). On the *soldadeiras*, see Francisco Nodar Manso, "La parodia de la literatura heroica y hagiográfica en las cantigas de escarnio y mal decir," *Dicenda: Cuadernos de filología hispánica* 9 (1990): 151–61; Liu, "'Affined to love the Moor,'" in Blackmore and Hutcheson, eds., *Queer Iberia*, 48–72, at 57–58; Filios, *Performing Women*, 33–82; eadem, "Jokes on *soldadeiras* in the *Cantigas de escarnio e de mal dizer*," *La corónica* 26 (1998): 29–39.

37. For example, the *soldadeira* Marinha Sabugal: *CEM*, no. 49.

38. *CEM*, no. 25; translation from Filios, *Performing Women*, 57. The *cantiga* in question is attributed to Alfonso X himself.

39. Filios, *Performing Women*, 58.

40. *CEM*, no. 189. Discussion in Liu, "'Affined to love the Moor,'" 64–65; Roy Rosenstein, "The Voiced and the Voiceless in the *Cancioneiros*: The Muslim, the Jew, and the Sexual Heretic as *Exclusus Amator*," *La Corónica* 26 (1998): 65–75, at 70; Filios, *Performing Women*, 70–74.

41. For example, *CEM*, nos. 11, 146, 195, 315, 321, 331, 337, 376, 425, 428.

42. *CEM*, no. 428.

43. Translation by Simon Doubleday, "The Ghost of María Pérez: Phantoms, Fantasies and Fictions of Thirteenth-Century Spain," *Society for Spanish and Portuguese Historical Studies Bulletin* 29, 2–3 (2004–5): 4–19, at 12–13.

44. Ramón Menéndez Pidal, *Poesía juglaresca y orígenes de las literaturas románicas: Problemas de historia literaria y cultural* (Madrid: Instituto de Estudios Políticos, 1957),

167–72; Carlos Álvar, "María Pérez, Balteira,'" *Archivo de filología aragonesa* 36–7 (1985): 11–40; Doubleday, "The Ghost of María Pérez"; idem, "Looking for María Pérez," *Rethinking History* 16.1 (2012): 27–40.

45. Antonio Ballesteros-Beretta, *Alfonso X el Sabio* (Barcelona-Madrid: Salvat Editores, 1963), 381.

46. "Este escarnho seria um documento histórico de grande importância, se o tomássemos a sério": *CEM*, no. 428.

47. Doubleday, "The Ghost of María Pérez," 12; idem, "Looking for María Pérez," 33.

48. Cf. Nirenberg, "Conversion," 1074–75.

49. *Cantigas de Santa María*, 2: no. 186; trans. Kulp-Hill, *Songs of Holy Mary*, no. 186.

50. Albert J. Bagby, "The Moslem in the Cantigas of Alfonso X, El Sabio," *Kentucky Romance Quarterly* 20 (1973): 173–207, at 195. The illustrations are reproduced in Figure 2 of this book. On the relationship between the "monstrous corporality" and lack of reason that were associated with Muslims in the medieval period, see Jeffrey Cohen, *Medieval Identity Machines* (Minneapolis: University of Minnesota Press, 2003), 196–99.

51. Nirenberg, "Conversion," 1074–75; Catlos, *The Victors*, 308–11.

52. Pelayo de Oviedo, *Crónica*, 87; English trans. in Barton and Fletcher, *The World of El Cid*, 87–88.

53. There is an exhaustive study of the various literary portraits of Zaida by Montaner Frutos, "La mora Zaida." See also Jaime Salazar y Acha, "Contribución al estudio del reinado de Alfonso VI de Castilla: algunas aclaraciones sobre su política matrimonial," *Anales de la Real Academia Matritense de Heráldica y Genealogía* 2 (1992–93): 299–343; idem, "De nuevo sobre la mora Zaida," *Hidalguía* 54 (2007): 225–42; Gambra, *Alfonso VI*, 1: 440–45, 475–76. On the background to the liaison between Alfonso and "Zaida," see Évariste Lévi-Provençal, "Hispano-Arabica: La 'Mora Zaida,' femme d'Alphonse VI de Castille, et leur fils l'infant D. Sancho," *Hespéris* 18 (1934): 1–8, at 6 and n. 1.

54. *Chronicon Floriacense*, in *Recueil des Historiens des Gaules et de la France*, 12, ed. Dom Martin Bouquet; new ed. Léopold Delisle (Paris: Victor Palmé, 1877), 7.

55. Ibn Idhārī al-Marrākushī, *Al-Bayān*, 1: 50. The memory of the relationship between Zaida and the Christian king lingered in the collective memory for centuries to come. When, late in the fifteenth century, the North African jurist al-Wansharīshī sought to persuade a Muslim to leave the Peninsula and cross to the Maghreb, he asserted that one of the reasons to do so was to avoid the crime of apostasy, "as occurred to the daughter-in-law of Almuʿtamid b. 'Abbād and her children": Évariste Lévi-Provençal, "La 'Mora Zaida,' belle-fille d'al-Muʿtamid," *Hespéris* 18 (1934): 200–201; cf. Montaner Frutos, "La mora Zaida," 277 and n. 11.

56. *Chronica Naierensis*, 179; *Chronicon Mundi*, 303–4.

57. *De Miraculis Sancti Isidori*: León, Biblioteca Capitular de la Real Colegiata de San Isidoro, MS.63; an edition of the Latin text is in preparation by Patrick Henriet for the *Corpus Christianorum: Continuatio Mediaeualis* series. I am grateful to Dr. Henriet for allowing me to consult his edition in advance of publication. For a Spanish translation, see *Milagros de San Isidoro*, trans. Juan de Robles, ed. José Manuel Martínez Rodríguez (León: Universidad de León; Cátedra de San Isidoro de la Real Colegiata de León, 1992), 8–9.

58. Al-Mu'tamid's supposed sympathy toward St. Isidore had first been reported in the *Translatio sancti Isidori*, an account of the translation of the relics of St. Isidore by a member of the religious community of San Juan Bautista in León, which was later incorporated by the author of the *Historia Silensis*: see *Historia Silense*, 199–204; English translation in Barton and Fletcher, *The World of El Cid*, 56–60.

59. Rodrigo Jiménez de Rada, *De rebus Hispanie*, 214.

60. One manuscript of the chronicle claimed that the king did marry Zaida, but this is almost certainly a later copyist's insertion: Montaner Frutos, "La mora Zaida," 309–10.

61. *La* Estoria de España, 463.

62. The list of towns follows that provided by Rodrigo Jiménez, but inserts Zorita between Huete and Amasatrigo.

63. *Primera Crónica General*, 2: 553.

64. Ibid., 2: 521.

65. María-Jesus Rubiera Mata, "Un insólito caso de conversas musulmanas al cristianismo: las princesas toledanas del siglo XI," in Ángela Muñoz Fernández, ed., *Las mujeres en el cristianismo medieval: Imagenes teóricas y cauces de actuación religiosa* (Madrid: Asociación Cultural Al-Mudayna, 1989), 341–48, at 342. On the use of the title *sayyida* in al-Andalus, see also Manuela Marín, "Ṣubḥ," *EI*[2], 9: 740–41. Alberto Montaner has suggested that Zaida's real name may have been Maryam or Māriya, that is, the Arabic form of Mary, which was the name recorded by Rodrigo Jiménez in the early thirteenth century: Montaner Frutos, "La mora Zaida," 310–14.

66. On al-Mu'tamid b. Abbād, see Evariste Lévi-Provençal, "'Abbādids (Banū 'Abbād)," *EI*[2], 1: 5–7; idem, "al-Mu'tamid ibn 'Abbād: 1. Life," *EI*[2], 7: 766–67.

67. Lévi-Provençal, "Hispano-Arabica," 6–7. Alternatively, Jaime Salazar y Acha has posited that Zaida was the daughter of al-Mutamid's elder brother, Ismā'īl b. 'Abbād: "Contribución," 319–20. On the problems this latter identification supposes, see Montaner Frutos, "La mora Zaida," 278–79.

68. Ramón Menéndez Pidal, *La España del Cid*, 5th ed., 2 vols. (Madrid: Espasa-Calpe, 1956), 1: 405–8 and 2: 764–65; Jacinto Bosch Vilá, *Los almorávides* (Granada: Universidad de Granada, 1990), 151–52.

69. For a detailed discussion of the likely chronology, see Montaner, "La mora Zaida," 297–99.

70. Rubiera Mata, "Un insólito caso," 344–45.

71. Lévi-Provençal, "Hispano-Arábica," 7. A similarly skeptical note is taken by Gambra, *Alfonso* VI, 1: 91, 442–44; and Gonzalo Martínez Díez, *El Cid histórico* (Barcelona: Planeta, 1999), 128–30.

72. For a useful overview, see Montaner Frutos, "La mora Zaida," 299–304.

73. Bernard F. Reilly, *The Kingdom of León-Castilla Under King Alfonso VI, 1065–1109* (Princeton, N.J.: Princeton University Press, 1988), 338–40 and 344–45.

74. Gonzalo Martínez Díez, *Alfonso VI: señor del Cid, conquistador de Toledo* (Madrid: Temas de Hoy, 2003), 121, 166, 171, 217–18, 227; cf. Salazar y Acha, "Contribución," 323–28.

75. On the problems of interpretation raised by the epitaph, see Montaner Frutos, "La mora Zaida," 283–95.

76. Menéndez Pidal, *Poesía juglaresca*, 263, 288; idem, *La España del Cid*, 2: 762.

77. Salvador Martínez, "Alfonso VI: Hero in Search of a Poet," *La Corónica* 15:1 (1986–87): 1–16, at 3–4; Deyermond, *La literatura perdida*, 127; Montaner Frutos, "La mora Zaida," 315 and n. 102 and 344.

78. For the influence of *Mainete* in the Peninsula, see Inés Fernández Ordóñez, "El tema épico-legendario de *Carlos Mainete* y la transformación de la historiografía medieval hispánica entre los siglos XIII y XIV," in Jean-Philippe Genet, ed., *L'Histoire et les nouveaux publics dans l'Europe médiévale (XIIIe-XVe siècles)* (Paris: Publications de la Sorbonne, 1997), 89–112; Francisco Bautista, "La tradición épica de las *Enfances* de Carlomagno y el *Cantar de Mainete* perdido," *Romance Philology* 56 (2003): 217–44; idem, *La materia de Francia en la literatura medieval española: La "Crónica carolingia"; Flores y Blancaflor; Berta y Carlomagno* (San Millán de la Cogolla: Instituto Biblioteca Hispánica del CiLengua, 2008), 73–83.

79. *La* Estoria de España, 426–33; *Primera Crónica General*, 2: 340–43. On the development of the Castilian *Cantar*, see Bautista, "La tradición épica."

80. Rodrigo Jiménez, *De rebus Hispanie*, 130.

81. Julio González, *El Reino de Castilla en la época de Alfonso VIII*, 3 vols. (Madrid: CSIC, 1960), 3: 179–86. On the subsequent military campaign against Navarre, see ibid., 1: 842–54.

82. Rodrigo Jiménez, *De rebus Hispanie*, 254; trans. Fernández Valverde, *Historia de los hechos*, 302.

83. King Sancho had already borrowed 70,000 solidi from the bishop to help fund the war effort against Castile and Aragon: *Colección diplomática de la Catedral de Pamplona, 829–1243*, ed. José Goñi Gaztambide (Pamplona: Gobierno de Navarra, Departamento de Educación y Cultura, 1997), no. 423.

84. Pedro Lino Munárriz y Velasco calculated the king's stay in al-Andalus to be no more than two years: "Viaje del rey don Sancho al África," *Boletín de la Comisión de monumentos históricos y artísticos de Navarra*, segunda época, año 3 (1912): 5–39, at 30. See further Nevill Barbour, "The relations of King Sancho VII of Navarre with the Almohads," *Revue de l'Occident Musulman et de la Méditerranée* 4 (1967): 9–21.

85. "Chronica Latina Regum Castellae," ed. Luis Charlo Brea, in *Chronica Hispana saeculi XIII*, eds. Luis Charlo Brea, Juan Antonio Estévez Sola, and Rocío Carande Herrero. *CCCM* 73 (Turnhout: Brepols, 1997), 7–118, at 51; English trans. by Joseph F. O'Callaghan, *The Latin Chronicle of the Kings of Castile* (Tempe: Arizona Center for Medieval and Renaissance Studies, 2002), 33.

86. *Primera Crónica General*, 2: 684.

87. For what follows, see *Chronica Magistri Roger of Hovedon*, ed. William Stubbs, *Rolls Series* 51, 4 vols. (London: Longmans, Green, Reader and Dyer, 1868–71), 3: 90–92. The Latin text and English translation of Roger's account are provided by Colin Smith, ed., *Christians and Moors in Spain*, vol. 2: *1195–1614* (Warminster: Aris & Phillips, 1989), 6–11.

88. *Chronica Magistri Roger of Hovedon*, 4: 113.

89. Munárriz y Velasco, "Viaje del rey don Sancho," 16. The historicity of the tale was also dismissed by Ambrosio Huici Miranda, *Las grandes batallas de la Reconquista* (Madrid: CSIC, 1956), 220–23.

90. Smith, ed., *Christians and Moors*, 7.

91. On the popularity of the legend, see Patricia E. Grieve, Floire and Blancheflor *and the European Romance* (Cambridge: Cambridge University Press, 1997); Sharon Kinoshita, *Medieval Boundaries: Rethinking Difference in Old French Literature* (Philadelphia: University of Pennsylvania Press, 2006), 77–104. See also Lynn Shutters, "Christian Love or Pagan Transgression? Marriage and Conversion in *Floire et Blancheflor*," in Albrecht Classen, ed., *Discourses on Love, Marriage, and Transgression in Medieval and Early Modern Literature* (Tempe: Arizona Center for Medieval Studies, 2004), 85–108. On the possible Arabic origins of some versions of the tale, see Cynthia Robinson, *Medieval Andalusian Courtly Culture: Ḥadīth Bayāḍ wa Riyāḍ* (London: Routledge, 2007), chap. 4.

92. A late thirteenth-century date of composition is defended by Nieves Baranda, "Los problemas de la historia medieval de Flores y Blancaflor," *Dicenda* 10 (1991–2): 21–39; and Fernando Gómez Redondo, *Historia de la prosa medieval castellana. II. El desarrollo de los géneros. La ficción caballeresca y el orden religioso,* 2 vols. (Madrid: Crítica, 1999), 2: 1577–93. By contrast, Fernando Bautista has placed the date of composition a full century later: *La materia de Francia*, 29–38.

93. Kinoshita, *Medieval Boundaries*, 103–4.

94. Rocío Sánchez Ameijeiras, "Histories and Stories of Love and Conversion in Fourteenth-Century Burgos," *Hispanic Research Journal* 13 (2012): 449–67.

95. Ibid., 458–60.

96. Ibid., 462.

97. Cynthia Robinson, "Arthur in the Alhambra? Narrative and Nasrid Courtly Self-Fashioning in The Hall Of Justice Ceiling Paintings," *Medieval Encounters* 14 (2008): 164–98.

98. Ibid., 185–89.

99. *Vita S. Petri Oxomensis, episcopi in Hispania ab anonymo suppari conscripta*, ed. Francis Plaine, *Analecta Bollandiana* 4 (1885): 10–29. On the *Vita*, see Javier Pérez-Embid, *Hagiologia y sociedad en la España medieval: Castilla y León (siglos XI–XIII)* (Huelva: Universidad de Huelva, 2002), 153–67; Patrick Henriet, "Les saints et la frontière en *Hispania* au cours du moyen âge central," in Klaus Herbers and Nikolas Jaspert, eds., *Grenzräume und Grenzüberschreitungen im Vergleich: Der Osten und der Western des mittelalterlichen Lateineuropa* (Berlin: Akademie Verlag, 2007), 361–86, at 362–63, nn. 4 and 7; and especially Anthony John Lappin, "Between the Chisel and the Quill: The Development of the Cult of Peter of Osma during the Middle Ages," in Barry Taylor, Geoffrey West, and Jane Whetnall, eds., *Text, Manuscript, and Print in Medieval and Modern Iberia: Studies in Honour of David Hook* (New York: Hispanic Seminary of Medieval Studies, 2013), 41–87.

100. *Vita S. Petri Oxomensis*, 19–21.

101. Roger Boase, *The Origin and Meaning of Courtly Love* (Manchester: Manchester University Press, 1977).

102. *The Songs of Jaufré Rudel*, ed. Rupert T. Pickens (Toronto: Pontifical Institute of Mediaeval Studies, 1978).

103. At least twenty-four poems involving Muslim princess figures have been identified by Jacqueline de Weever, *Sheba's Daughters: whitening and demonizing the Saracen*

woman in medieval French Epic (New York: Garland, 1998), xvii. On the literary depiction of Muslim women, see also Paul Bancourt, *Les Musulmans dans les chansons de geste du Cycle du Roi*, 2 vols. (Aix-en-Provence: Université de Provence, 1982), 2: 666–734; F. M. Warren, "The Enamoured Moslem Princess in Orderic Vital and the French Epic," *PMLA* 29 (1914): 341–58; Charles A. Knudson, "La thème de la princesse sarrasine dans *la Prise d'Orange*," *Romance Philology* 22 (1969): 449–62; Micheline de Combarieu, "Un personnage épique: la jeune musulmane," in *Mélanges de langue et littérature françaises du Moyen-Age offerts à Pierre Jonin*: *Senéfiance* 7 (1979): 181–96; Lynn Tarte Ramey, *Christian, Saracen and Genre in Medieval French Literature* (New York: Routledge, 2001); and Kinoshita, *Medieval Boundaries*, 46–73.

104. Remensnyder, "Christian Captives," 665.

105. Cf. Kinoshita, *Medieval Boundaries*, 47–48; Mohja Kahf, *Western Representations of the Muslim Woman: From Termagant to Odalisque* (Austin: University of Texas Press, 1999), 37–38.

106. Mirrer, *Women, Jews, and Muslims* 17–30; Juan Victorio Martínez, "La ciudad-mujer en los romances fronterizos," *AEM* 15 (1985): 553–60.

107. *La* Estoria de España, 334–46, 349–50.

108. *Primera Crónica General*, 2: 431b–442b, 446b–448a; *Crónica geral de Espanha de 1344*, ed. Luís Felipe Lindley Cintra, 3 vols. (Lisbon: Acadêmia de História, 1951–61), 3: 112–16, 122–71.

109. The essential work on the legend and its multiple literary variants is Ramón Menéndez Pidal, *La leyenda de los Infantes de Lara*, 3rd ed. (Madrid: Espasa-Calpe, 1971). This may be supplemented by Thomas A. Lathrop, *The Legend of the* Siete Infantes de Lara (*Refundición toledana de la crónica de 1344* version) (Chapel Hill: University of North Carolina Press, 1971); John G. Cummins, "The Chronicle Text of the Legend of the *Infantes de Lara*," *Bulletin of Hispanic Studies* 53 (1976): 101–16.

110. Menéndez Pidal, *La leyenda*, 451, 459.

111. Irene Zaderenko, "Acerca de la fecha de composición del *Cantar de los siete infantes de Lara*," *La Corónica* 26 (1997): 247–55.

112. Eukene Lacarra Lanz, "Sobre la historicidad de la leyenda de los *Siete Infantes de Lara*," in *Historicist Essays on Hispano-Medieval Narrative in Memory of Roger M. Walker*, ed. Barry Taylor and Geoffrey West (London: Maney; Modern Humanities Research Association, 2005), 201–27.

113. For a useful introduction, see Irene Zaderenko, "El tema de la traición en *Los siete infantes de Lara* y su tradición en la épica románica," *Bulletin of Hispanic Studies* 78 (2001): 177–90; Thomas Montgomery, "Cycles, Parallels, and Inversions in the *Leyenda de los Siete Infantes*," *Olifant* 13 (1988): 41–54.

114. John K. Walsh, "Religious Motifs in the Early Spanish Epic," *Revista Histórica Moderna* 36 (1970–71): 165–72, at 167–68.

115. Deyermond, "La sexualidad," 769–74.

116. Samuel Amago, "Sexual Pollution, Social Legitimacy, and the Economies of Power in the Legend of the *Siete Infantes de Lara*," *Revista de Estudios Hispanicos* 36 (2002): 3–22, at 9 and 13–14. See also Carolyn A. Bluestine, "The Power of Blood in the *Siete*

Infantes de Lara," *Hispanic Review* 50 (1982): 201–17; John R. Burt, "The Bloody Cucumber and Related Matters in the *Siete Infantes de Lara*," *Hispanic Review* 50 (1982): 345–52.

117. *Crónica geral de Espanha de 1344*, 3: 148; Castilian version in Menéndez Pidal, *La leyenda*, 284. In another Portuguese source the noblewoman becomes Almanzor's cousin: *Livro de Linhagens do Conde D. Pedro*, 147–48.

118. *Crónica geral de Espanha de 1344*, 3: 149–50; Menéndez Pidal, *La leyenda*, 286. However, in another version of the *Crónica*, the early fifteenth-century *Refundición toledana*, the sexual encounter is once more transformed into a love affair: Lathrop, *The Legend*, 64–65.

119. *Crónica geral de Espanha de 1344*, 3: 150; Menéndez Pidal, *La leyenda*, 286.

120. Mirrer, *Women, Jews, and Muslims*, 18.

121. Ibid., 22.

122. Alberto Montaner Frutos, "La historia del capitán cautivo y la tradición épica de frontera," *Letras* (Buenos Aires) 52–53 (2005–6) [= *Studia Hispanica Medievalia VII: Actas de las VIII Jornadas Internacionales de Literatura Española Medieval y de Homenaje al "Quijote"*], 73–115. The trope of the Muslim woman enamored of a Christian captive was to enjoy a long literary life well into the modern period: Manuela Marín, "'Amar a cristianos moras.' Ecos de un tema cervantino en textos españoles sobre Marruecos (s. XIX–XX)," *Bulletin Hispanique* 109 (2007): 235–62.

123. Orderic Vitalis, *The Ecclesiastical* History, ed. Marjorie Chibnall, 6 vols. (Oxford: Clarendon, 1968–80), 5: 358–78. By contrast, Albert of Aachen claimed that Bohemond was ransomed: Albert of Aachen, *Historia Ierosolomitana: History of the Journey to Jerusalem*, ed. Susan B. Edgington (Oxford: Clarendon, 2007), 680–87.

124. *La Chanson de Guillaume at La Prise d'Orange*, ed. Philip E. Bennett (London: Grant & Cutler, 2000).

125. Simon Yarrow, "Prince Bohemond, Princess Melaz, and the Gendering of Religious Difference in the *Ecclesiastical History* of Orderic Vitalis," in Cordelia Beattie and Kirsten A. Fenton, eds., *Intersections of Gender, Religion and Ethnicity in the Middle Ages* (London: Palgrave Macmillan, 2010), 140–57, at 150.

126. *Livro de Linhagens do Conde D. Pedro*, 148.

127. Kinoshita, *Medieval Boundaries*, 47.

128. Cf. Edward Said, *Orientalism: Western Conceptions of the Orient* (London: Routledge & Kegan Paul, 1978), 6.

CONCLUSION

1. Catlos, *Victors and Vanquished*, 296–98, 397–99.

2. Richard Fletcher, *The Cross and the Crescent: Christianity and Islam from Muhammad to the Reformation* (London: Allen Lane, 2003), 114.

3. Cf. Fredrik Barth, "Enduring and Emerging Issues in the Analysis of Ethnicity." In Hans Vermeulen and Cora Govers, eds., *The Anthropology of Ethnicity: Beyond "Ethnic Groups and Boundaries"* (Amsterdam: Het Spinhus, 1994), 11–32, at 20–21; Jennifer

Connolly, "Forbidden Intimacies: Christian-Muslim Intermarriage in East Kalimantan, Indonesia," *American Ethnologist* 36 (2009): 492–506.

4. Robert I. Burns, "Jews and Moors in the *Siete Partidas* of Alfonso X the Learned: A Background Perspective," in Roger Collins and Anthony Goodman, eds., *Medieval Spain: Culture, Conflict and Coexistence: Studies in Honour of Angus MacKay* (Basingstoke: Palgrave Macmillan, 2002), 46–62, at 49.

5. Stoler, *Carnal Knowledge*, 44.

6. Barth, *Ethnic Groups and Boundaries*, 15.

7. Stoler, *Carnal Knowledge*, 44.

8. Rafael Narbona Vizcaíno, *Pueblo, poder y sexo: Valencia medieval (1306–1420)* (Valencia: Diputación Provincial de Valencia, 1992), 75; cf. Nirenberg, "Conversion, Sex, and Segregation," 1076–84.

9. Letter of 1480 establishing the Inquisition in Castile in Jon Cowans, ed., *Early Modern Spain: A Documentary History* (Philadelphia: University of Pennsylvania Press, 2003), 10–11.

10. Helen Rawlings, *The Spanish Inquisition* (Oxford: Blackwell, 2006), 50–56.

11. The essential guide is Barbara Fuchs, *Exotic Nation: Maurophilia and the Construction of Early Modern Spain* (Philadelphia: University of Pennsylvania Press, 2009); see also María Soledad Carrasco Urgoiti, *El moro de Granada en la literatura: del siglo XV al XX* (Madrid: Revista de Occidente, 1956; repr. Granada: Universidad de Granada, 1989).

12. For a good introduction to the subject, see Marlène Albert-Llorca and José Antonio González Alcantud, eds., *Moros y cristianos: representaciones del otro en las fiestas del Mediterráneo occidental* (Toulouse: Presses Universitaires du Mirail; Granada: Centro de Investigaciones Etnológicas Ángel Ganivet, 2003); Daniela Flesler, *The Return of the Moor: Spanish Responses to Contemporary Moroccan Immigration* (West Lafayette, Ind.: Purdue University Press, 2008), 97–129. See also Demetrio E. Brisset Martín, "Fiestas hispanas de moros y cristianos: historia y significados," *Gazeta de Antropología* 17 (2001). For a description of one such theatrical representation of Christian-Muslim conflict, held at Jaén during the Christmas festivities of 1463, see *Hechos del Condestable Don Miguel Lucas de Iranzo: crónica del siglo XV*, ed. Juan de Mata Carriazo (Madrid: Espasa-Calpe, 1940), 98–100.

13. Robert Ricard, "Contribution à l'étude des fêtes de 'moros y cristianos' au Mexique," *Journal de la Société des Américanistes* 24 (1932): 51–84; José Rivair Macedo, "Mouros e cristãos: a ritualização da conquista no velho e no Novo Mundo", *Bulletin du Centre d'études Médiévales d'Auxerre*, Hors-série 2: *Le Moyen Âge vu d'ailleurs* (2008): http://cem.revues.org/8632 [last accessed 17.7.13]; Luis Weckmann, *The Medieval Heritage of Mexico*, trans. Frances N. López-Morillas (New York: Fordham University Press, 1992), 542–46; Max Harris, *Aztecs, Moors, and Christians* (Austin: University of Texas Press, 2000).

14. For what follows, see Ricard, "Contribution," 54–57.

15. Ibid., 66.

16. Rivair Macedo, "Mouros e cristãos," 6.

17. Flesler, *The Return of the Moor*, 65–76; Maria J. C. Krom, "Festivals of Moors and Christians: Performance, Commodity and Identity in Folk Celebrations in Southern Spain," *Journal of Mediterranean Studies* 18 (2008): 119–38; and Sina Lucia Kottmann,

"Mocking and Miming the 'Moor': Staging of the 'Self' and 'Other' on Spain's Borders with Morocco," *Journal of Mediterranean Studies* 20 (2011): 107–36.

18. On the ideological factors that have colored Spain's relations with the Islamic world in the present, see Hishaam D. Aidi, "The Interference of al-Andalus: Spain, Islam, and the West," *Social Text* 24 (2006): 67–88. On Spanish responses to contemporary Moroccan immigration, see Flesler, *The Return of the Moor*. Contemporary political sensitivities have given rise to a number of modifications to the content and choreography of certain festivals: Flesler, *The Return of the Moor*, 112–15; Kottmann, "Mocking and Miming," 124–25.

19. Kottmann, "Mocking and Miming."

20. Harris, *Aztecs, Moors, and Christians*, 59. Harris's suggestion that the festivals of *moros y cristianos* "were more about a yearning for peace and *convivencia* than they were about war" is less convincing: 39 and 62.

Selected Bibliography

PRIMARY SOURCES

Unpublished

León, Biblioteca Capitular de la Real Colegiata de San Isidoro, MS.63: *De Miraculis Sancti Isidori.*

Santiago de Compostela, Archivo de la Catedral, carpeta 7, no. 1.

Published

'Abd al-Malik b. Ḥabīb. *Kitāb al-Ta'rīj (La historia).* Ed. Jorge Aguadé. Madrid: CSIC, 1991.

Akhbār majmū'a fī fath al-Andalus. Ed. and trans. Emilio Lafuente y Alcántara. Madrid: Real Academia de la Historia, 1867.

Albar, Paul. *Indiculus luminosus. CSM* 1: 270–315.

———. *Vita Eulogii. CSM* 1: 330–43.

Albert of Aachen. *Historia Ierosolomitana: History of the Journey to Jerusalem.* Ed. Susan B. Edgington. Oxford: Clarendon, 2007.

Alfonso X el Sabio. *Fuero Real.* Ed. Azucena Palacios Alcaine. Barcelona: Promociones y Publicaciones Universitarias, 1991.

———. *Las Siete Partidas.* Trans. Samuel Parsons Scott, ed. Robert I. Burns. 5 vols. Philadelphia: University of Pennsylvania Press, 2001.

———. *Las Siete Partidas: el libro del fuero de las leyes.* Ed. José Sánchez-Arcilla Bernal. Madrid: Reus, 2004.

Aquinas, Thomas. *The "Summa Theologica" of St. Thomas Aquinas.* Trans. Fathers of the English Dominican Province, 22 vols. London: Burns Oates & Washbourne, 1920–24.

Assises de la cour des bourgeois. Ed. Conte de Beugnot, *Recueil des Historiens des Croisades: Lois, 2.* Paris: Académie Royal des Inscriptions et Belles-Lettres, 1843.

Baeza, Hernando de. "Las cosas que pasaron entre los reyes de Granada desde el tiempo de el rrey don Juan de Castilla, segundo de este nonbre, hasta que los Catholicos Reyes ganaron el rreyno de Granada." In *Relaciones de algunos sucesos de los últimos tiempos del reino de Granada*. Madrid: Sociedad de Bibliófilos Españoles, 1868. 1–44.

Berceo, Gonzalo de. *La "Vida de San Millán de la Cogolla" de Gonzalo de Berceo (Estudio y edición crítica)*. Ed. Brian Dutton. 2nd ed. London: Tamesis, 1984.

Cantigas d'escarnho e de mal dizer dos cancioneiros medievais galego-portugueses. Ed. Manuel Rodrigues Lapa. 2nd ed. Vigo: Editorial Galaxia, 1970.

Cantigas de Santa María. Ed. Walter Mettmann. 3 vols. Madrid: Castalia, 1986–89.

Los cartularios de San Salvador de Zaragoza. Ed. Ángel Canellas López. 4 vols. Zaragoza: IberCaja, 1989–90.

Castigos del rey don Sancho IV. Ed. Hugo Oscar Bizzarri. Frankfurt-Madrid: Vervuert; Iberoamericana, 2001.

Chancelarias Portuguesas. D. Pedro I (1357–1367). Lisbon: Instituto Nacional de Investigação Científica; Centro de Estudos Históricos da Universidade Nova de Lisboa, 1984.

La Chanson de Guillaume and la Prise d'Orange. Ed. Philip E. Bennett. London: Grant & Cutler, 2000.

Christians and Moors in Spain. Vol. 2, *1195–1614*. Ed. and trans. Colin Smith. Warminster: Aris & Phillips, 1989.

Christians and Moors in Spain. Vol. 3, *Arabic Sources*. Ed. and trans. Charles Melville and Ahmad Ubaydli. Warminster: Aris & Phillips, 1992.

"Chronica Latina Regum Castellae." Ed. Luis Charlo Brea. In *Chronica Hispana saeculi XIII*, ed. Luis Charlo Brea, Juan Antonio Estévez Sola, and Rocío Carande Herrero. *CCCM* 73. Turnhout: Brepols, 1997. 7–118.

Chronica Magistri Roger of Hovedon. Ed. William Stubbs. Rolls Series 51. 4 vols. London: Longmans, Green, Reader and Dyer, 1868–71.

Chronica Naierensis. Ed. Juan Antonio Estévez Sola. *CCCM* 71A. Turnhout: Brepols, 1995.

Chronica regia Coloniensis, ed. Georg Waitz, *MGH: Scriptores rerum Germanicarum*, 18i. Hanover: Impensis Bibliopoli Hahniani, 1880. 1–299.

Chronicon Floriacense. In *Recueil des Historiens des Gaules et de la France*, 12. Ed. Dom Martin Bouquet; new ed. Léopold Delisle. Paris: Victor Palmé, 1877.

The Code of Cuenca: Municipal Law on the Twelfth-Century Castilian Frontier. Trans. James F. Powers. Philadelphia: University of Pennsylvania Press, 2000.

La colección canónica hispana 4: *Monumenta Hispaniae Sacra*. Ed. Gonzalo Martínez Díez and Félix Rodríguez. Madrid: CSIC, 1984.

La colección canónica hispana 5: *Concilios hispanos: segunda parte*. Ed. Gonzalo Martínez Díez and Felix Rodríguez. Madrid: CSIC, 1992.

Colección de cánones y de todos los concilios de la iglesia española y de América. Ed. Francisco Antonio Gonzalez and Juan Tejada y Ramiro. 7 vols. Madrid: José María Alonso, 1849–62.

Colección de crónicas árabes de la Reconquista, 4. Trans. Ambrosio Huici Miranda. Tetuán: Editora Marroquí, 1955.

Colección de fueros municipales y cartas pueblas de los reinos de Castilla, Leon, Corona de Aragon y Navarra. Ed. Tomás Muñoz y Romero. Madrid: Imprenta de Don José María Alonso, 1847.

Colección diplomática de la Catedral de Pamplona, 829–1243. Ed. José Goñi Gaztambide. Pamplona: Gobierno de Navarra, Departamento de Educación y Cultura, 1997.

Colección diplomática del Archivo Histórico Municipal de Jaén. Siglos XIV y XV. Ed. José Rodríguez Molina et al. Jaén: Ayuntamiento de Jaén, 1985.

Colección diplomática del concejo de Zaragoza. Ed. Ángel Canellas López. 2 vols. Zaragoza: Ayuntamiento de Zaragoza, 1972.

Colección diplomática del monasterio de Sahagún (857–1230): II (1000–1073). Ed. Marta Herrero de la Fuente. León: CEISI; Caja de Ahorros y Monte de Piedad; Archivo Histórico Diocesano, 1988.

Colección diplomática de los condes de Castilla. Ed. Manuel Zabalza Duque. Valladolid: Junta de Castilla y León, 1998.

Colección documental del Archivo de la catedral de León (775–1230), III (986–1031). Ed. José Manuel Ruiz Asencio. León: CEISI; CSIC-CECEL; Caja de Ahorros y Monte de Piedad; Archivo Histórico Diocesano, 1987.

La colección diplomática de Sancho Ramírez. Ed. Ángel Canellas López. Zaragoza: Real Sociedad Económica Aragonesa de Amigos del País, 1993.

Conquerors and Chroniclers of Early Medieval Spain. Trans. Kenneth Baxter Wolf. 2nd ed. Liverpool: Liverpool University Press, 1999.

La conquista de al-Andalus. Trans. Mayte Penelas. Madrid: CSIC, 2002.

Constitutiones concilii quarti lateranensis una cum commentariis glossatorum. Ed. Antonio García y García. *Monumenta Iuris Canonici, Corpus glossatorum*, 2. Vatican City: Biblioteca Apostolica Vaticana, 1981.

Corpus Scriptorum Muzarabicorum. Ed. Juan Gil. 2 vols. Madrid: Consejo Superior de Investigaciones Científicas, 1973.

Costums de Tortosa. Ed. Jesús Massip i Fonollosa. Barcelona: Fundació Noguera, 1996.

"Crónica de la Población de Ávila." Ed. Manuel Gómez Moreno. *Boletín de la Real Academia de la Historia* 113 (1943): 11–56.

Crónica de la Población de Ávila. Ed. Amparo Hernández Segura. Valencia: Anúbar, 1966.

Crónica del Moro Rasis: versión del ajbār mulūk al-Andalus de aḥmad ibn muḥammad ibn mūsa al-rāzī, 899–955; romanzada para el rey don Dionís de Portugal hacia 1300 por mahomad, alarife, y Gil Pérez, clérigo de don perianes porçel. Ed. Diego Catalán and María Soledad de Andrés. Madrid: Editorial Gredos-Seminario Menéndez Pidal, 1970.

Crónica geral de Espanha de 1344. Ed. Luís Felipe Lindley Cintra. 3 vols. Lisbon: Acadêmia de História, 1951–61.

Crónica latina de los reyes de Castilla. Ed. Luis Charlo Brea. Cádiz: Universidad de Cadiz, 1984.

Crónica mozárabe de 754: edición crítica y traducción. Ed. José Eduardo López Pereira. Zaragoza: Anubar Ediciones, 1980.

Crónica Najerense. Trans. Juan Antonio Estévez Sola. Madrid: Ediciones Akal, 2003.

Crónicas asturianas. Ed. Juan Gil Fernández, José L. Moralejo, and Juan I. Ruiz de la Peña. Oviedo: Universidad de Oviedo, 1985.

Crónicas de los Reyes de Castilla. Desde don Alfonso el Sabio, hasta los Católicos don Fernando y doña Isabel. Ed. Cayetano Rosell. 3 vols. Madrid: Ediciones Atlas, 1953.

"El *Cronicón Iriense*, estudio preliminar, edición crítica y notas históricas." Ed. Manuel Ruben García Alvarez. *Memorial Histórico Español* 50 (1963): 1–204.

Deux récits de voyage inédits en Afrique du Nord au XVe siècle: Abdalbasit b. Halil et Adorne. Ed. and trans. Robert Brunschvig. Paris: Larose Editeurs, 1936; repr. Paris: Maisonneuve & Larose, 2001.

Diplomatari de la Catedral de Barcelona: Documents dels anys 844–1260. Ed. Àngel Fàbrega i Grau, 1. Barcelona: Fundació Noguera; Pagés Editors, 1995.

Disciplinary Decrees of the General Councils: Text, Translation and Commentary. Ed. H. J. Schroeder. St. Louis: B. Herder, 1937.

La documentación del Tumbo A de la catedral de Santiago de Compostela: estudio y edición. Ed. Manuel Lucas Álvarez. León: CEISI; Caja España de Inversiones, Caja de Ahorros y Monte de Piedad; Archivo Histórico Diocesano, 1997.

La documentación real astur-leonesa (718–1072). Ed. Manuel Lucas Álvarez. *El Reino de León en la Alta Edad Media,* 8. León: CEISI; Caja España de Inversiones, Caja de Ahorros y Monte de Piedad; Archivo Histórico Diocesano, 1995.

Documentos correspondientes al reinado de Sancio Ramirez: Documentos reales procedentes de la real casa y monasterio de San Juan de la Peña. Ed. José Salarrullana y de Dios and Eduardo Ibarra y Rodríguez. 2 vols. Zaragoza: M. Escar, 1907–13.

Documentos de los Archivos Catedralicio y Diocesano de Salamanca (siglos XII–XIII). Ed. José Luis Martín Martín et al. Salamanca: Universidad de Salamanca, 1977.

Los documentos reales del periódo astur. Ed. Antonio Floriano Cumbreño. 2 vols. Oviedo: Instituto de Estudios Asturianos, 1949–51.

Early Modern Spain: A Documentary History. Ed. Jon Cowans. Philadelphia: University of Pennsylvania Press, 2003.

Edición crítica del texto español de la Crónica de 1344 que ordenó el Conde de Barcelos don Pedro Alfonso. Ed. Diego Catalán and María Soledad de Andrés. Madrid: Editorial Gredos-Seminario Menéndez Pidal, 1970.

Epistolae Merowingici et Karolini Aevi, 1. *MGH: Epistolae* 3. Ed. Wilhelm Gundlach, Ernst Dümmler, et al. Berlin: Weidmann, 1892.

La Estoria de España *de Alfonso X: Estudio y edición de la* Versión Crítica *desde Fruela II hasta la muerte de Fernando II.* Ed. Mariano de la Campa Gutiérrez. *Anejos de Analecta Malacitana* 75. Málaga: Universidad de Málaga, 2009.

Eulogius. *Memoriale Sanctorum, CSM* 2: 363–459.

———. *Documentum martyriale, CSM* 2: 459–75.

———. *Liber apologeticus martyrum, CSM* 2: 475–95.

———. *Obras completas de San Eulogio: Introducción, traducción, y notas.* Trans. María Jesús Aldana García. Córdoba: Universidad de Córdoba, 1998.

Ex historia expeditionum in Terram Sanctam a. 1217–1219. Ed. Georg Waitz. *MGH: Scriptores rerum Germanicarum* 18. Hanover: Impensis Bibliopoli Hahniani, 1880. 339–43.

Fatḥ al-Andalus (La conquista de al-Andalus). Ed. Luis Molina. Madrid: CSIC; Agencia española de cooperación internacional, 1994.

El fuero de Baeza: Edición, estudio y vocabulario. Ed. Jean Marie Victor Roudil. The Hague: G.B. van Goor Zonen, 1962.

Fuero de Béjar. Ed. Juan Gutiérrez Cuadrado. Salamanca: Universidad de Salamanca, 1975.

El fuero de Brihuega. Ed. Juan Catalina García. Madrid: Tipografía de Manuel G. Hernández, 1887.

Fuero de Calatayud. Ed. Jesús Ignacio Algora and Felicísimo Arranz Sacristán. Zaragoza: Diputación Provincial; Institución Fernando el Católico, 1982.

El fuero de Coria: estudio histórico-jurídico. Ed. José Maldonado y Fernández del Torco et al. Madrid: Instituto de Estudios de Administracion Local, 1949.

Fuero de Cuenca (formas primordial y sistemática: texto latino, texto castellano y adaptación del Fuero de Iznatoraf). Ed. Rafael de Ureña y Smenjaud. Madrid: Tipografía de Archivos, 1935.

El fuero de Plasencia: estudio histórico y edición crítica del texto. Ed. Eloísa Ramírez Vaquero. Mérida: Editora Regional de Extremadura, 1987.

El Fuero de Teruel. Ed. Max Gorosch. Stockholm: Almqvist and Wiksell, 1950.

Fuero de Usagre (siglo XIII) anotado con las variantes dél de Cáceres. Ed. Rafael de Ureña y Smenjaud and Adolfo Bonilla y San Martín. Madrid: Hijos de Reus, 1907.

El Fuero de Zorita de los Canes. Ed. Rafael de Ureña y Smenjaud. Madrid: Establecimiento Tipográfico de Fortanet, 1911.

El fuero latino de Teruel. Ed. Jaime Caruana Gómez de Barreda. Teruel: Instituto de Estudios Turolenses, 1974.

Fueros castellanos de Soria y Alcalá de Henares. Ed. Galo Sánchez. Madrid: Junta para ampliación de estudios e investigaciones científicas; Centro de estudios históricos, 1919.

Les fueros d'Alcaraz et d'Alarcon. Ed. Jean Roudil. 2 vols. Paris: Librairie Klincksiek, 1968.

Los fueros del Reino de León. Ed. Justiniano Rodríguez Fernández. 2 vols. León: Ediciones Leonesas, 1981.

Los fueros de Sepúlveda: edición crítica y apéndice documental. Ed. Emilo Sáez et al. Segovia: Diputación Provincial de Segovia, 1953.

Los fueros de Villaescusa de Haro y Huete. Ed. María Teresa Martín Palma. Málaga: Universidad de Málaga, 1984.

Los fueros municipales de Cáceres: su derecho público. Ed. Pedro Lumbreras Valiente. Cáceres: Ayuntamiento, 1974.

Furs de València. Ed. Germà Colòn and Arcadi García. 5 vols. Barcelona: Barcino, 1970–90.

García de Salazar, Lope. *Las bienandanzas e fortunas. Códice del siglo XV*. Ed. Ángel Rodríguez Herrero. 4 vols. Bilbao: Diputación Provincial de Vizcaya, 1967.

Gesta crucigerorum Rhenanorum. Ed. Reinhold Röhricht. In *Quinti belli sacri: Scriptores minores*. Geneva: J.-G. Fick, 1879. 27–56.

Gosuini de expugnatione Salaciae carmen. In Monumenta Portugalia Historica, a saeculo octavo post Christum usque ad quintum decimum: Scriptores, vol. I, fascículo II. Ed. Alexandre Herculano. Lisbon: Academia Real das Ciências, 1860. *101–4*.

Guibert of Nogent. *Dei Gesta per Francos et cinq autres textes*. Ed. Robert B. C. Huygens. *CCCM* 127a. Turnhout: Brepols, 1996.

———. *The Deeds of God Through the Franks*. Trans. Robert Levine. Woodbridge: Boydell, 1997.

Hechos del Condestable Don Miguel Lucas de Iranzo: Crónica del siglo XV. Ed. Juan de Mata Carriazo. Madrid: Espasa-Calpe, 1940.

Historia Compostellana. Ed. Emma Falque Rey. *CCCM* 70. Turnhout: Brepols, 1988.

Historia Silense: Edición crítica e introducción. Ed. Justo Pérez de Urbel and Atilano González Ruiz-Zorrilla. Madrid: CSIC, 1959.

Huneberc of Heidenheim. *Vita Willibaldi episcope Eichstetensis*. Ed. Oswald Holder-Egger. *MGH: Scriptores* 15:1. Hanover: *Impensis Bibliopolii Hahniani*, 1887, 80–117.

Ibn ʿAbd al-Ḥakam. *The History of the Conquest of Egypt, North Africa, and Spain Known as the Futūḥ Miṣr of Ibn ʿAbd al-Ḥakam*. Ed. Charles C. Torrey. New Haven, Conn.: Yale University Press, 1922; repr. Piscataway, N.J.: Gorgias Press, 2002.

Ibn Darrāj al-Qasṭallī. *Almanzor en los poemas de Ibn Darrāŷ*. Trans. Margarita la Chica Garrido. Zaragoza: Anubar, 1979.

———. *Diwān*. Ed. Maḥmūd ʿAlī Makkī. Beirut: al-Maktab al-Islāmī, 1969.

———. Ibn Ḥawqal. *Kitāb ṣūrat al-arḍ*. Beirut: Dār Maktabat al-Ḥayāh, 1964.

———. *Configuración del mundo*. Trans. María José Romaní Suay. Valencia: Anúbar, 1971.

Ibn Ḥayyān. *Al-Muqtabas V*. Ed. Pedro Chalmeta et al. Madrid-Rabat: Instituto Hispano-Arabe de Cultura, 1979.

———. *Crónica del califa ʿAbarraḥmān III an-Nāṣir entre los años 912 y 942 (al-Muqtabis V)*. Trans. María Jesús Viguera and Federico Corriente. Zaragoza: Anubar Ediciones; Instituto Árabe de Cultura, 1981.

———. *Crónica de los emires Alḥakam I y ʿAbdarraḥmān II entre los años 796 y 847 [Al-muqtabis II–1]*. Trans. M. A. Makki and F. Corriente. Zaragoza: Instituto de Estudios Islámicos y del Oriente Próximo, 2001.

Ibn Ḥazm. *Kitāb Jamharat ansāb al-ʿArab*. Ed. ʿAbd al-Salām Muḥammad Hārūn. Cairo: Dār al-Maʿārif, 1962. Partial Spanish translations by Elías Terés, "Linajes árabes en al-Andalus, según la 'Ŷamhara' de Ibn Ḥazm," *Al-Andalus* 22 (1957): 55–112; and Fernando de la Granja, "La marca superior en la obra de al-ʿUdrí," *EEMCA* 8 (1967): 447–545, at 532–34.

———. *Naqṭ al-ʿarūs*. Ed. C.F. Seybold; trans. Luis Seco de Lucena. Valencia: Universidad de Valencia, 1974.

———. *Ṭawq al-Ḥamama fi al-ulfa wa-al-ullāf*. Ed. Al-Tahir Ahmad Makki. 3rd ed. Cairo: Dār al-Maʿārif, 1980.

———. *The Ring of the Dove by Ibn Hazm: A Treatise on the Art and Practice of Arab Love*. Trans. A. J. Arberry. London: Luzac Oriental, 1953.

Ibn Idhārī al-Marrākushī. *Al-Bayān al-mughrib fi akhbār al-Andalus waʾl-Maghrib*. Ed. Évariste Lévi-Provençal, Georges S. Colin, and Iḥsān ʿAbbas. 4 vols. Paris: Geuthner, 1930; Leiden: Brill, 1948–51; Beirut: Dār al-Thaqāfah, 1967.

———. *La caída del Califato de Córdoba y los Reyes de Taifas (al-Bayān al-Mugrib)*. Ed. and trans. Felipe Maíllo Salgado. Salamanca: Estudios Árabes e Islámicos, Universidad de Salamanca, 1993.

Ibn al-Qūṭīya, *Ta'rīkh iftitāḥ al-Andalus*. Ed. Ibrāhīm al-Abyārī. Cairo: Dār al-Kitāb al-Miṣrī; Beirut: Dār al-Kitāb al-Lubnānī, 1982.

———. *Early Islamic Spain: the History of Ibn al-Qutiya*. Trans. David James. London: Routledge, 2009.

The Koran. Trans. N. J. Dawood. 4th ed. Harmondsworth: Penguin, 1974.

The Latin Chronicle of the Kings of Castile. Trans. Joseph F. O'Callaghan. Tempe: Arizona Center for Medieval and Renaissance Studies, 2002.

Liber testamentorum coenobii laurbanensis. Ed. Aires A. Nascimento and José María Fernández Catón. 2 vols. León: CEISI, 2008.

Libro de los Testamentos de la catedral de Oviedo. Ed. Francisco Javier Fernández Conde. Rome: Iglesia Nacional Española, 1971.

Lives of the Visigothic Fathers. Trans. A. T. Fear. Liverpool: Liverpool University Press, 1997.

Livro de Linhagens do Conde D. Pedro. Ed. José Mattoso. In *Portugaliae Monumenta Historica - Nova Serie*. 2 vols. Lisbon: Academia das Ciências, 1980.

Livros Velhos de Linhagens. Ed. Joseph Piel and José Mattoso. In *Portugaliae Monumenta Historica - Nova Serie*. Lisbon: Academia das Ciências, 1980.

López de Úbeda, Francisco. *La pícara Justina*. Ed. Bruno Mario Damiani. Madrid: José Porrúa Turanzas/Studio Humanitatis, 1982.

Lucas of Tuy. *Chronicon Mundi*. Ed. Emma Falque. *CCCM* 74. Turnhout: Brepols, 2003.

———. *Milagros de San Isidoro*. Trans. Juan de Robles, ed. José Manuel Martínez Rodríguez. León: Universidad de León; Cátedra de San Isidoro de la Real Colegiata de León, 1992.

al-Maqqarī, Aḥmad b. Muḥammad. *The History of the Mohammedan Dynasties in Spain*. Trans. Pascual de Gayangos. 2 vols. London: Oriental Translation Fund of Great Britain and Ireland, 1840–43.

al-Marrākushī, 'Abd al-Wāḥid. *Kitāb al-Mu'jib fī talkhīṣ akhbār al-Maghrib. The History of the Almohades by Abdo-'l-Wahid al-Marrekoshî*. Ed. Reinhardt Dozy. 2nd ed. Amsterdam: Oriental Press, 1968.

Medieval Iberia: Readings from Christian, Muslim, and Jewish Sources. Ed. Olivia R. Constable. 2nd ed. Philadelphia: University of Pennsylvania Press, 2011.

Memorias del rey D. Fernando IV de Castilla. Ed. Antonio Benavides. 2 vols. Madrid: Imprenta de José Rodríguez, 1860.

Los "miraculos romançados" de Pero Marín: Edición crítica. Ed. Karl-Heinz Anton. Burgos: Abadía de Silos, 1988.

El monasterio de San Pelayo de Oviedo. Historia y fuentes, I: Coleccion diplomatica (996–1325). Ed. Francisco Javier Fernández Conde, Isabel Torrente Fernández, and Guadalupe de la Noval Menéndez. Oviedo: Monasterio de San Pelayo, 1978.

Monumenta Portugalia Historica, a saeculo octavo post Christum usque ad quintum decimum: Leges et Consuetudines. Ed. Alexandre Herculano and Joaquim J. da Silva Mendes Leal. 2 vols. Lisbon: Academia Real das Ciências, 1856–68.

Muḥammad b. Waḍḍaḥ, *Kitāb al-bida' (Tratado contra las innovaciones)*. Ed. María Isabel Fierro. Madrid: CSIC, 1988.

Orderic Vitalis. *The Ecclesiastical History*. Ed. Marjorie Chibnall. 6 vols. Oxford: Clarendon, 1968–80.

Pelayo de Oviedo. *Crónica del Obispo Don Pelayo*. Ed. Benito Sánchez Alonso. Madrid: Centro de Estudios Históricos, 1924.

Peter the Venerable. *Contra Petrobrusianos hereticos*. Ed. James Fearns. *CCCM* 10. Turnhout: Brepols, 1968.

Poema de Fernán González. Ed. Alonso Zamora Vicente. Madrid: Espasa Calpe, 1946.

Primavera y flor de romances o Colección de los más viejos y más populares romances castellanos. Ed. José Fernando Wolf and Conrado Hofmann. Berlin: A. Asher, 1856.

Primera crónica general de España. Ed. Ramón Menéndez Pidal. 2 vols. Madrid: Editorial Gredos, 1977.

al-Qayrawānī, Ibn Abī Zayd. *Risala ou traité abrégé de Droit Malékite et Morale Musulmane*. Trans. Edmond Fagnan. Paris: Geuthner, 1914.

Records of the Past. 2nd ser. Ed. A. H. Sayce, 6 vols. London: Samuel Bagster, 1888–92; http://www.sacred-texts.com/ane/rp/rp204/rp20413.htm.

Regesta Pontificum Romanorum ab condita ecclesia ad annum post Christum natum MCXCVIII. Ed. Philip Jaffé. 2 vols. Leipzig: Veit, 1885–88. Reprint Graz: Akademische Druck- u. Verlagsanstalt, 1956.

Rodrigo Jiménez de Rada. *Historia de rebus Hispanie sive Historica Gothica*. Ed. Juan Fernández Valverde. *CCCM* 72. Turnhout: Brepols, 1987.

———. *Historia de los hechos de España*. Trans. Juan Fernández Valverde. Madrid: Alianza Editorial, 1989.

Romancero general o colección de romances castellanos anteriores al siglo XVIII. Ed. Agustín Durán. 2 vols. Madrid: Atlas, 1945.

The Songs of Jaufré Rudel. Ed. Rupert T. Pickens. Toronto: Pontifical Institute of Mediaeval Studies, 1978.

Songs of Holy Mary of Alfonso X, The Wise: A Translation of the Cantigas de Santa María. Trans. Kathleen Kulp-Hill. Tempe: Arizona Center for Medieval and Renaissance Studies, 2000.

Textos de derecho local español en la Edad Media. Ed. Ana María Barrero García and María Luz Alonso Martín. Madrid: CSIC; Instituto de Ciencias Jurídicas, 1989.

Al-ʿUdhrī, *Nuṣūṣ ʿan al-Andalus min kitāb Tarṣī al-akhbār wa-tanwīʿ al-āthār wa l-bustān fi garāʾib al-buldān wa-al-masālik ilā jamīʿ al-mamālik*. Ed. ʿAbd al-ʿAzīz al-Ahwani. Madrid: Instituto de Estudios Islámicos, 1965. Partial Spanish translation, Fernando de la Granja, "La Marca Superior en la obra de al-ʿUdrí." *EEMCA* 8. Zaragoza, 1967: 447–545.

Una descripción anónima de al-Andalus. Ed. and trans. Luis Molina. 2 vols. Madrid: CSIC, 1983.

Vega, Lope de. *Las doncellas de Simancas*. In *Obras de Lope de Vega*, 16. Ed. Marcelino Menéndez y Pelayo. Madrid: Atlas, 1966. 395–431.

———. *El Labrador Venturoso*. Charleston, S.C.: BiblioBazaar, 2007.

Versión crítica de la Estoria de España. *Estudio y edición desde Pelayo hasta Ordoño II*. Ed. Inés Fernández-Ordóñez. Madrid: Fundación Ramón Menéndez Pidal; Universidad Autónoma de Madrid, 1993.

Vita S. Emiliani: edición crítica. Ed. Luis Vázquez de Parga. Madrid: CSIC, 1943.
Vita S. Petri Oxomensis episcopi in Hispania ab anonymo suppari conscripta. Ed. Francis Plaine. *Analecta Bollandiana* 4 (1885): 10–29.
The World of El Cid: Chronicles of the Spanish Reconquest. Ed. and trans. Simon Barton and Richard Fletcher. Manchester: Manchester University Press, 2000.

SECONDARY SOURCES

ʿAbbādī, Aḥmad Mukhtār ʿAbd al-Fattāḥ. *El reino de Granada en la época de Muhammad V*. Madrid: Instituto de Estudios Islámicos, 1973.
Abeledo, Manuel. "La crónica de la población de Ávila: un estado actual de la cuestión desde su primera publicación." *Estudios de Historia de España* 11 (2009): 13–47.
Abulafia, David. "Introduction: Seven Types of Ambiguity, c.1100–c.1500." In David Abulafia and Nora Berend, eds., *Medieval Frontiers: Concepts and Practices*. Aldershot: Ashgate, 2002. 1–34.
Aidi, Hishaam D. "The Interference of al-Andalus: Spain, Islam, and the West." *Social Text* 24 (2006): 67–88.
Alarcón Román, Concepción. "La antigua ceremonia de las doncellas *Cantaderas* en León." *Revista de dialectología y tradiciones populares* 50 (1995): 179–95.
Albert-Llorca, Marlène, and José Antonio González Alcantud, eds. *Moros y cristianos: representaciones del otro en las fiestas del Mediterráneo occidental*. Toulouse: Presses Universitaires du Mirail, 2003.
Ali, Kecia. *Marriage and Slavery in Early Islam*. Cambridge, Mass.: Harvard University Press, 2010.
Altschul, Nadia R. "Postcolonialism and the Study of the Middle Ages." *History Compass* 6, 2 (2008): 588–606.
———. "The Future of Postcolonial Approaches to Medieval Iberian Studies." *JMIS* 1 (2009): 5–17.
Alvar, Carlos. "María Pérez, Balteira." *Archivo de filología aragonesa* 36–37 (1985): 11–40.
Amago, Samuel. "Sexual Pollution, Social Legitimacy, and the Economies of Power in the Legend of the *Siete Infantes de Lara*." *Revista de Estudios Hispanicos* 36 (2002): 3–22.
Argente del Castillo Ocaña, Carmen. "Los cautivos en la frontera entre Jaén y Granada." In Cristina Segura Graíño, ed., *Relaciones Exteriores del Reino de Granada: IV Coloquio de Historia Medieval Andaluza*. Almería: Instituto de Estudios Almerienses, 1988. 211–25.
———. "Cautiverio y martirio de doncellas en La Frontera." In Francisco Toro Ceballos and José Rodríguez Molina, eds., *IV estudios de Frontera: Historia, tradiciones y leyendas en La Frontera*. Jaén: Diputación Provincial de Jaén, 2002. 31–72.
Argote de Molina, Gonzalo. *Nobleza de Andalucía*. Ed. Manuel Muñoz y Garnica. Jaén: Francisco López Vizcaíno, 1886; repr. Jaén: Instituto de Estudios Giennenses, 1957.
Arias Bautista, María Teresa. *Barraganas y concubinas en la España medieval*. Seville: Arcibel, 2010.

Arias Fernández, Ana Isabel. "Tradiciones y celebraciones en León, 1690–1700." In María Antonia de Morán Suárez and María del Carmen Rodríguez López, eds., *La documentación para investigación: homenaje a José Antonio Martín Fuertes*. León: Universidad de León, 2002. 71–97.

———. "Las cantaderas o el tributo de las cien doncellas." *Argutorio* 15 (2005): 11–15.

ʿAthamina, Khalil. "How did Islam Contribute to Change the Status of Women: The Case of the *jawārī*, or the Female Slaves." *Al-Qanṭara* 28 (2007): 383–408.

Aurell, Jaume. "Le médiévisme espagnol au XXème siècle: de l'isolationnisme à la modernisation." *Cahiers de civilisation médiévale* 48 (2005): 201–18.

Ayala Martínez, Carlos de, Pascal Buresi, and Philippe Josserand, eds. *Identidad y representación de la frontera en la España medieval (siglos XI-XIV)*. Madrid: Casa de Velázquez/Universidad Autónoma de Madrid, 2001.

Azcárate, Pilar, Julio Escalona, Cristina Jular, and Miguel Larrañaga. "Volver a nacer: historia e identidad en los monasterios de Arlanza, San Millán y Silos (siglos XII–XIII)." *Cahiers de linguistique hispanique médiévale* 29 (2006): 359–94.

Baer, Yitzhak. *A History of the Jews in Christian Spain*. 2 vols. Philadelphia: Jewish Publication Society, 1961.

Bagby, Albert J. "The Moslem in the Cantigas of Alfonso X, El Sabio." *Kentucky Romance Quarterly* 20 (1973): 173–207.

Ballesteros-Beretta, Antonio. *Alfonso X el Sabio*. Barcelona-Madrid: Salvat Editores, 1963.

Bancourt, Paul. *Les Musulmans dans les chansons de geste du Cycle du Roi*. 2 vols. Aix-en-Provence: Université de Provence, 1982.

Baranda, Nieves. "Los problemas de la historia medieval de Flores y Blancaflor." *Dicenda* 10 (1991–92): 21–39.

Barbour, Nevill. "The Relations of King Sancho VII of Navarre with the Almohads." *Revue de l'Occident Musulman et de la Méditerranée* 4 (1967): 9–21.

Bariani, Laura. "De las relaciones entre Ṣubḥ y Muḥammad Ibn Abī ʿĀmir al-Manṣūr, con especial referencia a su "ruptura" (waḥša) en 386–388/996–998." *Qurṭuba* 1 (1996): 39–57.

Barrau Dihigo, Louis. "Études sur les actes des rois asturiens (718–910)." *Revue Hispanique* 46 (1919): 1–192.

Barrero García, Ana María. *El Fuero de Teruel: su historia, proceso de formación y reconstrucción crítica de sus fuentes*. Madrid: Instituto de Estudios Turolenses, 1979.

Barth, Fredrik. "Introduction." In Fredrik Barth, ed., *Ethnic Groups and Boundaries: The Social Organization of Culture Difference*. Boston: Little, Brown, 1969. 9–37.

———. "Enduring and Emerging Issues in the Analysis of Ethnicity." In Hans Vermeulen and Cora Govers, eds., *The Anthropology of Ethnicity: Beyond "Ethnic Groups and Boundaries."* Amsterdam: Het Spinhus, 1994. 11–32.

Bartlett, Robert. *The Making of Europe: Conquest, Colonization and Cultural Change, 950–1350*. London: Allen Lane, 1993.

Barton, Simon. "El Cid, Cluny and the Spanish *Reconquista*." *English Historical Review* 126 (2011): 517–43.

———. "From Mercenary to Crusader: The Career of Álvar Pérez de Castro (d. 1239)

Reconsidered." In Julie Harris and Therese Martin, eds., *Church, State, Vellum and Stone: Essays on Medieval Spain in Honor of John Williams*. Leiden: Brill, 2005. 111–29.

———. "From Tyrants to Soldiers of Christ: The Nobility of Twelfth-Century León-Castile and the Struggle Against Islam." *Nottingham Medieval Studies* 44 (2000): 28–48.

———. "In Search of the Eternal Nation: Ramón Menéndez Pidal and the History of Spain." In Juan-Carlos Conde, ed., *Ramón Menéndez Pidal After Forty Years: A Reassessment*. London: Department of Hispanic Studies, Queen Mary, University of London, 2010. 97–112.

———. "Marriage Across Frontiers: Sexual Mixing, Power and Identity in Medieval Iberia." *JMIS* 3 (2011): 1–25.

———. "Traitors to the Faith? Christian Mercenaries in al-Andalus and the Maghreb, *c.*1100–1300." In Roger Collins and Anthony Goodman, eds., *Medieval Spain: Culture, Conflict and Coexistence: Studies in Honour of Angus MacKay*. Basingstoke: Palgrave Macmillan, 2002. 23–45.

Bautista, Francisco. *La materia de Francia en la literatura medieval española: La "Crónica carolingia"; Flores y Blancaflor; Berta y Carlomagno*. San Millán de la Cogolla: Instituto Biblioteca Hispánica del CiLengua, 2008.

———. "Pseudo-historia y leyenda en la historiografía medieval: la Condesa Traidora." In Francisco Bautista, ed., *El relato historiográfico: textos y tradiciones en la España medieval*. London: Department of Hispanic Studies, Queen Mary, University of London, 2006. 59–101.

———. "La tradición épica de las *Enfances* de Carlomagno y el *Cantar de Mainete* perdido." *Romance Philology* 56 (2003): 217–44.

Beckwith, John. *Caskets from Cordoba*. London: H.M. Stationery Office, 1960.

Bensch, Stephen. "From Prizes of War to Domestic Merchandise: The Changing Face of Slavery in Catalonia and Aragon, 1000–1300." *Viator* 25 (1994): 63–94.

Berend, Nora. *At the Gate of Christendom: Jews, Muslims and "Pagans" in Medieval Hungary, c.1000–c.1300*. Cambridge: Cambridge University Press, 2001.

Beresford, Andrew M. "'Cortol la cabeça e atola del petral ca la querie dar en donas a Galiana': On the Relationship Between Death and Sexuality in Four Epic Legends." In David G. Pattison, ed., *Textos épicos castellanos: problemas de edición y crítica*. London: Department of Hispanic Studies, Queen Mary and Westfield College, 2000. 41–63.

Bishko, Charles J. *Spanish and Portuguese Monastic History, 600–1300*. London: Variorum, 1984.

———. *Studies in Medieval Spanish Frontier History*. London: Variorum, 1980.

Bjørnlund, Matthias. "'A Fate Worse than Dying': Sexual Violence During the Armenian Genocide." In Dagmar Herzog, ed., *Brutality and Desire: War and Sexuality in Europe's Twentieth Century*. Basingstoke: Palgrave, 2008. 16–58.

Blachère, Régis. "La vie et l'oeuvre du poète-épistolier andalou Ibn Darrâğ al-Kasṭallī." *Hespéris* 36 (1933): 99–121.

Blackmore, Josiah, and Gregory S. Hutcheson, eds. *Queer Iberia: Sexualities, Cultures, and Crossings from the Middle Ages to the Renaissance*. Durham, N.C.: Duke University Press, 1999.

Bluestine, Carolyn A. "The Power of Blood in the *Siete Infantes de Lara.*" *Hispanic Review* 50 (1982): 201–17.

Boase, Roger. *The Origin and Meaning of Courtly Love*. Manchester: Manchester University Press, 1977.

Boloix, Barbara. *Las sultanas de la Alhambra (siglos XIII–XV): las grandes desconocidas del reino nazarí de Granada*. Granada: Editorial Comares, 2013.

Bonnassie, Pierre. *La Catalogne du milieu du Xe a la fin du XIe siècle: croissance et mutations d'une société*. 2 vols. Toulouse: Université de Toulouse-Le Mirail, 1975–76.

Bosch Vilá, Jacinto. *Los Almorávides*. Granada: Universidad de Granada, 1990.

Boswell, John. *Christianity, Social Tolerance and Homosexuality: Gay People in Western Europe from the Beginning of the Christian Era to the Fourteenth Century*. Chicago: University of Chicago Press, 1980.

———. *The Royal Treasure: Muslim Communities Under the Crown of Aragon in the Fourteenth Century*. New Haven, Conn.: Yale University Press, 1977.

Bourdieu, Pierre. *Masculine Domination*. Stanford, Calif.: Stanford University Press, 2001.

Bourke, Joanna. "Fear and Anxiety: Writing About Emotion in Modern History." *History Workshop Journal* 55 (2003): 113–33.

Bousquet, Georges Henri. *L'éthique sexuelle de l'Islam*. Paris: Maisonneuve et Larose, 1966.

Braga, Teófilo. *Epopêas da raça moçárabe*. Porto: Imprensa Portuguesa, 1871.

———. *As lendas cristãs*. Porto: Lugan & Genelioux, 1892.

Brisset Martín, Demetrio E. "Fiestas hispanas de moros y cristianos: historia y significados." *Gazeta de Antropología* 17 (2001).

Brodman, James. *Ransoming Captives in Crusader Spain: The Order of Merced on the Christian-Islamic Frontier*. Philadelphia: University of Pennsylvania Press, 1986.

Brundage, James. *The Crusades, Holy War and Canon Law*. Aldershot: Ashgate, 1991.

———. *Law, Sex, and Christian Society in Medieval Europe*. Chicago: University of Chicago Press, 1987.

———. "Marriage Law in the Latin Kingdom of Jerusalem." In Benjamin Z. Kedar, Hans Eberhard Mayer, and R. C. Smail, eds., *Outremer: Studies in the History of the Crusading Kingdom of Jerusalem Presented to Joshua Prawer*. Jerusalem: Yad Izhak Ben Zvi Institute, 1982. 258–71.

———. "Prostitution, Miscegenation and Sexual Purity in the First Crusade." In Peter W. Edbury, ed., *Crusade and Settlement. Papers Read at the First Conference of the Society for the Study of the Crusades and the Latin East and Presented to R. C. Smail*. Cardiff: University College Cardiff Press, 1985. 57–65.

Brunschvig, Robert. "'Abd." *EI*², 1: 24–40.

Bryder, Linda. "Sex, race, and colonialism: an historiographical review." *International History Review* 20 (1998): 806–54.

Bull, Marcus. *Knightly Piety and the Lay Response to the First Crusade*. Oxford: Oxford University Press, 1993.

Bulliet, Richard. *Conversion to Islam in the Medieval Period*. Cambridge, Mass.: Harvard University Press, 1979.

Buresi, Pascal. *La Frontière entre chrétienté et Islam dans la péninsule Ibérique: Du Tage à la Sierra Morena (fin XIe–milieu XIIIe siècle)*. Paris: Publibook, 2004.

Burns, Robert I. "Jews and Moors in the *Siete Partidas* of Alfonso X the Learned: A Background Perspective." In Roger Collins and Anthony Goodman, eds., *Medieval Spain: Culture, Conflict and Coexistence: Studies in Honour of Angus MacKay*. Basingstoke: Palgrave Macmillan, 2002. 46–62.

———. "Renegades, Adventurers and Sharp Businessmen: The Thirteenth-Century Spaniard in the Cause of Islam." *Catholic Historical Review* 58 (1972): 341–66.

Burt, John R. "The Bloody Cucumber and Related Matters in the *Siete Infantes de Lara*." *Hispanic Review* 50 (1982): 345–52.

Bussi, Emilio. "La condizione giuridica dei musulmani nel diritto canonico." *Rivista di storia del diritto italiano* 8 (1935): 459–94.

Cabeza de Vaca Quiñones y Guzmán, Francisco. *Resumen de las políticas ceremonias con que se gobierna la noble, leal y antigua ciudad de León, cabeza de su reino*. Valladolid: Imprenta de Valdivielso, 1693.

Cabrera Muñoz, Emilio. "Cautivos cristianos en el reino de Granada durante la segunda mitad del siglo XV." In Cristina Segura Graíño, ed., *Relaciones Exteriores del Reino de Granada: IV Coloquio de Historia Medieval Andaluza*. Almería: Instituto de Estudios Almerienses, 1988. 227–36.

Cañada Juste, Alberto. "Los Banu Qasi (714–924)." *Príncipe de Viana* 48–49 (1980): 5–95.

———. "El posible solar originario de los Banū Qasī." In *Homenaje a José María Lacarra en su jubilación del profesorado: Estudios Medievales*, 2 vols. Zaragoza: Anubar, 1977, 1: 33–38.

Canellas López, Ángel. "Aragón y la empresa del Estrecho en el siglo XIV: Nuevos documentos del Archivo Municipal de Zaragoza." *EEMCA* 2 (1946): 7–73.

Cantera Orive, Julián. *La batalla de Clavijo y aparición en ella de nuestro patrón Santiago*. Vitoria: Editorial Social Católica, 1944; repr. Logroño: Editorial La Rioja, 1997.

Card, Claudia. "Rape as a Weapon of War." *Hypatia* 11 (1996): 5–18.

Carpenter, Dwayne E. *Alfonso X and the Jews: An Edition and Commentary on the* Siete Partidas *7.24 "De los judios."* Berkeley: University of California Press, 1986.

———. "Minorities in Medieval Spain: the legal status of Jews and Muslims in the *Siete Partidas*." *Romance Quarterly* 33 (1986): 275–87.

Carrasco Urgoiti, María Soledad. *El moro de Granada en la literatura: del siglo XV al XX*. Madrid: Revista de Occidente, 1956; repr. Granada: Universidad de Granada, 1989.

Carriazo, Juan de Mata. "Relaciones fronterizas entre Jaén y Granada en el año 1479." *Revista de archivos, bibliotecas y museos* 61 (1955): 23–51.

Casey, James. *Early Modern Spain: A Social History*. London: Routledge, 1999.

Castro, Américo. *España en su historia. Cristianos, moros y judíos*. Buenos Aires: Editorial Losada, 1948; trans. Edmund L. King, *The Structure of Spanish History*. Princeton, N.J.: Princeton University Press, 1954. A revised and expanded edition was published as *La realidad histórica de España*. Mexico City: Porrúa, 1954; trans. Willard F. King and Selma Margarretten, *The Spaniards: An Introduction to Their History*. Berkeley: University of California Press, 1971.

Castro Lingl, Vera. "The Count's Wife in *La condesa traidora*, the *Poema de Fernan González*, and the *Romanz del infant Garçía*: How Many Sanchas?" *Bulletin of Hispanic Studies* (Glasgow) 73 (1997): 373–80.

———. "The Two Wives of Count Garçi Fernández: Assertive Women in *La condesa traidora*." In Andrew M. Beresford, ed., *Quien hubiese tal ventura: Medieval Hispanic Studies in Honour of Alan Deyermond*. London: Department of Hispanic Studies, Queen Mary and Westfield College, 1997. 9–21.

Catalán, Diego. *De la silva textual al taller historiográfico alfonsí: Códices, crónicas, versiones y cuadernos de trabajo*. Madrid: Fundación Ramón Menéndez Pidal; Universidad Autónoma de Madrid, 1997.

Catlos, Brian A. "Contexto y conveniencia en la corona de Aragon: propuesta de un modelo de interacción entre grupos etno-religiosos minoritarios y mayoritarios." *Revista d'História Medieval* 12 (2001–2): 259–68.

———. "Mahomet Abenadalill: A Muslim Mercenary in the Service of the Kings of Aragon (1290–1291)." In Harvey J. Hames, ed., *Jews, Muslims, and Christians in and Around the Crown of Aragon: Essays in honour of Professor Elena Lourie*. Leiden: Brill, 2004. 257–302.

———. *Muslims of Medieval Latin Christendom, c.1050–1614*. Cambridge: Cambridge University Press, 2014.

———. *The Victors and the Vanquished: Christians and Muslims of Catalonia and Aragon, 1050–1300*. Cambridge: Cambridge University Press, 2004.

Cavadini, John C. *The Last Christology of the West: Adoptionism in Spain and Gaul, 785–820*. Philadelphia: University of Pennylvania Press, 1993.

Chalmeta Gendrón, Pedro. *Invasión e islamización: La sumisión de Hispania y la formación de al-Andalus*. 2nd ed. Jaén: Universidad de Jaén, 2003.

Chalon, Louis. "La historicidad de la leyenda de la Condesa Traidora." *Journal of Hispanic Philology* 2 (1977–78): 153–63.

Christys, Ann. "Christian-Muslim Frontiers in Early Medieval Spain." *Bulletin of International Medieval Research* 5 (1999): 1–19.

———. *Christians in al-Andalus, 711–1000*. Richmond, UK: Curzon Press, 2002.

———. "Crossing the Frontier of Ninth-Century Hispania." In David Abulafia and Nora Berend, eds., *Medieval Frontiers: Concepts and Practices*. Aldershot: Ashgate, 2002. 35–53.

Clarke, Nicola. "Medieval Arabic accounts of the conquest of Córdoba: Creating a narrative for a provincial capital." *Bulletin of the School of Oriental and African Studies* 74 (2011): 41–57.

———. *The Muslim Conquest of Iberia: Medieval Arabic Narratives*. Abingdon: Routledge, 2011.

Cochelin, Isabelle. "Orders and Exclusions." *Early Medieval Europe* 13 (2005): 395–403.

Cohen, Jeffrey. *Medieval Identity Machines*. Minneapolis: University of Minnesota Press, 2003.

Cohen, Raymond, and Raymond Westbrook, eds. *Amarna Diplomacy: The Beginnings of International Relations*. Baltimore: Johns Hopkins University Press, 2000.

Collard, Frank. "*Venenosa mulier coronata:* variations sur la figure de la reine empoisonneuse dans l'Occident médiéval." In Marcel Faure, ed., *Reines et princesses au Moyen Âge: Actes du Cinquième Colloque International de Montpellier, Université Paul-Valéry, 24–27 novembre 1999*. 2 vols. Montpellier: Université Paul-Valéry, 2001. 1: 303–22.

Collins, Roger. *The Arab Conquest of Spain, 710–797*. Oxford: Blackwell, 1989.

———. *The Basques*, 2nd ed. Oxford: Blackwell, 1990.

———. *Early Medieval Spain: Unity in Diversity, 400–1000*. 2nd ed. Basingstoke: Macmillan, 1995.

———. "Queens-Dowager and Queens-Regnant in Tenth-Century León and Navarre." In John Carmi Parsons, ed., *Medieval Queenship*. Basingstoke: Palgrave Macmillan, 1997. 79–92.

———. *Visigothic Spain, 409–711*. Oxford: Blackwell, 2004.

Collins, Roger, and Anthony Goodman, eds., *Medieval Spain: Culture, Conflict and Coexistence; Studies in Honour of Angus MacKay*. Basingstoke: Palgrave Macmillan, 2002.

Combarieu, Micheline de. "Un personnage épique: la jeune musulmane." In *Mélanges de langue et littérature françaises du Moyen-Age offerts à Pierre Jonin*. Sénéfiance 7. Aix-en-Provence : CUERMA, 1979. 181–96.

Connolly, Jennifer. "Forbidden Intimacies: Christian-Muslim Intermarriage in East Kalimantan, Indonesia." *American Ethnologist* 36 (2009): 492–506.

Constable, Olivia Remie. "Muslim Spain and Mediterranean Slavery: The Medieval Slave Trade as an Aspect of Muslim-Christian Relations." In Scott L. Waugh and Peter D. Diehl, eds., *Christendom and Its Discontents: Exclusion, Persecution and Rebellion, 1000–1500*. Cambridge: Cambridge University Press, 1996. 264–84.

———. *Trade and Traders in Muslim Spain: The Commercial Realignment of the Iberian Peninsula, 900–1500*. Cambridge: Cambridge University Press, 1994.

Coope, Jessica A. "Marriage, Kinship, and Islamic Law in Al-Andalus: Reflections on Pierre Guichard's *Al-Ándalus*." *Al-Masāq* 20 (2008): 161–77.

———. *The Martyrs of Córdoba: Community and Family Conflict in an Age of Mass Conversion*. Lincoln: University of Nebraska Press, 1995.

Cossío, José María de. "Cautivos de moros en el siglo XIII." *Al-Andalus* 7 (1942): 49–112.

Cotarelo, E. "El supuesto casamiento de Almanzor con una hija de Bermudo II." *España Moderna* 169 (1903): 42–55.

Cowdrey, H. E. J. *The Cluniacs and the Gregorian Reform*. Oxford: Clarendon, 1970.

Cuadrado Lorenzo, María Flora. "La iglesia de Santa María de Carrión de los Condes y su programa escultórico." *Publicaciones de la Institución Tello Téllez de Meneses* 57 (1987): 203–92.

Cummins, John G. "The Chronicle Text of the Legend of the *Infantes de Lara*." *Bulletin of Hispanic Studies* 53 (1976): 101–16.

Daniel, Norman. *Islam and the West: The Making of an Image*. Edinburgh: Edinburgh University Press, 1960.

Davies, R. R. *Domination and Conquest: The Experience of Ireland, Scotland and Wales, 1100–1300*. Cambridge: Cambridge University Press, 1990.

Deswarte, Thomas. *Une Chrétienté romaine sans pape: L'Espagne et Rome (586–1085)*. Bibliothèque d'Histoire médiévale, 1. Paris : Classiques Garnier, 2010.

Deyermond, Alan. *La literatura perdida de la Edad Media castellana. Catálogo y estudio I: Épica y romances*. Salamanca: Universidad de Salamanca, 1995.

———. "La sexualidad en la épica medieval española." *Nueva Revista de Filología Hispánica* 36 (1988): 767–86.

Deyermond, Alan, and Margaret Chaplin. "Folk-Motifs in the Medieval Spanish Epic." *Philological Quarterly* 51 (1972): 36–53.

Díaz Borrás, Andrés. *El miedo al mediterráneo: La caridad popular valenciana y la redención de cautivos bajo poder musulmán, 1323–1539*. Barcelona: CSIC, 2001.

Díaz y Díaz, Manuel C. "La Pasión de S. Pelayo y su difusión." *AEM* 6 (1969): 97–116.

Dillard, Heath. *Daughters of the Reconquest: Women in Castilian Town Society, 1100–1300*. Cambridge: Cambridge University Press, 1984.

———. "Women in Reconquest Castile: The Fueros of Sepúlveda and Cuenca." In Susan Mosher Stuard, ed., *Women in Medieval Society*. Philadelphia: University of Pennsylvania Press, 1976. 71–94.

Dodds, Jerrilynn D., María Rosa Menocal, and Abigail Krasner Balbale. *The Arts of Intimacy: Christians, Jews, and Muslims in the Making of Castilian Culture*. New Haven, Conn.: Yale University Press, 2008.

Doubleday, Simon. "The Ghost of María Pérez: Phantoms, Fantasies and Fictions of Thirteenth-Century Spain." *Society for Spanish and Portuguese Historical Studies Bulletin* 29, 2–3 (2004–5): 4–19.

———. "Hacia la descolonización del concepto de *convivencia*: algunos apuntes sobre el contexto norteamericano." In Ariel Guiance, ed., *La influencia de la historiografía española en la producción histórica americana*. Madrid: Marcial Pons, 2011. 59–75.

———. "Looking for María Pérez." *Rethinking History* 16, 1 (2012): 27–40.

Doubleday, Simon, and David Coleman, eds. *In the Light of Medieval Spain: Islam, the West, and the Relevance of the Past*. New York: Palgrave, 2008.

Douglas, Mary. *Purity and Danger: An Analysis of Concepts of Pollution and Taboo*. London: Routledge, 1978.

Dozy, Reinhardt. *Recherches sur l'histoire et la littérature de l'Espagne pendant le Moyen Age*. 3rd ed. 2 vols. Paris-Leiden: Brill, 1881.

Drell, Joanna H. "The Aristocratic Family." In Graham Loud and Alex Metcalfe, eds., *The Society of Norman Italy*. Leiden: Brill, 2002. 97–113.

Driss, Abdelghaffar Ben. "Los cautivos entre Granada y Castilla en el siglo XV según las fuentes árabes.' In Pedro Segura Artero, ed., *Actas del Congreso "La Frontera Oriental Nazarí como Sujeto Histórico (S.XIII–XVI)": Lorca-Vera, 22 a 24 de noviembre de 1994*. Alicante: Instituto de Estudios Almerienses, 1997. 301–10.

Dutton, Brian. "Gonzalo de Berceo and the *Cantares de gesta*." *Bulletin of Hispanic Studies* 38 (1961): 197–205.

Echevarría Arsuaga, Ana. "Esclavos musulmanes en los hospitales de cautivos de la Orden militar de Santiago (siglos XII y XIII)." *Al-Qanṭara* 28 (2007): 465–88.

El Cheikh, Nadia Maria. "Gender and politics in the harem of al-Muqtadir." In Leslie Brubaker and Julia M. H. Smith, eds., *Gender in the Early Modern World: East and West, 300–900*. Cambridge: Cambridge University Press, 2004. 147–61.

El-Hajji, Abdurrahman Ali. "Intermarriage Between Andalusia and northern Spain in the Umayyad period." *Islamic Quarterly* 11 (1967): 3–7.

Escalona, Julio, Isabel Velázquez Soriano, and Paloma Juárez Benítez. "Identification of the sole extant charter issued by Fernán González, Count of Castile (932–970)." *JMIS* 4 (2012): 259–88.

Estepa Díez, Carlos. *Estructura social de la ciudad de León (siglos XI–XIII)*. León: CEISI; Archivo Histórico Diocesano; Caja de Ahorros y Monte de Piedad de León, 1977.

Falque Rey, Emma. "El llamado *Privilegio de los Votos*, fuente del *Chronicon Mundi* de Lucas de Tuy." *Habis* 33 (2002): 573–77.

Fälschungen im Mittelalter: Internationaler Kongress der Monumenta Germaniae Historica, München, 16.–19. September 1986: Schriften der Monumenta Germaniae Historica. 6 vols. Hanover: Hahnsche Buchhandlung, 1988–90.

Fernández-Armesto, Felipe. "The Survival of a Notion of *Reconquista* in Late Tenth- and Eleventh-Century León." In Timothy Reuter, ed., *Warriors and Churchmen in the High Middle Ages*. London: Hambledon, 1992. 123–43.

Fernández Conde, Francisco Javier. *Libro de los Testamentos de la catedral de Oviedo*. Rome: Iglesia Nacional Española, 1971.

Fernández del Pozo, José María. "Alfonso V, rey de León." In *León y su historia: miscelánea histórica* 5. León: CEISI, 1984. 9–262.

———. *Alfonso V (999–1028). Vermudo III (1028–1037)*. Burgos: La Olmeda, 1999.

Fernández Félix, Ana. "Children on the frontiers of Islam." In Mercedes García Arenal, ed., *Conversions islamiques: Identités religieuses en Islam méditerranéen*. Paris: Maisonneuve & Larose, 2002. 61–72.

———. *Cuestiones legales del islam temprano: la 'Utbiyya y el proceso de formación de la sociedad islámica andalusí*. Madrid: CSIC, 2003.

Fernández Ordóñez, Inés. "El tema épico-legendario de *Carlos Mainete* y la transformación de la historiografía medieval hispánica entre los siglos XIII y XIV." In Jean-Philippe Genet, ed., *L'Histoire et les nouveaux publics dans l'Europe médiévale (XIIIe–XVe siècles)*. Paris: Publications de la Sorbonne, 1997. 89–112.

Ferrer i Mallol, Maria Teresa. "La redempció de captius a la Corona de Aragon (segle XIV)." *Anuario de Estudios Medievales* 15 (1985): 237–97.

———. *Els sarraïns de la corona catalano-aragonesa en el segle XIV: segregació i discriminació*. Barcelona: CSIC, 1987.

———. *La frontera amb l'Islam en el segle XIV: Cristians i sarraïns al País Valencià*. Barcelona: CSIC, 1988.

———. "The Muslim 'aljama' of Tortosa in the Late Middle Ages: Notes on Its Organisation." *Scripta Mediterranea* 19–20 (1998–99): 143–64.

Ferrer i Mallol, Maria Teresa, and Josefa Mutgé i Vives, eds. *De l'esclavitud a la llibertat:*

esclaus i lliberts a l'Edat Mitjana: actes del col·loqui internacional celebrat a Barcelona, del 27 al 29 de maig de 1999. Barcelona: CSIC, 2000.

Fierro, Maribel. "El conde Casio, los Banu Qasi y los linajes godos en al-Andalus." *Studia Histórica: Historia Medieval* 27 (2009): 181–89.

———. "Genealogies of Power in al-Andalus: Politics, Religion and Ethnicity During the Second/Eighth–Fifth/Eleventh Centuries." *Annales Islamogiques* 42 (2008): 29–55.

———. *La heterodoxia en al-Andalus durante el periodo omeya*. Madrid: Instituto Hispano-Árabe de Cultura, 1987.

———. "La obra histórica de *Ibn al-Qūṭīya*." *Al-Qanṭara* 10 (1989): 485–511.

———. "On Political Legitimacy in al-Andalus: A Review Article." *Der Islam: Zeitschrift für Geschichte und Kultur des islamischen Orients* 73 (1996): 138–50.

———. "Pompa y ceremonia en los califatos del Occidente islámico (ss. II/VIII–IX/XV)." *Cuadernos del CEMYR* 17 (2009): 125–52.

———. "Violence Against Women in Andalusi Historical Sources (Third/Ninth-Seventh/Thirteenth Centuries)." In Robert Gleave and István Kristó-Nagy, eds., *Violence in Islamic Thought from the Qur'an to the Mongols*. Edinburgh: University of Edinburgh Press, forthcoming.

Filios, Denise K. "Jokes on *soldadeiras* in the *Cantigas de escarnio e de mal dizer*." *La Corónica* 26 (1998): 29–39.

———. *Performing Women: Sex, Gender, and the Medieval Iberian Lyric*. New York: Macmillan, 2005.

Flesler, Daniela. *The Return of the Moor: Spanish Responses to Contemporary Moroccan Immigration*. West Lafayette, Ind.: Purdue University Press, 2008.

Fletcher, Richard. *The Cross and the Crescent: Christianity and Islam from Muhammad to the Reformation*. London: Allen Lane, 2003.

———. *The Episcopate in the Kingdom of León in the Twelfth Century*. Oxford: Oxford University Press, 1978.

———. "Reconquest and Crusade in Spain, c.1050–1150." *Transactions of the Royal Historical Society* 5th ser. 37 (1987): 31–47.

———. *Saint James's Catapult: The Life and Times of Diego Gelmírez of Santiago de Compostela*. Oxford: Clarendon, 1984.

Flórez, Enrique et al. *España Sagrada: theatro geográfico-histórico de la iglesia de España*. 56 vols. Madrid: various publishers, 1747–1957.

Foard, Douglas W. "The Spanish Fichte: Menéndez y Pelayo." *Journal of Contemporary History* 14 (1979): 83–97.

Formes, Malia B. "Beyond Complicity Versus Resistance: Recent Work on Gender and European Imperialism." *Journal of Social History* 28 (1995): 629–41.

Foucault, Michel. *The History of Sexuality*. Vol. 1, *The Will to Knowledge*. Trans. Robert Hurley. Harmondsworth: Penguin, 1998.

Foulché-Delbosc, Raymond, and Alexander Krappe. "La légende du roi Ramire." *Revue Hispanique* 78 (1930): 489–543.

Fournes, Ghislaine. "Iconologie des infantes (*Tumbo* A et *Tumbo* B de la cathédrale de

Saint-Jacques de Compostelle et *Tumbo* de Touxos Outos)." *e-Spania* (6 December 2008) at e-spania.revues.org/index12033.html.

Francomano, Emily C. "The Legend of the *Tributo de las cien doncellas*: Women as War-weavers and the Coin of Salvation." *Revista Canadiense de Estudios Hispánicos* 32 (2007): 9–25.

Freidenreich, David M. "Muslims in Western Canon Law, 1000–1500." In David Thomas et al., eds., *Christian-Muslim Relations: A Bibliographic History*. 2 vols. Leiden: Brill, 2011. 2: 41–68.

Friedman, Yvonne. *Encounter Between Enemies: Captivity and Ransom in the Latin Kingdom of Jerusalem*. Leiden: Brill, 2002.

Friedmann, Yohanan. *Tolerance and Coercion in Islam: Interfaith Relations in the Muslim Tradition*. Cambridge: Cambridge University Press, 2003.

Fuchs, Barbara. *Exotic Nation: Maurophilia and the Construction of Early Modern Spain*. Philadelphia: University of Pennsylvania Press, 2009.

Gaca, Kathy L. "Girls, women, and the significance of sexual violence in ancient warfare." In Elizabeth D. Heineman, ed., *Sexual violence in conflict zones: From the Ancient World to the era of human rights*. Philadelphia: University of Pennsylvania Press, 2011. 73–88.

Gambra, Andrés, ed. *Alfonso VI: cancillería, curia e imperio*. 2 vols. León: CEISI; Caja España de Inversiones; Archivo Histórico Diocesano, 1997–98.

García de Cortázar, José Ángel. *El dominio del monasterio de San Millán de la Cogolla (siglos X a XIII): introducción a la historia rural de Castilla altomedieval*. Salamanca: Universidad de Salamanca, 1969.

García Gallo, Alfonso. "Aportación al estudio de los Fueros." *AHDE* 26 (1956): 387–446.

———. "El Concilio de Coyanza: Contribución al estudio del derecho canónico español en la Alta Edad Media." *AHDE* 20 (1950): 275–633.

García Isasti, Prudencio. *La España metafísica: Lectura crítica del pensamiento de Ramón Menéndez Pidal (1891–1936)*. Bilbao: Real Academia de la Lengua Vasca; Euskaltzaindia, 2004.

García Sanjuán, Alejandro. "Formas de sumisión del territorio y tratamiento de los vencidos en el derecho islámico clásico." In Maribel Fierro and Francisco García Fitz, eds., *El cuerpo derrotado: cómo trataban musulmanes y cristianos al enemigo vencido*. Madrid: CSIC, 2008. 61–112.

García Ulecia, Alberto. *Los factores de diferenciación entre las personas en los fueros de la Extremadura castellano-aragonesa*. Seville: Gráficas del Sur, 1975.

Garulo Muñoz, Teresa. "La biografía de Wallada, toda problemas." *Anaquel de Estudios Árabes* 20 (2009): 97–116.

Gilles, Henri. "Législation et doctrine canoniques sur les sarasins." *Cahiers de Fanjeaux* 18: *Islam et chrétiens du Midi (XII–XIVs.)*, ed. E. Privat. Toulouse: Centre d'Études Historiques de Fanjeaux, 1983. 195–213.

Giménez Soler, Andrés. "La Corona de Aragon y Granada." *Boletín de la Real Academia de Buenas Letras de Barcelona* 19 (1905): 101–34; 20 (1905): 186–224; 21 (1906): 295–324;

22 (1906): 333–65; 23 (1906): 450–76; 24 (1906): 485–96; 26 (1907): 49–91; 27 (1907): 146–80; 28 (1907): 200–25; 29 (1908): 271–98; 30 (1908): 342–75.

Glick, Thomas F., and Oriol Pi-Sunyer. "*Convivencia*: An Introductory Note." In Vivian B. Mann, Thomas F. Glick, and Jerrilyn D. Dodds, eds., *Convivencia: Jews, Muslims, and Christians in Medieval Spain*. New York: George Braziller, 1992. 1–10.

———. *Islamic and Christian Spain in the Early Middle Ages*. Rev. 2nd ed. Leiden: Brill, 2005.

Gómez Martínez, José Luis. *Américo Castro y el orígen de los españoles: historia de una polémica*. Madrid: Gredos, 1975.

Gómez Moreno, Manuel. "Las primeras crónicas de la Reconquista: el ciclo de Alfonso III." *Boletín de la Real Academia de la Historia* 100 (1932): 562–623.

Gómez Redondo, Fernando. *Historia de la prosa medieval castellana. II. El desarrollo de los géneros. La ficción caballeresca y el orden religioso,* 2 vols. Madrid: Crítica, 1999.

Goñi Gaztambide, José. *Historia de la bula de la Cruzada en España*. Vitoria: Editorial del Seminario, 1958.

González, Julio. *El Reino de Castilla en la época de Alfonso VIII*. 3 vols. Madrid: CSIC, 1960.

González Jiménez, Manuel. "Frontier and Settlement in the Kingdom of Castile (1085–1350)." In Robert Bartlett and Angus MacKay, eds., *Medieval Frontier Societies*. Oxford: Oxford University Press, 1989. 49–74.

Gonzalo Moreno, Jesús. "Aproximación a la procesión de las cien doncellas de Sorzano: orígenes y sentido actual." *Berceo* 122 (1992): 117–26.

Gordon, Murray. *Slavery in the Arab World*. New York: New Amsterdam Books, 1989.

Grande Quejigo, Francisco Javier. *Hagiografía y difusión en la vida de San Millán de la Cogolla de Gonzalo de Berceo*. Logroño: Gobierno de La Rioja; Instituto de Estudios Riojanos, 2000.

Grassotti, Hilda. "Vindicación de doña Teresa." In Hilda Grassotti, *Estudios medievales españoles*. Madrid: Fundación Universitaria Española, 1981. 449–58.

Grieve, Patricia E. Floire and Blancheflor *and the European Romance*. Cambridge: Cambridge University Press, 1997.

———. "Private Man, Public Woman: Trading Places in *Condesa traidora*." *Romance Quarterly* 34 (1987): 317–26.

———. *The Eve of Spain: Myths of Origins in the History of Christian, Muslim, and Jewish Conflict*. Baltimore: Johns Hopkins University Press, 2009.

Grimbert, Joan Tasker, ed. *Tristan and Isolde: A Casebook*. New York: Routledge, 2002.

Guichard, Pierre. *Al-Andalus: Estructura antropológica de una sociedad islámica en occidente*. Barcelona: Barral Editores, 1976.

———. "Les Arabes ont bien envahi l'Espagne: Les structures sociales de l'Espagne musulmane." *Annales. Economies. Sociétés. Civilisations* 29 (1974): 1483–1513.

———. "A propos de l'identité andalouse: quelques éléments pour un débat."*Arabica* 46 (1999): 97–110.

Hamilton, Bernard. "Women in the Crusader States: The Queens of Jerusalem (1100–1190)." In Derek Baker, ed., *Medieval Women*. Oxford: Blackwell, 1978. 143–74.

Harris, Max. *Aztecs, Moors, and Christians*. Austin: University of Texas Press, 2000.

Harrison, Alwyn. "Behind the Curve: Bulliet and Conversion to Islam in al-Andalus Revisited." *Al-Masaq* 24 (2012): 35–51.

Heers, Jacques. *Esclaves et domestiques au moyen âge dans le monde méditerranéan*. Paris: Fayard, 1981.

Henriet, Patrick. "*Ad regem Cordube militandi gratia perrexit:* Remarques sur la presence militaire chrétienne en al-Andalus (Xe–XIIIe siècle)." In Daniel Baloup and Philippe Josserand, eds., *Regards croisés sur la guerre sante. Guerre, idéologie et religion dans l'espace Méditerranéen latin (XIe–XIIIe siècle)*. Toulouse: CNRS-Université de Toulouse-Le Mirail, 2006. 359–79.

———. "Les saints et la frontière en *Hispania* au cours du moyen âge central." In Klaus Herbers and Nikolas Jaspert, eds., *Grenzräume und Grenzüberschreitungen im Vergleich: Der Osten und der Western des mittelalterlichen Lateineuropa*. Berlin: Akademie Verlag, 2007). 361–86.

Herbers, Klaus. "Politik und Heiligenverehrung auf der Iberischen Halbinsel: Die Entwicklung des '*politischen Jakobus.*'" In Jürgen Petersohn, ed., *Politik und Heiligenverehrung im Hochmittelalter*. Vorträge und Vorschungen 42. Sigmaringen: Thorbecke, 1994. 177–275.

Herde, Peter. "Christians and Saracens at the Time of the Crusades: Some Comments of Contemporary Medieval Canonists." *Studia Gratiana* 12 (1967): 360–76.

Hernando, Josep. *Els esclaus islàmics a Barcelona: Blancs, negres, llors i turcs. De l'esclavitud a la llibertat (S.XIV)*. Barcelona: CSIC, 2003.

Hillgarth, J. N. "Spanish Historiography and Iberian Reality." *History and Theory* 24 (1985): 23–43.

Hinojosa Montalvo, José. *Los mudéjares: La voz del Islam en la España cristiana*, 2 vols. Teruel: Centro de Estudios Mudéjares; Instituto de Estudios Turolenses, 2002.

Hodgson, Natasha. *Women, Crusading and the Holy Land in Historical Narrative*. Woodbridge: Boydell, 2007.

Hoenerbach, Wilhelm. "Notas para una caracterización de Wallāda." *Al-Andalus* 36 (1971): 467–73.

Huici Miranda, Ambrosio. *Las grandes batallas de la Reconquista*. Madrid: CSIC, 1956.

Iogna-Prat, Dominique. *Order & Exclusion: Cluny and Christendom Face Heresy, Judaism, and Islam (1000–1150)*. Ithaca, N.Y.: Cornell University Press, 2002.

———. "Ordering Christian Society Through Exclusion: The Strange History of Cluny." *Early Medieval Europe* 13 (2005): 413–18.

Isla Frez, Amancio. "Ensayo de historiografía medieval: El Cronicón Iriense." *En la España Medieval* 4 (1984): 413–32.

Jordan, Mark D. "Saint Pelagius, Ephebe and Martyr." In Josiah Blackmore and Gregory S. Hutcheson, eds., *Queer Iberia: Sexualities, Cultures, and Crossings from the Middle Ages to the Renaissance*. Durham, N.C.: Duke University Press, 1999. 23–47.

Jover Zamora, José María. "Corrientes historiográficas en la España contemporánea." In José María Jover Zamora, *Historiadores españoles de nuestro siglo*. Madrid: Real Academia de la Historia, 1999. 273–310.

Kahf, Mohja. *Western Representations of the Muslim Woman: From Termagant to Odalisque*. Austin: University of Texas Press, 1999.

Karge, Henrik. "'Hoc ego facio ad restaurationem portus Apostoli': Der Pórtico de la Gloria und die königliche *restauratio* von Santiago de Compostela in der 2. Hälfte des 12. Jahrhunderts." In Claudia Rückert and Jochen Staebel, eds., *Mittelalterliche Bauskulptur in Frankreich und Spanien: Im Spannungsfeld des Chartreser Königsportals und des Pórticode la Gloria in Santiago de Compostela*. Frankfurt: Vervuert-Iberoamericana, 2010. 321–40, with illustrations at 315–17.

Karras, Ruth Mazo. "Marriage, Concubinage, and the Law." In Ruth Mazo Karras, Joel Kaye, and E. Ann Matter, eds., *Law and the Illicit in Medieval Europe*. Philadelphia: University of Pennsylvania Press, 2008. 117–29.

———. *Sexuality in Medieval Europe: Doing unto Others*. New York: Routledge, 2005.

Kedar, Benjamin Z. "On the Origins of the Earliest Laws of Frankish Jerusalem: The Canons of Nablus, 1120." *Speculum* 74 (1999): 310–35.

Kendrick, T. D. *St. James in Spain*. London: Methuen, 1960.

Kennedy, Hugh. *The Court of the Caliphs: The Rise and Fall of Islam's Greatest Dynasty*. London: Weidenfeld & Nicolson, 2004.

———. *Muslim Spain and Portugal: A Political History of al-Andalus*. London: Longman, 1996.

Kenny, Gillian. *Anglo-Irish and Gaelic Women in Ireland*. Dublin: Four Courts Press, 2007.

Kinoshita, Sharon. *Medieval Boundaries: Rethinking Difference in Old French Literature*. Philadelphia: University of Pennsylvania Press, 2006.

Knudson, Charles A. "La thème de la princesse sarrasine dans *la Prise d'Orange*." *Romance Philology* 22 (1969): 449–62.

König, Daniel. "Caught Between Cultures? Bicultural Personalities as Cross-Cultural Transmitters in the Late Antique and Medieval Mediterranean." In Rania Abdellatif, Yassir Benhima, Daniel König, and Elisabeth Ruchaud, eds., *Acteurs des transferts culturels en Méditerranée médiévale*. Munich: Oldenbourg, 2012. 56–72.

Kosto, Adam J. "Reconquest, Renaissance, and the Histories of Iberia, ca.1000–1200." In Thomas F. X. Noble and John Van Engen, eds., *European Transformations: The Long Twelfth Century*. Notre Dame, Ind.: University of Notre Dame Press, 2012. 93–116.

Kottmann, Sina Lucia. "Mocking and Miming the 'Moor': Staging of the 'Self' and 'Other' on Spain's borders with Morocco." *Journal of Mediterranean Studies* 20 (2011): 107–36.

Krom, Maria J. C. "Festivals of Moors and Christians: Performance, Commodity and Identity in Folk Celebrations in Southern Spain." *Journal of Mediterranean Studies* 18 (2008): 119–38.

Krus, Luís. *A concepção nobiliárquica do espaço ibérico (1280–1380)*. Lisbon: Fundação Calouste Gulbenkian; Junta nacional de investigação científica e tecnológica, 1994.

Lacarra, José María. "Textos navarros del Códice de Roda." *EEMCA* 1 (1945): 194–283.

Lacarra, María Jesús. "La historia de Enalviellos (*Crónica de la Población de Ávila*)." In *Orígenes de la prosa*, vol. 4 of *Historia de la literatura española*, ed. María Jesús Lacarra and Francisco López Estrada. Madrid: Ediciones Júcar, 1993. 77–84.

Lacarra Lanz, Eukene. "Changing Boundaries of Licit and Illicit Unions: Concubinage and Prostitution." In Eukene Lacarra Lanz, ed., *Marriage and Sexuality in Medieval and Early Modern Iberia*. New York: Routledge, 2002. 158–94.

———. "La utilización del Cid de Menéndez Pidal en la ideología militar y franquista." *Ideologies and Literature* 3 (1980): 95–127.

———. "Sobre la historicidad de la leyenda de los *Siete Infantes de Lara*." In Barry Taylor and Geoffrey West, eds., *Historicist Essays on Hispano-Medieval Narrative In Memory of Roger M. Walker*. London: Maney Publishing; Modern Humanities Research Association, 2005. 201–27.

Lagardère, Vincent. *Histoire et société en Occident musulman au Moyen Âge: Analyse du* Mi'yār *d'al-Wanšarīsī*. Madrid: Casa de Velázquez; CSIC, 1995.

Lappin, Anthony. "Between the Chisel and the Quill: The Development of the Cult of Peter of Osma During the Middle Ages." In Barry Taylor, Geoffrey West, and Jane Whetnall, eds., *Text, Manuscript, and Print in Medieval and Modern Iberia: Studies in Honour of David Hook*. New York: Hispanic Seminary of Medieval Studies, 2013. 41–87.

———. *Gonzalo de Berceo: The Poet and His Verses*. Woodbridge: Tamesis, 2008.

———. *The Medieval Cult of St. Dominic of Silos*. Leeds: Maney Publishing; Modern Humanities Research Association, 2002.

———. "The Thaumaturgy of Regal Piety: Alfonso X and the *Cantigas de Santa Maria*." *Journal of Hispanic Research* 4 (1995–96): 39–59.

Lathrop, Thomas A. *The Legend of the* Siete Infantes de Lara (*Refundición toledana de la crónica de 1344* version). Chapel Hill: University of North Carolina Press, 1971.

León Tello, Pilar. "Disposiciones sobre judíos en los fueros de Castilla y León." *Medievalia* 8 (1999): 223–52.

Lévi-Provençal, Évariste. "'Abbādids (Banū 'Abbād)." *EI*², 1: 5–7.

———. "al-Mu'tamid ibn 'Abbād: 1. Life." *EI*², 7: 766–67.

———. "Hispano-Arabica: La 'Mora Zaida,' femme d'Alphonse VI de Castille, et leur fils l'infant D. Sancho." *Hespéris* 18 (1934): 1–8.

———. Histoire de l'Espagne Musulmane, 3 vols. Paris-Leiden: Maisonneuve; Brill, 1950–53.

———. "La 'Mora Zaida,' belle-fille d'al-Mu'tamid." *Hespéris* 18 (1934): 200–201.

Lévi-Strauss, Claude. *The Elementary Structures of Kinship*. Ed. Rodney Needham, trans. James Harle Bell, John Richard von Sturmer, and Rodney Needham. London: Eyre & Spottiswoode, 1969.

Lewis, Bernard. *Race and Slavery in the Middle East: An Historical Enquiry*. New York: Oxford University Press, 1990.

Lewis, David Levering. *God's Crucible: Islam and the Making of Europe, 570–1215*. New York: Norton, 2005.

Linage Conde, Antonio. *Los orígenes del monacato benedictino en la Península Ibérica*. 3 vols. León: CEISI; CSIC, 1973.

Linehan, Peter. "At the Spanish Frontier." In Peter Linehan and Janet L. Nelson, eds., *The Medieval World*. London: Routledge, 2001. 37–59.

———. "The Court Historiographer of Francoism? *La Leyenda oscura* of Ramón Menéndez Pidal." *Bulletin of Hispanic Studies* (Glasgow) 73 (1996): 437–50.

———. *History and the Historians of Medieval Spain.* Oxford: Clarendon, 1993.

———. "History in a Changing World." In Peter Linehan, *Past and Present in Medieval Spain.* Aldershot: Ashgate, 1992. Part 1, 1–22.

———. "Religion, nationalism and national identity in medieval Spain and Portugal." In Stuart Mews, ed., *Religion and National Identity*. Studies in Church History 18. Oxford: Blackwell/Ecclesiastical History Society, 1982. 161–99.

Lino Munárriz y Velasco, Pedro. "Viaje del rey don Sancho al África." *Boletín de la Comisión de monumentos históricos y artísticos de Navarra*, segunda época, año 3 (1912): 5–39.

Liu, Benjamin. "'Affined to love the Moor': Sexual Misalliance and Cultural Mixing in the *Cantigas d'escarnho e de mal dizer.*" In Josiah Blackmore and Gregory S. Hutcheson, eds., *Queer Iberia: Sexualities, Cultures, and Crossings from the Middle Ages to the Renaissance*. Durham, N.C.: Duke University Press, 1999. 48–72.

Lobera, Atanasio de. *Historia de las grandezas de la muy antigua e insigne ciudad y Iglesia de León y de su Obispo y Patrón sant Froylan, con las del glorioso San Atilano, obispo de Zamora*. Valladolid: Diego Fernandez de Cordoua, 1596.

Lopes de Barros, Maria Filomena. "Body, Baths and Cloth: Muslim and Christian Perceptions in Medieval Portugal." *Portuguese Studies* 21 (2005): 1–12.

López de Coca, José Enrique. "The Making of Isabel de Solis." In Roger Collins and Anthony Goodman, eds., *Medieval Spain: Culture, Conflict and Coexistence: Studies in honour of Angus MacKay*. Basingstoke: Palgrave Macmillan, 2002. 225–41.

López Alsina, Fernando. *La ciudad de Santiago de Compostela en la Alta Edad Media*. Santiago de Compostela: Ayuntamiento de Santiago de Compostela, Centro de Estudios Jacobeos, Museo Nacional de las Peregrinaciones, 1988.

López Ferreiro, Antonio. *Historia de la Santa A. M. Iglesia de Santiago de Compostela*. 5 vols. Santiago de Compostela: Impr. del Seminario conciliar central, 1898–1902.

López Rajadel, Fernando. *Datación de la "Historia de los Amantes de Teruel": A través de los datos socioeconómicos del "papel escrito de letra antigua" copiado por Yagüe de Salas*. Teruel: Centro de Documentación Hartzenbusch; Fundación Amantes de Teruel, 2008.

Lorenzo Jiménez, Jesús. "Algunas consideraciones acerca del conde Casio." *Studia Histórica: Historia medieval* 27 (2009): 173–80.

———. *La dawla de los Banū Qasī: Origen, auge y caída de un linaje muladí en la Frontera Superior de Al-Andalus*. Madrid: CSIC, 2010.

Lourie, Elena. "A Society Organized for War: Medieval Spain," *Past and Present* 35 (1966): 54–76.

Lowney, Christopher. *A Vanished World: Medieval Spain's Golden Age of Enlightenment*. New York: Free Press, 2005.

Lukes, Steven. *Durkheim: His Life and Work*. Harmondsworth: Penguin, 1973.

MacKay, Angus. *Spain in the Middle Ages: From Frontier to Empire, 1000–1500*. London: Macmillan, 1977.

Maier, Christoph T. "Crusade and rhetoric against the Muslim Colony of Lucera: Eudes of Châteuroux's *Sermones de Rebellione Sarracenorum Lucherie in Apulia.*" *Journal of Medieval History* 21 (1995): 343–85.

Makkī, Maḥmūd 'Alī. "La España cristiana en el diwan de Ibn Darrāŷ." *Boletín de la Real Academia de Buenas Letras de Barcelona* 30 (1963–64): 63–104.

Malti-Douglas, Fedwa. *Woman's Body, Woman's Word: Gender and Discourse in Arabo-Islamic Writing.* Princeton, N.J.: Princeton University Press, 1991.

Mansilla, Demetrio. "La supuesta metropolí de Oviedo." *Hispania Sacra* 8 (1955): 259–74.

Manzanares de Cirre, Manuela. "Las cien doncellas: Trayectoria de una leyenda." *PMLA* 81 (1966): 179–84.

Manzano Moreno, Eduardo. "Árabes, bereberes e indígenas: al-Andalus en su primer período de formación." In Miquel Barceló and Pierre Toubert, eds., *L'Incastellamento: Actas de las reuniones de Girona (26–27 November 1992) y de Roma (5–7 May 1994).* Rome: École française de Rome; Escuela española de historia y arqueología en Roma, 1998. 157–77.

———. *Conquistadores, emires y califas: Los omeyas y la formación de al-Andalus.* Barcelona: Crítica, 2006.

———. "The Creation of a Medieval Frontier: Islam and Christianity in the Iberian Peninsula, Eighth to Eleventh Centuries." In Daniel Power and Naomi Standen, eds., *Frontiers in Question: Eurasian Borderlands, 700–1700.* Basingstoke: Macmillan, 1999. 32–54.

———. *La frontera de al-Andalus en época de los omeyas.* Madrid: CSIC, 1991.

———. "Las fuentes árabes sobre la conquista de al-Andalus: una nueva interpretación." *Hispania* 202 (1999): 389–432.

———. "A vueltas con el conde Casio." *Studia Histórica: Historia Medieval* 31 (2013): 255–66.

Marca, Petro de. *Marca Hispanica sive Limes Hispanicus.* Paris: François Muguet, 1688.

Marín, Manuela. "'Amar a cristianos moras': Ecos de un tema cervantino en textos españoles sobre Marruecos (s. XIX–XX)." *Bulletin Hispanique* 109 (2007): 235–62.

———. *Mujeres en el-Ándalus: Estudios onomástico-biográficos de al-Andalus,* 11. Madrid: CSIC, 2000.

———. "Parentesco simbólico y matrimonio entre los ulemas Andalusies." *Al-Qantara* 16 (1995): 335–56.

———. "Ṣubḥ." *EI*², 9: 740–41.

———. "Una vida de mujer: Ṣubḥ." In María Luisa Ávila and Manuela Marín, eds., *Biografías y género biográfico en el occidente islámico.* Estudios onomástico-biográficos de al-Andalus 8. Madrid: CSIC, 1997. 425–45.

Mark, James. "Remembering Rape: Divided Social Memory and the Red Army in Hungary 1944–1945." *Past & Present* 188 (2005): 133–61.

Marmon, S. E. "Concubinage, Islamic." In *Dictionary of the Middle Ages,* ed. Joseph R. Strayer. 13 vols. New York: Scribner for American Council of Learned Societies, 1982–89. 3: 527–29.

Márquez Villanueva, Francisco. "Las lecturas del deán de Cádiz en una *cantiga de mal dizer*." In Israel J. Katz and John E. Keller, eds., *Studies on the* Cantigas de Santa María*: Art, Music, and Poetry. Proceedings of the International Symposium on the* Cantigas de Santa María *of Alfonso X, el Sabio (1221–1284) in Commemoration of Its 700th Anniversary Year–1981 (New York, November 9–21)*. Madison, Wis.: Hispanic Seminary of Medieval Studies, 1987. 329–54.

———. *Santiago: Trayectoria de un mito*. Barcelona: Edicions Bellaterra, 2004.

Martínez, Salvador. "Alfonso VI: Hero in Search of a Poet." *La Corónica* 15, 1 (1986–87): 1–16.

Martínez Carrillo, María de los Llanos. "Historicidad de los 'Miraculos romançados' de Pedro Marín (1232–1293): el territorio y la esclavitud granadinos." *AEM* 21 (1991): 69–96.

Martínez Díez, Gonzalo. *Alfonso VI: señor del Cid, conquistador de Toledo*. Madrid: Temas de Hoy, 2003.

———. "El concilio compostelano del reinado de Fernando I." *AEM* 1 (1964): 121–38.

———. *El Condado de Castilla (711–1038): La historia frente a la leyenda*. 2 vols. Madrid: Junta de Castilla y León/Marcial Pons, 2005.

———. *El Cid histórico*. Barcelona: Planeta, 1999.

Martinez-Gros, Gabriel. "Comment écrire l'histoire de l'Andalus? Réponse a Pierre Guichard." *Arabica* 47 (2000): 261–73.

———. *Identité andalouse*. Paris: Sindbad, 1997.

Martín Rodríguez, José Luis. *Orígenes de la Orden Militar de Santiago*. Barcelona: CSIC, 1974.

McCracken, Peggy. *The Romance of Adultery: Queenship and Sexual Transgression in Old French Literature*. Philadelphia: University of Pennsylvania Press, 1998.

Menéndez y Pelayo, Marcelino. *Historia de los heterodoxos españoles*. 2 vols. Madrid: Biblioteca de Autores Cristianos, 1956.

Menéndez Pidal, Ramón. *La España del Cid*. 5th ed. 2 vols. Madrid: Espasa-Calpe, 1956.

———. *Historia y epopeya. Obras de R. Menéndez Pidal*, 2. Madrid: Centro de Estudios Históricos; Imprenta de librería y casa editorial Hernando, 1934.

———. *La leyenda de los Infantes de Lara*. 3rd ed. Madrid: Espasa-Calpe, 1971.

———. *Poesía juglaresca y orígenes de las literaturas románicas: Problemas de historia literaria y cultural*. Madrid: Instituto de Estudios Políticos, 1957.

———. *The Spaniards in Their History.* Trans. Walter Starkie. London: Hollis & Carter, 1950.

Menocal, María Rosa. *The Ornament of the World: How Muslims, Jews and Christians Created a Culture of Tolerance in Medieval Spain*. Boston: Little, Brown, 2002.

Mermissi, Fatima. *The Forgotten Queens of Islam*. Trans. M. J. Lakeland. Minneapolis: University of Minnesota Press, 1993.

Meyerson, Mark D. "Prostitution of Muslim Women in the Kingdom of Valencia: Religious and Sexual Discrimination in a Medieval Plural Society." In Marilyn J. Chiat and Kathryn L. Reyerson, eds., *The Medieval Mediterranean: Cross-Cultural Contacts.* Medieval Studies at Minnesota 3. St. Cloud, Minn.: North Star, 1988. 87–95.

Millán Rubio, Joaquín. *La Orden de Nuestra Señora de la Merced.* Rome: Instituto Histórico de la Orden de la Merced, 1992.

Miller, Kathryn. *Guardians of Islam: Religious Authority and Muslim Communities of Late Medieval Spain*. New York: Columbia University Press, 2008.

Mirrer, Louise. *Women, Jews, and Muslims in the Texts of Reconquest Spain*. Ann Arbor: University of Michigan Press, 1996.

Mogrobejo, Endika, Irantzu, and Garikoitz de. *Diccionario Hispanoamericano de Heráldica Onomástica y Genealogía* 32 (17). Bilbao: Editorial Mogrobejo-Zabala, 2009.

Molina, Luis. "Los Banū Jaṭṭāb y los Banū Abī Ŷamra (siglos II–VIII/VIII–XIV)." In Manuela Marín and Jesús Zanón, eds., *Estudios onomástico-biográficos de al-Andalus*, 5. Madrid: CSIC, 1992. 289–307.

———. "Las campañas de Almanzor a la luz de un nuevo texto." *Al-Qanṭara* 2 (1981): 209–63.

Molina López, Emilio. "La cora de Tudmīr según al-'Uḏrī (s. XI): Aportaciones al estudio geográfico-descriptivo del SE. peninsular." *Cuadernos de Historia del Islam* 3 (1972): 1–113.

Montaner Frutos, Alberto. "La historia del capitán cautivo y la tradición épica de frontera." *Letras* (Buenos Aires) 52–53 (2005–6) [= *Studia Hispanica Medievalia VII: Actas de las VIII Jornadas Internacionales de Literatura Española Medieval y de Homenaje al "Quijote"*]: 73–115.

———. "La mora Zaida, entre historia y leyenda (con una reflexión sobre la técnica historiográfica alfonsí)." In Barry Taylor and Geoffrey West, eds., *Historicist Essays on Hispano-Medieval Narrative In Memory of Roger M. Walker.* London: Maney Publishing; Modern Humanities Research Association, 2005. 272–352.

Montgomery, Thomas. "Cycles, Parallels, and Inversions in the *Leyenda de los Siete Infantes.*" *Olifant* 13 (1988): 41–54.

Moore, R. I. *The Formation of a Persecuting Society: Power and Deviance in Western Europe, 950–1250*. 2nd ed. Oxford: Blackwell, 2007.

Morris, Colin. *The Papal Monarchy: The Western Church from 1050 to 1250*. Oxford: Clarendon, 1989.

Mourtada-Sabbah, Nada, and Adrian Gully. "'I am by God, fit for High Positions': On the Political Role of Women in al-Andalus." *British Journal of Middle Eastern Studies* 30 (2003): 183–209.

Mutgé Vives, Josefina. "La aljama sarracena en la Lleida cristiana: noticias y conclusiones." In *VII Simposio Internacional de Mudejarismo*. Teruel: Centro de Estudios Mudéjares; Instituto de Estudios Turolenses, 1999. 101–11.

———. *L'aljama sarraïna de Lleida a l'edat mitjana: aproximació a la seva historia*. Barcelona: CSIC, 1992.

Narbona Vizcaíno, Rafael. *Pueblo, poder y sexo: Valencia medieval (1306–1420)*. Valencia: Diputación Provincial de Valencia, 1992.

Nederman, Cary J. "Introduction: Discourses and Contexts of Tolerance in Medieval Europe." In John Christian Laursen and Cary J. Nederman, eds., *Beyond the Persecuting Society: Religious Toleration Before the Enlightenment*. Philadelphia: University of Pennsylvania Press, 1998. 13–24.

Nirenberg, David. *Communities of Violence: Persecution of Minorities in the Middle Ages.* Princeton, N.J.: Princeton University Press, 1996.

———. "Conversion, Sex, and Segregation: Jews and Christians in Medieval Spain." *American Historical Review* 107, 4 (2002): 1065–93.

———. "Deviant politics and Jewish love: Alfonso VIII and the Jewess of Toledo." *Jewish History* 21 (2007): 15–41.

———. "Engaging *Order and Exclusion*: Reflections on a Recent book by Dominique Iogna-Prat," *Early Medieval Europe* 13 (2005): 387–94.

———. "Enmity and Assimilation: Jews, Christians, and Converts in Medieval Spain." *Common Knowledge* 9 (2003): 137–55.

———. "Love Between Muslim and Jew in Medieval Spain: A Triangular Affair." In Harvey J. Hames, ed., *Jews, Muslims, and Christians in and Around the Crown of Aragon: Essays in honour of Professor Elena Lourie*. Leiden: Brill, 2004. 127–55.

———. "Religious and Sexual Boundaries in the Medieval Crown of Aragon." In Mark D. Meyerson and Edward D. English, eds., *Christians, Muslims, and Jews in Medieval and Early Modern Spain: Interaction and Cultural Change.* Notre Dame, Ind.: University of Notre Dame Press, 2000. 141–60.

Noble, Thomas F. X., and Thomas Head, eds., *Soldiers of Christ: Saints' Lives from Late Antiquity and the Early Middle Ages*. University Park: Pennsylvania State University Press, 1994.

Nodar Manso, Francisco. "La parodia de la literatura heroica y hagiográfica en las cantigas de escarnio y mal decir." *Dicenda: Cuadernos de Filología Hispánica* 9 (1990): 151–61.

Novikoff, Alex. "Between Tolerance and Intolerance in Medieval Spain: An Historiographical Engima." *Medieval Encounters* 11 (2005): 7–36.

O'Callaghan, Joseph F. *A History of Medieval Spain*. Ithaca, N.Y.: Cornell University Press, 1975.

———. "The Integration of Christian Spain into Europe: The Role of Alfonso VI of León-Castile." In Bernard F. Reilly, ed., *Santiago, St.-Denis, and St. Peter*. New York: Fordham University Press, 1985. 101–20.

———. *The Learned King: The Reign of Alfonso X of Castile*. Philadelphia: University of Pennsylvania Press, 1993.

———. *Reconquest and Crusade in Medieval Spain*. Philadelphia: University of Pennsylvania Press, 2003.

Ocampo, Florián de. *Corónica general de España que recopilaba el Maestro Florian de Ocampo coronista del rey nuestro señor Don Felipe II*. 8 vols. Madrid: Benito Cano, 1791.

Odd, Frank L. "Women of the Romanceros: A Voice of Reconciliation." *Hispania* 66 (1983): 360–68.

Olagüe, Ignacio. *Les Arabes n'ont jamais envahi l'Espagne*. Paris: Flammarion, 1969.

Olson, Glenn. "The Middle Ages in the History of Toleration: A Prolegomena." *Mediterranean Studies* 16 (2007): 1–20.

Paredes, Juan. *Las narraciones de los* Livros de Linhagens. Granada: Universidad de Granada, 1995.

Pastor de Togneri, Reyna. "Claudio Sánchez-Albornoz y sus claves de la historia de España." *Revista de Historia Jerónimo Zurita* 73 (1998): 117–31.

Pattison, David G. *From Legend to Chronicle: The Treatment of Epic Material in Alphonsine Historiography*. Oxford: Society for the Study of Mediaeval Languages and Literature, 1983.

Pavón Benito, Julia. "Muladíes. Lectura política de una conversión: los Banū Qasī (714–924)." *Anaquel de Estudios Árabes*, 17 (2006): 189–202.

Peirce, Leslie. *The Imperial Harem: Women and Sovereignty in the Ottoman Empire*. Oxford: Oxford University Press, 1993.

Peiró Martín, Ignacio. "La historiografía española del siglo XX: aspectos institucionales y políticos de un proceso histórico." In Antonio Morales Moya, ed., *Las claves de la España del siglo XX*, vol. 8, *La cultura*. Madrid: España Nuevo Milenio, 2001. 45–73.

Pérès, Henri. *La poésie andalouse en arabe classique au XIe siècle: ses aspects géneraux, ses principaux thèmes et sa valeur documentaire*. 2nd ed. Paris: Adrien-Maisonneuve, 1953.

Pérez-Embid, Javier. *Hagiologia y sociedad en la España medieval: Castilla y León (siglos XI–XIII)*. Huelva: Universidad de Huelva, 2002.

Pérez de Urbel, Justo. "Los primeros siglos de la Reconquista (Años 711–1038)." In Justo Pérez de Urbel and Ricardo del Arco y Garay, *España cristiana: Comienzo de la Reconquista (711–1038), Historia de España [dirigida por Ramón Menéndez Pidal]*, 6. Madrid: Espasa Calpe, 1956. 1–348.

Pérez Pascual, José Ignacio. *Ramón Menéndez Pidal: Ciencia y pasión*. Valladolid: Junta de Castilla y León, 1998.

Pérez Villanueva, Joaquín. *Ramón Menéndez Pidal: Su vida y su tiempo*. Madrid: Espasa-Calpe, 1991.

Peris, M. Carmen. "La prostitución valenciana en la segunda mitad del siglo XIV." *Revista d'Història Medieval* 1 (1990): 179–99.

Peristany, John, ed. *Honour and Shame: The Values of a Mediterranean Society*. London: Weidenfeld and Nicolson, 1965.

Pick, Lucy. "Peter the Venerable and the New World Order." *Early Medieval Europe* 13 (2005): 405–11.

Pitt-Rivers, Julian. *The Fate of Shechem, or the Politics of Sex: Six Essays in the Anthropology of the Mediterranean*. Cambridge: Cambridge University Press, 1977.

Pohl, Walter. "Alienigena coniuga: Bestrebungen zu einem Verbot auswärtiger Heiraten in der Karolingerzeit." In Andreas Pečar and Kai Trampedach, eds., *Die Bibel als politisches Argument*. Historische Zeitschrift 43. Munich: R. Oldenbourg, 2007. 159–88.

Porres Alonso, Bonifacio. *Libertad a los cautivos: Actividad redentora de la orden Trinitaria*, 2 vols.: Secretariado Trinitario, 1998.

Powers, James F. "Frontier Municipal Baths and Social Interaction in Thirteenth-Century Spain." *American Historical Review* 84 (1979): 649–67.

———. *A Society Organized for War: The Iberian Municipal Militias in the Central Middle Ages, 1000–1284*. Berkeley: University of California Press, 1988.

Prelog, Jan. *Die Chronik Alfons' III: Untersuchung und kritische Edition der vier Redaktionen*. Frankfurt am Main: Peter Lang, 1980.

Puente, Cristina de la. "La caracterización de Almanzor: entre la epopeya y la historia." In María Luisa Ávila and Manuela Marín, eds., *Biografías y género biográfico en el occidente islámico*, Estudios onomástico-biográficos de al-Andalus 8 (Madrid: CSIC, 1997), 367–402.

———. "Entre la esclavitud y la libertad: consecuencias legales de la manumisión según el derecho māliki." *Al-Qanṭara* 21 (2000): 339–60.

———. "Límites legales del concubinato: normas y tabúes en la esclavitud sexual según la *Bidāya* de Ibn Rušd." *Al-Qanṭara* 28 (2007): 409–33.

———. "Mujeres cautivas en 'la tierra del Islam'" *Al-Andalus-Magreb* 14 (2007): 19–37.

Purkis, William J. *Crusading Spirituality in the Holy Land and Iberia, c.1095–c.1187*. Woodbridge: Boydell, 2008.

———. "The Past as a Precedent: Crusade, Reconquest and Twelfth-Century Memories of Christian Iberia." In Lucie Doležalová, ed., *The Making of Memory in the Middle Ages*. Leiden: Brill, 2009. 441–61.

Quijera Pérez, José Antonio. "El tributo de las cien doncellas, un viejo mito mediterráneo." *Revista de Folklore* 13a (1993): 128–35.

Ragib, Youssef. "Les marchés aux esclaves en terre d'Islam." In *Mercati e mercanti nell'alto Medioevo: l'area euroasiastica e l'area mediterránea*. Settimane di studio del centro italiano di studi sull'alto Medioevo 40. Spoleto: Centro Italiano di Studi sull'alto Medioevo, 1993. 721–63.

Ramey, Lynn Tarte. *Christian, Saracen and Genre in Medieval French Literature*. New York: Routledge, 2001.

Ramos, María Ana. "Hestorja dell Rej dom Ramjro de lleom. . . . Nova versão de A Lenda de Gaia." Critica del Testo 7 (2004): 791–843.

———. "A intenção de inscrever na memória colectiva. O sucesso textual do motivo *a mulher de Salomão* na narrativa histórica portuguesa." In Márcio Ricardo Coelho Muniz, Maria de Fátima Maia Ribeiro, and Solange Santos Santana, eds., *Anais do XXII Congresso Internacional da Associação Brasileira de Professores de Literatura Portuguesa (2011). 625–53.* http://www.abraplip.org/anais_abraplip/documentos/mesas_tematicas/maria_ana_ramos.pdf.

Ramos y Loscertales, José María. *El cautiverio en la Corona de Aragon durante los siglos XIII, XIV y XV*. Zaragoza: Estudio de Filología de Aragón, 1915.

Rangel López, Noelia. "Moras, jóvenes y prostitutas: acerca de la prostitución valenciana a finales de la Edad Media." *Miscelánea Medieval Murciana* 32 (2008): 119–30.

Rawlings, Helen. *The Spanish Inquisition*. Oxford: Blackwell, 2006.

Ray, Jonathan. *The Sephardic Frontier: The* Reconquista *and the Jewish Community in Medieval Iberia*. Ithaca, N.Y.: Cornell University Press, 2006.

Reglero de la Fuente, Carlos Manuel. *Cluny en España: Los prioratos de la provincia y sus redes sociales (1073–ca. 1270)*. León: CEISI, 2008.

Reilly, Bernard F. *The Kingdom of León-Castilla Under King Alfonso VI, 1065–1109*. Princeton, N.J.: Princeton University Press, 1988.

Remensnyder, Amy G. "Christian Captives, Muslim Maidens, and Mary." *Speculum* 82 (2007): 642–77.

———. *La Conquistadora: The Virgin Mary at War and Peace in the Old World and the New.* Oxford: Oxford University Press, 2014.

Rey Castelao, Ofelia. "Historia e imaginación: la fiesta ficticia." In Manuel Núñez Rodríguez, ed., *El rostro y el discurso de la fiesta.* Santiago de Compostela: Universidad de Santiago, 1994. 185–96.

———. *La historiografía del Voto de Santiago: recopilación crítica de una polémica histórica.* Santiago de Compostela: Universidad de Santiago de Compostela, 1985.

———. *El Voto de Santiago: Claves de un conflicto.* Santiago de Compostela: Xunta de Galicia, 1993.

Ribeiro Miranda, José Carlos. "A *Lenda de Gaia* dos Livros de Linhagens: Uma questão de literatura?" *Revista da Faculdade de Letras: Línguas e Literaturas* 5 (1988): 483–516.

Ribera y Tarragó, Julián. *El cancionero de Abencuzmán*, in *Disertaciones y opúsculos*, 2 vols. Madrid: Imprenta de Estanislao Maestre, 1928.

Ricard, Robert. "Contribution à l'étude des fêtes de 'moros y cristianos' au Mexique." *Journal de la Société des Américanistes* 24 (1932): 51–84.

Riley-Smith, Jonathan. *The First Crusaders, 1095–1131.* Cambridge: Cambridge University Press, 1997.

Ríos Saloma, Martín F. *La Reconquista: Una construcción historiográfica (siglos XVI–XIX).* Madrid: Universidad Nacional Autónoma de Mexico; Marcial Pons, 2011.

Riquer, Martín de. "Crónica aragonesa del tiempo de Juan II." *Analecta Sacra Tarraconensia* 17 (1944): 1–29.

———. *La leyenda de Galcerán de Pinós y el rescate de las cien doncellas.* Barcelona: Talleres Gráficos Antonio J. Rovira, 1944.

———. "Una versión aragonesa de la leyenda de la enterrada viva." *Revista de Bibliografía Nacional* 6 (1945): 241–48.

Rivair Macedo, José. "Mouros e cristãos: A ritualização da conquista no velho e no Novo Mundo." *Bulletin du centre d'études médiévales d'Auxerre*, Hors-série 2: *Le Moyen Âge vu d'ailleurs* (2008): http://cem.revues.org/8632

Roberts, Anna. "Introduction: Violence Against Women and the Habits of Thought." In Anna Roberts, ed., *Violence Against Women in Medieval Texts.* Gainesville: University Press of Florida, 1998. 1–21.

Robinson, Chase F. *Empire and Elites After the Muslim Conquest: The Transformation of Northern Mesopotamia.* Cambridge: Cambridge University Press, 2000.

Robinson, Cynthia. "Arthur in the Alhambra? Narrative and Nasrid Courtly Self-Fashioning in the Hall of Justice Ceiling Paintings." *Medieval Encounters* 14 (2008): 164–98.

———. *Medieval Andalusian Courtly Culture: Ḥadīth Bayāḍ wa Riyāḍ.* London: Routledge, 2007.

Roca Franquesa, José María. "La leyenda 'El tributo de las cien doncellas.'" *Boletín del Instituto de Estudios Asturianos* 5 (1948): 129–63.

Rodriguez, Jarbel. *Captives and Their Saviors in the Medieval Crown of Aragon*. Washington, D.C.: Catholic University of America Press, 2007.

———. "Conversion Anxieties in the Crown of Aragón in the Later Middle Ages." *Al-Masāq* 22 (2010): 315–24.

Rodríguez Molina, José. "La frontera entre Granada y Jaén fuente de agrandecimiento para la nobleza (siglo XIV)." In Cristina Segura Graíño, ed., *Relaciones exteriores del Reino de Granada. IV Coloquio de Historia Medieval Andaluza*. Almería: Instituto de Estudios Almerienses, 1988. 237–50.

Rosenstein, Roy. "The Voiced and the Voiceless in the *Cancioneiros*: The Muslim, the Jew, and the Sexual Heretic as *Exclusus Amator*." *La Corónica* 26 (1998): 65–75.

Rubiera Mata, María-Jesus. "Un insólito caso de conversas musulmanas al cristianismo: las princesas toledanas del siglo XI." In Ángela Muñoz Fernández, ed., *Las mujeres en el cristianismo medieval. Imagenes teóricas y cauces de actuación religiosa*. Madrid: Asociación Cultural Al-Mudayna, 1989. 341–48.

Rubio Moreno, Laura María. "Crónica de la población de Avila: la polifonía textual en la historia de Nalvillos." In *Beatriz Díez Calleja, ed., El primitivo romance hispanico: de nuevo sobre la época de orígenes*. Burgos: Instituto Castellano y Leonés de la Lengua, 2008. 455–63.

Ruggles, D. Fairchild. "Mothers of a Hybrid Dynasty: Race, Genealogy, and Acculturation in al-Andalus." *Journal of Medieval and Early Modern Studies* 34 (2004): 65–94.

Safran, Janina M. *Defining Boundaries in al-Andalus: Muslims, Christians, and Jews in Islamic Iberia*. Ithaca, N.Y.: Cornell University Press, 2013.

———. "Identity and Differentiation in Ninth-Century al-Andalus." *Speculum* 76 (2001): 573–98.

———. *The Second Umayyad Caliphate: The Articulation of Caliphal Legitimacy in al-Andalus*. Cambridge, Mass.: Harvard University Press, 2000.

Sage, Carleton M. *Paul Albar of Cordoba: Studies on His Life and Writings*. Washington, D.C.: Catholic University of America Press, 1943.

Said, Edward. *Orientalism: Western Conceptions of the Orient*. London: Routledge, 1978.

Salazar y Acha, Jaime de. "Contribución al estudio del reinado de Alfonso VI de Castilla: algunas aclaraciones sobre su política matrimonial." *Anales de la Real Academia Matritense de Heráldica y Genealogía* 2 (1992–3): 299–343.

———. "De nuevo sobre la mora Zaida." *Hidalguía* 54 (2007): 225–42.

Sampedro Vizcaya, Benita, and Simon Doubleday. "Introduction." In Benito Sampedro Vizcaya and Simon Doubleday, eds., *Border Interrogations: Questioning Spanish Frontiers*. New York: Berghahn, 2008. 1–14.

Sánchez-Albornoz, Claudio. "La auténtica batalla de Clavijo." *Cuadernos de Historia de España* 9 (1948): 94–139.

———. *España: un enigma histórico*. 5th ed. Barcelona: Editora y Distribuidora Hispanoamericana, 1976. Trans. Colette Joly Dees and David-Sven Reher, *Spain, a Historical Enigma*. 2 vols. Madrid: Fundación Universitaria Española, 1975.

———. *Mi testamento histórico-político*. Barcelona: Planeta, 1975.

———. "El ejército y la guerra en el reino asturleonés, 718–1037." *Settimane di Studio del Centro Italiano de studi sull'alto medioevo* 15 (1968): 293–428.

Sánchez Ameijeiras, Rocío. "Histories and Stories of Love and Conversion in Fourteenth-Century Burgos." *Hispanic Research Journal* 13 (2012): 449–67.

Saunders, Corinne. "Sexual Violence in Wars: The Middle Ages." In Hans-Henning Kortüm, ed., *Transcultural Wars from the Middle Ages to the 21st Century*. Berlin: Akademie Verlag, 2006. 151–64.

Sayers, Jane E. *Innocent III: Leader of Europe, 1198–1216*. London: Longman, 1994.

Scales, Peter. *The Fall of the Caliphate of Córdoba: Berbers and Andalusis in Conflict*. Leiden: Brill, 1994.

Schacht, Joseph. "Umm al-Walad." *EI²*, 10: 857–59.

Schneider, Jane. "Of Vigilance and Virgins: Honor, Shame and Access to Resources in Mediterranean Societies." *Ethnology* 10 (1971): 1–24.

Schulenberg, Jane Tibbetts. *Forgetful of Their Sex: Female Sanctity and Society, ca. 500–1100*. Chicago: University of Chicago Press, 2001.

Searle, Eleanor. "Women and the Legitimisation of Succession at the Norman Conquest." In R. Allen Brown, ed., *Proceedings of the Battle Conference 1980*. Woodbridge: Boydell, 1981. 159–70.

Segl, Peter. *Königtum und Klosterreform in Spanien. Untersuchungen über die Cluniacenserklöster in Kastilien-León vom Beginn des 11. bis zur Mitte der 12. Jahrhunderts*. Kallmünz: Michael Lassleben, 1974.

Segura Urra, Félix. "Los mudéjares navarros y la justicia regia: cuestiones penales y pecularidades delictivas en el siglo XIV." *Anaquel de Estudios Árabes* 14 (2003): 239–58.

Seifert, Ruth. "The Second Front: The Logic of Sexual Violence in Wars." *Women's Studies International Forum* 19 (1996): 35–43.

Sénac, Philippe. *Al-Mansûr: Le fléau de l'an mil*. Paris: Perrin, 2006.

———. *La frontière et les hommes (VIIIe–XIIe siècle): Le peuplement musulman au nord de l'Ebre et les débuts de la reconquête aragonaise*. Paris: Maisonneuve et Larose, 2000.

———. "Note sur les musulmans dans les *Généalogies* de Roda." In Amaia Arizaleta, ed., *Poétique de la Chronique: l'écriture des textes historiographiques au Moyen Age (Péninsule Ibérique et France)*. Toulouse: Université de Toulouse-Le Mirail, 2008. 37–46.

———. "Les Seigneurs de la Marche (*aṣḥābu al-ṭagri*): les Banū 'Amrūs et les Banū Šabrīṭ de Huesca." *Cuadernos de Madīnat al-Zahrā* 7 (2010): 27–42.

Shatzmiller, Maya. "Marriage, Family, and the Faith: Women's Conversion to Islam." *Journal of Family History* 21 (1996) : 235–66.

Shepard, William P. "Two Assumed Epic Legends in Spanish." *Modern Language Notes* 23 (1908): 146–47.

Shutters, Lynn. "Christian Love or Pagan Transgression? Marriage and Conversion in *Floire et Blancheflor*." In Albrecht Classen, ed., *Discourses on Love, Marriage, and Transgression in Medieval and Early Modern Literature*. Tempe: Arizona Center for Medieval Studies, 2004. 85–108.

Simmel, Georg. *Conflict;* [and] *The Web of Group-Affiliations*. Trans. Kurt Wolf. New York: Free Press, 1955.

Smith, Colin. *The Making of the* Poema de mio Cid. Cambridge: Cambridge University Press, 1983.

Soifer, Maya. "Beyond *convivencia*: critical reflections on the historiography of interfaith relations in Christian Spain." *JMIS* 1 (2009): 19–35.

Souto Cabo, José António. *Os cavaleiros que fizeram as cantigas: aproximação às origens socioculturais da lírica galego-portuguesa*. Niterói: Editora da UFF, 2012.

Soyer, François. "Muslim slaves and freemen in Medieval Portugal." *Al-Qanṭara* 28 (2007): 489–516.

Stoler, Ann Laura. *Carnal Knowledge and Imperial Power: Race and the Intimate in Colonial Rule*. Berkeley: University of California Press, 2002.

Talbot, C. H. *The Anglo-Saxon Missionaries in Germany*. London: Sheed and Ward, 1954.

Tellenbach, Gerd. *The church in western Europe from the tenth to the early twelfth century.* Trans. Timothy Reuter. Cambridge: Cambridge University Press, 1993.

Thompson, Stith. *Motif-Index of Folk-Literature: A Classification of Narrative Elements in Folktales, Ballads, Fables, Mediaeval Romances, Exempla, Fabliaux, Jest-Books and Local Legends*. Copenhagen: Rosenkilde and Bagger, 1955.

Tolan, John. *Saracens: Islam in the Medieval European Imagination*. New York: Columbia University Press, 2002.

———. "Une *convivencia* bien précaire: la place des Juifs et des musulmans dans les sociétés chrétiennes ibériques au Moyen Âge." In Guy Saupin, Rémy Fabre, and Marcel Launay, eds., *La tolérance: Colloque international de Nantes, mai 1998, Quatrième centenaire de l'édit de Nantes*. Rennes: Presses Universitaires de Rennes, Centre de Recherche sur l'histoire du Monde Atlantique, 1999. 385–94.

———. "Using the Middle Ages to Construct Spanish Identity: Nineteenth- and Twentieth-Century Historiography of Reconquest." In Jan Piskorski, ed., *Historiographical Approaches to Medieval Colonization of East Central Europe*. Boulder, Colo.: East European Monographs, 2002. 329–47.

Torres Fontes, Juan, and Emilio Sáez. "Privilegios a la ciudad de Murcia." *AHDE* 14 (1943): 530–45.

Torres Sevilla-Quiñones de León, Margarita. *Las batallas legendarias y el oficio de la guerra*. Barcelona: Plaza & Janés: 2002.

———. *Linajes nobiliarios de León y Castilla (siglos IX–XIII)*. Valladolid: Junta de Castilla y León, Consejería de Educación y Cultura, 1999.

Ubieto Arteta, Antonio. "Los "Votos" de San Millán." In *Homenaje a Jaime Vicens Vives*, 2 vols. Barcelona: Universidad de Barcelona, 1965, 1: 304–24.

———. "Un tradicional ejemplo de confusión genealógica: a proposito de la muerte de Abd al-Rahman 'Sanchuelo' y Sancho ibn Gómez (1009)." *Estudios Humanísticos: Geografía, Historia, Arte* 19 (1997): 67–73.

van Herwaarden, Jan. *Between St. James and Erasmus: Studies in Late-Medieval Religious Life: Devotion and Pilgrimage in the Netherlands*. Leiden: Brill, 2003.

van Houts, Elisabeth. "Intermarriage in eleventh-century England." In David Crouch and Kathleen Thompson, eds., *Normandy and Its Neighbours 900–1250: Essays for David Bates*. Turnhout: Brepols, 2011. 237–70.

Vaquero, Mercedes. *Tradiciones orales en la historiografía de fines de la Edad Media*. Madison, Wis.: Hispanic Seminary of Medieval Studies, 1990.

Vázquez de Parga, Luis. *La División de Wamba*. Madrid: CSIC, 1943.

Vega Rodríguez, Pilar. "Teresa, la infanta (y el rey moro de Toledo)." In Leonardo Romero Tobar, ed., *Temas literarios hispánicos (I)*. Zaragoza: Universidad de Zaragoza, 2013. 243–70.

Vergara, Sebastián de. *Vida, y milagros de el thaumaturgo español Moyses Segundo, redemptor de cautivos, abogado de los felices partos, Sto. Domingo Manso, abad Benedictino, reparador de el Real Monasterio de Silos*. Madrid: Imprenta de los Herederos de Francisco del Hierro, 1736.

Verlinden, Charles. *L'esclavage dans l'Europe médiévale*. 2 vols. Bruges: De Tempel, 1955.

Victorio Martínez, Juan. "La ciudad-mujer en los romances fronterizos." *AEM* 15 (1985): 553–60.

Viguera Molins, María Jesús. *Aragón musulman: la presencia del Islam en el valle del Ebro*. Zaragoza: Mira Editores, 1988.

———. "Aṣluḥu li'l-ma'ālī: On the social status of Andalusī women." In Salma Khadra Jayyusi, ed., *The Legacy of Muslim Spain*. 2 vols. Leiden: Brill, 1992, 2: 709–24.

———. "Una andalusí en Galicia y sus cuatro 'transgresiones.'" In Francisco Toro Ceballos and José Rodríguez Molina, eds., *Mujeres y fronteras: Homenaje a Cristina Segura*. Estudios de Frontera 8. Jaén: Diputación de Jaén, 2010. 497–516.

Villanueva, Joaquin Lorenzo. *Viage literario a las iglesias de España*. 22 vols. Madrid: Imprenta Real, 1803–52.

Vindel Pérez, Ingrid. "Breves apuntes a la cantiga que Alfonso X dedicó a cierto deán de Cádiz." *Espéculo. Revista de Estudios Literarios* 14 (2000): published online at http://www.ucm.es/info/especulo/numero14/cantigas.html.

Wacks, David. *Framing Iberia: Maqāmāt and Frametale Narratives in Medieval Spain*. Leiden: Brill, 2007.

Walsh, John K. "Religious Motifs in the Early Spanish Epic." *Revista Histórica Moderna* 36 (1970–71): 165–72.

Warren, F. M. "The Enamoured Moslem Princess in Orderic Vital and the French Epic." *PMLA* 29 (1914): 341–58.

Wasserstein, David. "The Emergence of the Taifa Kingdom of Toledo." *Al-Qanṭara* 21 (2000): 17–56.

Watt, John A. *The Theory of Papal Monarchy in the Thirteenth Century: The Contribution of the Canonists*. New York: Fordham University Press, 1965.

Waugh, Scott L., and Peter. D. Diehl, eds. *Christendom and Its Discontents: Exclusion, Persecution and Rebellion, 1000–1500*. Cambridge: Cambridge University Press, 1996.

Webber, Ruth House. "The Spanish Epic in the Context of the Medieval European Epic." *Studia Riquer* 4 (1991): 333–44.

Weckmann, Luis. *The Medieval Heritage of Mexico*. Trans. Frances N. López-Morillas. New York: Fordham University Press, 1992.

Weever, Jacqueline de. *Sheba's Daughters: whitening and demonizing the Saracen woman in medieval French Epic*. New York: Garland, 1998.

Wolf, Kenneth Baxter. *Christian Martyrs in Muslim Spain*. Cambridge: Cambridge University Press, 1988.

———. "*Convivencia* in Medieval Spain: a Brief History of an Idea." *Religion Compass* 3 (2009): 72–85.

Ximena Jurado, Martín de. *Catálogo de los obispos de las iglesias catedrales de la diócesis de Jaén y anales eclesiásticos de este obispado*. Ed. José Rodríguez Molina and María José Osorio Pérez. Granada: Universidad de Granada, 1991.

Yarrow, Simon. "Prince Bohemond, Princess Melaz, and the Gendering of Religious Difference in the *Ecclesiastical History* of Orderic Vitalis." In Cordelia Beattie and Kirsten A. Fenton, eds., *Intersections of Gender, Religion and Ethnicity in the Middle Ages*. London: Palgrave Macmillan, 2010. 140–57.

Yepes, Antonio de. *Crónica general de la Orden de San Benito*, ed. Justo Pérez de Urbel. 3 vols. Madrid: Atlas, 1959–60.

Zaderenko, Irene. "Acerca de la fecha de composición del *Cantar de los siete infantes de Lara*," *La Corónica* 26 (1997): 247–55.

———. "El tema de la traición en *Los siete infantes de Lara* y su tradición en la épica románica." *Bulletin of Hispanic Studies* 78 (2001): 177–90.

Zorgati, Ragnhild Johnsrud. *Pluralism in the Middle Ages: Hybrid Identities, Conversion, and Mixed Marriages in Medieval Iberia*. New York: Routledge, 2012.

Index

Acknowledgments

In writing this book I have incurred many debts. First and foremost, I am deeply grateful to the Leverhulme Trust for the award of a Major Research Fellowship, during the course of which much of the work for this book was carried out. I am also indebted to the many kind colleagues who have helped this project in numerous ways, by sending me books or articles, offering advice and much-needed encouragement, and, above all, making me think. Particular thanks are due in this regard to Graham Barrett, Martin Brett, Francisco Bautista, Brian Catlos, Grace Davie, Jerrilynn Dodds, Amanda Dotseth, Patrick Henriet, David Hook, Antonella Liuzzo Scorpo, Emily Mantkelow, Manuela Marín, Youna Masset, Alberto Montaner, Tom Nickson, Armando de Sousa Pereira, Ofelia Rey Castelao, Jarbel Rodriguez, Laura Rubio, Catherine Rider, D. Fairchild Ruggles, Teresa Tinsley, Elisabeth van Houts, and Simon Yarrow. Special thanks are due to those steadfast individuals who went the extra mile and agreed to read the rough drafts of my chapters: Ann Christys, Isabel de Barros Dias, Simon Doubleday, Maribel Fierro, Sarah Hamilton, Fernando Luis Corral, Yolanda Plumley, Amy Remensnyder, Daniel Roach, and Geri Smith. Unless otherwise noted, all translations are my own. However, when linguistic problems presented themselves I was fortunate to be able to count on the expertise of others to help me: Alwyn Harrison was of inestimable assistance with some of the knottier passages of Latin I placed before him; Faraj Omar kindly lent a hand with some of the complexities of Ibn Darrāj's poetry; and Matthew Bailey and Anthony Lappin helped me to decode the deeper meaning of Gonzalo de Berceo's verse. Rocío Sánchez Ameijeiras kindly gave permission for me to reproduce her photograph of the carved depiction of Flores and Blancaflor in Burgos Cathedral, which is reproduced here. Sections of Chapter 1 have been adapted from my earlier article "Marriage Across Frontiers: Sexual Mixing, Power and Identity in Medieval Iberia," *Journal of Medieval*

Iberian Studies 3 (2011): 1–25; I am grateful to the publisher, Taylor & Francis (www.tandfonline.com), for granting me permission to do so. Last, but by no means least, my family and friends have provided me with much-needed moral support and have chivvied me along the bumpy road of authorship. To all I extend my heartfelt thanks.